PEOPLE, MARKETS, GOODS:
ECONOMIES AND SOCIETIES IN HISTORY

Volume 24

Mobility, Belonging and Identity in Freetown during the Era of Abolition

People, Markets, Goods: Economies and Societies in History

ISSN: 2051-7467

The interactions of economy and society, people and goods, transactions and actions are at the root of most human behaviours. Economic and social historians are participants in the same conversation about how markets have developed historically and how they have been constituted by economic actors and agencies in various social, institutional and geographical contexts. New debates now underpin much research in economic and social, cultural, demographic, urban and political history. Their themes have enduring resonance – financial stability and instability, the costs of health and welfare, the implications of poverty and riches, flows of trade and the centrality of communications. This paperback series aims to attract historians interested in economics and economists with an interest in history by publishing high quality, cutting edge academic research in the broad field of economic and social history from the late medieval/ early modern period to the present day. It encourages the interaction of qualitative and quantitative methods through both excellent monographs and collections offering path-breaking overviews of key research concerns. Taking as its benchmark international relevance and excellence it is open to scholars and subjects of any geographical areas from the case study to the multi-nation comparison.

PREVIOUSLY PUBLISHED TITLES IN THE SERIES
ARE LISTED AT THE BACK OF THIS VOLUME

Mobility, Belonging and Identity in Freetown during the Era of Abolition

Mégane L. Coulon

THE BOYDELL PRESS

First published 2026
The Boydell Press, Woodbridge

ISBN 978 1 83765 307 2

The Boydell Press is an imprint of Boydell & Brewer Ltd
and of Boydell & Brewer Inc.
website: www.boydellandbrewer.com

Our Authorised Representative for product safety in the EU
is Easy Access System Europe – Mustamäe tee 50, 10621 Tallinn, Estonia,
gpsr.requests@easproject.com

A catalogue record for this book is available
from the British Library

Contents

Figures, Graphs and Tables

Figures

Graphs

Tables

Acknowledgements

This book has taken shape over many years and through many conversations, guided by the support of people who entered this project at different moments and in different capacities, whether professional or personal, long-standing friends and more recent collaborators. I am deeply grateful to all who, in ways both large and small, helped me think through, challenge, and ultimately refine this work.

Among them, I owe particular thanks to the scholars who guided this project from its earliest phases. Suzanne Schwarz and Paul Lovejoy supported not only the drafts but also the earliest brainstorming, generously sharing their time, thoughts, and resources. They engaged closely with the first versions of this work, and their support, detailed comments, and thoughtful suggestions were indispensable to its completion. Their own scholarship inspired my research in numerous ways, and their expertise in the field helped me avoid many mistakes. Their mentorship continues to push me to do better, and I am grateful to have been able to rely on such generous guidance. At various stages of the project, Nemata Blyden and Mariana Candido provided valuable feedback, helping me clarify arguments and sharpen my analysis. From the beginning, I have been especially grateful to Érika Melek Delgado for her constant encouragement and for the many hours she devoted to helping me build a database for this research. Her support and persistence made an enormous difference; had I attempted this work on my own, it would have taken many months and many headaches. She has offered steady guidance and unwavering support throughout, and I am thankful for it. Several other scholars read portions of this manuscript, sometimes individual paragraphs, sometimes full sections, offered feedback, shared relevant articles, and engaged in conversations and brainstorming about this project or related work that indirectly shaped it. My thanks go to Henry Lovejoy, Leidy Alpízar Alpízar, Sean Kelley, Vanessa Oliveira, Trina Hogg, Nick Ungson, Kelly Brignac, Jeffrey Gunn, Fabio Cascadura, and Andreana Cunningham for their insight at these various stages.

I owe special thanks to Nualah Zahedieh, whose discussion of the book proposal at a conference helped move the project forward at a crucial and timely moment. At Boydell & Brewer, I am grateful to Michael Middeke and Crispin Peet for their availability, patience, and kindness in navigating countless emails and queries. Their guidance, prompt responses, and thoughtful attention made the editorial process smooth and much less daunting, and their support was invaluable in helping this book come to completion. I am also grateful for the insightful comments provided by the peer reviewers, which strengthened the manuscript in important ways.

I am indebted to Sophie Charvet, whose coffee time conversations and the many hours we have spent writing together in Selinsgrove and elsewhere have provided both inspiration and motivation to persevere, especially when the path forward felt challenging. As I write these lines during one of our regular coffee shop sessions, I am reminded of how steady and encouraging that support has been. I also thank Emmy Ribet for our online writing sessions and countless discussions about wording and phrasing. Likewise, I thank all the members of the Freedom Narratives team, past and current; our many Zoom meetings contributed greatly to reframing my thinking about biographies and micro-histories. I am equally grateful to the research team at Susquehanna University (SU), particularly the students who brought new cases to light and raised important questions about inconsistencies in the sources. I also thank the students in my various classes at SU with whom I shared primary sources as part of course activities; their comments pushed me to rethink, reshape, or more clearly explain key arguments. Special thanks go to Oak Parker, whose work toward the final stages of this project helped me stay on track and cross the finish line.

This research was made possible through the generous and sustained support of SU since I first joined the institution. I am particularly grateful for a faculty research grant and summer opportunities from the School of Humanities that funded research assistants and allowed me to advance the project at crucial stages. Additional support from the Department of History and the School of Humanities enabled me to attend conferences where I shared preliminary findings, received valuable feedback, and refined the arguments that would later shape this book. I am also thankful to colleagues at SU, especially from the History Department, who guided me toward resources on campus and generously shared their time, expertise, and advice throughout the research and writing process.

Likewise, I am grateful to the library services staff, whose help in locating materials beyond our own collections made this research possible. I also thank the staff at several archives, especially the National Archives at Kew and the British Library in London, for their assistance and expertise. In the same vein, I am indebted to Jody Butterworth for our conversations about the Endangered Archives Programme, both in relation to Sierra Leone and to other regions of the British Empire.

In Sierra Leone, I thank Albert Moore and the Sierra Leone Public Archives team for their guidance, generosity, and warm welcome. Being able to conduct research on site was essential to this project, and their openness made it possible for me to engage meaningfully with local archives and institutions. I owe particular thanks to Kartikay Chadha, who has been the best teammate in every collaboration we have undertaken. In this instance, Kartikay helped plan my research trip to Sierra Leone, shared resources, facilitated connections, and offered constant support, making this fieldwork not only possible but genuinely collaborative. Through Kartikay, I was also introduced to Yusif Kamara, who was kind enough to take me around Freetown and to sites he felt were especially relevant to my research. These exchanges enriched this book and helped lay the groundwork for future collaborations, some already underway, others still in development. I also wish to acknowledge the invitation from Muckson Sesay, the Chancellor of Central University, to give a talk at his institution, which allowed me to share insights with an engaged audience of students in Sierra Leone and made this research process all the more meaningful.

Finally, I could not have conducted this research without the unwavering support of my family. I am lucky to have a close-knit circle. My parents and sister have been my constant cheerleaders, and I know that my grandparents, uncles, aunts, and cousins are all very proud, always asking when the book will be out so they can have it proudly on their shelves. Special thanks go to Marélie and Alex for their help, whether tackling formatting nightmares or transcribing primary sources. And to all the important people in my life who now know far more about nineteenth-century Sierra Leone than they ever expected, I am grateful for your interest, encouragement, and good humour throughout this journey.

Abbreviations

BOA	British Online Archives
C.M.S.	Church Missionary Society
CO	Colonial Office
R.A.C.	Royal African Corps
RBF	Register of Births, Freetown
RLA	Register of Liberated Africans
SLPA	Sierra Leone Public Archives
TNA	The National Archives (UK)
W.I.R.	West India Regiments

Notes on the Text

A large number of people discussed in this book, though not all, were classified by colonial authorities as 'captured Negroes' until 1822, when the designation and legal term 'Liberated Africans' was introduced.[1] While this later term suggested freedom, scholars have demonstrated that the lived experiences of those so labelled were instead marked by coerced labour, restricted autonomy, and sustained colonial control.[2]

Throughout this book, the term 'Liberated Africans' appears in quotation marks to emphasise the disjunction between colonial language and historical reality. The quotation marks signal that liberation was often nominal rather than substantive, reflecting an administrative category rather than genuine freedom.

1 Christopher Fyfe, *A History of Sierra Leone* (Oxford, 1962), pp. 114–15, 138.

2 See Henry B. Lovejoy, 'Conceptualizing "Liberated Africans" and Slave Trade Abolition: Government Schemes to Indenture Enslaved People Captured from Slavery, 1800–1920', *Past & Present* (2024), 1–69; Richard Anderson and Henry B. Lovejoy (eds), *Liberated Africans and the Abolition of the Slave Trade: Digital Histories of Enslavement and Freedom* (Rochester, 2020); Maeve Ryan, *Humanitarian Governance and the British Antislavery World System* (New Haven, 2022).

Introduction

Archival material from mid-nineteenth-century Freetown preserve the lives of thousands of people in remarkably detailed ways. Names, ages, kinship ties, places of origin, occupations, disputes, apprenticeships, marriages, and illnesses appear in correspondence, court records, and various registers created by colonial administrations.[1] These records were not designed to tell personal stories, yet they contain a wealth of information about free, enslaved, and formerly enslaved people. This book draws on that density to centre individual lives, situating their histories within one of the largest forced movements of African people in the nineteenth century. Between 1808 and 1885, more than 111,000 people were relocated to the colony of Sierra Leone and subsequently classified as 'Liberated Africans', but their routes into the colony varied significantly. In the earlier decades, especially up to the 1860s, the majority were enslaved individuals taken from slave ships intercepted by the British Royal Navy. After 1875, however, most new arrivals were recorded through canoe seizures, the breakup of inland slave depots, and other small-scale coastal interdictions. Described at the time as humanitarian interventions, these relocations were acts of coercion, dislocation, and loss. In addition, a number of enslaved people entered the colony on their own, self-liberating by crossing into the colony to claim protection under British law.[2]

While Freetown received large numbers of formerly enslaved Africans, its population also included free populations from nearby regions and across West Africa. The colony depended on its hinterland for food, commerce, and labour, and rapid settlement reflected long-term trading links with Fuuta Jalon, the Kru Coast, and western Sudan. Fula, Kru, Limba, Loko, Mende, and Temne were among the many people who migrated there to take advantage of work

1 In different colonial contexts, the wealth of administrative archives has been noted by Mariana Candido, who shows that records preserve detailed personal information despite their bureaucratic purpose. Her work on Angola demonstrates how such materials allow historians to reconstruct individual lives. Mariana P. Candido, *Wealth, Land, and Property in Angola: A History of Dispossession, Slavery, and Inequality* (Cambridge, 2022), pp. 27–9; see various chapters in Paul E. Lovejoy, Henry B. Lovejoy, Érika Melek Delgado, and Kartikay Chadha, *Regenerated Identities: Documenting African Lives* (Trenton, 2022).

2 Henry B. Lovejoy, 'Conceptualizing "Liberated Africans" and Slave Trade Abolition: Government Schemes to Indenture Enslaved People Captured from Slavery, 1800–1920', *Past & Present* (2024), 1–69; Maeve Ryan, *Humanitarian Governance and the British Antislavery World System* (New Haven, 2022).

opportunities.[3] Freetown's status as the centre of a British colony also attracted individuals from Caribbean colonies and North America seeking professional advancement.[4] As put by Paul Lovejoy and Suzanne Schwarz, these movements made Freetown a 'frontier of the African diaspora', where diverse African-born and African-descended populations shaped its social, economic, and cultural life.[5] While only about 2,000 people lived there in 1809, by 1862, its population amounted to 17,800 inhabitants.[6]

This book is a social history of Freetown in the mid-nineteenth century. It evaluates social and residential segregations to reveal how various areas were affected by rapid settlement. To trace large patterns of social and economic interactions with people from coastal and inland areas, nearby or further afield, this study pays particular attention to the life experience of a broad cross-section of the population. It builds on Christopher Fyfe's scholarship on prominent 'Liberated Africans' and their descendants, whose stories he reconstructed through biographical information drawn from archival sources. By applying the same methodology to a broader sample of Freetown's population, this work attempts to recovers snapshots of life histories of individuals whose archival traces become legible through careful analysis.[7] By reconstructing biographical information where possible, the book aims to capture the diversity and complexity of individual experiences, whether from nearby regions, the hinterlands, and beyond the Atlantic world, providing a composite picture of

3 Barbara E. Harrell-Bond, Allen M. Howard, and David E. Skinner, *Community Leadership and the Transformation of Freetown (1801–1976)* (The Hague, 1978); Diane Frost, *Work and Community among West African Migrant Workers since the Nineteenth Century* (Liverpool, 1999); Jeffrey Gunn, *Outsourcing African Labor: Kru Migratory Workers in Global Ports, Estates and Battlefields until the End of the 19th Century* (Berlin, 2021).

4 Nemata Amelia Blyden, '"We Have the Cause of Africa at Heart": West Indians and African-Americans in 19th Century Freetown', in Mac Dixon-Fyle and Gibril Cole (eds), *New Perspectives on the Sierra Leone Krio* (New York, 2006), pp. 91–105, at p. 94.

5 Paul E. Lovejoy and Suzanne Schwarz, 'Introduction', in Paul E. Lovejoy and Suzanne Schwarz (eds), *Slavery, Abolition and the Transition to Colonialism in Sierra Leone* (Trenton, 2015), pp. 1–28; Richard Anderson, *Abolition in Sierra Leone: Re-Building Lives and Identities in Nineteenth-Century West Africa* (Cambridge, 2020), pp. 1–29.

6 Blue Books of Sierra Leone, 1862, British Online Archives [hereafter BOA], fol. 166; Gunn, *Outsourcing African Labor*, p. 77.

7 Christopher Fyfe, 'Four Sierra Leone Recaptives', *Journal of African History*, 11:1 (1961), 77–85; Christopher Fyfe, 'Peter Nicholls – Old Calabar and Freetown', *Journal of the Historical Society of Nigeria*, 2:1 (1960), 105–14; Christopher Fyfe, 'The Administration in 1885', *Sierra Leone Studies*, 1 (1955), 226–8; Christopher Fyfe, 'The Life and Times of John Ezzidio', *Sierra Leone Studies*, 1 (1955), 213–23; Christopher Fyfe, 'The Sierra Leone Press in the Nineteenth Century', *Sierra Leone Studies*, 8 (1957), 226–36; Christopher Fyfe, 'View of the New Burial Ground', *Sierra Leone Studies*, 2 (1954), 85–90.

Freetown and offering perspectives on urban life, emancipation, post-slavery societies, and the legacies of forced migration across West Africa.

Historical Context

Freetown emerged from a series of earlier initiatives, legal decisions, and resettlements. The colony of Sierra Leone was established in the aftermath of the 1772 Somerset v Stewart case that led to the abolition of slavery in the British Isles. In 1787, the Committee for the Relief of the Black Poor relocated 411 individuals to the Sierra Leone Peninsula, over 200 of whom were formerly enslaved people from Britain. In 1792, the Sierra Leone Company was created, and 1,192 Black Loyalists were relocated to Freetown. They were enslaved people who fought with the British during the American Revolution and had first been relocated to Nova Scotia. In 1800, Jamaican Maroons were also resettled in the colony of Sierra Leone. Maroons were Africans who escaped slavery and formed independent communities across the edges of plantation societies in the Americas. The term derives from the Spanish *cimarrón*, which evolved from describing runaway livestock to referring to Indigenous and then enslaved African people who had escaped.[8] Their exile followed the Second Maroon War of 1795–96, which opposed Maroon communities to British colonial authorities.[9]

This book begins in 1808, right after the British Abolition of the Slave Trade Act of 1807 under which the West Africa Squadron was established. Consisting of ships from the British Royal Navy, it chased foreign vessels carrying enslaved people from West Africa, West Central Africa, and South-east Africa. The anti-slavery ships patrolled about 2,000 miles between Cape Verde and the north of Luanda, leading to the relocation of Africans

8 See: Richard Price, 'Maroon Societies in the Americas', *Oxford Research Encyclopedia of African History* (Oxford, 2020) <https://doi.org/10.1093/acrefore/9780190277734.013.935> [accessed 17 April 2026].

9 Stephen J. Braidwood, *Black Poor and White Philanthropists: London's Blacks and the Foundation of the Sierra Leone Settlement, 1786–1791* (Liverpool, 1994); James W. St. G. Walker, *The Black Loyalists: The Search for a Promised Land in Nova Scotia and Sierra Leone, 1783–1870* (London, 1976); Mavis C. Campbell, *Back to Africa: George Ross & the Maroons – From Nova Scotia to Sierra Leone* (Trenton, 1995); Jeffrey A. Fortin, '"An Act of Deportation": The Jamaican Maroons' Journey from Freedom to Slavery and Back Again, 1796–1836', in Ana Lucia Araujo (ed.), *Paths of the Atlantic Slave Trade* (Amherst, 2011), pp. 71–106; Jeffrey A. Fortin, '"Blackened Beyond Our Native Hue": Removal, Identity and the Trelawney Maroons on the Margins of the Atlantic World, 1796–1800', *Citizenship Studies*, 10:1 (2006), 5–34.

from various areas, but mainly embarked in the Bight of Benin and in the Bight of Biafra, to the colony of Sierra Leone.[10]

Historiography

This book's historiographical significance lies in its engagement with multiple aspects of social, urban, and post-slavery history. A history of nineteenth-century Freetown and the wider colony of Sierra Leone forms part of a broad narrative on the forced displacement of Black people. Over the course of the long nineteenth century, more than 700,000 individuals enslaved in Africa were emancipated through legal processes over sea, land, and through seeking asylum at European consulates in the Atlantic world, in the Ottoman Empire, and in North Africa. As Henry Lovejoy points out, these forced relocations are both humanitarian efforts and a crime against humanity.[11] Among these vast movements, the colony of Sierra Leone represents one of the most significant concentrations of relocated Africans. The histories of 'Liberated Africans', *emancipados*, *libertos*, and *engagés* across the Atlantic and Indian Oceans, from the Cape Colony to Cuba, Mauritius, St Helena, Trinidad, and Zanzibar among others, continue to come to light as scholars question the consequences of abolition on the lives of thousands of people.[12] In June 2023, Henry Lovejoy

10 Mary Wills, *Envoys of Abolition: British Naval Officers and the Campaign against the Slave Trade in West Africa* (Liverpool, 2019), pp. 22, 27; Slave Voyages database <https://www.slavevoyages.org/voyages/SplVeiuY> [accessed 29 March 2022].

11 H. Lovejoy, 'Conceptualizing "Liberated Africans"', 1–69; Henry Lovejoy, '"Liberated Africans" in Global Perspective, 1800–1920', Liberated Africans database, <https://liberatedafricans.org/about/essays.php> [accessed 18 March 2024]; Henry B. Lovejoy, 'Condemned for Engaging in the Illicit Traffic: Mapping the Maritime Blockade of the African Slave Trade in Global Perspective, 1800–1902', *International Journal of Maritime History* (forthcoming).

12 A sample of that scholarship includes different chapters in Anderson and Lovejoy, *Liberated Africans and the Abolition of the Slave Trade*; Rosanne Marion Adderley, *"New Negroes from Africa", Slave Trade Abolition and Free African Settlement in the Nineteenth-Century Caribbean* (Bloomington, 2006); Andrew Pearson, *Distant Freedom: St. Helena and the Abolition of the Slave Trade, 1840–1872* (Liverpool, 2016); Kelly Brignac, *Immoral Debt: Abolition, Labor, and the End of Slavery in the French Empire* (Philadelphia, forthcoming); Marie-Pierre Ballarin, 'L'esclavage en héritage et l'émergence d'une mobilisation sociopolitique au Kenya', *Politique africaine*, 4:140 (2015), 41–59; Yaimara Izaguirre Martí, 'Emancipated Women in Cuba: Strategies of Freedom and Motherhood Inside of the Conflict', *Journal of Science*, 7:1 (2024), 84–93; Yaimara Izaguirre Martí, 'Las estrategias legales de los emancipados en Cuba (1856–1880)', *Oficio. Revista de Historia e Interdisciplina*, 18 (2024), 85–104; Roquinaldo Ferreira, *Worlds of Unfreedom: West Central Africa in the Era of Global Abolition* (Princeton, 2025); Antony Hopkins, *Capitalism in the Colonies: African Merchants in Lagos, 1851–1931* (New

launched a publicly accessible database on 'Liberated Africans'. It demonstrates the global significance of anti-slave trade legislations by providing demographic data and digital sources on emancipation and resettlement of over 200,000 individuals.[13]

The study of 'Liberated Africans' and their broader global significance is enriched by anthropological and archaeological research, which draws on artefacts, landscapes, and other forms of material culture to deepen historical understanding. In Sierra Leone, Agbelusi's research on the colonial village of Regent examines town lots through the analysis of landscape, architecture, and artefacts, demonstrating how yardscapes functioned as social spaces that enabled people to forge connections and mediate relationships between families.[14] In St Helena, the construction of the island's first airport led to the uncovering of burial grounds in Rupert's Valley. Excavations conducted between 2007 and 2008 brought to light the remains of 325 individuals, including 178 graves identified as those of 'Liberated Africans'. Genetic studies of these remains indicate ancestry connections with Bantu-speaking populations from regions such as Angola, Cameroon, and Gabon. The study of burial practices further provides insight into the experiences of 'Liberated Africans', as people were interred without shrouds or coffins in hurried, utilitarian burials. Unmarked graves highlight the anonymity of death and the absence of culturally grounded funerary practices. Only a small number of artefacts were recovered from the site, but some reflect possessions retained by individuals from before their Middle Passage journeys. Their presence is significant and offers rare glimpses into the lives of people prior to forced displacement.[15] As Andreana Cunningham explains, these objects suggest

Haven, 2024); Klara Boyer-Rossol, 'Les carnets manuscrits de l'ethnographe Eugène Huet de Froberville (1845–1847) : des noms et des voix de captifs déportés de l'Afrique orientale aux îles Mascareignes', *Esclavages & Post-esclavages*, 9 (2024) <doi.org/10.4000/1109y> [accessed 8 February 2026]; Céline Flory, 'L'engagisme africain au prisme du genre en Guyane française après l'abolition de l'esclavage de 1848', *Revue d'histoire du XIXe siècle*, 68 (2024), 107–27; Klara Boyer-Rossol, 'From East Africa to the Mascarenes: The Origins and Life Histories of 140 "Mozambiques" (1810s–1840s)', *Journal of Global Slavery*, 10:2–3 (2025), 223–44.

13 H. Lovejoy, 'Conceptualizing "Liberated Africans"', 1–69.

14 O. O. Agbelusi, 'Entangled Landscape: Spatial Discipline and Liminal Freedom in Coastal Sierra Leone', *American Antiquity*, 89:4 (2024), 574–90.

15 Marcela Sandoval-Velasco, Anuradha Jagadeesan, Jazmín Ramos-Madrigal, María C. Ávila-Arcos, Cesar A. Fortes-Lima, Judy Watson, et al., 'The Ancestry and Geographical Origins of St Helena's Liberated Africans', *The American Journal of Human Genetics*, 110:9 (2023), 1590–9; H. MacQuarrie and A. Pearson, 'Prize Possessions: Transported Material Culture of the Post-Abolition Enslaved – New Evidence from St Helena', *Slavery & Abolition*, 37:1 (2016), 45–72.

hurried departures, likely undertaken to avoid detection by the Royal Navy during anti-slavery patrols.[16]

A growing body of scholarship situates abolition and forced relocation of 'Liberated Africans' within Britain's broader colonial and capitalist agenda. Anti-slavery policies were shaped by economic ambitions that facilitated new forms of colonial governance and revealed abolition as a gateway to colonisation.[17] Scanlan demonstrates that anti-slavery reform was integral to economic and colonial logics. Anti-slavery functioned through financial incentives, including prize money from the capture of slave ships, as well as through the coerced labour of 'Liberated Africans', who cleared forests, repaired buildings, and undertook other forms of colonial work. Institutions such as the Courts of Mixed Commission and the Liberated African Department were not simply used to abolish slavery, they reorganised labour and economic life in ways that underpinned the colonial order.[18] Maeve Ryan highlights how abolitionist policy was developed with the recognition that coerced labour remained essential to imperial economies. She explains that the experiences of 'Liberated Africans' show how the policies put in place were structured around carceral practices, including confinement, surveillance, and labour regulation. Ryan shows that the portrayal of 'Liberated Africans' as being 'saved' and 'freed' relied on unequal relations of power, making assistance contingent on imperial authority. The possibility of framing their rescue as an act of care depended on the ability of colonial actors to control the lives and movements of 'Liberated Africans'.[19] Jake Richards extends this analysis through an Atlantic perspective that connects Sierra Leone to South Africa, Cuba, and Brazil. Through comparison across the Atlantic world, he shows that non-slave societies offered 'Liberated Africans' greater, if still limited, personal security and freedom. Richards also draws attention to the regulation of maritime captures, identifying significant gaps and loopholes within anti-slavery law that shaped the lives of those classified

16 Andreana Cunningham, 'Atlantic Crossings: Biosocial Interventions in African Diasporic Bioarchaeological Thought and Practice', *American Journal of Biological Anthropology*, 188:2 (2025), 1–10.

17 Ndubueze L. Mbah, 'Abolition Forgery: A History of the Afterlives of Slavery', Radcliffe Fellow's Presentation, Harvard Radcliffe Institute, April 2023 < https://www.radcliffe.harvard.edu/event/2023-ndubueze-l-mbah-fellow-presentation-virtual> [accessed 3 August 2025]; Ryan, *Humanitarian Governance*; Eric Williams, *Capitalism and Slavery* (Chapel Hill, 1944); Paul Lovejoy, *Transformations in Slavery: A History of Slavery in Africa* (Cambridge, 2012).

18 Padraic X. Scanlan, *Freedom's Debtors: British Antislavery in Sierra Leone in the Age of Revolution* (New Haven, 2017); Padraic X. Scanlan, 'The Colonial Rebirth of British Anti-Slavery: The Liberated African Villages of Sierra Leone, 1815–1824', *American Historical Review*, 121:4 (2016), 1085–113; Padraic X. Scanlan, 'The Rewards of Their Exertions: Prize Money and British Abolitionism in Sierra Leone, 1808–1823', *Past & Present*, 225 (2014), 113–42.

19 Ryan, *Humanitarian Governance.*

as 'liberated'. Yet within and against these regulatory frameworks, 'Liberated Africans' developed social, economic, and cultural practices that complicate narratives of complete domination.[20]

Recent historiography on the colony of Sierra Leone focuses on the identities and experiences of 'Liberated Africans'. Research demonstrates that their experience of survival meant that they preserved their heritage while adopting new cultural elements. Scholars of the colony of Sierra Leone explore abolition in detail by examining origins and the conditions of the relocation of 'Liberated Africans' to the British colony, drawing significant parallels with the experience of enslaved people disembarked in the Americas. Studies have shown that although 'Liberated Africans' were legally freed upon disembarkation, Nova Scotian and Jamaican Maroon settlers continued to regard them as commodities. These attitudes framed social hierarchies that emerged in early nineteenth-century Freetown. David Northrup's work on identity formation, alongside Richard Anderson's *Abolition in Sierra Leone*, provides detailed analysis of the origins of 'Liberated Africans' settled across the colony.[21] Érika Melek Delgado's work on the classification of children highlights their near-total lack of agency over their own lives, while studies by Schwarz and Howard examine the experiences of 'Liberated Africans' within apprenticeship systems, emphasising both coercion and opportunities for resistance and social mobility.[22]

Most 'Liberated Africans' settled in the colony were sent to villages on the Sierra Leone peninsula. In the early 1830s, about 70 per cent of the population of the colony lived there. There were five districts and over thirty villages under British jurisdiction. The First Mountain District was the largest with 5,267 inhabitants. It comprised the villages of Charlotte, Leopold, Old Bathurst, Gloucester, Leicester Mountain, and Regent.[23] At the time, the population of

20 Jake Subryan Richards, *The Bonds of Freedom: Liberated Africans and the End of the Slave Trade* (New Haven, 2025).

21 Anderson, *Abolition*; David Northrup, 'Becoming African: Identity Formation among Liberated Slaves in Nineteenth-Century Sierra Leone', *Slavery and Abolition*, 27:1 (2006), 1–21; David Northrup, 'Identity among Liberated Africans in Sierra Leone', in Jorge Cañizares-Esguerra, Matt D. Childs, and James Sidbury (eds), *The Black Urban Atlantic in the Age of the Slave Trade* (Philadelphia, 2013), pp. 21–41.

22 Érika Melek Delgado, 'Liberated African "Children" in Sierra Leone: Colonial Classifications of "Child" and "Childhood," 1808–19', in Richard Anderson and Henry B. Lovejoy (eds), *Liberated Africans and the Abolition of the Slave Trade: Digital Histories of Enslavement and Freedom* (Rochester, 2020), pp. 81–100, Suzanne Schwarz, 'The Impact of Liberated African "Disposal" Polices in Early Nineteenth-Century Sierra Leone', in Richard Anderson and Henry B. Lovejoy (eds), *Liberated Africans and the Abolition of the Slave Trade: Digital Histories of Enslavement and Freedom* (Rochester, 2020), pp. 45–65; Allen M. Howard, 'New Insights on Liberated Africans: The 1831 Freetown Census', in Richard Anderson and Henry B. Lovejoy (eds), *Liberated Africans and the Abolition of the Slave Trade: Digital Histories of Enslavement and Freedom* (Rochester, 2020), pp. 101–26.

23 Stefania Galli and Klas Rönnbäck, 'Land Distribution and Inequality in a Black Settler Colony: The Case of Sierra Leone, 1792–1831', *The Economic History Review* (2020), 1–23,

Freetown of 8,505 individuals was outstripped by the combined population of the villages but, as the colonial capital, Freetown was the commercial, administrative, industrial, and transport centre of the colony. Important rural-urban movements of people were exhibited when inhabitants of the villages travelled to the urban centre for employment, leisure, religious purposes, and the like.

A defining feature of Freetown's demographic composition was its location on the peninsula and its Atlantic orientation. As with other Atlantic ports in Africa, its commercial and political connections extended beyond the African continent, but the scale and diversity of immigration set Freetown apart. African Caribbean migrants from British colonies, as well as African American individuals shaped by slave societies, migrated voluntarily to the West African colony to improve their social and economic circumstances or to participate in what they understood as the moral and social renewal of Africa.[24] Nemata Blyden's work demonstrates the central role these Atlantic migrants played in the establishment of the colony Sierra Leone, as well as the sources of their influence in government positions. Her analysis fits within the broader historiography of the 'Back to Africa' movement, which emphasises Black Atlantic mobility, racial uplift, Christian reform, and the creation of autonomous Black political and social institutions in Africa.[25]

Although closely tied to Atlantic routes, Freetown was shaped as much by inland and coastal African connections as by transoceanic ones. British abolitionist activities and the expansion of legitimate commerce attracted significant numbers of African traders from both inland regions and neighbouring coastal areas. Located on the upper Guinea coast, the colony benefited from a complex network of rivers that facilitated transport and communication between coastal and inland areas, since roughly twenty-four main rivers flow from there into the Atlantic Ocean.[26] Known to the British as the Northern Rivers and to the French as the Southern Rivers, these include the Nunez, Pongo, Melikourie, Rokel, and the Small and Great Scarcies rivers,

---

at p. 8; *Reports to Secretary of State on Past and Present State of H.M. Colonial Possessions, 1850*, HC 1851, no. 1421, p. 183; TNA, CO 267/111, Census of Population and Liberated Africans, 1831, fol. 69.

24 Blyden, '"We Have the Cause of Africa at Heart"', p. 94.

25 Caree A. Banton, *More Auspicious Shores: Barbadian Migration to Liberia, Blackness, and the Making of an African Republic* (Cambridge, 2019); Lisa A. Lindsay, *Atlantic Bonds: A Nineteenth-Century Odyssey from America to Africa* (Chapel Hill, 2019); Joseph P. Stinnett, *Out of Virginia: Black Americans' Search for Freedom in Nineteenth-Century Liberia* (Charlottesville, 2026).

26 Henry B. Lovejoy, Paul Lovejoy, Walter Hawthrone, Edward A. Alpers, Mariana Candido, Matthew S. Hopper, Ghislaine Lydon, Colleen E. Kriger, and John Thornton, 'Defining Regions of Pre-Colonial Africa: A Controlled Vocabulary for Linking Open-Source Data in Digital History Projects', *History in Africa* (2021), 1–26, at p. 14; Walter Rodney, *A History of the Upper Guinea Coast 1545–1800* (New York, 1980), pp. 2, 16.

among others. These waterways directly connected Freetown to important trading centres such as Kambia and Port Loko.[27] Although less numerous than 'Liberated Africans', free African immigrants from areas along these rivers were important in the growth of Freetown, particularly because they had settled there voluntarily rather than being forcibly relocated.[28] Harrell-Bond, Howard, and Skinner have highlighted how these communities developed, from populations of Mende, Temne, and Krio, to Muslim resident groups among others, examining how they organised themselves, exercised leadership, and strategised for survival. Their study of these social structures extends beyond independence, continuing to into the 1970s.[29]

The Sierra Leone–Guinea corridors connected Freetown to the Muslim commercial interior through trade routes from Dinguiraye and Kankan. The kola trade attracted a steady flow of Muslim traders into the colony, while Freetown's proximity to the *jihād* states of Fuuta Toro and Fuuta Jalon, as well as the Rio Pongo region, reinforced its position within Atlantic and regional trade networks.[30] Fula, Mandinka, and Susu migrants from the interior were drawn to the colony for its religious and educational centres established by Muslim traders in Fourah Bay and Fula Town. Scholars such as David Skinner and Allen M. Howard in the late 1990s, and more recently Gibril Cole, have examined how Islam structured economic, commercial, and educational institutions, highlighting its central role in social networks and identity formation during the nineteenth and twentieth centuries.[31] Although voluntary

27 Winston McGowan, 'The Establishment of Long-Distance Trade between Sierra Leone and its Hinterland, 1787–1821', *Journal of African History*, 31 (1990), 25–41.

28 Kenneth Little, *The Mende of Sierra Leone: West African People in Transition* (London, 1998); Joseph Bangura, *The Temne of Sierra Leone: African Agency in the Making of a British Colony* (Cambridge, 2017); Frost, *Work and Community*; Gunn, *Outsourcing African Labor*.

29 Harrell-Bond, Howard, Skinner, *Community Leadership*.

30 Jan Jansen, 'Habitation and Warfare Strategies in 19th Century Mande – A View from the Kafu', in Allen M. Howard and Richard M. Shain (eds), *The Spatial Factor in African History: The Relationship of the Social, Material, and Perceptual* (Leiden: Brill, 2005), pp. 260–89, at pp. 263, 271; Richard L. Roberts, *Warriors, Merchants, and Slaves: The State and the Economy in the Middle Niger Valley, 1700–1914* (Stanford, 1987), p. 62; Allen M. Howard, 'Mande Kola Traders of Northwestern Sierra Leone, Late 1700s to 1930', *Mande Studies*, 9 (2007), 83–102, at p. 90; Rodney, *A History*, p. 206; Paul E. Lovejoy, *Caravans of Kola: The Hausa Kola Trade 1700–1900* (Zaria, 1980), p. 2; Harrell-Bond, Howard, Skinner, *Community Leadership*, p. 106; Paul Lovejoy, *Jihād in West Africa during the Age of Revolution* (Athens, 2016), pp. 17–19.

31 Allen M. Howard, 'Mande Identity Formation in the Economic and Political Context of North-West Sierra Leone, 1750–1900', *Paideuma*, 46 (2000), 13–35; Allen M. Howard, 'The Relevance of Spatial Analysis for African Economic History: The Sierra Leone-Guinea System', *Journal of African History*, 17:3 (1976), 365–88; Allen M. Howard, 'Trade and Islam in Sierra Leone, 18th–20th Centuries', in Alusine Jalloh and David E. Skinner (eds),

migration facilitated the spread of Islam in Freetown, approximately 10 per cent of 'Liberated Africans' in the colony were already Muslim upon arrival.[32] The broader significance of Islam in shaping trade, social interactions, and communal identities in West Africa is emphasised in the works of J. Spencer Trimingham and Paul Lovejoy.[33]

Within Freetown itself, Islam was also an important component for some members of the Krio community. The term Krio refers to the colony-born population of Freetown of the mid-nineteenth century and their descendants. The origin of the term was thought to derive from 'Creole' and to echo the exposure to British values for people known as Europeanised Africans, or Black Englishmen. Some scholars challenge this definition and posit instead that Krio more accurately captures the diverse influences that shaped the community, including those of Temne, Mende, and Mandinka peoples, as well as Muslim populations.[34]

Finally, the book situates the history of the colony within the wider histories of slavery and abolition in Africa. Although the slave trade was formally abolished, the colony remained embedded in commercial networks

Islam and Trade in Sierra Leone (Trenton, 1997), pp. 21–63; David E. Skinner, 'Islam and Education in the Colony and Hinterland of Sierra Leone (1750–1914)', *Canadian Journal of African Studies / Revue canadienne des études africaines*, 10:3 (1976), 499–520; David E. Skinner, 'The Incorporation of Muslim Elites into the Colonial Administrative Systems of Sierra Leone, The Gambia and the Gold Coast', *Journal of Muslim Minority Affairs*, 29:1 (2009), 91–108; David E. Skinner, 'The Influence of Islam in Sierra Leone History: Institutions, Practices, and Leadership', *Journal of West African History*, 2:1 (2016), 27–71; Gibril R. Cole, *The Krio of West Africa: Islam, Culture, Creolization, and Colonialism in the Nineteenth Century* (Athens, 2013); Gibril R. Cole, 'Liberated Slaves and Islam in Nineteenth-Century West Africa', in Toyin Falola and Matt D. Childs (eds), *Yoruba Diaspora in the Atlantic World* (Bloomington, 2005); Gibril R. Cole, 'Religious Plurality and Economic Sustainability: Muslim Merchants in the Colonial Economy of Nineteenth Century Freetown', *African Economic History*, 36 (2008), 79–93.

32 Harrell-Bond, Howard, Skinner, *Community Leadership*, pp. 107–8; Anderson, *Abolition*, p. 248; Fyfe, *A History*, p. 372.

33 J. Spencer Trimingham, *Islam in West Africa* (Oxford, 1959); J. Spencer Trimingham and Christopher Fyfe, 'The Early Expansion of Islam in Sierra Leone', *The Sierra Leone Bulletin of Religion*, 2:2 (1960), 33–40; P. Lovejoy, *Caravans of Kola*; P. Lovejoy, *Jihād in West Africa*; Paul E. Lovejoy, *Salt of the Desert Sun: A History of Salt Production and Trade in the Central Sudan* (Cambridge, 1986).

34 Akintola J. G. Wyse, 'On Misunderstandings Arising from the Use of the Term "Creole" in the Literature on Sierra Leone: A Rejoinder', *Africa*, 49:4 (1979), 408–17; C. Magbaily Fyle, 'The Yoruba Diaspora in Sierra Leone's Krio Society', in Toyin Falola and Matt D. Childs (eds), *Yoruba Diaspora in the Atlantic World* (Bloomington, 2005), pp. 366–82; Cole, *The Krio of West Africa*.

that continued to sustain slave trafficking. As Philip Misevich shows, these networks were closely tied to the production of 'legitimate' commodities. Trade in agricultural produce, such as rice, depended on the labour and transport of enslaved people in regions such as Sherbro and the Gallinas, which meant that the colony remained indirectly connected to systems of enslavement, even after abolition.[35] At the same time, the book treats abolition as a lived and contested process in which Africans played an active role. While scholarship has examined the end of slavery in Africa, Asia, and Latin America, it has paid comparatively less attention to Africans as agents in these transitions.[36] This study foregrounds the experiences of enslaved and self-liberated people in the colony's hinterland, particularly those who fled to Freetown and claimed freedom there.

This book draws on Benedetta Rossi's distinction between abolition and amelioration, where abolition reflects a moral rejection of slavery itself, and amelioration seeks only to improve the conditions of the enslaved. This study identifies as abolitionists those individuals who helped others secure freedom, whether driven by fear, empathy, or personal interest. Their actions are woven into the wider social fabric of Freetown.[37] These dynamics parallel studies such as Cheik Sène's analysis of French abolition, which explores the experiences of those freed upon entering colonial settlements, and Thiago Mota's work on Muslim responses to emancipation, which shows that, for free-born Muslims, abolition was both disruptive to the structure and organisation of labour, and liberatory.[38] Together, cases of continuing slave trading and ongoing abolition show the interplay of local leadership, treaty-making, and responses to abolition, revealing both the continuities of slavery and the diverse ways Africans shaped emancipation and social change across multiple spheres.

This study thus brings together a wide range of influences. The diversity of the population and the emergence of new social hierarchies had already been noted by scholars in the 1960s, who acknowledged the heterogeneity of Freetown's society but tended to focus on those who rose to prominence.[39] The

35 Philip Misevich, *Abolition and the Transformation of Atlantic Commerce in Southern Sierra Leone, 1790s to 1860s* (Trenton, 2019).

36 Benedetta Rossi, 'Introduction: African Approaches to the Abolition of Slavery', *Esclavages & Post-esclavages* 10 (2024), <https://doi.org/10.4000/12sh9> [accessed 29 November 2024].

37 Ibid.

38 Cheikh Sène, 'Le décret de l'émancipation des esclaves de 1848 : une application difficile au Sénégal (1848–1905)', *Esclavages & Post-esclavages* 10 (2024), <https://doi.org/10.4000/12sh5> [accessed 2 December 2024]; Thiago H. Mota, 'Muslims for and Against Slavery: Debates on the European Abolitionism within the Muslim Elite of Saint-Louis, Senegal (1844)', *Slavery & Abolition*, 46:1 (2025), 230–53.

39 See some of Fyfe's scholarship in footnote 7; Christopher Fyfe, 'A Royal Visit in 1860', *Sierra Leone Studies*, 2 (1959), 260–72; Christopher Fyfe, 'European and Creole Influences in the Interior of Sierra Leone before 1896', *Sierra Leone Studies*, 6 (1956), 113–23; Christopher

arrival of African Caribbean migrants further reinforced social distinctions within the port-city, while 'Liberated Africans', though legally free, were still treated as commodities by many settlers.[40] Building on Harrell-Bond, Skinner, and Howard's emphasis on community leadership, this study shows how individual life histories reveal the essential role of social networks in navigating these hierarchies. Drawing also on Schwarz's examination of how successive movements of people shaped Freetown's social structure in the late eighteenth and early nineteenth centuries, it demonstrates how these varied influences together make it possible to analyse interactions and networks in ways that bring underlying hierarchies into view.[41]

Within these hierarchies and networks, women's experiences reveal how gender intersected with social, economic, and religious life. Across multiple urban colonial settings in Africa, women became active agents of their own independence.[42] In Freetown, from the early days of the colony in the late eighteenth century, women held various economic roles and were active participants. Nova Scotian and Maroon women were able to reach some level of economic independence by entering trade and acting as intermediaries in

Fyfe, 'The Countess of Huntingdon's Connexion in 19th century Sierra Leone', *The Sierra Leone Bulletin of Religion*, 4 (1962), 53–61; Christopher Fyfe, *A Short History of Sierra Leone*, 2nd edn (London, 1979); Christopher Fyfe, *Sierra Leone Inheritance* (London, 1964); Fyfe, *A History*; Arthur Porter, *Creoledom: A Study of the Development of Freetown Society* (London, 1963); John Peterson, *Province of Freedom: A History of Sierra Leone, 1787–1870* (Evanston, 1969).

40 Bronwell Everill, *Abolition and Empire in Sierra Leone and Liberia* (Basingstoke, 2013); Fyfe, *A History*; Suzanne Schwarz, 'Reconstructing', 175–207; Schwarz, 'The Impact', pp. 45–65; Harrell-Bond, Howard, Skinner, *Community Leadership*; Walker, *The Black Loyalists*; Scanlan, *Freedom's Debtors*, pp. 165–95.

41 Suzanne Schwarz, 'Reconstructing', pp. 175–207; Suzanne Schwarz, '"A Just and Honourable Commerce": Abolitionist Experimentation in Sierra Leone in the Late Eighteenth and Early Nineteenth Century', *African Economic History*, 45:1 (2017), 1–45; Suzanne Schwarz, 'Adaptation in the Aftermath of Slavery: Women, Trade and Property in Sierra Leone, c.1790–1812', in Mariana P. Candido and Adam Jones (eds), *African Women in the Atlantic World: Property, Vulnerability & Mobility 1660–1880* (Woodbridge, 2019), pp. 19–37; Schwarz, 'The Impact', pp. 45–65.

42 Philip Havik, *Silences and Soundbites: The Gendered Dynamics of Trade and Brokerage in the Pre-Colonial Guinea Bissau Region* (Münster, 2004); Pernille Ipsen, *Daughters of the Trade: Atlantic Slavers and Interracial Marriage on the Gold Coast* (Philadelphia, 2015); Hilary Jones, *The Métis of Senegal: Urban Life and Politics in French West Africa* (Bloomington, 2013); Vanessa S. Oliveira, *Slave Trade and Abolition: Gender, Commerce, and Economic Transition in Luanda* (Madison, 2021); Mariana Candido and Eugénia Rodrigues, 'African Women's Access and Rights to Property in the Portuguese Empire', *African Economic History*, 43 (2015), 1–18, Lorelle D. Semley, *Mother is Gold, Father is Glass: Gender and Colonialism in a Yoruba Town* (Bloomington, 2011); Mariana P. Candido, *Wealth, Land, and Property in Angola: A History of Dispossession, Slavery, and Inequality* (Cambridge, 2022).

African–European commerce, drawing on skills from their regions of origin to cultivate foodstuffs and pursue multiple occupations. 'Liberated African' women later followed these models and entered trading themselves.[43] Maeve Ryan's work on forced marriage practices in the Liberated African Yard – the walled enclosure where 'Liberated Africans' waited for the adjudication of their cases – further highlights the complex and coercive conditions under which these women navigated freedom, offering a series of glimpses into the varied and uneven experiences of liberation.[44]

The colonial framework sometimes allowed women to challenge prejudice. The promotion of monogamy meant that trading and domesticity were not constrained by the hierarchies present in polygynous households.[45] As Mariana Candido and Adam Jones note, studies of colonial Africa tend to focus on women's economic life, households, and bodies, leaving scope for exploring women's experiences before the late nineteenth century.[46] Throughout this book, women emerge as central actors whose contributions shaped social, economic, and religious life. Their roles as wives, mothers, home carers, and educators intersected with broader economic and social networks, from managing domestic work to participating in labour opportunities provided by institutions such as the Liberated African Department. Women's experiences of migration and settlement reveal both continuities and differences compared with men, highlighting the multiple ways in which they exercised agency. They were also active participants in religious communities, nurturing social bonds and reinforcing communal life. While Chapter 4 specifically examines gender roles and expectations within households, stories of women and their contributions are interwoven throughout the book, showing how their labour, relationships, and networks were integral to everyday life.

The population of Freetown lived within a landscape shaped simultaneously by slavery and abolition, a context that helps underscore Orlando Patterson's argument that slavery produces a condition of 'social death', marked by the violent severing of kinship, ancestry, and social belonging. This framework is especially useful for understanding the experiences of those brought to the

43 Schwarz, 'Adaptation', pp. 19–37.

44 Maeve Ryan, '"It Was Necessary to do Something with Those Women"': Colonial Governance and the "Disposal" of Women and Girls in Early Nineteenth-Century Sierra Leone', *Gender & History* (2021), 491–510.

45 E. Frances White, *Sierra Leone's Settler Women Traders* (Ann Arbor, 1987); E. Frances White, 'Creole Women Traders in the Nineteenth Century', *The International Journal of African Historical Studies*, 14:4 (1981), 626–42; E. Frances White, 'Women, Work, and Ethnicity: The Sierra Leone Case', in Edna G. Bay (ed.), *Women and Work in Africa* (Boulder, 1982), pp. 19–34.

46 Mariana P. Candido and Adam Jones, 'Introduction', in Mariana P. Candido and Adam Jones (eds), *African Women in the Atlantic World: Property, Vulnerability & Mobility 1660–1880* (Woodbridge, 2019), pp. 1–18, at p. 1.

colony, who arrived having undergone profound forms of natal alienation.[47] As Baumeister and Leary demonstrate, the need to belong in a community is a basic human need; people form bonds because connections are essential to psychological well-being.[48] The destruction of prior social ties through natal alienation does not eliminate this need but intensifies the pressure to re-establish belonging in new social contexts. Research across psychology shows that shared identity and social connection shape how individuals cope with displacement, act collectively, and find purpose under conditions of trauma.[49] Upon arriving in Freetown, 'Liberated Africans' worked to reconstruct social ties that could provide belonging, stability, and mutual support. These dynamics extended beyond 'Liberated Africans', as voluntary migrants relied on existing contacts and kin-like ties when settling in the colony, reinforcing the importance of interpersonal networks. Across their life span, individuals sought to create new ties through employment, childbearing, religious conversion, and other social institutions.[50]

Methodology and Sources

Throughout this book, I show that a wide range of social, economic, familial, commercial, religious bonds and networks shaped everyday life in mid-nineteenth-century Freetown. As newcomers entered local economies, patterns of work, economic clustering, and inherited occupations produced social and spatial hierarchies that structured opportunity and status. Commercial partnerships further linked individuals and communities. Economic arrangements intersected with the formation and reshaping of families and households, where relationships and roles provided both stability and pathways for advancement. Religious communities and spiritual practices offered additional spaces for cultivating belonging, reinforcing bonds that connected economic, familial, and social life. Even before arrival in Freetown, migration, particularly when achieved through acts of self-liberation, was made possible by interpersonal

47 Orlando Patterson, *Slavery and Social Death* (Cambridge, 1982).

48 R. F. Baumeister and M. R. Leary, 'The Need to Belong: Desire for Interpersonal Attachments as a Fundamental Human Motivation', *Psychological Bulletin*, 117:3 (1995), 497–529.

49 A sample includes: Baumeister, and Leary, 'The Need to Belong'; M. N. Lambert, T. F. Stillman, J. A. Hicks, S. Kamble, R. F. Baumeister, and F. D. Fincham, 'To Belong Is to Matter: Sense of Belonging Enhances Meaning in Life', *Personality and Social Psychology Bulletin*, 39:11 (2013), 1418–27; J. Drury, 'The Role of Social Identity Processes in Mass Emergency Behaviour: An Integrative Review', *European Review of Social Psychology*, 29:1 (2018), 38–81.

50 Baumeister, and Leary, 'The Need to Belong', 505.

connections and the interventions of others. Taken together, these interconnected networks framed the diverse experiences of its inhabitants, including the roles played by women within households, commerce, and community life.

This research draws on an extensive collection of manuscript and printed evidence in Britain and Sierra Leone, which offers the opportunity to recover fragments of individual life experiences. Biographical details extracted across sources reveal the many layers of interaction within Freetown, shaped by legal status, geographical origins, employment, residential patterns, family and household structures, professional and business networks, and social spaces. Tracing these factors over half a century helps illustrate the evolution of social identity in one of the major ports of the West African coast during the era of abolition.

The Colonial Office records at the National Archives at Kew comprise Governor and Secretary of State despatches, issues from the Government's press *The Royal Gazette*; and *Sierra Leone Advertiser*, and annual reports. Although these records were instruments of colonial authority and reflect Western ideologies and imperial perspectives, they provide valuable insights.[51] Probate records include wills, which although they predominantly concern European merchants and colonial officials, offer important information about demographic and social change, including personal relationships, property ownership, and debt. To counterbalance the overwhelming number of wills from European men (there is only one surviving will from a 'Liberated African'), memorial inscriptions from St George's Cathedral and gravestones from the Circular Road cemetery have been incorporated. These inscriptions contain biographical information on roughly fifty individuals who lived in Freetown in the mid-nineteenth century.[52]

On 3 November 1831, Governor Findlay submitted to the Principal Secretary of State for War and the Colonies a detailed census of Freetown and the surrounding villages. The Freetown census listed names, occupations, and places of residence for 8,505 individuals, making it an invaluable source for reconstructing the demographic profile of the town and the lives of thousands of men and women. Its organisation suggests a household-by-household enumeration divided between the eastern and western sections, following a grid layout (figure I.1). House numbers were recorded sequentially as enumerators moved from dwelling to dwelling. Although houses on narrow streets such as

51 Assan Sarr, *Islam, Power, and Dependency in the Gambia River Basin: The Politics of Land Control, 1790–1940* (Rochester, 2016), p. 25; Alice Bellagamba, 'Slavery and Emancipation in the Colonial Archives: British Officials, Slave-Owners, and Slaves in the Protectorate of the Gambia (1890–1936)', *Canadian Journal of African Studies / Revue canadienne des études africaines*, 39:1 (2005), 5–41, at p. 14.

52 They were made available by the Arts and Humanities Research Council 'Remember Me' project at the University of Hull.

Frederick Street or George Street stood close together, consecutive entries in the census do not necessarily indicate immediate neighbours.[53] The 1831 census offers a rare view of a broad cross-section of the population.

In recent years, several studies have highlighted the socio-economic stratification of Freetown by analysing the 1831 census. This body of work shows that 'Liberated Africans' were builders of the port-city, but that labour was highly gendered. 'Liberated Africans' occupied the lowest income groups compared to Europeans and to free African immigrants. Informal and flexible labour became important with women being economic providers engaging in various activities.[54] Allen Howard has emphasised the value of linking the 1831 census to other primary sources and of using it as a starting point for historical reconstruction.[55] The presence of the colonial administration and creation of the Liberated African Department provides a wealth of documentation for 'Liberated Africans' and other members of the society.

Sources from the Sierra Leone Public Archives offer further evidence to construct a better understanding of the evolution and consequences of rapid settlement on Freetown. These include the Registers of Liberated Africans, birth and death registers, and the Register of Alien Children.[56] Between 1857 and 1862, birth registers comprise information on 1,117 births with the names, occupations, place of residence, and partners of 884 fathers. The Register of Alien Children from 1859 provides information on 112 children from outside the colony. This includes their names, occupation, residence in Freetown, ethnic group, as well as the name and residence of the parents and of the people with whom they lived within the port-city. Although these sources only provide information for a brief snapshot in time, their analysis brings to light voluntary migration patterns that reveal the multiplicity of experiences within different groups. Information extracted from the 1831 census, birth registers, and the Register of Alien Children has been transcribed and organised in

53 Edward Higgs, *A Clearer Sense of the Census: Victorian Censuses and Historical Research* (London, 1996), p. 60.

54 Stefania Galli, 'Socioeconomic Status and Group Belonging: Evidence from Early-Nineteenth-Century Colonial West Africa', *Social Science History* (2022), 1–24; Bronwen Everill, '"For the Services of Shipwrights, Coopers, and Grumettas": Freetown's Ship Repair Cluster in Nineteenth-Century Sierra Leone', *History of Science* (2020), 1–17; A. M. Howard, 'New Insights'; Everill and Laura Channing, 'On the Freetown Waterfront: Household Income and Informal Wage Labour in a Nineteenth Century Port City', *African Economic History Working*, 58 (2020), 1–36.

55 A. M. Howard, 'New Insights', pp. 101–26.

56 A large number of nineteenth-century sources held at the Sierra Leone Public Archives are available in digitised form through the British Library's Endangered Archives Programme. See 'Archival records from *Nineteenth century documents of the Sierra Leone Public Archives*' <https://eap.bl.uk/project/EAP443> [accessed 23 December 2025]; 'Preserving nineteenth-century records in the Sierra Leone Public Archives' <https://eap.bl.uk/project/EAP782> [accessed 23 December 2025].

Figure I.1 Street plan of Freetown, Sierra Leone.

Plan of Free Town, Sierra Leone, West Africa, Undertaken by J. T. F. Wallace (1885), Bibliothèque nationale de France, département Cartes et plans, GE D-21697.

an Excel database to trace nominal linkages between possible individuals through historical records. Using the dataset, which contains information on 9,972 individuals, makes it possible to identify occupational clusters, the formation of households, and the compositions of family units, among other patterns. This underscores various issues associated with the evolution of the social and economic profile of Freetown in the mid-nineteenth century.

The quantitative data of the census and birth registers is supplemented and cross-referenced to testimonies from seven volumes of police court records and police magistrate records, which contain 2,661 cases involving violence, public offences, property disputes, and taxation. These testimonies provide first-hand accounts of daily life, capturing glimpses of the voices of 'Liberated Africans', other African inhabitants, and enslaved people who escaped bondage and sought protection under British colonial law. Although these voices were mediated through clerks and officials, the records remain a rich source of evidence, particularly regarding women who made use of the judicial system.[57] The court cases reveal the varied degrees of freedom and constraint experienced

57 Candido, *Wealth, Land, and Property*, pp. 97, 111.

by Freetown's residents, as well as the complex dynamics of equality and inequality in a British West African colony.

Records from the courts of recovery of small debts between 1838 and 1840, and again in 1861, include 3,759 cases concerning debt ownership. Contrary to Victorian ideals of female domesticity, testimonies from African women show the breadth of their economic activities and their willingness to bring legal action, including against their husbands. Single women appear more frequently in the records, as they were not legally subsumed under a male household head. Married women, by contrast, were identified in relation to their husbands, which can obscure aspects of their individual identities. Although courtroom records offer only brief glimpses into the lives of Freetown's inhabitants, they nonetheless provide valuable insights into the lived experiences of both married and unmarried men and women.[58]

Chapter Outline

Chapter 1 examines the colonial framework that emerged in Freetown in the aftermath of the 1807 British Abolition Act. The city's infrastructure was outdated and not adequate for rapid demographic growth, creating harsh conditions of relocation for formerly enslaved people. As greater numbers of coerced migrants were settled in Freetown ('Liberated Africans', Barbadian exiles, discharged soldiers), the colonial government strengthened its policies controlling the life experience of African individuals. Yet, demographic growth also generated employment opportunities for members of the elite in sectors that supported the population through trade for local consumption, property ownership, and organisation of the Liberated African Department. At the time, forcibly relocated individuals were not passive actors and found ways to resist imposed structures, especially by leaving the colony or taking part in illegal slave trading activities.

Building on the examination of the colonial framework, Chapter 2 evaluates the diverse forms of settlement experiences that shaped Freetown's population. By the 1830s, more than half of the population was born outside the colony of Sierra Leone. Expectations of living conditions in the port-city were intrinsically different based on whether people were from Africa or from across the Atlantic, and on whether they were coerced to settle or freely migrated to Freetown. The town was perceived as an urban educational and trading centre, a place to secure freedom from war and slavery, or a place of forced relocation. The analysis of the inhabitants' urban background and the conditions and

58 Kristin Mann, *Slavery and the Birth of an African City: Lagos, 1760–1900* (Bloomington, 2007), p. 284.

circumstances of their journey to Freetown provides insight into the complex identity of the port-city, which was shaped by different perceptions of freedom and unfreedom.

Chapter 3 shifts from patterns of arrival to analysis of the employment profile and spatial distribution of the population to construct a socio-economic portrait of Freetown. It demonstrates how social status was not always fixed and that a small number of individuals were able to move upward within the colony's hierarchy. Time spent in the colony, education, knowledge of multiple languages, good working and social relationships were all factors that contributed to individuals attaining higher status. Wealth was expressed through land and property ownership, wearing apparel, jewellery, and furniture. For most coerced migrants, however, economic success was not typical, and the city remained segregated along lines of occupation, property ownership, and at times gender. Although new occupations became available to women and offered greater financial independence, they continued to be excluded from positions of influence.

Chapter 4 of this book examines the family and kinship networks that developed in Freetown. Households were central to the city's foundation and served as sites where communities were formed. Although domestic roles were often shaped by British social norms, African women actively challenged preconceived notions of domesticity. Despite the imposition of colonial family structures, cultural influences from people's homelands persisted. Polygyny continued to be practised, and women remained important social and economic contributors to their households. Through the analysis of women's testimonies preserved in police court records, the chapter shows the degree to which women were able to secure independence from violent and neglectful husbands. A comparative perspective further demonstrates that such acts of resistance were not unique to Freetown but formed part of broader patterns of women asserting agency across different colonial contexts.

While the previous chapter explores social interactions at the household level, Chapter 5 evaluates the dynamic and interconnected ways that commerce affected social relations. Family labour underpinned commercial activity, as children's contributions supported their parents' work. Islam was especially important to the expansion of the economy by securing trading partnerships between members of the Muslim community. Connected both to the Atlantic coast and to inland regions through extensive river networks, Freetown's expanding trade generated new forms of business relationships and created growing demand for transport services, food, accommodation, and translation for traders arriving from outside the colony. The development of these trading networks remained closely tied to the broader trajectory of legitimate commerce, which was periodically undermined by the persistence of slave-trading activities, even within the colony's own boundaries.

Beyond the spheres of household and work, Chapter 6, the last, focuses on religion, language, and ethnic affiliation as powerful markers of identity that fostered a sense of community belonging. Residents carved out social spaces for themselves in both public and private settings, extending beyond the boundaries imposed by colonial authorities. Yet social barriers were seldom fully dissolved since interactions remained closely tied to Christian or Muslim religious membership, to linguistic affiliations, or membership of clubs and initiation societies.

The study of Freetown's urban profile highlights the organisation and dynamics of its culturally diverse society. Population returns, birth registers, court records, and other archival materials offer rich evidence about many aspects of inhabitants' lives, revealing the identities of those who shaped, and were shaped by, the city's urban culture. Across the chapters, a comparative approach highlights both the parallels and distinctions between Freetown, other African Atlantic towns, and colonies throughout the British Empire, showing how this heterogeneous community was structured and sustained.

I

The Framework of Abolition

Held at the National Archives in Kew, London, the 1831 census of Freetown is the only detailed one available for the nineteenth century. It contains information on 8,505 inhabitants.[1] Studying the socio-economic profile of Freetown based on this document requires an understanding of how the society was shaped up to that date. Between 1808 and 1831, a total of 46,459 enslaved people were 'emancipated' in its harbour as 'Liberated Africans'.[2] Some of them were enlisted and later discharged from the Royal African Corps (R.A.C.), and the Second and Fourth West India Regiments (W.I.R.). In 1819, eighty-five enslaved people from Barbados were exiled to Freetown in the aftermath of an uprising on the island. Alongside these groups were free individuals drawn to the growing urban centre by economic and social connections. Although overlapping forms of voluntary and coerced displacement across the Atlantic world continued well into the 1860s, the aim of this chapter is to reconstruct the landscape of Freetown in the decades leading up to 1831. It outlines the structural framework that enabled and shaped successive waves of coerced settlement, showing how population growth created economic opportunities for some, while at the same time producing conditions that, for others, resembled slavery.[3] By examining both the composition of the population and the nature of the urban space, the chapter provides essential context for understanding the broader dynamics of life in Freetown that underpin the sources and life histories examined in later chapters of this book.

1 Census of Population and liberated Africans, 1831, TNA, CO 267/111.

2 Henry Lovejoy, Liberated Africans database, <https://liberatedafricans.org/databases/cases.php> [accessed 5 August 2025].

3 Suzanne Schwarz, 'The Impact of Liberated African "Disposal" Polices in Early Nineteenth-Century Sierra Leone', in Richard Anderson and Henry B. Lovejoy (eds), *Liberated Africans and the Abolition of the Slave Trade: Digital Histories of Enslavement and Freedom* (Rochester, 2020), pp. 45–65, at pp. 55–62; Richard Anderson, 'Abolition's Adolescence: Apprenticeship as "Liberation" in Sierra Leone, 1808–1848', *English Historical Review*, 137:586 (2022), 763–93; Christopher Fyfe, *A History of Sierra Leone* (Oxford, 1962), pp. 182–3; Henry Lovejoy, 'Defining "Liberated Africans" and Other Related Terms' <https://liberatedafricans.org/about/essays.php?id=3> [accessed 25 January 2024].

Demographic data about Freetown in the first decades of the nineteenth century is inconsistent, and the continuous arrival of 'Liberated Africans' impeded the undertaking of accurate enumeration. Some estimates are, however, available to trace demographic growth (Table 1.1). The first census was taken in 1802, followed by others in 1811 and 1817, but these excluded 'Liberated Africans', who were first included in 1818. Numerical data for 1818, 1820, and 1822 was transmitted to London in 1825 and is available in Parliamentary Papers. Although a census was conducted in 1826, it excluded children attending school and 'Liberated Africans' employed in the public works, and significantly underestimated the number of 'Liberated Africans' disembarked in the colony.[4] Additional demographic information appears in the Blue Books of the colony of Sierra Leone. While not entirely reliable, the numerical data compiled in different returns still offers a useful starting point for examining patterns of demographic growth and spatial organisation.

As in many British colonies, the nature and scope of demographic information was contingent on local concerns.[5] Categories used in the population returns thus reflect the evolution of the social landscape of Freetown, as shown in 1817 when the population was divided into 'Europeans', 'Settlers', 'Maroons', 'Natives', and 'Servants'.[6] By the end of 1818, the population was divided into 'Europeans', 'Nova Scotian settlers', 'Maroon settlers', 'Liberated Africans' listed as apprentices, 'Liberated Africans' who were not apprenticed, 'Kroo', and 'Natives'. Beyond 1822, and up to 1831, the numbers only refer to the overall population, without any indications on the proportion of 'Liberated Africans' and other members of the society.

Table 1.1 Population of Freetown and of the colony, 1802–1831.

Year	Freetown	Colony
1802	1,615	
1809	2,000	
1811	2,518	
1817	2,183	
1818	4,430	9,450

4 Kathrin Levitan, '"Sprung from Ourselves": British Interpretations of Mid-Nineteenth-Century Racial Demographics', in Andrew S. Thompson and Kent Fedorowich (eds), *Empire, Migration and Identity in the British World* (Manchester, 2013), pp. 60–81, at p. 60; Robert René Kuczynski, *Demographic Survey of the British Colonial Empire* (London, 1948), pp. 19–21.

5 A. J. Christopher, 'The Quest for a Census of the British Empire c.1840–1940', *Journal of Historical Geography*, 34 (2008), 268–85, at pp. 269, 272.

6 Cadbury Research Library, University of Birmingham, Birmingham, UK; Church Missionary Society Archives, Special Collections, Census of Freetown, March 1817.

Year	Freetown	Colony
1820	5,785	12,509
1822	5,643	15,081
1823		15,081
1824		14,094
1825		16,510
1826	5,790	17,354
1827		17,512
1831	8,505	31,288

Sources: David E. Skinner, *Thomas George Lawson: African Historian and Administrator in Sierra Leone* (Stanford, 1980), p. 5; Cadbury Research Library; University of Birmingham, Birmingham, UK, Church Missionary Society Archives, Special Collections; Census of Freetown, March 1817; *Sierra Leone. Accounts relating to the duties, exports, imports; population; schools, churches, marriages; &c. of the colony of Sierra Leone*, HC 1825, no. 520, pp. 19–21; Adam Jones, 'Recaptive Nations: Evidence Concerning the Demographic Impact of the Atlantic Slave Trade in the Early Nineteenth Century', *Slavery & Abolition*, 11 (1990), 42–57, at p. 55; BOA, Blue Books of Sierra Leone, 1824, fol. 53; BOA, Blue Books of Sierra Leone, 1825, fol. 32; BOA, Blue Books of Sierra Leone, 1826, fol. 43; BOA, Blue Books of Sierra Leone, 1827, fol. 48; BOA, Blue Books of Sierra Leone, 1828, fol. 48; BOA, Blue Books of Sierra Leone, 1829, fol. 58; BOA, Blue Books of Sierra Leone, 1831, fol. 58; Jeffrey Gunn, *Outsourcing African Labor: Kru Migratory Workers in Global Ports, Estates and Battlefields until the End of the 19th Century* (Berlin, 2021), p. 77.

This chapter focuses on coerced migrants who were settled in Freetown in the first decades of the nineteenth century, but it is important to consider other groups whose presence significantly shaped Freetown's landscape, and whose experiences ran parallel to those of coerced migrants. Small numbers of Europeans lived in Freetown as missionaries or as part of the colonial administration. By 1808, Nova Scotian settlers had been living there for sixteen years, and Maroons for eight years. Most of them lived near the harbour in an area that came to be known as Settler Town. Through the naming of streets, these communities inscribed their presence onto the landscape and left behind visible markers of their origins and identities. Nova Scotians' references are seen through street names related to figures from the American Revolutionary War, such as William Howe, Francis Rawdon, and Banastre Tarleton, while the Maroons' origin was referenced in names such as Trelawney Street, a nod to Trelawny Town in Jamaica.[7]

The 'Natives' category in the population returns indicates free movements of Africans, who also settled in specific areas of Freetown. These groups, fully discussed in Chapter 2, comprised nearby Fula, Loko, Mende, Susu, and Temne migrants, among others. Muslim migrants were among those who made a clear

7 Fyfe, *A History*, p. 99.

imprint on the urban landscape. In 1819, they established Bambara Town and Fula Town in the eastern part of Freetown. Their movements were influenced by networks of traders and scholars from north of the colony, especially from Forekaria and Timbo, and from more distant regions in Senegal and Mali.[8] In 1818, 1820, and 1822, the number of African immigrants recorded in official returns was 997, 646, and 1,387, respectively. It remains unclear how these figures were compiled since their arrival in the colony was not systematically documented. Free regional migrants also included Kru, who were maritime labourers from the Kru Coast, in modern-day southern Liberia and south-western Côte d'Ivoire. Some had arrived in Sierra Leone even before the founding of the Sierra Leone Company in 1792 and were employed at the British slave fort on Bunce Island. By the nineteenth century, they were employed on ships, working as firemen, stokers, and greasers, or on deck as stevedores and winchmen. The arrival of 'Liberated Africans' increased demand for their labour, especially for unloading ships, as Kru boats were essential for landing. Kru communities had been living by Kroo Bay since at least 1792, and, in 1816, they were settled in a reservation known as Kroo Town (Krutown). By 1820, 615 Kru people were officially recorded, a number that almost doubled to 1,100 by 1826.[9]

The focus now turns to coerced migrants, those whose arrival in the colony was shaped by various forms of forced displacement. Although this group is mostly represented by 'Liberated Africans', there is also a smaller number of enslaved individuals exiled from Barbados. On Easter Sunday 14 April 1816, Bussa's rebellion, the only major uprising led by enslaved people on the island, erupted across plantations in Barbados. It was swiftly suppressed within a few days, and martial law was declared. By 21 September 1816, 144 people were executed, another 70 were sentenced to death, and 123 were sentenced to deportation. On 25 January 1817, these 123 prisoners were embarked on board the *Francis & Mary* to be deported to British Honduras. On their arrival, the Lieutenant-Governor there, George Arthur, refused to let them permanently settle there. In 1819, 85 surviving African Barbadians were thus relocated to Freetown.[10] Their settlement in the West African colony was

8 R. J. Olu-Wright, 'The Physical Growth of Freetown', in Christopher Fyfe and Eldred Durosimi Jones (eds), *Freetown: A Symposium* (Oxford, 1968), pp. 24–37, at pp. 27–8; David E. Skinner, 'Islam and Education in the Colony and Hinterland of Sierra Leone (1750–1914)', *Canadian Journal of African Studies / Revue canadienne des études africaines*, 10:3 (1976), 499–520, at p. 501.

9 Gunn, *Outsourcing African Labor*; Diane Frost, 'Diasporan West African Communities: The Kru in Freetown & Liverpool', *Review of African Political Economy*, 29:92 (2002), 285–300, at pp. 291–2.

10 Hilary Beckles, 'The Slave-Drivers' War: Bussa and the 1816 Barbados Slave Rebellion', *Boletín de Estudios Latinoamericanos y del Caribe*, 39 (1985), 85–110; Hilary Beckles, *A History of Barbados: From Amerindian Settlement to Caribbean Single Market*, 2nd edn

part of their exile rather than a choice. Most had been born into slavery in Barbados and had no direct knowledge of the African continent. In the returns of 1820, they only appear in a brief note: '85 persons from Barbadoes [*sic*], last from Honduras'.

The largest and most important influx of coerced migrants to Freetown between 1808 and 1831 came in the form of 'Liberated Africans'. The British Vice-Admiralty Court legally 'freed' 38,747 people between 1808 and 1885, with 17,383 of them 'emancipated' between 1808 and 1831. Others were then 'emancipated' through a system of international cooperation against the trans-atlantic slave trade. On 28 July 1817, 23 September 1817, and 4 May 1818, Britain signed treaties with Portugal, Spain, and the Netherlands, respectively, granting the right to search these nations' merchant vessels suspected of carrying enslaved people. In 1819, three Courts of Mixed Commission were established to prosecute slave merchants and legally emancipate enslaved individuals found on captured ships: an Anglo-Portuguese, an Anglo-Spanish, and an Anglo-Dutch court. A treaty signed with Brazil on 23 November 1826 led to the opening of an Anglo-Brazilian court in 1828. These new legal mechanisms shaped demographic growth, since, between 1823 and 1829, the number of captured ships increased significantly, with 1829 marking the highest number of disembarkations within a single year (Graph 1.1). Between 1808 and 1831, these Mixed Commission courts 'emancipated' over 29,076 'Liberated Africans'. In total, they 'emancipated' over 72,000 individuals with the last significant influx in 1861. The last ship adjudicated by a Mixed Court in Freetown was Spanish vessel *America* in 1864.[11]

The sequence of steps that unfolded once a captured ship reached Freetown (waiting, adjudication, registration, and disembarkation) defined the initial phase of the 'Liberated African' legal emancipation process. After a vessel entered the harbour, people had to wait before disembarking and being sent to King's Yard (later known as Queen's Yard), the walled enclosure built in 1817 to contain newly landed individuals.[12] When the case was adjudicated, basic information on each individual was recorded by clerks of the Liberated African Department in the Registers of Liberated Africans.[13] In many cases, this registration was carried out on board the ships themselves. Clerks relied

(Cambridge, 2006), p. 109; Hilary Beckles, *Great House Rules: Landless Emancipation and Workers' Protest in Barbados* (Kingston, 2004), p. 91.

11 Leslie Bethell, 'The Mixed Commissions for the Suppression of the Transatlantic Slave Trade in the Nineteenth Century', *Journal of African History*, 7:1 (1966), 79–93; Henry Lovejoy, Liberated Africans database <https://liberatedafricans.org/databases/cases.php> [accessed 7 August 2025].

12 Fyfe, *A History*, p. 134; Anderson, *Abolition*, p. 87.

13 Suzanne Schwarz, 'Reconstructing the Life Histories of Liberated Africans: Sierra Leone in the Early Nineteenth Century', *History in Africa*, 39 (2012), 175–207.

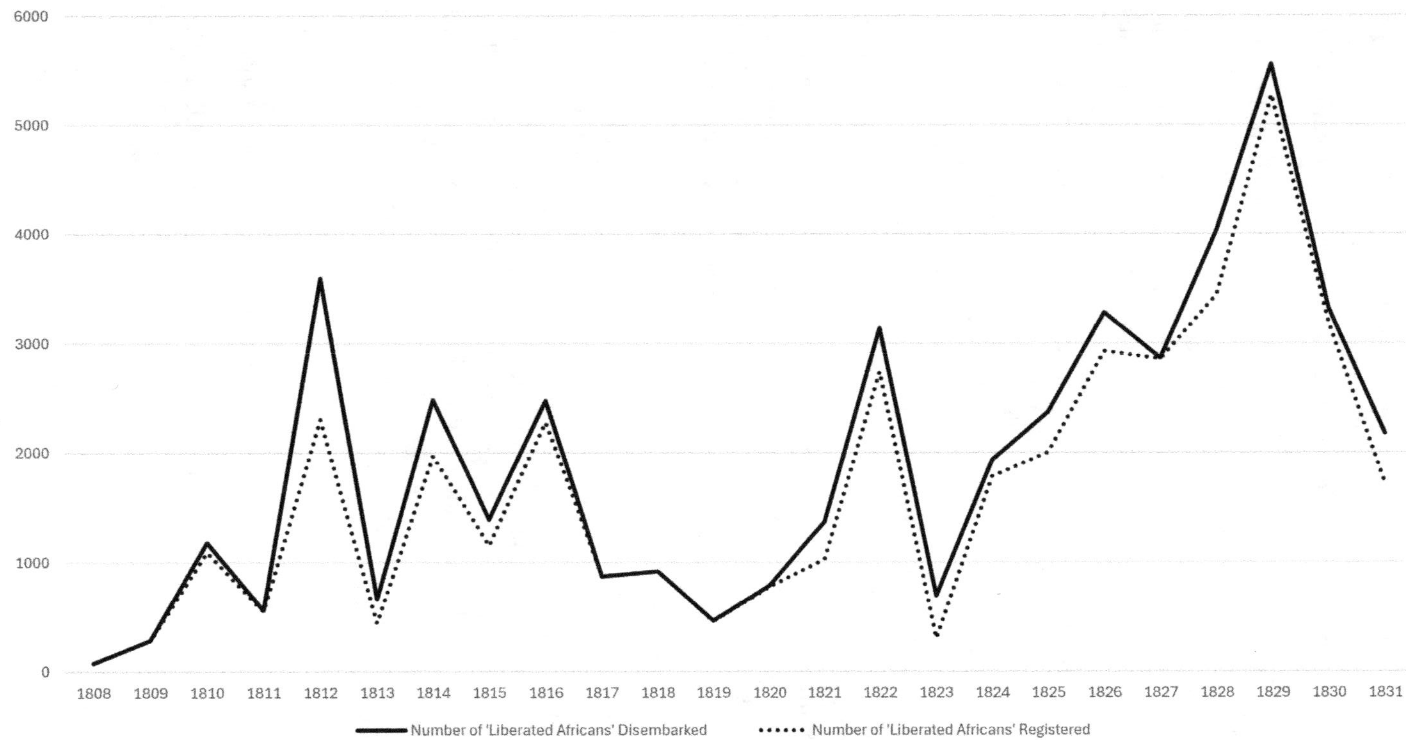

Graph 1.1 Number of 'Liberated Africans' disembarked at Freetown, 1808–1831.
Source: Liberated Africans database <https://liberatedafricans.org/databases/cases.php> [accessed 25 February 2026].

on interpreters, including some 'Liberated Africans', to complete the registers. Since small numbers of individuals died between the date of sentencing and the moment of registration, and since in certain cases no register was produced, the Liberated African database (liberatedafricans.org) distinguishes between the numbers of 'Liberated Africans' disembarked and the numbers of those who were registered.[14]

Delays in disembarkation were frequent, forcing them to remain on the ship longer. In 1812, officials noted that the Royal Navy's growing activity overwhelmed the Vice-Admiralty Court with paperwork. That year, twenty-two ships arrived, with five landing in March alone.[15] According to the colonial secretary, Joseph Reffell, during the early phase of the Court 'Liberated Africans' landed a day after their arrival, but under the Mixed Commission Courts, the process took up to twenty days. By 1826, Thomas Cole, the chief superintendent of the Liberated African Department, stated that an additional five to six days were needed before 'Liberated Africans' were officially registered. The amount of time varied according to the court overseeing the adjudication process. On 18 February 1829, there were already three slave vessels awaiting adjudication.[16] In March 1829, five ships, *União*, *Jules*, *Carolina*, *Jeune Eugénie*, and *Almirante* arrived, disembarking a total of 1,434 'Liberated Africans' over a period of twenty days. Other times vessels arrived on the same day. Brazilian schooner *Mensengeira* and Dutch schooner *Hirondelle* together landed a total of 334 'Liberated Africans' on 5 May 1829.[17]

'Liberated Africans' who were in poor health were brought on shore first. When the Spanish schooner *Iberia* arrived on 22 January 1826 with 417 enslaved individuals on board, 14 died shortly after at the smallpox hospital at Wilberforce – smallpox being one of the epidemiological factors connected with the slave trade.[18] In extreme cases, when conditions were dire, all survivors were landed immediately, as with Brazilian brig *Clementina*, which in 1828 had

14 Henry Lovejoy, Liberated Africans database <https://liberatedafricans.org/databases/cases.php> [accessed 2 March 2026].

15 *Extracts from the Report of the Commissioners Appointed for Investigating the State of the Settlements and Governments on the Coast of Africa*, HC 1812, p. 7; Slave Voyages database <https://www.slavevoyages.org/voyages/YAfluZ5f> [accessed 19 January 2024].

16 Appendix B, No. 9, 1827, TNA, CO 267/92, Commissioner's Report, Sierra Leone Commissioners of Enquiry: Appendices B and C., fol. 11; Appendix B, No. 10, 1827, TNA, CO 267/92, fol. 56; *Abstract Statement of Expenditure of Sierra Leone, 1812–28*, HC 1830, no. 57, p. 34.

17 Henry Lovejoy, Liberated Africans database <https://liberatedafricans.org/databases/cases.php> [accessed 5 August 2025].

18 Richard Anderson, *Abolition in Sierra Leone: Re-Building Lives and Identities in Nineteenth-Century West Africa* (Cambridge, 2020), pp. 82–3; 'Iberia', Liberated Africans database <https://liberatedafricans.org/event_details.php?EventID=3169> [accessed 4 March 2025]; 'Voyage ID: 2368' <http://www.slavevoyages.org/voyage/2368/variables>

lost 107 of the 271 enslaved people on board during the Middle Passage from the Cameroons River.[19]

The lack of adequate infrastructure meant that, between disembarkation and legal emancipation, some 'Liberated Africans' had to spend the night outside. Thomas Cole reported that accommodation was insufficient and not well adapted to the needs of 'Liberated Africans' after landing. With no shed or covering belonging to the Liberated African Department, individuals arriving during the rainy season had to wrap themselves in blankets and find shelter in shady places or arcades in public squares. In some cases, Cole admitted, the Department placed them in the gaol for lack of other accommodation.[20] Maeve Ryan notes that in 1815 'Liberated Africans' were roaming the streets and 'foraging for basic subsistence'. Some missionaries observed cases of a few of them dying of starvation.[21] In the late 1820s, the colonial administration became increasingly worried that the poor soil of the colony would drive 'Liberated Africans' to wander in the woods beyond the jurisdiction of the colony.[22] In April 1830, Commissioner William Smith reported that the Department was not in charge of any 'Liberated Africans' in Freetown. Yet, by 31 May 1830, 1,117 individuals recently disembarked were still awaiting 'emancipation'.[23] Many sought temporary shelter on the streets or waited in the King's Yard.

'Liberated Africans' transited through Freetown's harbour, but their fates diverged. Upon arrival, they were either conscripted, settled in the port-city, or dispersed into colonial villages. The Slave Trade Abolition Act stipulated that those released by the West African Squadron were to 'enter and enlist ... into His Majesty's Land or Sea Service, as Soldiers, Seamen, or Marines ... as if he had voluntarily so enlisted' or be bound as apprentices to older settlers for a period up to fourteen years. [24] Far from

[accessed 23 March 2022]; Philip D. Curtin 'Epidemiology and the Slave Trade', *Political Science Quarterly*, 83:2 (1968), 190–216.

19 *Abstract*, HC 1830, no. 57, p. 29, 'Clementina', Liberated Africans database, <https://liberatedafricans.org/event_details.php?EventID=3384> [accessed 5 August 2025].

20 Appendix B, No. 9, 1827, TNA, CO 267/92, fol. 43.

21 Maeve Ryan, '"A Most Promising Field for Future Usefulness": The Church Missionary Society and the Liberated Africans of Sierra Leone', in W. Mulligan and M. Bric (eds), *A Global History of Anti-Slavery Politics in the Nineteenth Century* (London, 2013), pp. 37–58, at. p. 39.

22 *Abstract*, HC 1830, no. 57, p. 6; *Liberated Africans. Papers relating to liberated Africans located in the colony of Sierra Leone*, HC 1826, no. 389, pp. 4–5.

23 *Charge delivered by Mr. Justice Jeffcott to Grand Jury of Sierra Leone and Correspondence on Slave Trade*, HC 1832, no. 364, p. 9; *Correspondence with British Coms. at Sierra Leone, Havana, Rio de Janeiro and Surinam, and with Foreign Powers on Slave Trade, 1830 (Class A & B)*, HC 1831, no. 004, p. 53.

24 Geo III Sess. 1 c. 36.

granting full freedom, legal emancipation marked the beginning of a new form of coercion, either through another coerced ship journey or coerced labour. 'Liberated Africans' came to be considered as products of the Crown colony, and their labour was instrumentalised for the expansion of the British Empire.[25]

Large numbers of 'Liberated Africans' were sent to farm across newly created colony villages on the Sierra Leone peninsula. In 1812, out of 2,569 individuals disembarked, 752 were settled in unauthorised villages, which were organically formed by the people rather than by the colonial administration. In 1816, Governor MacCarthy decided to administratively reorganise the colony and divided it into parishes with appointed superintendents.[26] On 6 March 1827, Spanish schooner *Emilia* landed 177 'Liberated Africans', with none of them settled in Freetown. Of the 172 'Liberated Africans' disembarked from Brazilian schooner *Não Lendia* on 1 April 1830, only Malfallarbay and Awosoo were settled in the port-city. Malfallarbay was apprenticed to Joseph DeGraft and was given the name of Frederick James and Awosoo was apprenticed to Harriet Gillard and was either renamed Nancy or Rosanna.[27] Despite the emphasis on village settlement, Freetown's population grew significantly by the late 1820s. After 1824, many who had been settled in villages began moving into the city in search of employment after the Church Missionary Society (C.M.S.) was relieved from their superintendence.[28] In 1818, 'Liberated Africans' represented 34 per cent of the population, increasingly slightly to 38 per cent in 1820 and 35 per cent in 1822. By the 1831 census, they represented almost 40 per cent of the population of Freetown.[29]

25 Érika Melek Delgado, 'Liberated African "Children" in Sierra Leone: Colonial Classifications of "Child" and "Childhood," 1808–19', in Richard Anderson and Henry B. Lovejoy (eds), *Liberated Africans and the Abolition of the Slave Trade: Digital Histories of Enslavement and Freedom* (Rochester, 2020), pp. 81–100, at p. 87; Padraic X. Scanlan, 'The Rewards of Their Exertions: Prize Money and British Abolitionism in Sierra Leone, 1808–1823', *Past & Present*, 225 (2014), 113–42; Henry Lovejoy, 'Defining'; Maeve Ryan, *Humanitarian Governance and the British Antislavery World System* (New Haven, 2022).

26 Anderson, *Abolition*, pp. 107, 111–12; Slave Voyages database <https://www.slavevoyages.org/voyages/NWsqilWs> [accessed 23 January 2024]; Fyfe, *A History*, p. 128.

27 SLPA, Liberated African Department; Miscellaneous return book (1826–1834), fol. 91; 'Emilia', Liberated Africans database, <https://liberatedafricans.org/event_details.php?EventID=3176> [accessed 10 February 2026]; 'Não Lendia', Liberated Africans database, <https://liberatedafricans.org/databases/event_details.php?EventID=3405> [accessed 10 February 2026]; Census, 1831, TNA, CO 267/111, fol. 299, 327.

28 *Coms. of Inquiry into State of Colony of Sierra Leone, Report (Part I.)*, HC 1827, no. 312, pp. 32–4.

29 *Sierra Leone*, HC 1825, no. 520, pp. 13–15.

Before 1811, 106 'Liberated Africans' had been enlisted into the R.A.C. or the British Royal Navy.[30] Recruitment efforts increased after 1812, when W.I.R. recruiters from Barbados established a depot at Bunce Island. The W.I.R. relied on the purchase of enslaved people for military service, but the abolition of the British transatlantic slave trade ended this practice and turned 'Liberated Africans' into replacements.[31] 'Liberated Africans' who were enlisted into the W.I.R. troops were recruited not only in the colony of Sierra Leone but also in parts of the Caribbean, such as Tortola (part of the British Virgin Islands) and the Bahamas.[32] Between 1808 and 1815, over 2,000 'Liberated Africans' were enlisted upon their 'emancipation' in Freetown and discharged at the end of the Napoleonic Wars. These individuals were deployed to the Caribbean, received pay, and were given the option to return to the colony of Sierra Leone after discharge, an option some exercised. Most of them were able-bodied men, but there were also over a hundred women recruited.[33]

Enlistment not only shaped the lives of 'Liberated Africans' but also laid the foundation for distinct areas in Freetown. By 1811, recruits from the R.A.C. were settled near Fort Thornton. As the barracks there required reconstruction, soldiers built huts and established what became known as Soldier Town.[34] Five companies of the Second W.I.R. were disbanded in 1819, joining approximately 1,222 soldiers and their families who had been discharged from the R.A.C. between 1817 and 1819.[35] The 1820 returns listed them as 'people discharged from the late 4th W. I. Regiment, Royal African Corps, and 2nd W. I. Regt'. In 1822, a designated 'discharged soldier' section was added. Officers of the W.I.R. were moved to colony villages, with only about 300 remaining in Freetown. They founded the area of Gibraltar Town, named after their service in Gibraltar. By

30 Daniel Domingues da Silva, David Eltis, Philip Misevich, and Olatunji Ojo, 'The Diaspora of Africans Liberated from Slave Ships in the Nineteenth Century', *Journal of African History*, 55 (2014), 347–69, at p. 359.

31 Richard Anderson, 'The Diaspora of Sierra Leone's Liberated Africans: Enlistment, Forced Migration, and "Liberation" at Freetown, 1808–1863', *African Economic History*, 41 (2013), 101–38, at pp. 105–6.

32 Sean M. Kelley, 'Precedents: The "Captured Negroes" of Tortola, 1802–22" in Richard Anderson and Henry B. Lovejoy (eds), *Liberated Africans and the Abolition of the Slave Trade: Digital Histories of Enslavement and Freedom* (Rochester, 2020), pp. 25–44, at p. 38; Laura Rosanne Adderley, 'Household Labor and Sexual Coercion Reconstructing Women's Experience of African Recaptive Settlement', in Richard Anderson and Henry B. Lovejoy (eds), *Liberated Africans and the Abolition of the Slave Trade: Digital Histories of Enslavement and Freedom* (Rochester, 2020), pp. 174–97, at p. 179.

33 Anderson, 'The Diaspora', pp. 105–6.

34 Fyfe, *A History*, p. 119; Anderson, 'The Diaspora', p. 105; Padraic X. Scanlan, 'The Colonial Rebirth of British Anti-Slavery: The Liberated African Villages of Sierra Leone, 1815–1824', *American Historical Review*, 121:4 (2016), 1085–113, at p. 1097.

35 Anderson, 'The Diaspora', pp. 110–1; Fyfe, *A History*, pp. 135–6, 146.

March 1826, there were 949 military pensioners in the colony although only 291 of them lived in Freetown.[36]

Some individuals were dispersed across different parts of the city to aid in its expansion. In 1808, 'Liberated African' men disembarking from French schooner the *Marie Paul* were each given two acres of land. In 1812, another group settled near the former site of Granville Town, on the eastern side of the city, in an area named Kissi Town. In 1813, others who had been purchased by Portuguese or Brazilian slave traders and bound to Brazil before being intercepted by the Royal Navy, settled in Pa Demba's Town, later renamed Portuguese Town. Others were settled according to their regions of origin. In 1816, a group of 'Liberated Africans' who were said to be 'Congo' people (a term referring their West Central Africa origin), was placed in an area along Whiteman's Bay, which became known as Congo Town.[37]

Apprenticeship became a preferred method for placing 'Liberated Africans' during Edward Henry Columbine's governorship (1810–1811). It reduced government costs by shifting responsibility to private households, which paid a nominal apprenticeship fee.[38] Authorities claimed this system ensured that apprentices would be housed with people able to feed and clothe them. In the mid-1830s, Governor Campbell raised the apprenticeship fee from 10 shillings to £1, increasing the cost of 'freedom'.[39] This was a significant amount since, as an example, the annual salary of a beadle was £7. 16s. and that of a church cleaner £5. 4s.[40] Several historians argue that the apprenticeship system bore strong similarities to slavery, with Henry Lovejoy defining it as an 'involuntary, unpaid labor contract assigned to an enslaved person emancipated through state intervention'.[41] This was not unique to the colony of Sierra Leone. In the French colonies of Senegal and Madagascar, formerly enslaved people were forced to 'pay' for their freedom through a system of engagement. In Brazil and Cuba, the conditions endured by *libertos* and *emancipados* are described as severe as, or worse than, those of slavery.[42] Such comparisons were already

36 *Sierra Leone. Accounts relating to the duties, exports, imports; population; schools, churches, marriages; &c. of the colony of Sierra Leone*, HC 1825, no. 520, p. 18; Anderson, 'The Diaspora', pp. 110–11.

37 Fyfe, *A History*, pp. 119–20; Anderson, *Abolition*, p. 135; Gwendolyn Midlo Hall, *Slavery and African Ethnicities in the Americas: Restoring the Links* (Chapel Hill, 2005), p. 88.

38 Anderson, *Abolition*, pp. 106–7.

39 Anderson, 'Abolition's Adolescence', pp. 784–5.

40 BOA, Blue Books of Sierra Leone, 1831, fol. 44.

41 Schwarz, 'The Impact', pp. 55–62; Anderson, 'Abolition's Adolescence', pp. 763–93; Fyfe, *A History*, pp. 182–3; Henry Lovejoy, 'Defining'.

42 Kelly Brignac, 'African Indentured Labor in Senegal and Ste. Marie, Madagascar, 1817–1830', *Slavery & Abolition*, 43:4 (2022), 779–97; Djiguatte Amédé Bassene, 'Continuité de la traite d'êtres humains, de la captivité et de l'asservissement des femmes et des enfants

being made during the early years of the colony. In 1808, Governor Thomas Perronet Thompson condemned the treatment of the first 167 'Liberated Africans' landed in Freetown, who were sold by colonial authorities to local inhabitants for US $20 each.[43] Despite oppressive conditions, 'Liberated Africans' sought to resist and assert their rights. They sometimes made use of colonial legal channels to report mistreatment as magistrates were required to treat their complaints as seriously as those of other settlers, although these efforts were not always successful.[44]

There were very few exceptions where apprenticeship offered economic opportunities. As part of a report commissioned in the mid-1820s, information was gathered on some members of the population, and twenty-five 'Liberated African' men were asked questions sent by the Commissioners.[45] Among them were Peter and Cato Preston, who were apprenticed to Judith Preston. They stated that they did not learn any trade from her, but that they were later apprenticed to Peter Scott, a butcher, who taught them his

en Sénégambie française du XIXe au début du XXe siècles', in Klara Boyer-Rossol and Marie-Pierre Ballarin (eds), *Les esclavages en Afrique. Passé(s), présent(s) et héritages* (Paris, 2024), pp. 179–94, at pp. 187–8; Inés Roldán de Montaud, 'The Misfortune of Liberated Africans in Colonial Cuba, 1824–76', in Richard Anderson and Henry B. Lovejoy (eds), *Liberated Africans and the Abolition of the Slave Trade: Digital Histories of Enslavement and Freedom* (Rochester, 2020), pp. 153–73, at p. 162; Daniela Carvalho Cavalheiro, '"I am not a Slave": Liberated Africans and their Usage of the Judicial System in Nineteenth Century Rio de Janeiro', in Vanicléia Silva Santos (ed.), *General History of Africa*, vol. X, *Africa and its Diasporas* (Paris, 2023), pp. 891–900; Ibrahima Thioub, 'L'abolition de l'esclavage en Afrique française : le principe du sol libérateur à l'épreuve du terrain', in Annie Fitte-Duval (ed.), *Droit et esclavages : Théorie et pratiques en Afrique et dans les Amériques (XVe-XIXe siècles)* (Paris, 2022), pp. 215–40, at p. 221; Roquinaldo Ferreira, *Worlds of Unfreedom: West Central Africa in the Era of Global Abolition* (Princeton, 2025), pp. 187–91.

43 Suzanne Schwarz, 'Reconstructing the Life Histories of Liberated Africans: Sierra Leone in the Early Nineteenth Century', *History in Africa*, 39 (2012), 175–207.

44 Schwarz, 'The Impact', pp. 45–65; Suzanne Schwarz, 'Fragments of the Life History of Fuseng-Be: A Temne Woman Sold in Freetown, Sierra Leone in the Early Nineteenth Century', in Vanicléia Silva Santos (ed.), *General History of Africa*, vol. X, *Africa and its Diasporas* (Paris, 2023), pp. 977–86.

45 On 23 March 1824, Joseph Hume, MP for Aberdeen, demanded that information should be supplied on the benefits that the colony of Sierra Leone was bringing to Britain. Economic pressure in Britain led members of the government to argue that the colony was unhealthy and poorly located to patrol the coast. As a result, Messrs Rowan and Wellington were sent to Freetown as Commissioners in late 1825. They returned to England in 1826. On 11 April 1827, they submitted a report on the state of the colony to Henry Bathurst, 3rd Earl Bathurst, Secretary of State for War and the Colonies. See HC, Debate, 12 March 1824, vol. 10 c962; Fyfe, *A History*, p. 163; *Coms. of Inquiry*, HC 1827, no. 312; David Lambert, 'Sierra Leone and Other Sites in the War of Representation over Slavery', *History Workshop Journal*, 64 (2007), 103–32.

trade before he passed away. Other men interviewed managed to use the skills they acquired during their apprenticeship. Samuel Bone, forcibly relocated in Freetown in 1810, was apprenticed as a mason for nine years to Adam Turner, a Nova Scotian settler. After completing his apprenticeship, Bone began selling wattles, which were branches of trees interlaced and used to build fences, walls, and roofs. He later worked as a mason at Îles de Los, before being employed by the authorities. Thomas Brown, who disembarked from a slave ship in Freetown around 1812, was apprenticed to and named after a mason named Thomas Brown. After three years of learning his trade, he was able to work on his own account.[46]

With demographic and spatial growth, 'Liberated Africans' who were not apprenticed and who were considered as unskilled labourers were employed on the public works.[47] Unlike other Atlantic ports in Africa, Freetown was not built on slave labour but on the work of newly 'freed' individuals forcibly relocated there. This was facilitated by the fact that, between 1808 and 1831, the majority of 'Liberated Africans' were male (65.6 per cent).[48] Employing men in construction was characteristic of other colonies as well. In St Helena and the Bahamas, 'Liberated Africans' were placed on public works after disembarkation, to repair roads and maintain government facilities.[49] They worked for a minimum of three months before being replaced by newly disembarked people. Information on disposal is not available for all those disembarked between 1808 and 1831, which makes it impossible to trace the exact number of men sent to the public works upon disembarkation. Men disembarked from the *Marie Paul* had to '[cut] a road to their place of settlement'.[50] Between 1808 and 1831, 370 additional men were recorded as labourers on the public works in the Registers of Liberated Africans. There were also 212 men employed as labourers at the barracks. As shown in Table 1.2, 19 per cent of the people disembarked from 10 slave ships between 1825 and 1826 went straight into public works.[51] On 30 June 1829, 66 men were employed in the public works with an allowance expiring on 15 October 1829. Another 104

46 'Wattle, n.1'. *OED Online* (Oxford, 2022 <http://www.oed.com/view/Entry/226365> [accessed 24 June 2022]; Appendix A, No. 11, 1827, TNA, CO 267/91, Commissioner's Report, Sierra Leone Commissioners of Enquiry; *Coms. of Inquiry*, HC 1827, no. 312, p. 32.

47 Scanlan, 'The Colonial Rebirth', p. 1099.

48 Slave Voyages database <https://www.slavevoyages.org/voyages/W8C4LYaE> [accessed 26 January 2024].

49 Andrew Pearson, *Distant Freedom: St. Helena and the Abolition of the Slave Trade, 1840–1872* (Liverpool, 2016), pp. 201–203; Howard Johnson, 'The Liberated Africans in the Bahamas, 1811–60', *Immigrants & Minorities*, 7:1 (1988), pp. 16–40, at p. 31.

50 Schwarz, 'Reconstructing', p. 190.

51 SLPA, RLA 19889 - 24205 (1825–1827).

men had an allowance ending on 27 December 1829.[52] During the first two to three years after their arrival in Freetown, exiled Barbadian men from Bussa's rebellion were also to repair roads. It was only after a few years that they were able to work on their own account.[53]

Table 1.2 'Liberated Africans' employed on public works, 1808–1826.

Year	Vessel	Number of 'Liberated Africans' employed on public works	Total number of 'Liberated Africans' disembarked
1808	*Marie Paul*	34	60
1825	*Segunda Gallega*	38	276
1825	*Teresa*	4	40
1825	*Ana*	15	71
1825	*Ninfa Habanera*	40	228
1825	*Paquete da Bahia*	126	385
1826	*Aimable Claudine*	10	32
1826	*Iberia*	75	417
1826	*Charles*	40	243
1826	*Fortunée*	17	198
1826	*Enterprize*	5	23
Total		**404**	**1,973**

Source: SLPA, RLA 1-3,773 (1808–1812); SLPA, RLA 19889–24205 (1825–1827).

The number of people assigned to public works was sometimes so excessive that, just as with apprenticeship, their conditions were comparable to those of enslaved peoples. On 14 December 1820, during a meeting organised by Joseph Reffell, William Johnson, the superintendent of the village of Regent, accused Reffell of turning 'Liberated Africans' into enslaved people and making superintendents into 'slave drivers'.[54] Reffell initially requested repairs for the roads leading from Freetown to the villages, but when his efforts were unsuccessful,

52 Anderson, *Abolition*, p. 124; SLPA, Liberated African Department, Miscellaneous return book (1826–1834), fol. 79.

53 Despatch No. 206, McCarthy to Bathurst, 25 June 1819, SLPA, Governor Despatches to the Secretary of State (1818–1822), pp. 88–9.

54 SLPA, Liberated African Department, Letterbook Vol. 1 (1820–1826), fol. 9.

he turned to 'Liberated Africans' living in the Mountain villages, asking them to mend the road. Even though this would require them to work more than six days a week, Reffell justified the request, arguing that the road was primarily used by those living in the area. Johnson deemed the measure unjust, and C. Taylor, the superintendent of the village of Charlotte, agreed. In response, Reffell threatened to withhold clothing from the 'Liberated Africans' until they repaired the road, which led to accusations of slavery practices. Reffell's line of defence was: 'Is it slavery to desire men who have received for years past clothing food and in fact all they enjoy from His Majesty's Bounty to bestow three days labour ... on a public road leading directly to their place of residence?'[55] In the end, Reffell showed little consideration, if any, for the plight of 'Liberated Africans'.

Colonial authorities imposed labour demands on 'Liberated Africans', while also exploring different methods of support and sustenance. As part of the broader emancipation process, the colonial government was responsible for providing support and resources, especially food, to newly arrived individuals. In the first groups of 'Liberated Africans', each adult was allocated daily subsistence rations of one quart of rice, half a gill of palm oil, and a quarter of a gill of salt, with a portion of beef (and three quarters of these for each child).[56] By 1 January 1822, 3,775 'Liberated Africans' were receiving government rations. That number increased to 5,539 in 1824 but was reduced to 2,737 in 1825 as Governor Turner sought to cut down expenses. On 26 June 1822, Governor MacCarthy reported to the Secretary for the Colonies, Earl Bathurst, that supplies were falling short due to the rapidly increasing number of 'Liberated Africans'.[57] A few years later, on 19 January 1827, Governor Campbell informed Bathurst that, beginning 1 January 1827, rations would no longer be issued to 'Liberated Africans' in Freetown or the villages. Instead, he proposed a daily allowance of three pence.[58] In the case of 'Liberated Africans' who were placed into apprenticeship, the daily allowance was not paid directly to them but to the individuals to whom they were apprenticed. Although Bathurst initially objected, Campbell was ultimately able to reform the policy. Under the new system, men received three pence per day for a period of six months and women for three months.[59]

55 Ibid., fol. 5, 8–10.

56 *Coms. of Inquiry*, HC 1827, no. 312, p. 27; Philip Misevich, *Abolition and the Transformation of Atlantic Commerce in Southern Sierra Leone, 1790s to 1860s* (Trenton, 2019), pp. 119–20.

57 *Abstract*, HC 1830, no. 57, p. 8; Enclosure in Despatch No. 286, McCarthy to Bathurst, 26 June 1822, SLPA, Governor Despatches to the Secretary of State (1818–1822).

58 *Abstract*, HC 1830, no. 57, pp. 12–13.

59 Misevich, *Abolition*, (Trenton, 2019), p. 120.

Rations for 'Liberated Africans', as well as Freetown markets, were supplied by the inhabitants of the colony and by individuals living in the surrounding areas.[60] Most of the food trade resulted from small-scale cultivation by women, whether 'Liberated African', Maroon or Nova Scotian. They sold their own produce and the food they prepared across several markets – especially Maroon women who were already used to selling foodstuff and livestock in Jamaica.[61] 'Liberated Africans' produced yams and cocoa. Fruit and vegetables were supplied from the Mountain villages. While fish was principally supplied by Nova Scotian fishermen, meat and rice were sourced outside the colony. Cattle were brought from Fuuta Jalon, and rice was obtained by traders from Port Loko, Rio Pongo, and Sherbro among other areas.[62] Between May and November 1824, acting Governor Daniel Molloy Hamilton permitted the import of beans, potatoes, salt fish, and sheep among other produce. In 1825, George Rendall, the acting Colonial Secretary, permitted the import of roots and vegetables, and other foodstuffs.[63] Fairs and market days made more food accessible to the population. *The Royal Gazette* advertised contracts for fresh beef to supply the troops at the stations for a year and a half. These contracts were secured by 'Liberated Africans' Thomas and Betsy Carew, and Nancy Hughes.[64]

Food preferences were tied to geographical origins, religious affiliations, or social status. As more 'Liberated Africans' arrived in Freetown from the Bight of Biafra, the consumption of yams became more common. By the mid-1820s, authorities in the colony villages thought that rice was not as central to the diet of 'Liberated Africans' as it used to be.[65] Meals included rice, yams, cocoa, cassava, maize, sweet potatoes, and ground nuts, with meat or fish. People

60 Stefania Galli, 'Socioeconomic Status and Group Belonging: Evidence from Early-Nineteenth-Century Colonial West Africa', *Social Science History*, 46:2 (2022), 349–72, at pp. 358–9.

61 E. Frances White, 'Creole Women Traders in the Nineteenth Century', *The International Journal of African Historical Studies*, 14:4 (1981), 626–42, at pp. 629–30; Suzanne Schwarz, 'Adaptation in the Aftermath of Slavery: Women, Trade and Property in Sierra Leone, c.1790–1812', in Mariana P. Candido and Adam Jones (eds), *African Women in the Atlantic World: Property, Vulnerability & Mobility 1660–1880* (Woodbridge, 2019), pp. 19–37, at 29–32.

62 *Report from the Select Committee on the Settlements of Sierra Leone and Fernando Po*, HC 1830, no. 661, pp. 38, 42–3; *Abstract*, HC 1830, no. 57, p. 17; Misevich, *Abolition*, pp. 132–45.

63 London, British Library, *The Royal Gazette and Sierra Leone Advertiser*, 15 May 1824, BLL01013918484, p. 281; London, British Library, *The Royal Gazette and Sierra Leone Advertiser*, 25 June 1825, BLL01013918484, p. 513.

64 *Royal Gazette and Sierra Leone Advertiser*, 16 June 1821, TNA, CO 271/2, p. 606; Fyfe, *A History*, p. 191.

65 Misevich, *Abolition*, p. 124; *Coms. of Inquiry*, HC 1827, no. 312, p. 40.

ate stews, cassava rolls, and couscous based on local produce cultivated by the people of the colony.[66] Members of the Muslim community favoured kola (the only stimulant available allowed by Islam) and Yoruba 'Liberated Africans', from west of the Niger River, cooked dishes with black-eyed peas among others.[67] Concerns over food quality, especially from influential people, surfaced in the government press. An article published in *The Royal Gazette* on 8 September 1821, complained about poor meat and scarce turkeys, suggesting that the Agricultural Society promote turkey farming and distribute geese to the villages.[68] This mirrored Vanessa Oliveira's observation that new crops were often introduced in Africa to meet European settlers' needs. In Luanda, beef remained a luxury for the elite, whereas pork, goat, and chicken were more affordable.[69]

Coerced migrants were relocated to a colony still grappling with the challenges of adjusting to a large influx of inhabitants. As previously mentioned, there was a significant lack of facilities for the newly arrived 'Liberated African', many of whom were left wandering the streets of Freetown. On 20 September 1828, acting Governor Samuel Smart suggested the construction of a building near the seaside or a floating lazaretto (a building used to quarantine the diseased) to receive 'Liberated Africans' while they awaited adjudication. Smart envisioned a structure that could accommodate up to 1,000 people. In 1830, Governor Findlay equally envisioned a lazaretto as an extension of the hospital built in Kissy in 1827.[70] The colony was in desperate need of additional buildings, and several public structures belonging to the Liberated African Department required repairs. These ranged from the stone walls of a house in Regent Square to the roofs, doors, and windows of offices and warehouses in MacCarthy Square. The brick house and sheds used for the newly arrived 'Liberated Africans' required doors and windows to be repaired.[71]

66 Robert B. Clarke, 'Sketches of the Colony of Sierra Leone and its Inhabitants', *Transactions of the Ethnological Society of London*, 2 (1863), 320–63, at pp. 341–2.

67 Walter Rodney, *A History of the Upper Guinea Coast 1545–1800* (New York, 1980), p. 206; Paul E. Lovejoy, *Caravans of Kola: The Hausa Kola Trade 1700–1900* (Zaria, 1980), p. 2; Paul E. Lovejoy, 'Kola in the History of West Africa (La kola dans l'histoire de l'Afrique occidentale)', *Cahiers d'études africaines*, 20:77/78 (1980), 97–134; C. Magbaily Fyle, 'The Yoruba Diaspora in Sierra Leone's Krio Society', in Toyin Falola and Matt D. Childs (eds), *Yoruba Diaspora in the Atlantic World* (Bloomington, 2005), pp. 366–82, at p. 376.

68 *Royal Gazette and Sierra Leone Advertiser*, 8 September 1821, TNA, CO 271/2, pp. 652–3; Fyfe, *A History*, p. 174.

69 Vanessa S. Oliveira, *Slave Trade and Abolition: Gender, Commerce, and Economic Transition in Luanda* (Madison, 2021), pp. 40, 53.

70 *Abstract*, HC 1830, no. 57, pp. 29–31; Anderson, *Abolition*, pp. 84–5.

71 SLPA, Liberated African Department, Miscellaneous return book (1826–1834), fol. 205–8.

Not only were the facilities of the Liberated African Department inadequate, but other architectural aspects of the city were in a poor state. An article published in *The Royal Gazette* on 9 May 1818 observed that the facades of buildings were not well ordered. In 1829, the market house located on Water Street was unfinished.[72] At the end of the rainy season, streets needed to be cleared, and roads repaired, especially the roads leading to the Mountain villages of Leicester, Gloucester, Bathurst, and Wilberforce. Repairs were further required for military facilities. Barracks were in a ruinous state, and in August 1824 Governor Turner wrote to the Under-Secretary for War and the Colonies that he thought it was necessary to improve them and to have 'proper accommodation' for European troops. He requested the barracks to be prepared for 300 men arriving in early November 1824.[73]

Some improvements were undertaken in the late 1810s and continued throughout the 1820s. In 1817, an author in *The Royal Gazette* remarked that more houses had been built in the past two years than seemed possible. Freetown saw a building boom under Governor MacCarthy in the 1820s.[74] Most of the expansion, however, was focused on the needs of the garrison or the city's layout, rather than improving conditions for 'Liberated Africans'. In 1812, a reduction in government expenditure meant that 'Liberated Africans' were expected to rely on themselves while comfortable lodgings were being built for the troops.[75] In 1819, MacCarthy secured an increase of the annual expenditure for public works from £4,000 to £10,000. He supervised the enlargement of the wharf and the construction of stone steps and bridges to replace the older wooden ones, which connected Freetown to the extremity of the peninsula.[76] In 1814, there were only 6 stone houses, mostly inhabited by Europeans, but by 1818, that number had grown to 80 and reached 117 by 1823.[77] On 2 July 1825, 200 men of the Royal African Colonial Corps landed and marched to the barracks, which were said to be 'the most healthy and delightful in the whole

72 Catherine Coquery-Vidrovitch, *Histoire des villes d'Afrique noire : Des origines à la colonisation* (Paris, 1993), p. 304 ; *Report*, HC 1830, no. 661, p. 130.

73 SLPA, Liberated African Department; Letterbook; vol. 1 (1820–1826), fol. 77; Charles Turner to Robert John Wilmot-Horton, 23 August 1824, SLPA, Governor Despatch (14 August 1824 – 24 July 1826), pp. 3–4.

74 London, British Library, *The Royal Gazette and Sierra Leone Advertiser*, 9 August 1817, BLL01013918573, p. 1; Christopher Fyfe, *A Short History of Sierra Leone*, 2nd edn (London, 1979), p. 42; Fyfe, *A History*, pp. 141, 117.

75 *Extracts*, HC 1812, pp. 5–6.

76 London, British Library, *The Royal Gazette and Sierra Leone Advertiser*, 7 December 1822, BLL01013918484, p. 287.

77 *Abstract*, HC 1830, no. 57, p. 19; Fyfe, *A Short History*, p. 43, Fyfe, *A History*, p. 135; *Coms. of Inquiry*, HC 1827, no. 312, p. 7.

Peninsula'.[78] An officer's house and one barrack were built before Governor Turner's death in March 1826, and they were all completed by December 1827. By 24 June 1830, 168 barracks had been erected on the hill with bricks and artisans sent from Britain.[79]

As the city continued to grow, various groups, particularly the Nova Scotians and Maroons, found themselves benefiting from the expanding labour market. Most of these settlers held occupations that reflected the city's growth, contributing to construction, administration, food supply, and various services.[80] A report from 1827 on the state of the colony, which includes population returns from 1826, reveals that a significant portion of Nova Scotian men were employed in construction, particularly as carpenters, masons, and sawyers.[81] Out of 109 Nova Scotian men with an occupation listed, 62 (57 per cent) were linked to construction. While construction was an important sector, the expanding bureaucracy also created opportunities in administration. Six Nova Scotians and five Maroons worked as clerks for the Liberated African Department. The food supply sector included farmers and fishermen, as well as traders. Eight Nova Scotians were fishermen, and one was a farmer. Among the Maroons, eleven men were farmers. Trading also emerged as a significant activity, with 29 Nova Scotians (over a quarter of the total) engaged in trade, and with 76 out of 105 Maroon men (72 per cent).[82]

Occupations provided in the appendix to the Commissioners' report likewise reveal that settler women benefited from the growth of the population in domestic services as washerwomen and seamstresses. Maroons Nancy Barnett, Francis Bucknor, Carroll Downer, and Betsy McFarguer were washerwomen. Of the 29 Nova Scotian women for whom occupation was given, 14 were also washerwomen.[83] Most women from this sample were connected to services as there were three nurses and midwives, and two seamstresses. The names of most settler women are not provided, they are listed numerically under the male head of household. However, among the 166 Maroon families, 61 were headed by women, indicating that they were the main economic providers for their households.[84] There were only two women for whom occupation differed. A woman who was described as 'very old' lived with Edward Willoughby Jr and

78 London, British Library, *The Royal Gazette and Sierra Leone Advertiser*, 2 July 1825, BLL01013918484, p. 519.

79 *Report*, HC 1830, no. 661, pp. 37–40.

80 James W. St. G. Walker, *The Black Loyalists: The Search for a Promised Land in Nova Scotia and Sierra Leone, 1783–1870* (London, 1976), pp. 315–16.

81 Appendix A, No. 1, 1827, TNA, CO 267/91.

82 Appendix A, No. 1, 1827, TNA, CO 267/91; Appendix A, No. 2, 1827, TNA, CO 267/91.

83 Appendix A, No. 1, 1827, TNA, CO 267/91; Appendix A, No. 2, 1827, TNA, CO 267/91.

84 *Coms. of Inquiry*, HC 1827, no. 312, p. 14.

was also said to be 'very industrious', which might have included some work as a seamstress or pastoral labour. Nathaniel Snowball's mother was a brewer of beer, which suggests that she worked in or owned a tavern. Women were heavily involved in trading and food supplies, as demonstrated by the scholarship of E. Frances White.[85] There were five Nova Scotian women who were recorded as selling small articles, and two others who earned a living by working in a shop. Charlotte Simpson was a shopkeeper and David George Jr's wife was a shopwoman (her name was not recorded). Since the days of the Sierra Leone Company, women have been leaders in the trading sectors. As early as 1794, there were six shops established by licence of the Sierra Leone Company and three of them were owned by Nova Scotian women. By 1811, twenty-seven of them even held licences for the sale of spirits.[86] Out of the five Maroon women for whom an occupation was given, Elizabeth Parkinson was the only one employed in trade as a shopkeeper.[87]

While Nova Scotian and Maroon settlers benefited from demographic growth, some coerced migrants, such as Barbadian exiles and 'Liberated Africans' enlisted and later discharged from the R.A.C. and W.I.R., also gained access to certain resources, though to a more limited extent. The 1827 report reveals that in 1826 about one third of the exiled Barbadians held an occupation that directly resulted from settlement policies.[88] As Freetown's population grew, so did demand for trades like shoemaking, tailoring, coopering, and roles in commerce and domestic service. Earnings varied widely. James Giddins was one of three shopmen and earned 20 shillings a month, while William Coopers who was described as a good tradesman gained 'a good livelihood'. Of the four coopers, Dicky earned £3 a month, and Castella earned £4 a month. Servants such as John Probert, Monsieur Barrow, and John Trial earned about 30 shillings, and cook John Barrow earned £3. Grooms William Lord and Prince William reportedly had 'a great deal of money' and were said to be 'better off than any one of the Barbadians'. A few men, Pridie, Drummers, Morgan, and Lane, worked as masons or carpenters, possibly drawing on experience from public works, earning between £1 and £4 a month. Of the thirty-four Barbadian men listed, the largest group (eleven) were labourers. They served as overseers on farms, supervising 'Liberated Africans', with wages ranging from 15 to 30 shillings. They were financially struggling since Samuel Lane earned 30 shillings

85 E. Frances White, *Sierra Leone's Settler Women Traders* (Ann Arbor, 1987); E. Frances White, 'Creole Women', 626–42; E. Frances White, 'Women, Work, and Ethnicity: The Sierra Leone Case', in Edna G. Bay (ed.), *Women and Work in Africa* (Boulder, 1982), pp. 19–34.

86 Schwarz, 'Adaptation', p. 29.

87 Appendix A, No. 2, 1827, TNA, CO 267/91.

88 Appendix B, No. 8, 1827, TNA, CO 267/92; Evelyn O'Callaghan, *The Earliest Patriots: Being the True Adventures of Certain Survivors of Bussa's Rebellion (1816 In the Island of Barbados and Abroad)* (London, 1986).

and explained that it was not enough to support himself and his wife, while Mundy reportedly earned 'nearly nothing'.[89]

Ten discharged soldiers were also interviewed as part of the 1827 report. Although it is a very small sample, it offers insight into how population growth impacted their lives. Marquis Granby, discharged in 1819 in the village of Wellington, learned to make shingles and sold them in Freetown, allowing him to build a house, which he rented to a clergyman.[90] Likewise, Serjeant Maitland, who lived with his wife Iris Jones, a Nova Scotian settler, in the village of Kent, owned a farm where he grew cassava, selling it to the Liberated African Department. He also ran a shop selling spirits and tobacco, and owned a house in Freetown with his wife that they rented out for £4 per month. These, however, are rare examples that highlight successful experiences of discharged soldiers. Most of the other former soldiers, who were primarily farmers or small artisans, used their pensions to merely survive, rather than to accumulate wealth.[91]

For the majority of the population, economic conditions remained precarious. Since inhabitants had to find additional resources, some of them turned to slave trafficking, which, although illegal in the colony of Sierra Leone, remained profitable in surrounding regions. In 1830, Chief Justice Jeffcott addressed the Grand Jury, stating that the slave trade was active within the colony, prompting the formation of a Committee of Enquiry.[92] Many European traders and colonial officials believed the rise in slave trading stemmed from a lack of economic opportunities. On 20 January 1831, Irish merchant John MacCormack testified that kidnapping had increased, largely because colonial support for 'Liberated Africans' was only for a short period. Other officials echoed this concern. John Dean Lake, of the Mixed Commission Court, noted that reduced public works meant fewer opportunities to earn money. William Cole, commissioner of appraisement and sale to the Mixed Commission Court, shared a similar view the following month.[93] Yet, the surge in kidnapping was not unique to Freetown but was part of broader regional trends. Sean Kelley analysed a sample of 103 testimonies from upper Guinea and found that a third of those enslaved between 1686 and 1820 had been kidnapped, with the practice increasing after 1820 due to drought, famine, and slave trading activities that developed around Rio Pongo, just north of the colony.[94]

89 O'Callaghan, *The Earliest Patriots*, 55–8.

90 Appendix A, No. 11, 1827, TNA, CO 267/91.

91 Fyfe, *A History*, p. 168.

92 Philip Misevich, 'Freetown and "Freedom?" Colonialism and Slavery in Sierra Leone, 1790s to 1861', in Paul E. Lovejoy and Suzanne Schwarz (eds), *Slavery, Abolition and the Transition to Colonialism in Sierra Leone* (Trenton, 2015), pp. 189–216, at p. 198.

93 *Charge*, HC 1832, no. 364, pp. 13–14, 21.

94 Sean Kelley, 'Enslavement in Upper Guinea during the Era of the Transatlantic Slave Trade: Biographical Perspectives', *African Economic History*, 48:1 (2020), 46–73, at pp. 57–60.

The participation of the inhabitants of Freetown in slave trafficking activities complicates the port-city's narrative around freedom. While seeking to improve their economic conditions, some inhabitants made the lives of others more precarious. The Liberated African Department's Miscellaneous return book (1826–1834) records thirty-four individuals who had been 'freed' by the colony, enslaved again, and subsequently 'rescued' and re-liberated.[95] In most cases, it is impossible to trace the exact circumstances of their rescue since the clerks of the Liberated African Department only entered the names of the person who rescued them and where from. There were eight 'Liberated Africans' who experienced embarkation on a slave ship and subsequent capture by the Royal Navy twice. Carafalla, Cota, John Davis, and George King were respectively enslaved by Billy Grant, Doucahahi, Thomas Black, and Pa Foory al John Fooday. All four were sold in Rio Pongo and were embarked on the French schooner *Caroline*, which was captured by H.M.S. *Conflict*, and landed in Freetown in December 1830.[96] Likewise, Sarboo also known as John Brown, Joseph Wright, Sam Thorpe, and Sabo Al Abraham were kidnapped by Jonas Davis, William Day, William Brown, Jem Wilhelm, and William Kennedy. They were all children embarked on the Portuguese schooner *Nimpha* in Rio Pongo, which was also captured by H.M.S. *Conflict* in 1830.[97]

They had been kidnapped and quickly sent away from the colony since the slave traders had to conceal their illegal activities. Many strategies were deployed for that purpose and one of the most common ones was to kidnap children rather than adults. Children were easier to kidnap, control, and conceal from the authorities.[98] Among the thirty-four individuals, nineteen were children. It is unclear whether they knew their enslavers. As Ojo notes in the context of Igbo communities, kidnappers might have known the children they targeted, which made it easier to gain their trust and lure them away.[99] Such acts would have been controversial in other communities where the enslavement of known individuals was socially and religiously condemned, especially among

95 SLPA, Liberated African Department, Miscellaneous return book (1826–1834), fol. 249–56.

96 Registration No. 38,550-38,553, SLPA, RLA 37430–43537 (1829–1832); 'Caroline', Liberated Africans database <https://liberatedafricans.org/databases/event_details.php?EventID=3520> [accessed 9 February 2026].

97 Registration No. 38,535-38.538, SLPA, RLA 37430–43537 (1829–1832); 'Nimpha', Liberated Africans database <https://liberatedafricans.org/event_details.php?EventID=3204> [accessed 9 February 2026].

98 Kelley, 'Enslavement', p. 65; Misevich, *Abolition*, p. 175.

99 Olatunji Ojo, 'Child Slaves in Pre-colonial Nigeria, c.1725–1860', *Slavery & Abolition*, 33:3 (2012), 417–34 p. 422; Roquinaldo Ferreira, *Cross-Cultural Exchange in the Atlantic World: Angola and Brazil during the Era of the Slave Trade* (Cambridge, 2012), p. 98.

members of the Muslim community who believed freeborn Muslims should not be enslaved.[100]

Engaging in slave trafficking activities in the colony supposes developing knowledge and networks. In nine cases, people were enslaved by 'Liberated Africans', and in five of those, the enslavers did not act alone. Hannah was captured and sold by Thomas and Nancy Showers, a 'Liberated African' couple from Kissy. Kanawah al John was sold by two 'Liberated Africans' named James Howall and William Dawes. While some inhabitants worked together, others were helped by people from surrounding areas. Duncan Campbell kidnapped and sold two adults, one named James and another named Thomas Wilberforce, with the help of William Johnson, a Temne man. William Kennedy sold Sabo Al Abraham with the help of Surra Gabboo, a Mandinka man, likely associated with Muslim slave trafficking networks operating the Northern Rivers.[101] In fifteen other cases, the enslavers were not from the colony and were identified as Mandinka and Temne men. After being apprehended, they were sentenced to five to ten years hard labour in the House of Correction.

It is unclear how long individuals were in the colony before they engaged in slave trafficking, but it usually did not take long. Shortly after their arrival, Nova Scotians were involved in the slave trade and in the early nineteenth century, one of them, Betsey Walker, managed a slave factory at Crawford Island on the Îles de Los.[102] Among the enslavers from the Miscellaneous return book, there were three settlers: a Maroon, John Ellis, and two Nova Scotian settlers named Jonas Davis and Jacob Johnson. Settled in Freetown for decades, they still participated in the trade, highlighting how difficult it was to eradicate slavery and deter inhabitants from partaking in it. The cases also reveal that people from surrounding areas came to the colony to kidnap individuals, as fifteen instances were recorded.

Resorting to slave trading was not the only way inhabitants found to overcome Freetown's limited opportunities. Even though forced relocation meant that 'Liberated Africans' who chose to leave the colony were considered as 'runaways', many sought to self-liberate from the colonial system. In 1808, twenty-one people disembarked from the *Eliza* and the *Baltimore* attempted to flee about eight miles from the colony but were soon arrested and taken back to Freetown. In contrast, about two thirds of individuals disembarked between March 1808 and July 1810 were said to have left the colony by the end of 1811. Between 1808 and

100 Jennifer Lofkrantz and Olatunji Ojo, 'Slavery, Freedom, and Failed Ransom Negotiations in West Africa, 1730–1900', *Journal of African History*, 53:1 (2012), 25–44, pp. 27–8.

101 Misevich, *Abolition*, pp. 157–9, 169–75.

102 James Sidbury, '"African" Settlers in the Founding of Freetown', in Paul E. Lovejoy and Suzanne Schwarz (eds), *Slavery, Abolition and the Transition to Colonialism in Sierra Leone* (Trenton, 2015), pp. 127–42, at p. 132; Schwarz, 'Adaptation', p. 33.

1831, the Registers of Liberated Africans occasionally recorded escapes before or shortly after emancipation, although the records are inconsistent. At least twenty-five individuals were considered as fugitives, but the actual number was likely higher.[103] Leaving before apprenticeship provided more opportunities to evade surveillance, a strategy common among 'Liberated Africans' and enslaved populations across the Atlantic, as seen by Sean Kelley in Tortola with the case of William Jennings, who left within twenty-four hours of his indenture.[104]

The main motivation to leave was proximity to the homeland and the possibility of returning to their communities, especially for nearby Bullom, Loko, Mende, Sherbro, Susu, and Temne people. They might have been familiar with the environment or have connections that allowed them to plan their escape. Richard Rathbone suggests that in the late eighteenth century, clusters of islands on the upper Guinea coast offered protection sites for people who escaped slavery.[105] Those who returned home had likely been enslaved as prisoners of war or were people who had been kidnapped, since people enslaved due to legal processes or debts would have been seen as outcasts by their communities.[106] People who were from more distant regions were also inclined to leave near the time of their emancipation. Adoyra was twenty-two years old when he was embarked on the Spanish vessel *Veloz Pasagera* in 1830. The ship departed from the port of Jakin, located in Godomey, on the south-west shores of Lake Nokoue that borders the north of Cotonou, before it was captured. The case of the *Veloz Pasagera* was adjudicated on 16 October 1830, but by 2 November, Adoyra had managed to leave.[107] Ackeboo,

103 Schwarz, 'The Impact', pp. 47–8; *Report*, HC 1830, no. 661, pp. 118–19.

104 Érika Melek Delgado, 'Children, Childhood and Slavery in Sierra Leone: The Experiences of Liberated African Children c. 1808–1834' (Unpublished PhD dissertation, University of Worcester, 2017), p. 173; Schwarz, 'The Impact', p. 47; Kelley, 'Precedents', p. 40. Works on the topic include Hilary McD. Beckles, 'Running in Jamaica: A Slavery Ecosystem', *The William and Mary Quarterly*, 76:1 (2019), 9–14; Shauna J. Sweeney, 'Market Marronage: Fugitive Women and the Internal Marketing System in Jamaica, 1781–1834', *The William and Mary Quarterly*, 76:2 (2019), 197–222; Daylet Domínguez and Víctor Goldgel Carballo, 'Slavery, Mobility, and Networks in Nineteenth-Century Cuba', *Atlantic Studies*, 18:1 (2021), 1–6.

105 Richard Rathbone, 'Some Thoughts on Resistance to Enslavement in West Africa', in Gad Heuman (ed.), *Out of the House of Bondage: Runaways, Resistance and Marronage in Africa and the New World* (London, 1986), pp. 11–22, at p. 19.

106 *Charge*, HC 1832, no. 364, p. 13; Schwarz, 'The Impact', p. 49.

107 Registration No. 37,555, SLPA , RLA 37430 - 43537 (1829–1832); 'Veloz Pasagera', Liberated Africans database <https://liberatedafricans.org/event_details.php?EventID=3203> [accessed 9 February 2026]; Robin Law, 'Between the Sea and the Lagoons: The Interaction of Maritime and Inland Navigation on the Precolonial Slave Coast (Entre mer et lagune : les interactions de la navigation maritime et continentale sur la Côte des Esclaves avant la colonisation)', *Cahiers d'études africaines*, 29:114,1 (1989), 209–37, at p. 210.

Ahdakereber, Omoloo, and Ahcallah were embarked on board the Spanish brig *Segunda Teresa* in Ouidah in 1832. They fled shortly after their arrival on 14 April and were recorded as runaways by 26 July.[108]

Conditions upon arrival drove people to seek self-liberation. In September 1829, Jimmay, Karee, Fannah, Imboh, and Konah, all between five and nine years old, were embarked on the Spanish schooner *Emanuel* in Sherbro. The ship was wrecked, and they were moved with 371 other enslaved Africans onboard the French schooner *La Laure*. Alexander Gordon, captain of British ship *Atholl*, captured the ship and landed in Aberdeen in October 1829 but due to bureaucratic delays, the enslaved people onboard were forced to remain on the ship. The British and Spanish Mixed Court commissioners refused to process the case because they arrived on board a French ship rather than the Spanish schooner *Emanuel*. The matter was then handed over to the Secretary of State for Foreign Affairs, but over a year later, by 31 December 1830, no instructions had been received. The enslaved people were ultimately delivered to the Liberated African Department on 1 January 1831. When the clerks recorded their details in the Registers, thirty-five of them had already died, and Jimmay, Karee, Fannah, Imboh, and Konah had successfully escaped. Since they were young children, they had been helped by other people.[109]

The act of self-liberation from colonial authorities contrasted with the experience of other inhabitants, who could leave the colony without being labelled as runaways. In 1826, Mr Jewitt, a Nova Scotian preacher at the Methodist chapel, reported that twenty-four Nova Scotian families left the colony with the majority going to England (fifteen out of twenty-four).[110] In addition, the 1827 report lists seven Nova Scotian adult males as having gone to England by themselves as well as three other family units. Jewitt also stated that one family went to America, and the return indicates one man went there as a sailor, without specifying an exact location. Padraic Scanlan observes that children of settlers sought employment as sailors on merchant vessels because of the growing numbers of 'Liberated Africans', who were considered as cheap workers and too strong a competition.[111] Settlers also moved to different areas in the colony's hinterland, which suggests the existence of social and commercial networks. There are several examples of Nova Scotian settlers who left the

108 Registration No. 40,790, 40,792, 40,793, 40,799, SLPA, RLA 37430–43537 (1829–1832); 'Segunda Teresa', Liberated Africans database <https://liberatedafricans.org/event_details.php?EventID=3207> [accessed 9 February 2026].

109 Registration No. 38,602, 38,603, 38,604, 38,619, 38,626, SLPA, RLA 37430–43537 (1829–1832); 'Laure', Liberated Africans database <https://liberatedafricans.org/databases/event_details.php?EventID=3327> [accessed 9 February 2026].

110 *Coms. of Inquiry*, HC 1827, no. 312, pp. 11–12.

111 Scanlan, 'The Colonial Rebirth', p. 1095.

colony to expand their trade networks.[112] As early as 1796, John Kizell, a Nova Scotian settler born in the coastal region, permanently relocated to Sherbro thanks to previously established trading networks.[113] In 1826, Phillis Battes and Thomas Gray were at Cape Mount where Gray was born. Rose and Mary Murray went to Rio Pongo and Abraham Newman to Gambia. Two exiled Barbadian settlers were also said to have gone to the Îles de Los and three to the Gambia.[114]

Wealthier individuals were able to leave by paying for cabins on vessels advertised in *The Royal Gazette*. On 30 November 1819, the brig *Palemon* was to sail for Barbados and Antigua, and its captain offered cabins for four passengers. The issue of 11 January 1823 read that the brig *Lively* had good accommodation for individuals wanting to travel to London. The ship was set to sail on 1 February, and people had to apply for passage to Thomas Craig. Another ship, the *Betsy and Ann*, was to depart for England on 25 March 1823. In that same month, the *Triton* was said to have 'very superior accommodations'. On 10 May 1823, the gazette advertised passage to England on board the *Elizabeth*, the *Glory*, the *Sir John Cameron*, and the *Hadlow*.[115] Individuals who did not have the financial means to travel on these ships had the opportunity to offer their services to wealthier people. On 7 May 1825, a young woman, whose name was not printed, was seeking a position as 'waiting maid to any Lady' who was returning to England.[116]

Conclusion

As increasing numbers of 'Liberated Africans' disembarked in the harbour of Freetown, they followed the same line of work as those who arrived before them by providing a labour force to improve infrastructure. A few of them were able to secure opportunities resulting from spatial and demographic

112 Schwarz, 'Adaptation', p. 32.

113 Kevin G. Lowther and Joseph Opala, *The African American Odyssey of John Kizell: A South Carolina Slave Returns to Fight the Slave Trade in His African Homeland* (Columbia, 2012), pp. 136, 139, 143.

114 Appendix A, No. 1, 1827, TNA, CO 267/91.

115 London, British Library, *The Royal Gazette and Sierra Leone Advertiser*, 13 November 1819, BLL01013918573; London, British Library, *The Royal Gazette and Sierra Leone Advertiser*, 11 January 1823, BLL01013918484, p. 8; London, British Library, *The Royal Gazette and Sierra Leone Advertiser*, 8 February 1823, BLL01013918484, p. 24; London, British Library, *The Royal Gazette and Sierra Leone Advertiser*, 15 March 1823, BLL01013918484, p. 44; London, British Library, *The Royal Gazette and Sierra Leone Advertiser*, 10 May 1823, BLL01013918484, p. 76.

116 London, British Library, *The Royal Gazette and Sierra Leone Advertiser*, 7 May 1825, BLL01013918484, p. 488.

growth through employment in sectors that supported the population. The majority of coerced migrants, however, lived in a colony that secured and strengthened its policies around the exploitation of individuals for colonial and financial benefits. Being advantageous for older settlers, experiences of relocation were intrinsically different among various groups of people. Greater colonial management and control defined the population structure and its spatial distribution although individuals tried to find ways to improve their conditions. These experiences set precedents for an even larger number of 'Liberated Africans' (56,740) who were to be relocated in the colony in subsequent decades, between 1832 and 1864.[117] While management and resistance were both at play in Freetown, the city developed into a hybrid diverse society based on a system that British administrators tried to implement and that recently emancipated individuals tried to resist.

117 Henry Lovejoy, Liberated Africans database <https://liberatedafricans.org/databases/cases.php> [accessed 11 August 2025].

2

Free and Coerced Settlements

By 1831, Freetown had become a 'a place of absorption' of the African diaspora. More than 60 per cent of its population comprised African people and people of African descent born outside the boundaries of the colony.[1] Over the next three decades, large numbers of formerly enslaved people (known as 'Liberated Africans'), free people from within the continent (African immigrants), and smaller numbers of free individuals from the Caribbean and Europe continued to be settled or chose to settle there. According to the 'Laws of Migrations' proposed by Ernest George Ravenstein in 1889, migration is driven by economic 'push' and 'pull' factors. There exist conditions that compel people to leave their homelands, and incentives that attract them to new environments.[2] Although Ravenstein's Laws were formulated in the context of Britain and do not map onto the realities of a colonial West African port-city, they offer a useful framework for understanding voluntary migration and a valuable lens through which to explore the socio-economic dynamics of Freetown. They must be applied cautiously, however, since migration to Freetown was mainly coerced and directly influenced by the intervention of the Royal Navy. This chapter delves into both coerced and voluntary forms of settlement, tracing migration experiences and geographical origins of its inhabitants. It is based on personal stories which, though they might appear as anecdotal and full of numerous details, together paint a rich socio-cultural mosaic. Examining the diverse paths that led people to Freetown reveals varying perceptions of freedom and unfreedom, which together shaped the social and cultural fabric of the city.

1 Paul E. Lovejoy and Suzanne Schwarz, 'Sierra Leone in the Eighteenth and Nineteenth Centuries', in Paul E. Lovejoy and Suzanne Schwarz (eds), *Slavery, Abolition and the Transition to Colonialism in Sierra Leone* (Trenton, 2015), pp. 1–28; Richard Anderson, *Abolition in Sierra Leone: Re-Building Lives and Identities in Nineteenth-Century West Africa* (Cambridge, 2020), pp. 1–29; Census of Population and liberated Africans, 1831, TNA, CO 267/111.

2 E. G. Ravenstein, 'The Laws of Migration', *Journal of the Statistical Society of London*, 48:2 (1885), 167–235; E. G. Ravenstein, 'The Laws of Migration', *Journal of the Royal Statistical Society*, 52:2 (1889), 241–305; Glenda Garelli and Martina Tazzioli, 'Migration and "Pull Factor' Traps", *Migration Studies*, 9:3 (2021), 383–99, at p. 388.

The first part of this chapter examines patterns of coerced and voluntary migration from the 1831 census up to the last major arrival of 'Liberated Africans' disembarked from slave ships in the early 1860s. The factors influencing the settlement of many free migrants differed significantly from those affecting 'Liberated Africans'. Evidence shows that motivations for migration included the pursuit of economic opportunity, reunification with family, and the need to escape armed conflict. The second part of this chapter scrutinises the geographical origins of individuals who settled in Freetown between the 1830s and 1860s. As Paul Lovejoy argues, identity and expectations in a new environment were shaped by individuals' urban backgrounds, which were associated with commerce, literacy, and awareness of slavery.[3] Accordingly, the chapter includes a discussion of ethnonyms and of the urban or rural backgrounds of individuals, as factors defining experiences and identities in Freetown.

By 1862, 17,829 individuals lived in Freetown, but the most important demographic growth was observed between 1831 and 1848 when the population doubled in just a little over fifteen years. This sharp increase was the result of the arrival of 22,818 'Liberated Africans' between 1836 and 1840.[4] Demographic growth later decreased (Table 2.1). Governor Norman Macdonald attributed the apparent population decline from 18,551 to 16,679 between 1849 and 1850 to clerical errors, suggesting that residents were not always truthful or forthcoming with census enumerators. Between 15 February 1839 and 10 January 1840, six individuals were charged for refusing to cooperate with census officials. Ann Shepard was taken to the police office because, on 4 March 1839, she declined to answer the census enumerator's questions and instructed one of her daughters to pretend that she was not home.[5] While inaccuracies in population returns and censuses contributed to some distortions, the sharp decline in population between 1848 and 1850 was driven primarily by large scale emigration. From the 1840s onward, significant numbers of people were sent to the British Caribbean, where planters sought new labourers after emancipation. During the nineteenth century, around 15,000 were transported across the Atlantic once again, under indenture contracts that placed them alongside indentured workers from Asia on Caribbean plantations.[6]

3 Paul E. Lovejoy, 'The Urban Background of Enslaved Muslims in the Americas', *Slavery and Abolition*, 26:3 (2005), 349–76.

4 Henry Lovejoy, Liberated Africans database, <https://liberatedafricans.org/databases/cases.php> [accessed 24 February 2026].

5 William Hirst Wise v. Ann Shepard, 4 March 1839, SLPA, Police Magistrate Record (15 February 1839 – 10 January 1840), fol. 10-11.

6 Philip D. Curtin and Jan Vansina, 'Sources of the Nineteenth Century Slave Trade', *Journal of African History*, 5:2 (1964), 185–208, at p. 186; Céline Flory, 'Sierra Leone Indentured Workers in Guyana and Martinique in the Nineteenth Century', in Paul E.

Table 2.1 Demographic evolution of Freetown, 1831–1862.

Year	Population
1831	8,505
1833	9,937
1840	13,741
1848	18,190
1849	18,551
1850	16,679
1851	18,027
1854	16,022
1860	17,523
1862	17,829

Sources: Census of Population and liberated Africans, 1831, TNA, CO 267/111, fol. 261; David E. Skinner, *Thomas George Lawson: African Historian and Administrator in Sierra Leone* (Stanford, 1980), p. 5; Robert René Kuczynski, *Demographic Survey of the British Colonial Empire* (London, 1948), p. 23; *Reports to Secretary of State on Past and Present State of H.M. Colonial Possessions, 1848 (Maps and Plans)*, HC 1849, no. 1126, p. 304; *Reports to Secretary of State on Past and Present State of H.M. Colonial Possessions, 1850*, HC 1851, no. 1421, p. 184; *Reports to Secretary of State on Past and Present State of H.M. Colonial Possessions, 1851*, HC 1852, no. 1539, p. 182; *Reports to Secretary of State on Past and Present State of H.M. Colonial Possessions, 1854*, HC 1856, no. 2050, p. 187; *Reports to Secretary of State on Past and Present State of H.M. Colonial Possessions, 1860*, HC 1862, no. 2955–1, p. 24; Blue Books of Sierra Leone, 1862, British Online Archives, p. 166.

As before 1831, the census and population returns are organised according to descriptive categories that represent a colonial interpretation of the society (Appendix A).[7] People are listed as 'Europeans', 'Mulattoes', 'Colonial Residents and Freeborn Blacks', 'Discharged Soldiers and Their Families', 'Liberated Africans', 'Kroomen', and 'Native Strangers'. Some of the categories changed by 1850 with the census returns accounting for

Lovejoy and Suzanne Schwarz (eds), *Slavery, Abolition and the Transition to Colonialism in Sierra Leone* (Trenton, 2015), pp. 257–72; Richard Anderson, 'The Diaspora of Sierra Leone's Liberated Africans: Enlistment, Forced Migration, and "Liberation" at Freetown, 1808–1863', *African Economic History*, 41 (2013), 101–38; Céline Flory, *De l'esclavage à la liberté forcée. Histoire des travailleurs africains engagés dans la Caraïbe française au XIXe siècle* (Paris, 2015).

7 A. J. Christopher, 'The Quest for a Census of the British Empire c.1840–1940', *Journal of Historical Geography*, 34 (2008), 268–85, at pp. 269, 272; Stefania Galli, 'Socioeconomic Status and Group Belonging: Evidence from Early-Nineteenth-Century Colonial West Africa', *Social Science History*, 46:2 (2022), 349–72, at p. 354.

'Europeans', 'Maroons', 'Nova Scotians', 'Liberated Africans', 'Native Creoles', 'West Indians', 'Americans', 'Kroomen', and 'Native Strangers'. By 1860, 'Native Creoles' was changed to 'Colony-born'. Unearthing the meaning behind the terms used by the Liberated African Department is important to trace geographical backgrounds and circumstances of settlement in Freetown. Allen Howard notes that these categories are socio-racial or ethno-legal as they provide information on the inhabitants' social or legal status.[8] They refer to people's status, but they can be used to trace information on identities, origins, and migration experience.

During the first half of the nineteenth century, the largest group of the population was that of 'Liberated Africans'. In 1831 and 1850, they represented about 40 per cent of the population. About 39,426 of them arrived in the colony during the 1830s, followed by another 20,738 in the 1840s. By 1860, however, their share of the population had fallen to 29 per cent. This decrease stemmed from the collapse of the slave trade in the Bight of Biafra, the main region of embarkation, as well as the suppression of the Brazilian slave trade in 1850. As a result, only 6,497 'Liberated Africans' arrived in the 1850s, and only a small portion of them were ultimately settled in Freetown.[9]

As coerced migrants, 'Liberated Africans' had already endured a series of traumatic events through enslavement. Some were prisoners of war, some victims of armed conflicts, while others had been sold into slavery as outsiders within their communities.[10] After capture, they were marched to the coast and spent about six months to a year in the hands of various enslavers before boarding slave ships. Violence frequently accompanied their capture by the Royal Navy, with confrontations sometimes lasting several hours and resulting in injuries or deaths.[11] On 7 September 1830, 556 enslaved individuals were embarked at Jakin on the *Veloz Pasagera*. The ship was seized the same day by H.M.S. *Primrose*,

8 Allen M. Howard, 'New Insights on Liberated Africans: The 1831 Freetown Census', in Richard Anderson and Henry B. Lovejoy (eds), *Liberated Africans and the Abolition of the Slave Trade: Digital Histories of Enslavement and Freedom* (Rochester, 2020), pp. 101–26, at p. 109.

9 Liberated Africans database, <https://liberatedafricans.org/databases/cases.php> [accessed 25 February 2026]; Anderson, *Abolition*, pp. 31–4; Leslie Bethell, 'The Mixed Commissions for the Suppression of the Transatlantic Slave Trade in the Nineteenth Century', *Journal of African History*, 7:1 (1966), 79–93, p. 92; *Reports to Secretary of State on Past and Present State of H.M. Colonial Possessions, 1850*, HC 1851, no. 1421, p. 184.

10 G. Ugo Nwokeji, *The Slave Trade and Culture in the Bight of Biafra: An African Society in the Atlantic World* (Cambridge, 2010), p. 118.

11 Mary Wills, *Envoys of Abolition: British Naval Officers and the Campaign against the Slave Trade in West Africa* (Liverpool, 2019), p. 109; Enclosure 10 in No. 9, Commander Oake to Captain Jones, 30 September 1844, *Correspondence with British Coms. at Sierra Leone, Havana, Cape of Good Hope, Jamaica, Loanda, and Cape Verd Islands; Reports from British Vice-Admiralty Courts and Naval Officers on Slave Trade: 1845 (Class A)*, HC 1846, no. 723, pp. 12–13; Enclosure 24 in No. 9, Commander Hay to Commodore Jones, 13 September 1844, *Correspondence*, HC 1846, no. 723, p. 17;

during which one enslaved man, Jack Primrose, sustained injuries that led to the amputation of his right arm.[12] Following such captures, trauma continued. Royal Navy officers used Yoruba translations to assert authority, with phrases like 'silence or you'll get punished'.[13] Yet, some officers displayed paternalistic or sympathetic behaviour; in 1815, Commander John Tailour removed the shackles from the enslaved people onboard, showed them the chains, which he threw into the sea.[14]

Table 2.2 Numbers of 'Liberated Africans' disembarked and registered, 1808–1885.

2.2.1 Sum of 'Liberated Africans' disembarked.

	British and Brazilian Court of Mixed Commission, Freetown	British and Netherlands Court of Mixed Commission, Freetown	British and Portuguese Court of Mixed Commission, Freetown	British and Spanish Court of Mixed Commission, Freetown	Court of Vice Admiralty, Freetown	Total Sum of 'Liberated Africans' Disembarked
1808					78	78
1809					285	285
1810					1,179	1,179
1811					560	560
1812					3,596	3,596
1813					661	661
1814					2,484	2,484
1815					1,389	1,389
1816					2,477	2,477
1817					869	869

Enclosure 35 in No. 9, Lieutenant Hockin to Commodore Jones, 21 November 1844, *Correspondence*, HC 1846, no. 723, p. 21.

12 Registration No. 37,654, SLPA, Register of Liberated Africans 37,430–43,537 (1829–1832); Henry Lovejoy, Liberated Africans database, <https://liberatedafricans.org/event_details.php?EventID=3203> [accessed 7 February 2024].

13 Mary Wills, 'At War with the "Detestable Traffic": The Royal Navy's Anti-Slavery Cause in the Atlantic Ocean', in John McAleer and Christer Petley (eds), *The Royal Navy and the British Atlantic World, c.1750–1820* (London, 2016), pp. 123–46, at p. 132; Wills, *Envoys of Abolition*, p. 104.

14 Wills, *Envoys of Abolition*, p. 104.

	British and Brazilian Court of Mixed Commission, Freetown	British and Netherlands Court of Mixed Commission, Freetown	British and Portuguese Court of Mixed Commission, Freetown	British and Spanish Court of Mixed Commission, Freetown	Court of Vice Admiralty, Freetown	Total Sum of 'Liberated Africans' Disembarked
1818					916	916
1819		36		63	365	464
1820		92	97	528	69	786
1821		178	757	507	102	1,366
1822			1,603	474	884	3,139
1823			280	390	21	691
1824			1,600	170	160	1,930
1825			1,049	582	544	2,373
1826		198	1,392	1,223	167	3,280
1827		498	2,133	463	15	2,862
1828	1,380	251	995	1,025		4,032
1829	2,774	632	420	1,449	372	5,548
1830	1,224	533	202	1,892	4	3,322
1831			157	1,829	186	2,172
1832			385	1,342	17	1,744
1833			317	1,539		1,856
1834			1,233	2,361		3,594
1835			915	3,832	4	4,751
1836			4,872	2,201		7,073
1837	596		5,141	445		6,182
1838			5,420			5,420
1839	226		1,545	1,524	17	3,312
1840	44		434	352	1	831
1841			290		16	306
1842			446			446
1843	283		290			819
1844	1,306		446	1,020		2,381
1845	417		536	378	1,542	3,314
1846			55		550	550

	British and Brazilian Court of Mixed Commission, Freetown	British and Netherlands Court of Mixed Commission, Freetown	British and Portuguese Court of Mixed Commission, Freetown	British and Spanish Court of Mixed Commission, Freetown	Court of Vice Admiralty, Freetown	Total Sum of 'Liberated Africans' Disembarked
1847			977		443	4,434
1848					2,530	5,418
1849			1		2,239	2,239
1850			2,915		1,867	1,867
1851					796	796
1852					124	124
1853					49	49
1854					495	495
1855					199	199
1856					155	155
1857					1,555	1,555
1858						
1859					1,257	1,257
1860					624	624
1861					1,763	1,793
1862						
1863					368	368
1864						
1875					34	34
1876					81	81
1877					79	79
1878					64	64
1879					70	70
1880					70	70
1881					44	44
1882					105	105
1883					98	98
1884					144	144
1885					1	1
Grand Total	8,250	2,418	36,167	25,589	38,474	111,171

2.2.2 Sum of 'Liberated Africans' registered

	British and Brazilian Court of Mixed Commission, Freetown	British and Netherlands Court of Mixed Commission, Freetown	British and Portuguese Court of Mixed Commission, Freetown	British and Spanish Court of Mixed Commission, Freetown	Court of Vice Admiralty, Freetown	Total Sum of 'Liberated Africans' Registered
1808					78	78
1809					281	281
1810					1,088	1,088
1811					548	548
1812					2,303	2,303
1813					442	442
1814					1,970	1,970
1815					1,149	1,149
1816					2,279	2,279
1817					869	869
1818					915	915
1819		33		62	365	460
1820		92	96	158	69	775
1821			517	507		1,024
1822		178	1,585	472	506	2,741
1823			280		20	300
1824			1,504	118	160	1,782
1825		125	1,046	580	251	2,002
1826		425	1,181	1,189	132	2,927
1827		251	2,132	459	15	2,857
1828	1,373	559	763	750		3,445
1829	2,598	497	415	1,427	335	5,272
1830	1,123		202	1,862	4	3,191
1831				1,532	185	1,717
1832				1,316	17	1,333
1833			315	1,532		1,847
1834				434	2,178	2,612
1835				870	3,682	4,552
1836			3,449	2,177		5,626

	British and Brazilian Court of Mixed Commission, Freetown	British and Netherlands Court of Mixed Commission, Freetown	British and Portuguese Court of Mixed Commission, Freetown	British and Spanish Court of Mixed Commission, Freetown	Court of Vice Admiralty, Freetown	Total Sum of 'Liberated Africans' Registered
1837	586		3,425	429		4,440
1838			3,402			3,402
1839	225		1,171	1,310	17	2,723
1840	44		369	349	1	763
1841			290		16	306
1842			439			439
1843	276		529			805
1844	1,257		55	1,015		2,327
1845	411		399	377	1,490	2,677
1846					550	550
1847					4,425	4,425
1848					2,458	2,458
1849						
1850						
1851						
1852						
1853						
1854					263	263
1855						
1856						
1857						
1858						
1859						
1860						
1861						
1862						
1863						
1864						
1875					34	34

	British and Brazilian Court of Mixed Commission, Freetown	British and Netherlands Court of Mixed Commission, Freetown	British and Portuguese Court of Mixed Commission, Freetown	British and Spanish Court of Mixed Commission, Freetown	Court of Vice Admiralty, Freetown	**Total Sum of 'Liberated Africans' Registered**
1876					81	81
1877					79	79
1878					64	64
1879					70	70
1880					70	70
1881					44	44
1882					105	105
1883					98	98
1884					144	144
1885					1	1
Grand Total	**7,893**	**2,160**	**24,868**	**24,841**	**23,991**	**82,753w**

Table 2.2 Source: Liberated Africans database, <https://liberatedafricans.org/databases/cases.php> [accessed 25 February 2026]
Note: No data is available for the years 1865–1874.

The length of the journey after interception and the harsh shipboard conditions further harmed the health of 'Liberated Africans'. The voyage to Freetown was nearly as long as the Middle Passage to the Americas, averaging 40.4 days compared to 42.5 days.[15] In response, some mitigation efforts were made. On 4 March 1845, the surgeon aboard H.M.S. *Hydra* ordered seventy-eight boys and four sick adults to be removed from the slave deck of the *Pepito*, where they were being crushed by adult men.[16] Officers were also equipped with Yoruba translations, not only to assert authority but to understand medical complaints, such as 'my belly is sick'.[17] Despite such efforts, illness and death were common. The ship *Incompreensível*, which

15 Anderson, *Abolition*, pp. 74, 80; Daniel Domingues da Silva, David Eltis, Philip Misevich, and Olatunji Ojo, 'The Diaspora of Africans Liberated from Slave Ships in the Nineteenth Century', *Journal of African History*, 55:3 (2014), 347–69, at p. 352.

16 Enclosure 127 in No. 9, Commander Young to Commodore Jones, *Correspondence*, HC 1846, no. 723, pp. 63–4.

17 Wills, *Envoys of Abolition*, p. 104.

departed Mozambique on 15 November 1836 with 785 enslaved people, arrived in Freetown 73 days later with 189 dead, which represents 24 per cent of those on board. It was the only ship in the 1830s traced to south-east Africa and the only one captured south of the equator.[18] Upon disembarkation many 'Liberated Africans' were sent to the Colonial Hospital, where death rates remained high. Between August 1861 and June 1862, 22 individuals recorded as 'Liberated African Congo' died after arriving from the *Clara Windsor* and the *Fairy (a) Flight*, which had embarked 840 and 504 enslaved individuals from Cabinda and the Congo River respectively.[19] The term 'Congo' refers to their West Central Africa origin and Kikongo language.[20] Nine of them suffered from dysentery, the deadliest gastrointestinal illness of the Middle Passage. In 1856, Robert Clarke, surgeon at Kissy Hospital, noted that most dysentery patients there did not survive. Others succumbed to pneumonia, enteritis, rheumatism, diarrhoea, and bronchitis.[21]

Not all people categorised as 'Liberated Africans' experienced the Middle Passage, since enslaved individuals who crossed the boundaries of the colony could also claim their freedom there. The act of crossing certain borders to secure freedom is known as the principle of 'Free Soil', a tradition prevalent across the Atlantic in relation to the abolition of the slave trade.[22] In Senegal, the 27 April 1848 decree emancipated enslaved people who crossed into French territory.[23] At times, such laws were more about deterring slave trafficking than

18 Slave Voyage database <https://www.slavevoyages.org/voyage/3072> [accessed 10 March 2026]; Leslie Bethell, *The Abolition of the Brazilian Slave Trade: Britain, Brazil and the Slave Trade Question* (Cambridge, 1970), p. 127.

19 Slave Voyages database <https://www.slavevoyages.org/voyages/Joeqv9u4> [accessed 1 November 2021].

20 Anderson, *Abolition*, p. 135; Gwendolyn Midlo Hall, *Slavery and African Ethnicities in the Americas: Restoring the Links* (Chapel Hill, 2005), p. 88.

21 Steven T. Katz, *The Holocaust and New World Slavery: A Comparative History*, vols 1 and 2 (Cambridge, 2019), p. 89; Robert Clarke, 'Short Notes of the Prevailing Diseases in the Colony of Sierra Leone, with a Return of the Sick Africans Sent to Hospital in Eleven Years, and Classified Medical Returns for the Years 1853–4. Also Tables Showing the Number of Lunatics Admitted to Hospital in a Period of Thirteen Years, and the Number Treated from 1st April, 1842, to 31st March, 1853', *Journal of the Statistical Society of London*, 19:1 (1856), 60–81, at p. 67; P. Lovejoy and Schwarz, 'Sierra Leone', pp. 1–28; Anderson, *Abolition*, pp. 1–29; Registration No. 1, 3, 4, 5, 14, 28, 29 30, 42, 43, 45, 46, 80, 127, 128, 129, 157, 192, 204, 156, 320, 433, SLPA, Register of Deaths, Freetown district (1861–1862).

22 Sue Peabody and Keila Grinberg, 'Free Soil: The Generation and Circulation of an Atlantic Legal Principle', *Slavery & Abolition*, 32:3 (2011), 331–9, at pp. 331, 334; Philip J. Havik, *Silences and Soundbites: The Gendered Dynamics of Trade and Brokerage in the Pre-Colonial Guinea Bissau Region* (Münster, 2004), p. 72.

23 Cheikh Sène, 'Le décret de l'émancipation des esclaves de 1848 : une application difficile au Sénégal (1848–1905)', *Esclavages & Post-esclavages*, 10 (2024) <https://doi.org/10.4000/12sh5> [accessed 2 December 2024].

protecting enslaved people. In 1761, the king of Portugal declared enslaved people free if they entered his kingdom, not out of desire to grant freedom, but as a strategy to prevent slave traders' traffic.[24] The exact number of 'Liberated Africans' who did not experience the Middle Passage is unclear, but Registers of Liberated Africans and a sample of thirty-seven testimonies included in police court records held at the Sierra Leone Public Archives provide information on some of them. Although cases analysed here are small in number and anecdotal, they still provide insights into the experience of diverse people.

As interactions with and knowledge about the colony spread, enslaved people increasingly used to their advantage expeditions, trading journeys, and encounters with colonial authorities. As the enslavement of Freetown inhabitants became more common, colonial authorities organised inland expeditions to recover those who had been kidnapped. Some enslaved individuals, particularly those who spoke English, falsely claimed to be from the colony in order to obtain British protection.[25] Others benefited from the enforcement of the Free Soil principle. Enslaved people transported in slaving canoes (long boats used in coastal trade) could be declared free if their vessels entered British waters and were seized by the authorities.[26] Court records contain the case of Kamah, an enslaved boy given to John Macaulay at Foredugu. While being transported to Sherbro, the canoe carrying him passed through the colony and was seized on charges of slave dealing, resulting in Kamah's liberation as a 'Liberated African'.[27] Police constables also became an important resource for enslaved people sent to the colony by their enslavers to trade. Foerry's testimony recounts that he had been captured in war and sent to Freetown to sell rice. When Lamina Moody attempted to carry him away by force, the police intervened and declared him free.[28]

Evidence of acts of self-liberation appear in police court testimonies and in the Registers of Liberated Africans. On 8 May 1838, Saboo, a Sherbro boy, appeared at the police office and explained that he fled from Bonko on the Bereire River. The authorities subsequently sent him to the Queen's Yard with

24 Cristina Nogueira Da Silva and Keila Grinberg, 'Soil Free from Slaves: Slave Law in Late Eighteenth- and Early Nineteenth-Century Portugal, *Slavery & Abolition*, 32:3 (2011), 431–46, at pp. 431–2.

25 Philip Misevich, 'Freetown and "Freedom?" Colonialism and Slavery in Sierra Leone, 1790s to 1861', in Paul E. Lovejoy and Suzanne Schwarz (eds), *Slavery, Abolition and the Transition to Colonialism in Sierra Leone* (Trenton, 2015), pp. 189–216, at p. 199.

26 Philip Misevich, *Abolition and the Transformation of Atlantic Commerce in Southern Sierra Leone, 1790s to 1860s* (Trenton, 2019), pp. 177–8, 204.

27 Kamah, 26 July 1854, SLPA, Police Court Record (1 June 1854 – 21 October 1854).

28 Foerry, 15 May 1839, SLPA, Police Magistrate Record (27 February 1839 – 10 January 1840), fol. 139.

'Liberated Africans' disembarked from slave ships.[29] Likewise, in 1847, Sabbah, Kanray, Joroo, Osoomodumoo, and Melombo were recorded in the Registers of Liberated Africans as individuals who had 'made their escape to the Colony for protection' and were therefore received under the authority of the department.[30] Many enslaved people living near the colony sought escape not only from mistreatment and hunger but also from the constant threat of being sold. The prospect of sale could be as feared as whipping on plantations in the Americas, as it meant exportation out of Africa.[31]

Some enslaved individuals who had first attempted to escape elsewhere eventually turned to Freetown. They may not have known precisely what freedom in the colony would entail, but they understood that reaching it could offer protection from re-enslavement. Phayeemah, sold around 1841 and taken to Fula country, first escaped to Susu country before being captured and sold again at Rio Pongo. He was later transported to Matakong Island (a small island north of the Melakori River), from where he ultimately managed to escape to Freetown.[32] Foerry, born at Bullom Shore and later sold in the Scarcies (rivers at the borders of modern-day Guinea and Sierra Leone), was enslaved for four years to a woman named Macont before fleeing to his grandfather. When some of Macont's people came to reclaim him, he escaped once more and made his way to Freetown.[33]

The thirty-seven testimonies reveal that successful cases of liberation include individuals fleeing in groups, which offered better protection and broke patterns of alienation from communities, caused by slavery.[34] On 15 August 1839, Foerry and Packet explained that they escaped together from a farm in a town in the Scarcies.[35] On 21 December 1839, Gabanman, Bital, Marrah, Tallah, and Bosoom, fled together after being enslaved to a man named Booweelah.[36] On 18

29 Saboo, 8 May 1838, SLPA, Police Court Record (22 August 1837 – 8 May 1838).

30 Henry Lovejoy, Liberated Africans database, <https://liberatedafricans.org/event_details.php?EventID=469> [accessed 7 February 2024]; Registration No. 82,689–82,693, SLPA, Register of Liberated Africans 75,357–84,420 (1845).

31 Paul Lovejoy, *Transformations in Slavery: A History of Slavery in Africa* (Cambridge, 2012), p. 271; Myles Ali, '"Here in the Queen's Territory, Every Man and Woman Are Free": Slavery and the Lives of the Enslaved in Late Nineteenth Century Sierra Leone' (Unpublished PhD dissertation, York University, 2020), pp. 118–56.

32 Phayeemah, 6 September 1854, SLPA, Police Court Record (1 June 1854 – 21 October 1854).

33 Foerry and Packet, 15 August 1839, SLPA, Police Magistrate Record (27 February 1839 – 10 January 1840), fol. 266.

34 Ali, '"Here in the Queen's Territory"', pp. 121, 153.

35 Foerry and Packet, 15 August 1839, SLPA, Police Magistrate Record (27 February 1839 – 10 January 1840), fol. 266.

36 Gabanman, Bital, Marrah, Tallah, Bosoom, 21 December 1839, SLPA, Police Magistrate Record (27 February 1839 – 10 January 1840), fol. 427.

August 1854, Bangah, Baratah, and Lamgah escaped from Matakong Island.[37] In some cases, larger groups fled; on 6 September 1854, Phayeemah also escaped from Matakong Island with his wife, child, and seventeen other enslaved individuals.[38] In 1859, a list of fifty-six 'fugitives' from slavery was included in Governor's despatches from 1859, and they all arrived in thirteen groups.[39]

To be able to reach Freetown, they sometimes relied on the help of its inhabitants, who acted as abolitionists by helping people secure their freedom. Forah came to the police office on 16 September 1854 and stated that he had been put in pawn, as a collateral for a loan translation, to a trader named Joseph Reffell.[40] He was handed over to Sosah who complained to Mr Samson that Reffell placed Forah with him. Samson decided to bring Forah to Freetown and told him he was free. In another case, Fangiah, a woman enslaved by William Donald McIntyre (who was from the colony) at Petifu, escaped with the help of William Johnson, a deserter from one of the W.I.R. Johnson, who had freed himself by deserting, now helped another gain freedom. He brought her to the colony village of Waterloo to protect her, and Mamadoo Thompson took her to Freetown to claim her freedom. At court, Johnson recalled: 'I told her to run away with me as it was not right for Sierra Leone people to keep her as a slave'.[41] Favourable conditions such as unsupervised agricultural work also facilitated flight. Mohammed Bashir Salau argues that, in the Sokoto Caliphate, those who worked on plantations were less monitored than those in households, making their escape more likely. On the upper Guinea coast, some enslaved individuals cultivated their own plots of lands, which also provided opportunities to escape.[42] Of the thirty-seven testimonies traced in the police court records, thirty were of people able to flee as they were working as labourers or on farms.

The location of Freetown on the Atlantic coast made it accessible to enslaved people from distant places. Foerry and Packet escaped by taking a canoe lying at the wharf. Phayeemah planned his group's escape from Matakong Island by boarding a British man-of-war. At the police office, his testimony was translated by Thomas George Lawson, the Government interpreter, which reveals that he did not speak English. He must have been able to negotiate

37 Bangah, 25 August 1854, SLPA, Police Court Record (1 June 1854 – 21 October 1854).

38 Phayeemah, 6 September 1854, SLPA, Police Court Record (1 June 1854 – 21 October 1854).

39 Despatch No. 9146, 19 August 1859, TNA, CO 267/264.

40 Paul E. Lovejoy, 'Pawnship, Debt, and "Freedom" in Atlantic Africa during the Era of the Slave Trade', *Journal of African History*, 55:1 (2014), 55–78.

41 Regina v. William Donald McIntyre, 2 June 1854, SLPA, Police Court Record (1 June 1854 – 21 October 1854).

42 Mohammed Bashir Salau, *Plantation Slavery in the Sokoto Caliphate: A Historical and Comparative Study* (Rochester, 2018), p. 112; Walter Rodney, *A History of the Upper Guinea Coast 1545–1800* (New York, 1980), p. 261.

his escape with sailors who spoke his language, likely local Mende or Susu. Similarly, on 19 October 1854, Barrasah was able to escape by fleeing on a fishing boat, eventually claiming his freedom in Freetown.[43] In 1859, five enslaved men, John Mymidon, Lavers Mymidon, Moses Hawkins, Makondah also known as George Williams, and Tom Yalloh, were able to escape from Calabar, possibly on the Royal Navy ship *Myrmidion*. They reached Ascension Island, a Royal Navy base, where they boarded H.M.S. *Hecla* bound for Freetown.[44] Instances of enslaved individuals escaping on British ships were observed across the Atlantic and Indian Oceans in Havana and Bahia, as well as in Mozambique and Madagascar among other locations, demonstrating the significant role maritime life played in providing opportunities for enslaved people to escape slavery.[45]

Tracing migration experiences of enslaved people in the police court records highlights the growing influence of colonial agents in shaping relationships with local African leaders.[46] They show the complexities of implementing abolitionist policies in a slave trading area. Since the days of the Sierra Leone Company, individuals enslaved in the vicinity of the colony such as on Îles de Los, fled to Freetown. At the time, Governor Zachary Macaulay discouraged Nova Scotian settlers from harbouring enslaved people to avoid difficulties with their enslavers.[47] Later, treaties between Governor Campbell and local African leaders, including some ratified in 1836 with Temne and Loko, facilitated the surrender of enslaved individuals who had escaped to Freetown. Sections on this were shortly annulled by Doherty, Campbell's successor.[48] The issue of surrendering enslaved people was significant, as it undermined the authority of nearby African rulers and slave traders. In Dakar, some leaders threatened

43 Phayeemah, 6 September 1854, SLPA, Police Court Record (1 June 1854 – 21 October 1854); Barrasah, 19 October 1854, SLPA, Police Court Record (1 June 1854 – 21 October 1854); Christopher Fyfe, *A History of Sierra Leone* (Oxford, 1962), p. 258.

44 Despatch No. 9146, 19 August 1859, TNA, CO 267/264; Érika Melek Delgado, 'Children, Childhood and Slavery in Sierra Leone: The Experiences of Liberated African Children c. 1808–1834' (Unpublished PhD dissertation, University of Worcester, 2017), p. 215; Jeffrey Gunn, *Outsourcing African Labor: Kru Migratory Workers in Global Ports, Estates and Battlefields until the End of the 19th Century* (Berlin, 2021), pp. 107–9; Clifford Pereira, 'Black Liberators: The Role of Africans & Arabs sailors in the Royal Navy within the Indian Ocean 1841–1941', paper delivered at The Slave Route UNESCO Symposium Rabat, 2007, p. 3.

45 Fugitive Slaves Commission: Reception of fugitive slaves on board British ships in foreign territorial waters, 1837–1871, TNA, FO 84/1433; Roquinaldo Ferreira, *Worlds of Unfreedom: West Central Africa in the Era of Global Abolition* (Princeton, 2025), p. 77.

46 Mariana P. Candido, 'African Freedom Suits and Portuguese Vassal Status: Legal Mechanisms for Fighting Enslavement in Benguela, Angola, 1800–1830', *Slavery & Abolition*, 32:3 (2011), 447–59, at pp. 453–5.

47 Fyfe, *A History*, p. 53.

48 Ibid., pp. 206–7.

embargoes against the French, halting food supplies and provisions to their colony. As a result, there were instances when enslaved people were returned to their enslavers.[49]

The analysis of the origins of 'Liberated Africans' through court testimonies, especially that of Phayeemah, also reveal that British subjects sometimes continued to engage in slave trading activities. In 1844, Nathaniel Isaacs, a British trader already operating in the Gambia, purchased Matakong Island for £215 from William Gabbidon, a Maroon settler. Isaacs exported groundnuts and reportedly despatched as many as sixteen ships per year. He was also involved in the slave trade, a fact that came to light due to rising tensions with Gabbidon. In late March 1853, Governor Kennedy despatched H.M.S. *Bloodhound* to investigate slave trading accusations. The captain of the *Bloodhound* questioned people on Matakong Island about their status, but all denied being enslaved after having been warned to do so by Isaacs's partner, Hannah Hayes.[50] Yet, by August 1854 individuals like Phayeemah and his group managed to escape from slavery on Matakong Island and reach Freetown. Their testimonies, along with others, prompted authorities to pursue Isaacs. Forewarned by one of his agents, he managed to flee before he could be apprehended.[51]

The role of Freetown as an abolitionist town was multifaceted. It attracted enslaved people and immigrants with its 'pull' factors, such as opportunities for legitimate trade, education, or to reunite with family members, among other reasons. In the 1831 census and subsequent population returns, free Africans who chose to reside in Freetown were categorised as 'Native Strangers'. 'Native' refers to their being from Africa but 'strangers' highlights that they were not from the colony. Not all voluntary African immigrants were included in this category since Kru were allocated their own group in the different returns. This

49 Sène, 'Le décret', p. 4; Djiguatte Amédé Bassene, 'Continuité de la traite d'êtres humains, de la captivité et de l'asservissement des femmes et des enfants en Sénégambie française du XIXe au début du XXe siècles', in Klara Boyer-Rossol and Marie-Pierre Ballarin (eds), *Les esclavages en Afrique. Passé(s), présent(s) et héritages* (Paris, 2024), pp. 179–94, at p. 192; Ibrahima Thioub, 'L'abolition de l'esclavage en Afrique française : le principe du sol libérateur à l'épreuve du terrain', in Annie Fitte-Duval (ed.), *Droit et esclavages : Théorie et pratiques en Afrique et dans les Amériques (XVe-XIXe siècles)* (Paris, 2022), pp. 215–40, at p. 221.

50 When Gabbidon went bankrupt in 1852, he accused Isaacs of illegally occupying Matakong Island. He tried to rally support from local leaders and Governor Macdonald but failed. Later that year, Arthur Kennedy assumed the governorship of the colony of Sierra Leone and soon discovered that the colonial surveyor had been secretly importing and exporting goods. The surveyor fled to Matakong Island and escaped with Isaacs's assistance. Seeing an opportunity, Gabbidon informed Kennedy that Isaacs was, in fact, running a slave factory on the island. Adam Rovner, *The Jew Who Would Be King: A True Story of Shipwreck, Survival, and Scandal in Victorian Africa* (Oakland, 2025), pp. 195–215.

51 Fyfe, *A History*, pp. 240, 258, 275.

was characteristic of the colony of Sierra Leone – other colonies of the British Empire did not separate Kru from other African immigrants. In Freetown, they had a distinct identity and established a permanent community.[52] In 1831, 1850, and 1860, the proportion of 'Native Strangers' remained stable, ranging between 8 and 10 per cent, increasing proportionally to the total population of the city. Kru numbers remained stable between 1831 and 1850 as 501 and 560 were recorded, but their numbers decreased to 338 by 1860 as there were fewer Royal Navy ships, reducing employment opportunities for Kru.

Many of these individuals travelled to Freetown with some of their relatives or to reunite with them. Parents sometimes migrated alone, and their children later joined them. Michiel de Haas and Ewout Frankema note that migration to new trading centres was first dominated by men, but family members later joined.[53] In 1853, an ordinance made compulsory the registration of 'free African children of free African parents residing in the neighbouring territories [placed] in accordance with long usage under the guardianship of their friends or connections in the colony for the purpose of education and training in useful occupations'.[54] Their arrival was recorded in the Register of Alien Children, as was that of Mousu and Merry, two Susu girls from Bullom, who arrived on 30 July 1859. Mousu and Merry, along with twenty-seven other children listed in the Register in 1859, already had a parent living in Freetown or in one of the colony villages before they were registered.[55]

In other cases, children travelled with close relatives and arrived in Freetown as wards. The institution of wardship, or foster parenthood, was widespread in West Africa and across communities living in river towns close to the colony. Children were placed among relatives for multiple reasons and sometimes out of necessity when families were unable to provide for their children in cases of famine or illness. The placement of children as wards was also voluntary in cases when children were placed with educated relatives to improve their behaviour, make connections for marriage prospects, or to learn a trade.[56] Communities living close to European colonies would send their children to the urban centre

52 Gunn, *Outsourcing African Labor*, pp. 72–102, 160–1.

53 Michiel de Haas and Ewout Frankema, 'Introduction: The Age of Intra-African Migration – A Synthesis', in Michiel de Haas and Ewout Frankema (eds), *Migration in Africa: Shifting Patterns of Mobility from the 19th to the 21st Century* (London, 2022), 1–34, at p. 21.

54 Despatch no. 31, Arthur E. Kennedy to Henry Pelham-Clinton, 5th Duke of Newcastle, 10 February 1854, SLPA, Governor's despatches to Secretary of State for the Colonies (20 February 1853 – 22 July 1854), pp. 291–2.

55 Registration No. 48, 50, 109, 128, 129, 132, 144, 148, 164, 165, SLPA, Register of Alien Children (1859).

56 Kristin Mann, *Marrying Well: Marriage, Status and Social Change among the Educated Elite in Colonial Lagos* (Cambridge, 1985), p. 106; Havik, *Silences and Soundbites*, p. 65; Esther N. Goody, *Parenthood and Social Reproduction: Fostering and Occupational Roles in West Africa* (Cambridge Press, 1982), pp. 23, 152; Jessica Catherine Reuther, *The Bonds of*

since new trades opened, such as carpentry, bricklaying, or masonry.[57] Of the 112 children recorded in the Register of Alien Children in Freetown that year, 31 were brought by their parents who did not live in the colony. Arriving as wards did not necessarily mean that children were isolated from their families, since sixteen children in the 1859 Register arrived with a sibling. Six of them had no parents present in the colony, making their siblings their only known immediate family.[58] In seven of these sibling groups, the children travelled together. Only Bargay and his brother Yaneh arrived a few days apart. Bargay arrived in Freetown on 2 May 1859 with George William and lived with John Caulker. Two days later, on 4 May 1859, George William returned with Bargay's brother. While some children from this sample arrived with or were reunited with their parents or close relatives, they did not represent the majority. These eight-sibling groups only accounted for seventeen of the 112 children registered.

Additional sporadic evidence further underscores that free immigrants tended to settle in Freetown with relatives. The 1831 census recorded 28 'Native Strangers' as 'traders and their families' indicating the presence of family members in the household. The census does not include the precise relationship between the members of the family units, but it is likely that they were partners, children, or siblings. Similar patterns can be observed in police court records, as shown for example by the testimony of Sardia, a woman who lived in Freetown in 1839. When testifying about slavery, she explained that she was born in Bendu and came to settle in Krutown with her mother Cabaray.[59] Likewise, some Europeans came with their siblings or joined them later. English trader Abraham Lemon settled in Freetown by 1831. His brother Edward Lemon joined him by 1843. Hamburg traders and brothers Theodore and William John Charles Rosenbush were both settled in Freetown by 1860.[60]

Not all immigrants came with family members, but networks facilitated travel to Freetown.[61] During interviews conducted in 1849–1850 for his work *Polyglotta Africana*, German missionary Sigismund Wilhelm Koelle talked to

---

Kinship in Dahomey: Portraits of West African Girlhood, 1720–1940 (Bloomington, 2025), pp. 8–9, 28, 114.

57 Goody, *Parenthood*, p. 198.

58 Registration Nos 30–1, 32–4, 45–6, 58–9, 124–6, 128–9, 139–40, 164–5, SLPA, Register of Alien Children (1859).

59 Sardia, 9 July 1839, SLPA, Police Magistrate Record (27 February 1839 – 10 January 1840), fol. 225.

60 Census, 1831, TNA, CO 267/111, fol. 271; Edward Lemon v. Thomas Terry, James Johnson, and Peter Johnson, 16 June 1843, SLPA, Police Magistrate Record (1 June 1843 – 27 June 1844); Registration No. 92; SLPA, Register of Births, Freetown [hereafter RBF] (1857–1860); An Ordinance for the Naturalization of William John Charles Rosenbush, in the Colony of Sierra Leone 20 December 1860, British Library BLL01003380621.

61 de Haas and Frankema, 'Introduction', p. 13.

Gbā, also known as Thomas Samson, who explained that he left his hometown around Monrovia and was taken to Freetown by a friend.[62] There were thirty-four children in the Register of Alien Children who travelled with the people they were to live with. There are, however, forty-seven cases in which a third person was involved. It is not possible to trace the connection between the parents, the person who brought the child to the colony, and the person the child was to live with in Freetown. The parents sent children away with people they knew were able to take their children safely to the colony. For these children, the individuals could be family members, relatives, or strangers. Joe was registered on 17 May 1859 and his entry states that he was brought by a woman from a town near Rokon. Dahai was registered a day later, and the same information was entered.[63]

Trading networks also encouraged settlement as people from various places in West Africa travelled in caravans of varying sizes. Caravans have been interpreted as institutions for moving goods, armed convoys, or groups of people travelling together.[64] They were composed of about 1,000 to 2,000 men in the Volta markets, while in the Middle Niger Valley, Maraka caravans were composed of no more than thirty or forty merchants.[65] The extent of the relationship between the members of a caravan travelling to Freetown is unknown, but they were part of the same extended networks. As seen with enslaved people who self-liberated, travelling in groups provided a sense of protection, especially when traders travelled across politically unsettled areas. People needed to be aware of different rules when they went through places such as *jihād* states that were controlled by Muslims. The colonial government also worked with traders and rulers outside the colony to protect trade caravans. In his role as acting Governor in 1855, Robert Dougan assured Susu Muslim traders of their safe passage to the colony in a letter to Alikali Modu, a ruler of Medina – Alikali was the title given to a sub-chief, and the term itself derives from the Arabic word *qadi*, meaning a judge or legal authority.[66] Knowledge of the routes was essential, since in Fuuta Jalon, where cattle traders originated, the mountainous landscape was an obstacle to caravan commerce, and areas

62 Sigismund Wilhelm Koelle, *Polyglotta Africana; or A Comparative Vocabulary of Nearly Three Hundred Words and Phrases in more than One Hundred Distinct African Languages* (London, 1854), p. 4.

63 Registration No. 72–3, SLPA, Register of Alien Children (1859).

64 Bruce L. Mouser, '"Walking Caravans" of Nineteenth Century Fuuta Jaloo, Western Africa', *Mande Studies*, 12 (2010), 19–104, at p. 32.

65 Paul E. Lovejoy, *Caravans of Kola: The Hausa Kola Trade 1700–1900* (Zaria, 1980), p. 102; Richard L. Roberts, *Warriors, Merchants, and Slaves: The State and the Economy in the Middle Niger Valley, 1700–1914* (Stanford, 1987), p. 63.

66 Gibril R. Cole, *The Krio of West Africa: Islam, Culture, Creolization, and Colonialism in the Nineteenth Century* (Athens, 2013), p. 99; E. Ade Ijagbemi, 'A History of the Temne in the Nineteenth Century' (Unpublished PhD dissertation, University of Edinburgh, 1968), p. 80.

needed to be crossed on foot. The currents of the rivers were dangerous, impeding travel by boat. Bruce Mouser noted that guides followed well-known and national roads.[67]

Voluntary migration was sometimes dictated by conditions beyond people's control. Although not listed as a reason in the Register of Alien Children, food shortage was an important factor connected to the institution of wardship.[68] The Register does, however, list Freetown as a temporary solution to secure safety from slavery and warfare. Of the 112 children recorded in the Register of Alien Children, Mousu and Merry came seeking protection from slavery and sixteen other children were sent to escape from war. Ten of these children were listed as from Bullom, where people had already turned to the British colony for protection against Susu who invaded their territory in 1846. In early 1859, Temne people from Port Loko and Bullom Shore people together attacked the Susu.[69] Some children escaped this conflict by coming to Freetown for some time. Six others escaped war conflicts from Rotubong, Robari, Kagboroh, Taiama, and Foredugu. In Foredugu, Bokari Sila was in a dispute with Thomas Theophilus Caulker, over ownership of land by the Rossolo Creek, south of the Ribi River. The conflict was ultimately resolved by a peace treaty signed in August 1859.[70] Ten of the children who escaped from a war were to return home after the conflict was over. The abolition of the slave trade by European countries contributed to the growth of their colonies and created new opportunities for safety and relief. In Senegal, several children were also sent to the French colony of Saint Louis during wartime, especially in the second half of the nineteenth century when people sought to escape warfare led by the *jihād* of Al-Hajj Umar Tal in Fuuta Toro.[71] In Sierra Leone, Freetown was not the only place of refuge from warfare: outlying 'Liberated African' settlements were too. In the late 1820s, Loko people were displaced because of the Temne-Loko wars that started in 1828. They sought refuge with Kossoh 'Liberated Africans' settled in Koya Country.[72]

Freetown was also attractive to people who lived on the other side of the Atlantic Ocean, especially African Caribbean and African American men.

67 Mouser, '"Walking Caravans"', pp. 2, 63

68 Allen M. Howard, 'Pawning in Coastal Northwest Sierra Leone, 1870–1910', in Toyin Falola and Paul E. Lovejoy (eds), *Pawnship in Africa: Debt Bondage in Historical Perspective* (Boulder, 1994), pp. 267–84, at p. 271.

69 Fyfe, *A History*, p. 297.

70 Ijagbemi, 'A History of the Temne'.

71 Bernard Moitt, *Child Slavery and Guardianship in Colonial Senegal* (Cambridge, 2024), p. 92.

72 Adeleye Ijagbemi, 'The Kossoh War 1838–41: A Study in Temne/Colony Relations in the Nineteenth Century', *Journal of the Historical Society of Nigeria*, 5:4 (1971), 549–64, at pp. 552–3.

Analysis of the categories of the 1831 census reveals that they were not always classified under the same headings. Robert Dougan, an African Caribbean man, arrived in 1822 and was listed as 'mulatto', while Thomas Williams and Alexander Harleston, respectively arriving in the 1810s and early 1820s, were African American men listed as 'colonial residents'. Both categories also included Nova Scotian and Maroon settlers without a clear distinction. By 1850 and 1860, people from the Caribbean and from the United States of America were distinctly identified. The returns comprise 'Nova Scotians', 'Maroons', 'West Indians', and 'Americans', which were more straightforward categories. In 1850, there were 121 'Americans' recorded in Freetown and 90 'West Indians'.[73] Ten years later, the number of 'Americans' dropped to 50 and 'West Indians' still accounted for 90 individuals. To a small degree, these categories make it possible to consider voluntary migration from the Caribbean and the U.S. in the cultural landscape of Freetown.

The migration of transatlantic people of African descent also relied on constraints experienced in their home communities. They left their homeland because of poor living conditions and lack of opportunities for Black people who faced continuing discrimination after the abolition of slavery. As Atlantic migrants they were able to take up new opportunities across the British Empire. Those who came to Freetown were often men who came alone to further their economic and professional advancement. Others longed to return to the land of their ancestors and sought to bring religious knowledge and promote Christianity.[74] These movements of people were possible because of established links between colonies in the Caribbean and West Africa. As Caree Banton notes, newspapers, letters, gossip and propaganda created a discourse between the two sides of the Atlantic and advertised new opportunities. Barbadian newspapers such as *The Liberal* printed articles about the colony of Sierra Leone, the lives people led there, and what prospective migrants could acquire.[75]

Wealthier people could afford the trip to Freetown, while others, such as sailors and mariners, deserted upon arrival in the harbour. They chose to do so because of mistreatment, and despite the loss of pay and rank that would ensue. On 12 November 1839, John Fleming, Alexander Richie, and Henry Skey,

73 *Reports*, HC 1851, no. 1421, pp. 184–5.

74 Nemata Amelia Blyden, *African Americans and Africa: A New History* (New Haven, 2019), pp. 80–97; Nemata Amelia Blyden, *West Indians in West Africa, 1808–1880: The African Diaspora in Reverse* (Rochester, 2000), pp. 40, 114–15; Abioseh Nicol, 'West Indians in West Africa', *Sierra Leone Studies*, 13 (1958), 14–23, at p. 15; Julie Hardwick, Sarah M. S. Pearsall, and Karin Wulf, "Introduction: Centering Families in Atlantic Histories," *The William and Mary Quarterly*, 70: 2 (2013), 205–24, at p. 211.

75 Caree A. Banton, *More Auspicious Shores: Barbadian Migration to Liberia, Blackness, and the Making of an African Republic* (Cambridge, 2019), pp. 77, 105, 121, 129.

respectively chief mate, second mate, and seaman of the brig *Oscur*, deserted the ship as they claimed they were ill-used by the captain.[76] Several deserters were found wandering the streets of Freetown. On 26 February 1838, William Olway, the second mate of the barque *Bernard*, deserted the vessel with three men at Tombo Ward, all of whom were found wandering the streets. At two o'clock in the morning on 30 April 1838, Samuel Ellis, George Miller, and Dick Tom were found in the public streets and admitted to having run away and deserted. Not all deserters were without money, and some were able to afford lodgings. In August 1837, sailors named Carpenter and Frederick stayed at Maria Mattop's boarding house. In April 1851, Joseph Smith, a seaman from H.M.S. *Volcano* stayed with Jim Gray.[77]

Transatlantic immigrants also included white people who were separated from those of colour in the population returns. There is no distinction between people who migrated from Britain, France, or Brazil: if they were white, they were considered as 'Europeans', indicating that the European category refers to race rather than origins. By 1831, Commissary judge Jose de Paiva moved from Brazil with his wife and their son. In the census, he was categorised as European. Marcus Rediker argues that when a slave ship arrived on the African coast, sailors became 'white' regardless of cultural or ethnic background.[78] These cultural negotiations were frequent since in Cacheu, in the late eighteenth century, baptised Africans were considered as Christian, white, and Portuguese.[79] In 1850 and 1860, white transatlantic immigrants were listed among the 89 and 117 Europeans accounted for, respectively. These were, however, only rare cases in the category. De Paiva had been appointed to the Anglo-Brazilian Court of Mixed Commission, which was only intermittently represented between 1836 and 1844. The category was not significant in the population as they never represented more than 1 per cent.

The categories used in the 1831 census and the population returns offer a useful starting point for analysing the migration experiences of individuals who lived in Freetown during the mid-nineteenth century. These experiences constructed identities and expectations about what they life might look like. However, such expectations were not formed solely through the act of migration itself. They were also influenced by individuals' experiences prior to their arrival in Freetown. As Sylvie Kandé notes, Freetown's urban space and cultural

76 John Fleming, Alexander Richie, and Henry Skey, 12 November 1839, SLPA, Police Magistrate Record (15 February 1839 – 10 January 1840), fol. 395.

77 William Olway, Thomas Jenkins, Thomas Smith, John Leigh, 28 February 1838, Samuel Ellis, George Miller, and Dick Tom, 30 April 1838, Maria Mattop, 22 August 1838, SLPA, Police Court Record (22 August 1837 – 8 May 1838); Regina v. Jim Gray, 12 April 1851, SLPA, Police Court Record (1851 – 1852).

78 Nicol, 'West Indians', p. 14; Marcus Rediker, *The Slave Ship* (London, 2007), p. 260.

79 Rodney, *A History*, pp. 202–3.

landscape were shaped both by British authorities and by 'Liberated Africans' and African immigrants who brought with them diverse urban traditions.[80] Urban areas developed distinct identities, characterised by their biological environment, political structures, social dynamics, and commercial activities.[81]

Migrants came from various regions across Africa and sometimes across the Atlantic in North America, the Caribbean, or Brazil. They arrived under different circumstances, some as free individuals, others at various stages of enslavement. The urban experiences of some 'Liberated Africans' and a small sample of African immigrants are documented in Sigismund Wilhem Koelle's *Polyglotta Africana*. Between 1849 and 1850, Koelle interviewed eighty-six individuals in Freetown, recording the birthplace of seventy-nine of them, noting whether they were born in a hamlet, village, or town. In some cases, he also included information about other places they had lived in, whether as free persons or during their enslavement. Birthplaces, other place names, and ethnonyms can also be traced in the Register of Alien Children, testimonies from the police court records, and in a list of fifty-six 'fugitives' from slavery included in a despatch from the Governor and dated 19 August 1859. Although these sources make it possible to trace the geographical origins of only a small number of inhabitants, they help contextualise identities and expectations within both African and Atlantic histories of migration.

Only a small number of 'Liberated Africans' originated from areas near the colony of Sierra Leone, meaning that most were unfamiliar with its surrounding environment. Less than 14 per cent of embarkation ports were located in Sierra Leone and Senegambia, regions from which groups such as the Fula, Kossoh, Susu, and Temne originated, accounting for their limited numerical presence among 'Liberated Africans'. The 1848 census reflects this limited representation among Freetown residents, with 609 individuals identified as Kossoh (a term referring to Mende speakers from the south-east of Freetown), alongside only 51 Susu, 14 Fula, and 5 Temne.[82]

By contrast, individuals from these neighbouring areas were more prominent among people who self-liberated from slavery. British naval blockades of coastal ports disrupted the Atlantic slave trade and redirected enslaved labour inland, particularly onto agricultural estates. Although colonial governors sought to suppress slave trading beyond the coast, the expansion of so-called 'legitimate commerce' intensified internal slave trading networks. Foodstuffs and resources sold in Freetown were frequently produced through coerced labour, creating conditions in which escape to the nearby colony became an option for enslaved

80 Sylvie Kandé, *Terres, urbanisme et architecture « créoles » en Sierra Leone, XIIe-XIXe siècles* (Paris, 1998), p. 151.

81 Catherine Coquery-Vidrovitch, *Histoire des villes d'Afrique noire : Des origines à la colonisation* (Paris, 1993), pp. 15–16.

82 Anderson, *Abolition*, pp. 31, 134.

people.[83] Of the thirty-seven fugitives traced in police court records, twenty-two escaped from Matakong, twelve from Bullom, and thirteen from Bumpe, which are areas all situated relatively close to the colony.[84] The fifty-six individuals listed in the Governor's despatches were also mainly Kossoh, Sherbro, and Temne (Table 2.3).

Cultural and social structures also influenced who fled and who did not. Carol MacCormack argues that Temne people were less likely to escape to the colony due to internalised obedience reinforced through Poro and Bundu initiation societies.[85] These gender-specific institutions, which transcended ethnic boundaries, regulated family life, spiritual beliefs, and political and economic conduct. In the region surrounding the colony, the Poro (male) and its female counterpart, Sande or Bundu, were especially widespread, shaping norms that could discourage flight.[86] At times, enslaved people were allocated land to farm, which could produce living conditions perceived as preferable to those of free labourers, further complicating decisions to flee. However, the British annexation of parts of the Sherbro coast in 1861 altered this balance. Both the colony and the newly annexed coastal zones offered increased opportunities for liberation.[87] Between 1858 and 1861, 288 people self-liberated in Freetown, all from areas close to the colony. Over time, as Philip Misevich notes, the origins of fugitives gradually extended further inland.[88]

83 Allen M. Howard, 'Nineteenth-Century Coastal Slave Trading and the British Abolition Campaign in Sierra Leone', *Slavery & Abolition*, 27:1 (2006), 23–49.

84 Fyfe, *A History*, p. 240.

85 Carol P. MacCormack, 'Wono: Institutionalized Dependency in Sherbro Descent Groups (Sierra Leone)', in Suzanne Miers and Igor Kopytoff (eds), *Slavery in Africa: Historical and Anthropological Perspectives* (Madison, 1977), pp. 181–203, at pp. 189–91.

86 Kenneth Little, *The Mende of Sierra Leone: West African People in Transition* (London, 1998), p. 8; Katrina Keefer, 'Mission Education in Sierra Leone, 1793–1820' (Unpublished PhD dissertation, York University Toronto, 2015), p. 13; Kenneth Little, 'The Political Function of the Poro. Part I', *Africa: Journal of the International African Institute*, 35:4 (1965), 349–65, at p. 249; Christine Whyte, 'Mothering Solidarity: Infant-Feeding, Vulnerability and Poverty in West Africa since the Seventeenth Century', *Past & Present*, 246:15 (2020), 54–92, at p. 62; Katrina Keefer, 'Poro, Witchcraft and Red Water in Early Colonial Sierra Leone: G. R. Nylander's *Ethnography and Systems of Authority on the Bullom Shore*', *Canadian Journal of African Studies / Revue canadienne des études africaines*, 55:1 (2021), 39–55, at pp. 41–3; Trina Leah Hogg, *The Paradox of Protection: The Making of Indirect Rule in Southern Sierra Leone, 1850–1915* (East Lansing, 2026), pp. xxii–xxiii.

87 MacCormack, 'Wono', at pp. 189–91; Keefer, 'Poro, Witchcraft and Red Water', 39–55; K. L. Little, 'The Role of the Secret Society in Cultural Specialization', *American Anthropologist* 51:2 (1949): 199–212.

88 Misevich, 'Freetown and "Freedom?"', p. 204.

Table 2.3 Ethnonyms of 'fugitives' from slavery included in the Governor's despatches in 1859.

Place of origins	Number of fugitives
Igbo	2
Kalabar	1
Koranko	2
Kosso	18
Loko	2
Moko	2
Sherbro	12
Temne	17
Total	**56**

Source: Despatch No. 9146, 19 August 1859, TNA, CO 267/264.

People from areas close to the colony were also more numerous among free African immigrants. In the population return for 1850, 'Native Strangers' were identified as Temne, Sherbro, Fula, and Mandinka. Temne lived in the hinterland of Sierra Leone, and Sherbro initially occupied the coastal area. Fula and Mandinka originated from Guinea but came from various regions in West Africa.[89] Koelle interviewed eleven voluntary immigrants in Freetown, nine of whom came from places located on the upper Guinea coast, including Port Loko and Timbo. Other places were Balanser, located on the coast opposite the Îles de Los, Gbẹgbẽwīli, in the vicinity of Monrovia, Gbẽn·a, opposite York Island, and Tor on Bissau Island (Figure 2.1). The two farthest areas were Kaba and Timbuktu. African immigrants came from nearby areas connected to market towns such as Port Loko, Gbinti, Makeni, or Kukuna, having come into contact with traders or inhabitants from the colony of Sierra Leone before they moved there. Ambre, also known as Stephen, explained to Koelle that he was born at Balanser, where British traders lived.[90] Of 112 children in the Register of Alien Children, 107 were recorded as Baga, Bullom, Kono, Koranko, Kossoh, Gallinas, Limba, Loko, Mende, Sarakuli, Sherbro, Susu, and Temne (95.5 per cent).[91] Of the 327 'alien' children counted in the different despatches sent from the Governor to the Secretary of State, 305 were identified as part of

89 Anderson, *Abolition*, p. 134; Joseph Bangura, *The Temne of Sierra Leone: African Agency in the Making of a British Colony* (Cambridge, 2017), p. 3.

90 Koelle, *Polyglotta Africana*, pp. 1–2

91 A. P. Kup, 'An Account of the Tribal Distribution of Sierra Leone', *Man*, 60 (1960), 116–19.

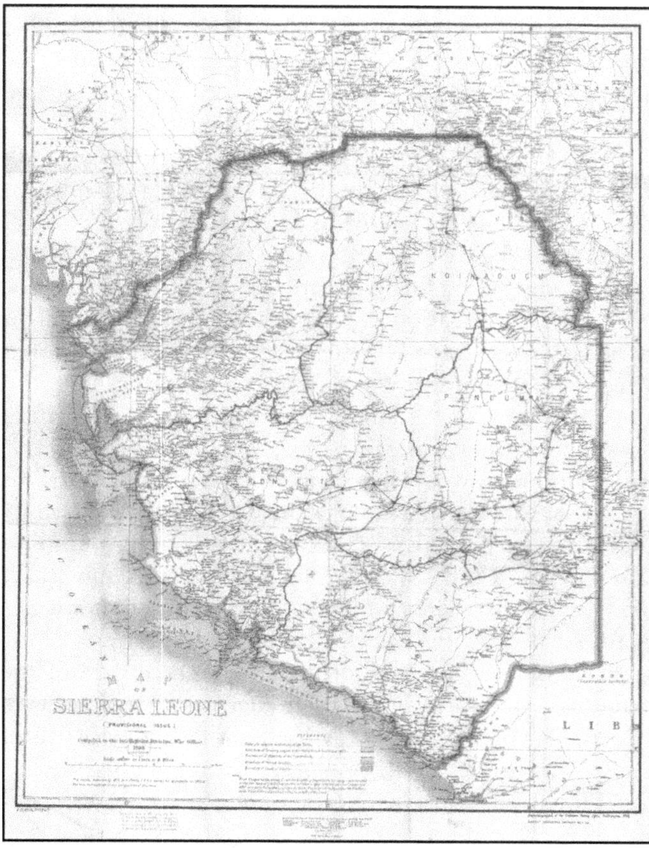

Figure 2.1 Map of Sierra Leone.

Source: Map of Sierra Leone (Provisional Issue) Compiled in the Intelligence Division, War Office, 1898, Barry Lawrence Ruderman Antique Maps Inc. ©

these groups (93.2 per cent, see appendix B). This also indicates that many of these children were part of Muslim communities.[92]

The majority of 'Liberated Africans' interviewed by Koelle had no prior experience or knowledge of the urban centre of Freetown, but they were born in or near a town, which are settings associated with commerce, craft production, religion, and literacy. Urban environments were multilingual and diverse, shaping the identities and worldviews of the individuals who lived in them.[93] Koelle identified sixty 'Liberated Africans' who were born in towns, while others, though born in villages or hamlets, were still closely connected to urban life through proximity. Gúmbo was born in Ndṣődọ, a hamlet in the

92 Anderson, *Abolition*, p. 231; Despatch No. 1448, 9 February 1859, TNA, CO 267/263; Despatch No. 9141, 1 August 1859, TNA, CO 267/264; Despatch No. 11209, 13 October 1859, TNA, CO 267/264; SLPA, Register of Alien Children (1859).

93 P. Lovejoy, 'The Urban Background', p. 349.

Salum district. Kõmi was born in the village of Adắmẹ, which is now part of Anfoega in Ghana, located just a mile from Akukome, the seat of the Anfoega ruler.[94] Mōhámmadu, also known as Jacob Brown, was born in Bérni Ndắda, half a day from Katsina, where he later moved with his parents.[95]

Parts of the urban areas from which many enslaved Africans came were important religious centres, and this significantly shaped the religious landscape of Freetown. A notable portion of enslaved individuals from urban backgrounds were Muslims. In the colony of Sierra Leone about 10 per cent of 'Liberated Africans' were already Muslims before being resettled.[96] Ali Eisami was born in Borno and began receiving an education in Arabic around the age of eight years. His case was not unique since many Muslims receive Islamic education.[97] Likewise, Muslim Africans who voluntarily moved to Freetown brought with them a background in Arabic literacy. 'Abdallihi Sérif was born in Timbuktu and lived in several prominent Muslim centres (Djenné, Segu, and Futa country) before eventually settling in Freetown. These experiences shaped both his education and identity, and he later became an Arabic teacher in the colony.[98]

The analysis of ethnonyms also helps deepen understanding of how familiar people were with urban settings. The 1848 census for Freetown accounted for 'Liberated Africans' and their descendants and recorded the presence of 7,114 Yoruba, the most urbanised people in West Africa. They were a politically and ethnically diverse group of people from Yorubaland, located west of the Niger River, east of Dahomey, and north of the Bight of Benin.[99] In Freetown, they were referred to as Aku, a colonial term only used in the colony of Sierra Leone, deriving from *e ku*, a common Yoruba greeting. Yoruba represented 53 per cent of the total of 'Liberated Africans' and their descendants (7,114 out

94 Koelle, *Polyglotta Africana*, pp. 4, 16; Veronika Bendt, 'Some Aspects of Legal Minority in the Tradition of the Anfoe Ewe, Ghana', *Zeitschrift für Ethnologie*, 104:1 (1979), 155–162, at p. 155.

95 Koelle, *Polyglotta Africana*, p. 17.

96 P. Lovejoy, 'The Urban Background', p. 350; Barbara E. Harrell-Bond, Allen M. Howard, and David E. Skinner, *Community Leadership and the Transformation of Freetown (1801–1976)* (The Hague, 1978), p. 106.

97 Paul E. Lovejoy, 'Ali Eisami's Enslavement in Jihad and Emancipation as a Liberated African', in Richard Anderson and Henry B. Lovejoy (eds), *Liberated Africans and the Abolition of the Slave Trade: Digital Histories of Enslavement and Freedom* (Rochester, 2020), pp. 127–52, at p. 131; Paul Lovejoy, *Jihād in West Africa during the Age of Revolution* (Athens, 2016), p. 81.

98 Koelle, *Polyglotta Africana*, p. 17; J. Spencer Trimingham, *Islam in West Africa* (Oxford, 1959), p. 246.

99 Matt D. Childs and Toyin Falola, 'The Yoruba Diaspora in the Atlantic World: Methodology and Research', in Toyin Falola and Matt D. Childs (eds), *Yoruba Diaspora in the Atlantic World* (Bloomington, 2005), pp. 1–16.

of 13,273 individuals).[100] Yoruba towns mentioned by Koelle's informants were located one to six days walk from Ilorin and five to six days from Abeokuta, two of the largest towns in Yoruba country.[101] Abeokuta was established around 1830 by Egba refugees from 154 places. Its population was estimated at 55,000 inhabitants in the mid-nineteenth century, more than three times the size of Freetown.[102] Some Yoruba cities had long traditions of urbanism, such as Ife, while others expanded in the eighteenth (Ilesha), or nineteenth century (Ogbomoso), which were cities identified as birthplaces of some of Koelle's informants.[103] Although of different sizes, being from large urban centres meant that these individuals were accustomed to large marketplaces with regional and imported goods available such as glassware, stoneware, or even European blue plates. Akinwumi Ogundiran notes that hundreds of markets in Yoruba provincial towns were well supplied.[104]

Some Yoruba people were already familiar with displacement and adaptation to a new urban environment before their enslavement. The *jihād* that began in Hausa states in 1804 and spread to Nupe in 1810, triggered an uprising of Muslim enslaved people in Ilorin in 1817. Subsequent Yoruba wars led to the collapse of the Oyo Empire (the largest Yoruba kingdom) in 1836. As a result, many refugees were forced to migrate southward within Yorubaland, to newly established settlements in places such as Abeokuta, Ibadan, or New Oyo.[105] For some, this was only the first of multiple displacements. 'Liberated Africans' uprooted by these conflicts experienced a second displacement when they were captured and enslaved. The story of John Taylor illustrates this layered history. A memorial in the Circular Road Cemetery remembers him as 'John Taylor, Native of Ilawo Abeokuta, in the Egba territory'. Since his son, William Ray Taylor, was born in Freetown in 1839, John Taylor was enslaved, embarked, subsequently 'liberated' from a slave ship, and brought to the colony of Sierra Leone prior to that date and thus had first been displaced to Abeokuta.[106]

100 Anderson, *Abolition*, pp. 155–65, 269; Coquery-Vidrovitch, *Histoire des villes*, p. 286; Akinwumi Ogundiran, *The Yoruba: A New History* (Bloomington, 2020), p. 266.

101 Samuel Johnson, *The History of the Yorubas*, 1897 (London, 1921), p. 94.

102 Coquery-Vidrovitch, *Histoire des villes*, p. 255; P. Lovejoy, 'The Urban Background', p. 353.

103 Coquery-Vidrovitch, *Histoire des villes*, p. 174; J. D. Y. Peel, 'Kings, Titles, and Quarters: A Conjectural History of Ilesha I – The Traditions Reviewed', *History in Africa*, 6 (1979), 109–53, at p. 109; B. A. Agiri, 'When was Ogbomoso Founded? An Analysis of the Traditions of Origin of an Oyo-Yoruba Town with Special Reference to Problems of Chronology and Feedback', *Transafrican Journal of History*, 5:1 (1976), 32–51, at p. 32; Koelle, *Polyglotta Africana*, pp. 5–6.

104 Ogundiran, *The Yoruba*, p. 268.

105 P. Lovejoy, *Jihād*, pp. 42–9.

106 Memorial to John Taylor, Circular Road Cemetery, Freetown, Sierra Leone, 2 October 1876. University of Hull, Remember Me project.

In 1848, the second largest group of 'Liberated Africans' (and their descendants) were Igbo, who accounted for 1,231 individuals in the census. They did not have experience of large urban centres, although they came from densely populated areas and lived in decentralised communities in which multiple villages formed village groups centred around a market in the senior village.[107] One of Koelle's Igbo informants, Akowi·lo, was born in the town of Umozuō. Igbo people spoke different dialects and did not have a common identity in their homeland. As with more than half of the 'Liberated Africans' disembarked in Freetown, they came from distant areas. They were from along and east of the lower Niger.[108] Their alienation was further reinforced by the fact that the enslavement of Igbo people in the Bight of Biafra often resulted from warfare and kidnapping. They had not been enslaved as outsiders by their communities and were active members of the societies from which they were forcibly removed.[109]

Exposure, even brief, to different cultures in Africa helped individuals develop adaptability skills. 'Liberated Africans' who were not from urban centres travelled through some of them during their march to the coast and spent some time in Atlantic ports. Enslaved Africans thereby became exposed to different cultures and languages, which shaped their identity and tied them to ethnicity and religious expression. They went through a process similar to creolisation, as they identified and were identified differently than before enslavement.[110] Ndán·ga told Koelle he was taken as a war prisoner by the 'Muhammadan Tíbāle', indicating his exposure to Islamic culture.[111] In Atlantic ports, enslaved individuals sometimes acquired knowledge of European languages.[112] A few examples in Koelle's research include Mámāde who was enslaved and taken to Bissau where he stayed for fifteen years. Bissau was an entrepôt and an incorporated enclave of the Portuguese Crown, where Mámāde learned some Portuguese. N·gōn·ga stayed for two years in the hands of Portuguese traders although he did not specify where. Musēwo, also known as Toki Petro, was enslaved, and stayed in Luanda for twenty-one years.[113] Musēwo's other name, Toki Petro, underscores his experience in Portuguese Luanda rather than in

107 David Northrup, 'The Growth of Trade among the Igbo before 1800', *Journal of African History*, 13:2 (1972), 217–36, at p. 226.

108 David Northrup, 'Becoming African: Identity Formation among Liberated Slaves in Nineteenth-Century Sierra Leone', *Slavery and Abolition*, 27:1 (2006), pp. 1–21, at pp. 9–11; Anderson, *Abolition*, pp. 139–45.

109 Nwokeji, *The Slave Trade*, p. 128.

110 P. Lovejoy, 'The Urban Background', p. 352; Paul Lovejoy, *Slavery in the Global Diaspora of Africa* (London, 2019), p. 259.

111 Koelle, *Polyglotta Africana*, p. 12; P. Lovejoy, *Jihād*, pp. 80, 92.

112 Northrup, 'Becoming African', p. 6.

113 Koelle, *Polyglotta Africana*, p. 2; Philip J. Havick, 'Gendering the Black Atlantic: Women's Agency in Coastal Trade Settlements in the Guinea Bissau Region', in Douglas Catterall and Jodi Campbell (eds), *Women in Port: Gendering Communities, Economies, and Social Networks in Atlantic Port Cities, 1500–1800* (Leiden, 2012), pp. 315–56, at p. 322.

Freetown. Koelle noted that there was one Dőei man (west of Bornu in northern Nigeria) in the colony of Sierra Leone who had been sold as a child and, due to alienation and exposure to other cultures, had forgotten his native language. The same was true for another Dőei woman.[114]

Others experienced different societies beyond the Atlantic. Kindṣĩmbi, also known as Dṣindṣĩmbi or John Baptist, was taken to Brazil where he spent fifteen years before escaping on a merchant vessel bound for Sierra Leone. Bẽmbi, also known as William Davis, was sold and taken to Demerara, where he likely acquired some knowledge of English.[115] At his master's death Musẽwo went to Brazil as a free man. There, a Portuguese merchant employed him in the slave trade for six years. When the ship on which he served was seized, Musẽwo was classed as a 'Liberated African', alongside the enslaved people he traded. Muhammadu was kidnapped at seventeen years and taken to Jamaica, where he remained for nine years before being sent to Sierra Leone to serve as a soldier. He was discharged around 1830. Individuals enslaved in the Caribbean who joined the W.I.R. and arrived in Freetown already possessed some familiarity with British society and the English language, an advantage that eased their integration. A significant number of these soldiers were discharged in the 1820s, but, in 1843, a company of the 1st W.I.R. came from Barbados, followed by a company from Jamaica in 1848, which remained until 1854. Additional companies set out from Demerara and Barbados in January 1857 and arrived the following month.[116]

Experience of different settings with European presence was not limited to 'Liberated Africans' disembarked from slave ships. Although these cases were rare, a few individuals who self-liberated and a few children sent as wards experienced colonial settings or direct interactions with Europeans. John Mymidon, Lavers Mymidon, Moses Hawkins, George Williams, and Tom Yalloh already had English names when they arrived. They might have had European enslavers, prior interactions with Europeans on Ascension Island (two of them were named after a Royal Navy ship), and possibly some knowledge of the English language. Three children sent as wards (from the Register of Alien children) also experienced interactions with other Europeans or colonial settings. Thomas Joaque was from Cacheu, a Portuguese trading post located on the south bank of the Cacheu River.[117] Catharine Higgins was the only

114 Koelle, *Polyglotta Africana*, p. 10.

115 Ibid., pp. 13–15.

116 S. C. Ukpabi, 'West Indian Troops and the Defence of British West Africa in the Nineteenth Century', *African Studies Review*, 17:1 (1974), 133–50, at p. 137; A. B. Ellis, *The History of the First West India Regiments* (London, 1885), pp. 218, 232, 258.

117 Registration No. 12, SLPA, Register of Alien Children (1859); Patrick Gantly, *Histoire de la Société des missions africaines (SMA) 1856–1907*, tome premier, traduit par Joseph Hardy et Pierre Trichet (Paris, 2009), p. 40; Filipa Ribeiro da Silva, *Dutch and Portuguese in Western Africa: Empires, Merchants and the Atlantic System, 1580–1674* (Leiden, 2011), pp. 154–8.

child who was recorded as American. She was about seven years old and had been brought to Freetown from the Nunez River by Jane Joseph. Three years later, in 1862, she was removed to Liberia.[118] She might have been the child of African Americans settled in Monrovia. Cesar Ciococo came from the most distant town of Epe, established by Kosoko, the exiled King of Lagos, on the north-eastern shore of the lagoon, where both French and British merchants traded for palm oil.[119] Sent for his education, Cesar arrived with French naval captain Aristide Vallon, who had previously taken royal Dahomean children to France. In June 1859, Vallon stopped in Epe, where Cesar Ciococo and his parents lived. Before returning to France, he left Cesar in the care of Father Louis Reymond, a French Catholic priest in Freetown.[120] Unlike most children, Cesar came from a Yoruba town and was from an influential family since his parents sent him away with a French captain.

By the 1860s, the demographic profile of Freetown had shifted significantly. While earlier generations were shaped by their direct experiences of migration, whether from diverse areas in Africa, the Caribbean, the Americas, or across the Atlantic, the majority of the population by this time was born within the colony itself. These later generations inherited traditions and cultural memories of migration, but they no longer shared first-hand experiences of the journeys that had defined their ancestors' identities. As a result, the lived reality of migration ceased to be a first-hand experience in shaping individual identities in Freetown, marking a new chapter in the colony's social history.

The proportion of these generations in the society grew from 38 per cent of the population in 1831, to 45 and 57 per cent in 1850 and 1860 respectively. The terminology around this group of the population was fluid. In 1831, they were referred to as 'freeborn blacks', in 1850 they were 'Native Creoles', and by 1860, 'colony-born'. They are now referred to as Krio. Historians debate the origin of the term 'Krio', with some scholars arguing that the term derives from 'Creole', and others that it derives from the Yoruba term *akiriyo*, which means 'those who go about paying visits'.[121] In the 1960s, the term 'Creole' was used to refer to individuals born in the colony and 'Krio' to refer to the *lingua franca*

118 Registration No. 68, SLPA, Register of Alien Children (1859).

119 Kristin Mann, *Slavery and the Birth of an African City: Lagos, 1760–1900* (Bloomington, 2007), pp. 49, 122, 142; Robin Law, 'Trade and Politics Behind the Slave Coast: The Lagoon Traffic and the Rise of Lagos, 1500–1800', *Journal of African History*, 24:3 (1983), 321–48, p. 326; Registration No. 99, SLPA, Register of Alien Children (1859).

120 Fyfe, *A History*, p. 288; Patrick Gantly, *Histoire de la Société des missions africaines*, p. 39; Bibliothèque nationale de France, *Revue Maritime et Coloniale* (Paris : Librarie de Challamel Ainé, 1862), pp. 320–3; Bibliothèque nationale de France, *Moniteur du Sénégal et Dépendances*, 134 (19 October 1858), p. 4.

121 P. E. H. Hair, 'Aspects of the Prehistory of Freetown and Creoledom', *History in Africa*, 25 (1998), pp. 111–18; C. Magbaily Fyle, 'The Yoruba Diaspora in Sierra Leone's Krio Society', in Toyin Falola and Matt D. Childs (eds), *Yoruba Diaspora in the Atlantic World* (Bloomington, 2005), pp. 366–82.

that emerged in the nineteenth century.[122] With the exposure to British values, the meaning of Creole shifted to refer to Europeanised Africans and Black Britons. Other historians reject this definition and state that Creoles should in fact be called Krio, a term that would include influence from other African groups – including Temne, Mende, and Mandinka peoples – or Muslims.[123] Fyfe argued that the Krio identity did not develop in Freetown until at least 1859, since members of the population united under associations such as 'The National Society of the Liberated Africans and Their Descendants', and 'The Nova Scotian and Maroon Descendants' Association'.[124]

Conclusion

The analysis of migration patterns in Freetown reveals diverse and paradoxical experiences of freedom of movement, the movement of people to secure their freedom, and the coerced movement of the 'Liberated Africans', which shaped a complex social landscape. These experiences framed Freetown as a place of African diaspora where the degree of alienation was influenced by their geographical background and migration experience. Adaptation was shaped by these experiences and by the reasons behind their relocation to the British colony. For 'Liberated Africans', Freetown further represented the lack of agency in their enforced movement. They arrived in the colony in poor health conditions, and without a complete understanding of their new life. In contrast, people who self-liberated from slavery risked being captured during their escape but, being aware of opportunities lying ahead, they were prepared to take the risk. Voluntary immigrants came for greater economic, educational, or familial opportunities. Labour migrants or migrants who came with family members travelled more safely and had guidance once in Freetown. This chapter puts forth complex and diverging histories of migration, showing how different factors driving migration, combined with different circumstances of arrival, conditioned migrants' understanding of their new environment and of their status within it.

122 John Peterson, *Province of Freedom: A History of Sierra Leone, 1787–1870* (Evanston, 1969); Leo Spitzer, *The Creoles of Sierra Leone: Responses to Colonialism 1870–1945* (Madison, 1974).

123 Akintola J. G. Wyse, 'On Misunderstandings Arising from the Use of the Term "Creole" in the Literature on Sierra Leone: A Rejoinder', *Africa*, 49:4 (1979), 408–17; Fyle, 'The Yoruba Diaspora'.

124 Fyfe, *A History*, p. 293; Kandé, *Terres, urbanisme*, p. 286.

3

The Economic and Social Profile of Freetown

By the mid-nineteenth century, Freetown experienced rapid population growth. Between 1831 and 1862, its population more than doubled, growing from 8,505 to 17,829 inhabitants.[1] Despite being a relatively recent settlement, founded in the late eighteenth century, the pace of its growth was striking when compared to other major ports along the Atlantic coast in Africa. Its population had already surpassed or was catching up to that of older coastal towns. Luanda, established in 1575, had 12,656 inhabitants by 1850, and even though Ouidah had been a main port since the 1670s, in the 1850s, its population was similar to that of Freetown and ranged between 18,000 and 20,000. Likewise, Lagos, founded as *Èkó* in the sixteenth century, had a population of about 20,000.[2] Rapid population growth has clear consequences on the economy as more people need to find ways to provide for themselves. This chapter traces the nature of the economy and society by first assessing the employment profile of the city. This sheds light on hierarchical distinctions between inhabitants, and the implications for social stratification and social mobility. Christopher Fyfe and Allen M. Howard identified examples of 'Liberated Africans' who achieved considerable economic and social success in the colony.[3] This chapter demonstrates that the experience of these individuals, although significant, was

1 Census of Population and liberated Africans, 1831, TNA, CO 267/111; Blue Books of Sierra Leone, 1862, British Online Archives [hereafter BOA], p. 166.

2 Vanessa Oliveira, *Slave Trade and Abolition: Gender, Commerce, and Economic Transition in Luanda* (Madison, 2021), p. 12; Robin Law, 'Ouidah as a Multiethnic Community', in Jorge Cañizares-Esguerra, Matt D. Childs, James Sidbury (eds), *The Black Urban Atlantic in the Age of the Slave Trade* (Philadelphia, 2013), pp. 42–62, at p. 42; Mariana P. Candido, *An African Slaving Port and the Atlantic World: Benguela and its Hinterland* (Cambridge, 2013), p. 112; Kristin Mann, *Slavery and the Birth of an African City: Lagos, 1760–1900* (Bloomington, 2007).

3 Christopher Fyfe, 'Four Sierra Leone Recaptives', *Journal of African History*, 11:1 (1961), 77–85; Allen M. Howard, 'New Insights on Liberated Africans: The 1831 Freetown Census', in Richard Anderson and Henry B. Lovejoy (eds), *Liberated Africans and the Abolition of the Slave Trade: Digital Histories of Enslavement and Freedom* (Rochester, 2020), pp. 101–26.

an exception and not typical of the overall experience of 'Liberated Africans' and of other members of the society.

Occupation is an important factor in measuring social status as it reveals levels of wealth and education, providing a basis for drawing inferences about the social profile of Freetown. A number of sources created by the colonial administration provide valuable information for tracing the occupational profile of Freetown; these include the 1831 census, birth registers, statistical returns, and Blue Books. The 1831 census provides a detailed breakdown of its population and it records information on the locations of 8,505 residents listed in 37 streets and 6 areas. It provides occupational descriptions for 4,983 of the people listed (59 per cent). Of these, 3,635 were provided for adults, meaning that an occupation is listed for 70 per cent of the adult population. On 18 August 1851, Governor Norman Macdonald transmitted to Earl Grey a numerical breakdown of 16,679 people, distributing them into eleven occupational categories. Birth registers from 1857 to 1862, provide information on 1,117 births recorded with information on the fathers' occupations. There were 884 different fathers and 1,053 mothers. As men sometimes held multiple jobs, a number of 906 occupational descriptions are provided for the fathers, but not for mothers. Street addresses are included for all but five fathers, and occupations are provided for 873 of those listed (92 per cent). The last source used is the Blue Books, which contain information on 10,951 appointments in the colony.[4]

Together, the sources bring a total number of different occupational designations to 267, although some occupational labels were used for the same occupations. To understand the economic profile of Freetown, these various occupations were organised into seventeen categories based on Charles Booth and W. A. Armstrong's works of occupations in Britain. Their classifications are relevant to nineteenth-century Freetown as decision making about occupations contained in censuses and birth registers followed British systems of record keeping.[5] On 18 May 1886, Booth presented before the Statistical

4 The Blue Books of Sierra Leone provide information on the occupations in these sectors. Between 1831 and 1862, there were 10,951 occupations listed by the civil, judicial, and ecclesiastical establishments in Freetown and by the Liberated African Department in Freetown and the colony villages. The civil establishment included occupations ranging from governor, and colonial surveyor to clerks, occupations in education and at the Colonial Hospital. The judicial establishment included the chief justice, registrars at the Vice Admiralty Court, gaolers, or police inspectors. The ecclesiastical establishment included chaplains, organists, and church cleaners. The section on the Liberated African Department recorded superintendents, managers, writers, labourers, coxswain, and any other residents employed by the Department in Freetown and in the colony villages.

5 Alistair Tough and Paul Lihoma, 'The Development of Recordkeeping Systems in the British Empire and Commonwealth, 1870s–1960s', *Archives and Manuscripts*, 40:3 (2012), 191–216.

Society his 'Occupations of the people of the United Kingdom, 1808–81', in which he compiled tables that distributed occupations listed in British censuses. These were divided into eleven categories: agriculture; fishing; mining; building; manufacturing; transport; dealing; industrial service; public and professional service; domestic service; property owning independent, and indefinite. In 1972, W. A. Armstrong amended that list and divided economic activities in Britain into nine occupational groups: agriculture and fishing; mining; building; manufacturing; transport; dealing; industrial service; public service and professional; and domestic service.[6]

All the occupations listed in the sources used in this chapter are divided into sixteen categories with an additional category for individuals without any recorded occupation who are listed as 'not recorded'. Eight of the nine categories used by Armstrong are used for the purposes of this analysis, except for 'industrial service'. This includes activities related to banking, insurance, and accountancy, which are concealed in trading occupations. For Armstrong, 'public service' referred to administration, the army and the navy, the police, law, medicine, arts, literature, science, education, and religion. The group contains occupations that need to be separated into distinct categories for a better understanding of the social profile of Freetown. Consequently, this group is divided into six smaller ones: administration, ecclesiastical, education, medical, military, and public service. For clarity, the category 'dealing' is changed to 'trade'.

A few occupational titles are more ambiguous than others. A shoemaker could manufacture and sell the product. It is impossible to know whether all the inhabitants listed as making goods sold their products, but some cases are clearer cut. May Copeland lived with a woman named Venus, on 22 East Street. While May was a pancake maker, Venus was a pancake seller, a clear distinction between the making of the goods and its sale. Following this example, individuals making goods are considered as manufacturers.[7] Another ambiguous group is that of 'labourers'. The term referred to various sectors from building to moving goods at the wharf, and other forms of manual labour. The same is true

6 Charles Booth, 'Occupations of the People of the United Kingdom, 1801–81', *Journal of the Statistical Society of London*, 49:2 (1886), 314–444, at p. 416; W. A. Armstrong, 'The Use of Information about Occupation', in E. A. Wrigley (ed.), *Nineteenth-Century Society: Essays in the Use of Quantitative Methods for the Study of Social Data* (Cambridge, 1972), pp. 191–310; Matthew Woollard, 'The Classification of Occupations in the 1881 Census of England and Wales', *Historical Censuses and Social Surveys Research Group Occasional Paper No. 1* (Essex, 1999), 1–57, at p. 6.

7 Marco H. D. van Leeuwen, Ineke Maas, and Andrew Miles, 'Creating a Historical International Standard Classification of Occupations an Exercise in Multinational Interdisciplinary Cooperation', *Historical Methods: A Journal of Quantitative and Interdisciplinary History*, 37:4 (2004), 186–97, at p. 191; Census, 1831, TNA, CO 267/111, fol. 291.

for 'woman of all work' and 'workman/woman'. These three occupations are grouped together under the category 'manual labour'. A category for apprentices has been added to reflect the specific context of Freetown where, between 1808 and 1848, large numbers of 'Liberated Africans' were allocated to masters or mistresses for a period. Not all inhabitants without an occupation listed were unemployed, but for the purpose of clarity the 'working population' refers to people listed with an occupation.

Analysing the occupational profile of Freetown first requires understanding that there are three economic sectors: one based on raw material and natural growth, another on the derivation of products and mechanical factors, and the tertiary sector is the service industry that relies on human skills.[8] In 1831, the primary sector comprised agriculture, fishing, and mining and employed 322 inhabitants. The secondary sector comprised occupations in building, manual labour, and manufacturing, and employed 1,152 inhabitants. The tertiary sector employed individuals in administration, apprenticeship, domestic service, ecclesiastical, educational, medical, military, public service, trade, and transport. It represented the largest proportion of occupational descriptions with 3,509 residents. In the birth registers, the primary sector employed 181 fathers, the secondary 260, and tertiary 449, which follows the same trend as the data contained in the census of 1831. Trade and crafts expanded rapidly, but agriculture remained marginal in the urban area. Between 1857 and 1862, the birth registers listed 106 fathers working in agriculture and 51 in fishing, which represents 17 per cent of the total number of fathers in the registers (see Appendix C). As this is only a small sample, this number does not accurately reflect the proportion of agricultural workers in Freetown but suggests that it was close to that indicated in the census of 1831.

In 1831, 270 inhabitants were employed in agriculture and fishing. Of these, 124 were recorded as farmers and 135 as fishermen. The majority of them (166 individuals, 62 per cent) were listed as 'Liberated Africans' (See Appendix D, Table 1), reflecting colonial policy that allocated them plots of land to cultivate, especially in the colony villages.[9] As an urban centre, agriculture only represented 3 per cent of the total of occupations (270 out of 8,505 inhabitants) and 5 per cent of the working population (270 out of 4,983 inhabitants). In addition, and in common with Lagos, land on the Sierra Leone peninsula

8 Martin Wolfe, 'The Concept of Economic Sectors', *The Quarterly Journal of Economics*, 69:3 (1955), 403–20.

9 Richard Anderson, *Abolition in Sierra Leone: Re-Building Lives and Identities in Nineteenth-Century West Africa* (Cambridge, 2020), p. 105; Padraic X. Scanlan, 'The Colonial Rebirth of British Anti-Slavery: The Liberated African Villages of Sierra Leone, 1815–1824', *American Historical Review*, 121:4 (2016), 1085–113, at p. 1099.

was not suitable for agriculture.[10] In 1851, Norman Macdonald informed Earl Grey that boats were used for fishery and that all pilots of the colony were fishermen. They were grouped along with seamen under one category, comprising 588 inhabitants.[11]

The analysis of the employment profile of Freetown over three decades does not depict a static picture but one in which socio-economic dynamics were based on age and sex. People engaged in agricultural labour and fishing were all male, and included 268 adults, two of whom did not have their sex recorded (see Tables 2 and 3 in Appendix D). The only child was Goodwill Drake, a 'Liberated African' boy who was likely apprenticed to George Drake, another farmer. No women were listed with an occupation in agriculture or fishing in the census, but this does not mean that they were not involved in either or both. British censuses were taken by men who tended to under-record occupational descriptions for women, especially if they were not household heads. This underreporting, which also applied to colonial records, was influenced by the domestic ideology of women as wives and mothers. Wives of innkeepers, lodging-house keepers, shopkeepers, butchers, farmers, and shoemakers, who were listed by their social status as 'wife', were active in the businesses run by their husbands.[12] In Freetown, 650 men and 925 women were not ascribed an occupational designation, but more women were following the same line of work as their spouse. Nine women were listed with the title 'wife'. Six might have been working with their husbands who were merchants and traders, and shoemakers. They might also have had independent occupations as European colonies in Africa saw growing numbers of business-women in the eighteenth and nineteenth centuries.[13]

10 James W. St. G. Walker, *The Black Loyalists: The Search for a Promised Land in Nova Scotia and Sierra Leone, 1783–1870* (London, 1976), p. 193; Mann, *Slavery*, p. 64.

11 Governor Norman William Macdonald to Secretary of State for War and the Colonies, Henry Grey, 3rd Earl Grey, 18 August 1851, SLPA, Governor's Despatches to the Secretary of State (13 July 1851 – 26 December 1851), fol. 35.

12 Edward Higgs and Amanda Wilkinson, 'Women, Occupations and Work in the Victorian Censuses Revisited', *History Workshop Journal*, 81 (2016), 17–38, at pp. 17–18, 22, 28; Jody Benjamin, *The Texture of Change: Dress, Self-Fashioning, and History in Western Africa, 1700–1850* (Athens, 2024), p. 98.

13 Jane Hamlett, 'Review of *The Foundations of Female Entrepreneurship: Enterprise, Home and Household in London, c. 1800–1870* by Alison C. Kay', *The Economic History Review*, 64:1 (2011), 310–11; Mariana Candido, 'African Women in Ecclesiastical Documents, Benguela, 1760–1860', *Social Sciences and Missions*, 28 (2015), 235–60, p. 260; Vanessa S. Oliveira, 'Dona Ana Joaquina Dos Santos Silva: A Woman Merchant of Nineteenth Century Luanda', in Vanicléia Silva Santos (ed.), *General History of Africa*, vol X, *Africa and its Diasporas* (Paris, 2023), pp. 913–24; Philip J. Havik, *Silences and Soundbites: The Gendered Dynamics of Trade and Brokerage in the Pre-Colonial Guinea Bissau Region* (Münster, 2004).

Many wives of fishermen and farmers were selling their husbands' products. Out of 75 fishermen-identified spouses, 41 (55 per cent) were 'market women' as well as 15 (29 per cent) of 51 farmers' spouses. There were more women selling their husbands' products, but their occupations differed. Damba, a cow-keeper, lived with Sarah, a milk woman on 46 Grassfield East.[14] Market people were predominantly females, as 592 of the 688 market people recorded in the census were women. On 24 June 1830, George Clack stated that 'Liberated Africans' cultivated their country lots for their own use and that they only sold small quantities to Freetown markets.[15] By 1851, 18 per cent of the working population was in the category of farmers, farm labourers, and market people (see Appendix E).[16] Farming was more arable than pastoral, and local consumption rested on yams, cocoa, Indian corn, sugar cane, sweet potatoes, and bananas. In the villages, farmers planted rice, patches of cassava, and coconut, which were sold to the Liberated African Department.[17]

Selling produce and other forms of trade employed 1,081 inhabitants in 1831, which represented 13 per cent of the population and 22 per cent of the working population. Throughout the nineteenth century, trade remained the most important economic sector. The Blue Books' returns on the city's population in 1855 and 1857 recorded employment for 9,310 of its 16,022 inhabitants who worked in agriculture, manufacture, and commerce. Of the three sectors, trade was the largest with 4,079 (44 per cent) residents.[18] Trading also emerged as the main economic sector in the birth registers between 1857 and 1862. From the sample of 906 occupational descriptions, 264 (29 per cent) held an occupation in trade. 'Trade' in Freetown was a diverse group comprising gold traders, hawkers, market people, merchants, tobacconists, traders, shopkeepers, and storekeepers among others. These different occupations within this group highlight wide variations in terms of short- and long-distance trade, the material they were trading in, and the levels of wealth. While markets were based on small quantities of perishable foodstuffs and livestock, long-distance

14 Census, 1831, TNA, CO 267/111, fol. 262; E. Frances White, *Sierra Leone's Settler Women Traders* (Ann Arbor, 1987), p. 25.

15 *Report from the Select Committee on the Settlements of Sierra Leone and Fernando Po*, HC 1830, no. 661, p. 38.

16 Macdonald to Grey, 18 August 1851, SLPA, Governor's Despatches 1851, fol. 64.

17 Padraic X. Scanlan, *Freedom's Debtors: British Antislavery in Sierra Leone in the Age of Revolution* (New Haven, 2017), pp. 184–5.

18 Blue Books of Sierra Leone, BOA, 1855, p. 163; Blue Books of Sierra Leone, 1857, BOA, p. 153.

trade was based on the bulking of produce.[19] Goods were sold in stalls, along the streets, and at the market site near the harbour on Water Street. In the 1850s, materials were shipped from England to construct a formal market. Completed in 1861, it became known as the Big Market. Today, the *Big Markit* remains a trading centre with food, crafts, jewellery, and more.[20]

A growing number of African immigrants came to Freetown in response to the increasing European demand for timber, groundnuts, and palm produce. Scholarship on Sierra Leone has focused on the importance of trade in the colony, as well as on trading links with the interior.[21] In 1831, there were 203 traders listed in Freetown and 104 (51 per cent) of these were listed as 'Native Strangers' (African immigrants), but these numbers are not necessarily accurate. There are only 41 women listed as traders even though women participated in long-distance trade.[22] There are no 'Liberated African' women and only 12 'Liberated African' men specifically recorded as 'traders', even though many acted as intermediaries between people from the interior and Freetown-based merchants. Others stayed in the colony out of fear of re-enslavement when they travelled outside of it.[23]

Muslim traders expanded trade networks with regional centres such as Timbo, Kankan, and Dinguiraye in present-day Guinea, which were central to the economy of Freetown and of the whole colony.[24] Fluctuating numbers

19 C. W. Newbury, 'Credit in Early Nineteenth Century West African Trade', *Journal of African History*, 13:1 (1972), 81–95, at p. 81.

20 Christopher Fyfe, *A History of Sierra Leone* (Oxford, 1962), p. 303; 'Siera Leone: Explore Freedom', <https://tourismsierraleone.com/attractions/big-market/> [accessed 23 May 2025].

21 White, *Sierra Leone's Settler Women Traders*; Suzanne Schwarz, 'Adaptation in the Aftermath of Slavery: Women, Trade and Property in Sierra Leone, c.1790–1812', in Mariana P. Candido and Adam Jones (eds), *African Women in the Atlantic World: Property, Vulnerability & Mobility 1660–1880* (Woodbridge, 2019), pp. 19–37, at p. 32; Barbara E. Harrell-Bond, Allen M. Howard, and David E. Skinner, *Community Leadership and the Transformation of Freetown (1801–1976)* (The Hague, 1978); Gibril R. Cole, 'Liberated Slaves and Islam in Nineteenth-Century West Africa', in Toyin Falola and Matt D. Childs (eds), *Yoruba Diaspora in the Atlantic World* (Bloomington, 2005), pp. 383–403; Christopher Fyfe, 'The Foundation of Freetown', in Christopher Fyfe and Eldred Durosimi Jones (eds), *Freetown: A Symposium* (Oxford, 1968), pp. 1–8, at p. 3; Philip Misevich, 'The Sierra Leone Hinterland and the Provisioning of Early Freetown, 1792–1803', *Journal of Colonialism & Colonial History*, 9:3 (2008), <https://doi.org/10.1353/cch.0.0032> [accessed 25 April 2026].

22 Cole, 'Liberated Slaves', p. 396.

23 Bronwen Everill, *Abolition and Empire in Sierra Leone and Liberia* (Basingstoke, 2013), p. 38; Philip Misevich, 'Freetown and "Freedom?" Colonialism and Slavery in Sierra Leone, 1790s to 1861', in Paul E. Lovejoy and Suzanne Schwarz (eds), *Slavery, Abolition and the Transition to Colonialism in Sierra Leone* (Trenton, 2015), pp. 189–216, at p. 200.

24 Gibril R. Cole, *The Krio of West Africa: Islam, Culture, Creolization, and Colonialism in the Nineteenth Century* (Athens, 2013), p. 98; Gibril R. Cole, 'Religious Plurality and

of non-resident Muslim traders came from regions including the Upper Niger, Fuuta Jalon, and around Port Loko. Itinerant traders stayed with resident hosts, also called *diatigi*, who spoke Temne, Limba, Loko, and Mende, among other languages.[25] They sold items imported from the interior including kola nuts, benni seed, and shea butter but also cattle, hide, and ginger. Some also engaged in the kola trade extending to Senegal and the Gambia. Kola nuts, a highly valued commodity in West Africa, were primarily produced in the forests of Sierra Leone and areas eastward to Asante.[26] Following the British founding of Freetown, the north-west coast of Sierra Leone became a supply zone in the early nineteenth century, linking it to the broader Coastal Corridor between the Nunez River and southern Sierra Leone, a central region to kola growing. The growth of this trade drew leaders of Mande-speaking communities from Kankan, Segu, Touba, and Timbo to Freetown.[27] Colony-born Muslims were also integrated into these networks. Mohammed Sitta, born to Yoruba 'Liberated Africans' in Waterloo in 1824, had relocated to Lagos by the 1850s and traded in cotton cloths, hides, egusi (seeds of some cucurbitaceous plants), gum copal (aromatic resin from the copal tree), and kola nuts.[28] While thirty-two Muslim traders were identified in birth registers, their actual number was underreported, as the registers most likely include Christian births over that of Muslim families or non-registered marriages.

Products such as kola, palm oil, teak timber, ginger, groundnuts, or camwood were bought in the interior markets and shipped back to Freetown in canoes where merchants sold them to Europe.[29] There were thirty-three merchants recorded in the census and twenty-two in the birth registers. Although fewer in number than market sellers and traders, these men controlled more substantial financial capital and engaged in long-distance trade. By the mid-nineteenth century, demand for palm oil surged in Britain due to its use in manufacturing candles, soaps, and tinplate. In response, palm oil exports began in 1824 and

Economic Sustainability: Muslim Merchants in the Colonial Economy of Nineteenth Century Freetown', *African Economic History*, 36 (2008), 79–93, at p. 81; David E. Skinner, 'The Influence of Islam in Sierra Leone History: Institutions, Practices, and Leadership', *Journal of West African History*, 2:1 (2016), 27–71, at p. 32; Allen M. Howard, 'Trade and Islam in Sierra Leone, 18th–20th Centuries', in Alusine Jalloh and David E. Skinner (eds), *Islam and Trade in Sierra Leone* (Trenton, 1997), pp. 21–63, at p. 22.

25 Howard, 'Trade and Islam', p. 27.

26 Paul E. Lovejoy, *Jihād in West Africa during the Age of Revolution* (Athens, 2016), p. 141.

27 Allen M. Howard, 'Mande Kola Traders of Northwestern Sierra Leone, Late 1700s to 1930', *Mande Studies*, 9 (2007), 83–102, at pp. 85, 89–90.

28 Cole, 'Liberated Slaves', pp. 396–8; Antony Hopkins, *Capitalism in the Colonies: African Merchants in Lagos, 1851–1931* (New Haven, 2024), pp. 88–9.

29 Martin Lynn, *Commerce and Economic Change in West Africa* (Cambridge, 1997), p. 64.

expanded significantly during the 1830s, followed by the first kernel exports in 1846.[30] The use of steamships further contributed to the expansion of trade and intensified regional competition. In 1855, Peter Nicholls, a 'Liberated African' who returned home to Old Calabar (a city-state in present-day Calabar in south-eastern Nigeria) used steamers to send oil to Britain. Other merchants soon followed, and by 1856, between fifteen and twenty colony-born merchants exported palm oil from Lagos.[31]

The example of Peter Nicholls is not unique and illustrates the potential for social mobility among 'Liberated Africans' who became merchants; however, while these cases are highlighted here, they were exceptional and did not represent the typical experience of most 'Liberated Africans'. Some 'Liberated African' merchants were able to bid on the cargo of condemned ships, but only three or four possessed capital between £50 and £500, enabling them to retire with sums of £1,000 to £1,500.[32] Memorial inscriptions in Freetown's churches reveal that a few 'Liberated Africans' rose to prominence as merchants and members of the Legislative Council, leaving a lasting mark.[33] Isadore, later known as John Ezzidio, began as an apprentice to Jean Billaud before rising to wealth and political influence as a merchant and member of the Legislative Council.[34] He requested a marble tablet to be erected at Wesley Chapel in Trelawney Street at his death, symbolising his material success and immortalising his legacy.[35] Today, the basement hall of Wesley Church bears his name.

30 Everill, *Abolition and Empire*, p. 159; Martin Lynn, 'From Sail to Steam: The Impact of the Steamship Services on the British Palm Oil Trade with West Africa, 1850–1890', *Journal of African History*, 30 (1989), 227–45, at p. 228; Lynn, *Commerce*, pp. 14, 24; *Reports*, HC 1852, no. 1539, p. 143.

31 Lynn, *Commerce*, p. 140; Antony Hopkins, 'Property Rights and Empire Building: Britain's Annexation of Lagos, 1861', *The Journal of Economic History*, 40:4 (1980), pp. 777–98, at p. 785; Christopher Fyfe, 'Peter Nicholls – Old Calabar and Freetown', *Journal of the Historical Society of Nigeria*, 2:1 (1960), 105–14; Mann, *Slavery*, p. 127.

32 *Report from the Select Committee on the West Coast of Africa; together with the minutes of evidence, appendix, and index. Part I – Report and evidence*, HC 1842, no. 551, p. 253.

33 Anderson, *Abolition*, pp. 161, 275.

34 Fyfe, *A History*, pp. 217, 231; Christopher Fyfe, 'The Life and Times of John Ezzidio', *Sierra Leone Studies*, 1 (1955), 213–23; John Peterson, *Province of Freedom*, p. 294; Everill, *Abolition and Empire*, p. 161; Gustav Kashop Deveneaux, 'Public Opinion and Colonial Policy in Nineteenth-Century Sierra Leone', *The International Journal of African Historical Studies*, 9:1 (1976), 47–67, at p. 48; Census, 1831, TNA, CO 267/111, fol. 310; Registration No. 48, SLPA, Register of Deaths, Freetown district (1872–1873).

35 The Will of John Ezzidio, 18 December 1872, Principal Registry of Her Majesty's Court of Probate, *Find A Will*, <www.probatesearch.service.gov.uk/Calendar?surname=Ezzidio&yearOfDeath=1872&page=3#calendar> [accessed 23 April 2021]; Sarah Tarlow, *Bereavement and Commemoration: An Archaeology of Mortality* (Oxford, 1999), p. 117.

Trade also stimulated various forms of employment, particularly in transport and boat building. In 1831, 163 inhabitants worked in transport, a sector tied to Freetown's role as a port. Much as in Lagos, where European merchants hired workers from the Kru Coast and the Gold Coast to load ships, Kru were employed on ships, at the harbour, or as pilots.[36] Other port-related occupations included clerks at the custom house. In 1831, this occupation was held by Thomas Pinches and in 1862 by Charles Bucknor Bucknor. In the birth registers Bucknor Bucknor was listed as 'second landing waiter customs', showing the increasing need for multiple customs officials.[37] The expansion of trade likewise boosted boat building and ship repair industries. During the 1850s, Freetown's harbour was 'full of small craft' headed to the Northern Rivers and Lagos.[38] The census and the birth registers combined recorded seven occupational descriptions related to boat building (including boat builder, mat maker, rope maker, ship carpenter). In 1831 alone, there were thirteen ship carpenters, three sail makers, and a sailmaker's apprentice named Hannah Black.[39] Birth registers also list nineteen fathers working as ship carpenters and shipwrights.

Ship carpenters were part of the manufacturing sector, which employed 335 inhabitants in 1831. This sector included a wide range of trades, from blacksmiths and boatbuilders to cabinet makers, sawyers, shingle makers, and seamstresses. Manufacturing activities supported the production of goods such as shoes, rope, and cigars. Between 1857 and 1862, 121 fathers were recorded with occupations in manufacturing, underscoring diversification in production from palm wine maker to bamboo maker, and clapboard maker. Combined data from the census and birth registers reveal forty-two distinct occupations within the manufacturing sector. Seven were linked to construction (e.g., blacksmiths, sawyers, joiners), another seven to boat building, and two to military production (armourer and mortar maker). The majority, however, provided essential goods and services, including bakers, barbers, sausage makers, shoemakers, seamstresses, and straw-hat makers. Six occupations served both domestic and agricultural needs (e.g., basket and fence makers), while two were associated with tavern-related trades – brewers and palm wine makers. This sector produced everyday goods for local consumption, while also supporting trade and agricultural work. By the 1850s, groundnut oil had become an important manufactured product. Nuts were pressed in two mercantile houses

36 Mann, *Slavery*, p. 151.

37 Registration No. 245, SLPA, Register of Births, Freetown district [hereafter RBF] (1860–1861).

38 Bronwen Everill, '"For the Services of Shipwrights, Coopers, and Grumettas": Freetown's Ship Repair Cluster in Nineteenth-Century Sierra Leone', *History of Science* (2020), 1–17, at p. 3; Fyfe, *A History*, p. 317.

39 Census, 1831, TNA, CO 267/111, fol. 291.

owned by Mr Oldfield and Mr Burnett, the latter having introduced screw presses to Freetown in the early 1840s. In 1851, these presses were operated by twenty Kru workers, producing oil used for cooking and lighting.[40] The birth registers for 1861 list William Gerber as a soap maker, a trade dependent on the palm oil produced and sold within the colony.[41]

There are marked gender divisions in the manufacturing sector, with most skilled occupations requiring previous knowledge or training largely restricted to men (77 per cent). Only seventy-three women were listed in manufacturing and, of these, sixty-seven were described as seamstresses (91 per cent). The six women who were not categorised as seamstresses each had a different occupation: brewer, cigar maker, sausage maker, pancake maker, starch maker, and straw-hat maker. The dominance of seamstresses was partly due to the nature of education provided at missionary schools, where needlework was used to teach African girls to learn literacy, numeracy, and virtues such as perseverance and obedience.[42] According to census data, 92 per cent of the seamstresses were listed as colonial inhabitants, 'Liberated Africans', and discharged soldiers and their families. Manufacturing women were all adults, except Maria Fraser and Hannah Black, the sail girl. Maria Fraser was learning the trade followed by her mother, Anne Fraser, who was a seamstress.[43] Maria Fraser's training alongside her mother was not uncommon, as many women in manufacturing worked within family and household networks.[44]

While women clothed Freetown, 'Liberated Africans' were instrumental in building the city itself.[45] Out of the 870 individuals in the census with an occupation in building, labour or mining, 499 (57 per cent) were categorised as 'Liberated Africans'. The majority of men among that group were in construction roles with 382 inhabitants listed as bricklayers, carpenters, masons, and shingle carpenters. Less skilled manual labour was also predominantly male. Of the 436 individuals listed as work people, women of all work, and labourers, 379 (87 per cent) were male. Labourers were employed in various ways, from the construction of barracks and carrying of timber and iron.[46] Mining occupations including lime burners, stone breakers, and stone cutters,

40 Macdonald to Grey, 18 August 1851, SLPA, Governor's Despatches 1851. fol. 33; Fyfe, *A History*, p. 258.

41 Registration No. 181, SLPA, RBF (1861–1862).

42 Howard, 'New Insights', p. 114; Silke Strickrodt, 'African Girls' Samplers from Mission Schools in Sierra Leone (1820s to 1840s)', *History in Africa*, 37 (2010), 189–245.

43 Census, 1831, TNA, CO 267/111, fol. 304.

44 Ibid, fol. 311.

45 Daniel Augustine Vonque Stephen, 'A History of the Settlement of Liberated Africans in the Colony of Sierra Leone during the First Half of the 19th Century' (Unpublished PhD dissertation, Durham University, 1963), p. 20; Howard, 'New Insights', p. 116.

46 *Coms. of Inquiry into State of Colony of Sierra Leone, Report (Part I.)*, HC 1827, no. 312, p. 78.

were exclusively male. These occupations collectively accounted for 52 men in the census, focusing on extracting and preparing construction materials (although lime was also used to improve soil quality). In the birth registers, 45 of the 906 occupational descriptions (5 per cent) fell into the building category, with 94 (10 per cent) engaged in manual labour, and 12 (1 per cent) in mining. As in Britain, however, women and girls likely contributed to the sorting and transport of mined materials as 'work women' or 'women of all work'.[47]

Women's work was largely centred within households. In 1831, 671 inhabitants were recorded in domestic service roles, of whom 473 (71 per cent) were women. These occupations included charwoman, housekeeper, laundress, and washerwoman. By 1851, women in these roles were grouped under the miscellaneous category with seamstresses and washerwomen. They amounted to 2,014 inhabitants and represented 16 per cent of the working population. The image of the African woman as a domestic servant is vividly captured in a watercolour from Henry Needs collection titled 'Katherine Murray, Washerwoman, Sierra Leone', which depicts an African woman ironing. Women like her shaped the everyday life of Freetown. It was common to see laundresses washing clothes at watering spots such as King Tom Bridge and Ravine Bridge.[48]

Even though predominantly a female occupation, some contemporary accounts underscore the presence of men in domestic service. Both Elizabeth Helen Melville, the wife of Michael Melville, Registrar of the Mixed Court Commission, and W. L. Neville, superintendent of the Mission of the West Indian Church on the Rio Pongas (in present-day Guinea), wrote about having male servants in their household. In 1851, male servants were included in a diverse category that included 'grumettas, predial labourers, and house servants' (amounting to 4,121 individuals). Grumettas were maritime labourers, working along the waterways, and predial labourers cultivated the land. This makes it impossible to probe the proportion of house servants in the society for that year.[49] In the birth registers, only 27 fathers were recorded in domestic service as cooks, dressers, house servants, servants, and waiters. Men employed in domestic service were cooks or house servants while women took care of the upkeep of the house with the washing.

There is an unclear distinction between servants and apprentices and in the census, 1,598 residents were recorded as such. The term servant indicates that

47 Angela V. John, *Coalmining Women: Victorian Lives and Campaigns* (Cambridge, 1984).

48 Caroline Sheridan Norton (ed.), *A Residence at Sierra Leone. Described from a Journal Kept on the Spot, and from Letters Written to Friends at Home* (London, 1849), p. 203.

49 Macdonald to Grey, 18 August 1851, SLPA, Governor's Despatches 1851, fol. 64; Norton (ed.), *A Residence*, p. 13; W. L. Neville, *Journal of a Voyage from Plymouth to Sierra Leone* (London, 1858), p. 30.

Figure 3.1 Katherine Murray, a washerwoman in Sierra Leone.
© National Maritime Museum, Greenwich, London, ART/10/1, Volume of 143 watercolours by Henry Need covering the commission of the sloop LINNET on the suppression of slavery on the west coast of Africa, 1852–1856.

the individuals worked in domestic service, and the use of the term apprentice suggests that they were supposed to learn their masters' or mistresses' trade. Because the census was taken by two writers from the Liberated African Department, the terms could also refer to the same condition. Throughout the nineteenth century, apprentices came to be considered as 'cheap additional labour' and a new form of labour supply to settlers and to other 'Liberated Africans'.[50] Out of the fifty European households of the census, only five did not have any servants listed. There are a few examples of 'Liberated African' households with their own servants or apprentices. John and Fanny Newby lived with three children, including their son Joseph Newby, and with Hannah and Mary, two apprentices. Martin and Mary Haffner lived with five apprentices, and John Ogoo and his wife Charlotte Ogoo lived with seven apprentices and three other people.[51]

A large proportion of servants and apprentices were children (1,298 out of 1,598 individuals, or 75 per cent). Prior to the abolition of the apprenticeship system in 1848, the majority of these children were 'Liberated Africans', who made up 76 per cent of this group in 1831. From the 1850s onward, the number of African immigrant children, or wards, sent to Freetown increased, and these children gradually replaced the 'Liberated Africans' as unpaid servants.[52] Of the 112 wards recorded in the Register of Alien Children in 1859, 27 were allocated as domestic servants and 8 came to learn to wash and sew, which represents 31 per cent of the children who arrived during that time. It is very likely that 36 children (32 per cent) listed as coming for education were employed in domestic service in their respective households.

A small number of individuals, mostly men, were employed in public service roles under colonial administration, though they remained a minority. In 1831, 100 residents worked in administration, with wide disparities in income. While top officials such as the Lieutenant-Governor and Chief Justice earned £1,500–£2,000 annually, clerks earned just £50–£100.[53] The Liberated African

50 Schwarz, 'Adaptation', pp. 34–5; Suzanne Schwarz, 'The Impact of Liberated African "Disposal" Polices in Early Nineteenth-Century Sierra Leone', in Richard Anderson and Henry B. Lovejoy (eds), *Liberated Africans and the Abolition of the Slave Trade: Digital Histories of Enslavement and Freedom* (Rochester, 2020), pp. 45–65; Maeve Ryan, '"A Moral Millstone"? British Humanitarian Governance and the Policy of Liberated African Apprenticeship, 1808–1848', *Slavery & Abolition*, 37:2 (2016), 399–422, at pp. 405–6.

51 Maeve Ryan, 'A "Very Extensive System of Peculation and Jobbing": The Liberated African Department of Sierra Leone, Humanitarian Governance and the Fraud Inquiry of 1848,' *Journal of Colonialism & Colonial History*, 17:3 (2016) <https://doi.org/10.1353/cch.2016.0041> [accessed 25 April 2026].

52 Christine Whyte, '"Freedom but Nothing Else": The Legacies of Slavery and Abolition in Post-Slavery Sierra Leone, 1928–1956', *The International Journal of African Historical Studies*, 48:2 (2015), 231–50, at p. 233; Fyfe, *A History*, p. 270.

53 Blue Books of Sierra Leone, 1831, BOA, fol. 32, 33, 38.

Department was a major focus of activity and employment. In 1841, it employed more than 200 inhabitants, whose names are listed in colonial Blue Books, making it the largest single employer in the colony.[54] By 1851, 31 government officers, likely clerks in the Liberated African Department, were recorded.[55] Of 85 fathers listed as working in administration in the birth registers, 40 were clerks or writers, a group more inclined to register their children's births due to the nature of their roles.

Occupations related to religion, education, the medical sector, or the military were rare. The census listed six: four missionaries, a church beadle, and a man named Johnson, described as a 'Jew'. Clearly, Johnson's does not indicate his occupation, but other Jewish people were not identified for their religion. Abraham Lemon, a Jewish resident was identified as a trader and not as a Jewish man.[56] Other public service roles included forty-six individuals in education, twenty-three in the medical sector, and three in the military. In the birth registers, eleven fathers were clergymen or catechists, fifteen worked in education, two in medicine, and thirteen in the military. Twelve 'bandsmen' were part of a military band, though only Alexander Bonard appeared in the birth registers with this occupation.[57] In legal professions, William Henry Savage, an African European (person of African and European descent) and advocate for the 'Liberated African' Muslim community, was listed as a solicitor, while John Thorpe, a colony-born son of Maroon John Thorpe, was an attorney.[58]

Of the 195 occupational descriptions listed in the census within public service categories, only thirty-two were held by women (16 per cent). Of these, twenty women worked in the medical field as nurses, midwives, or matrons. There were also three schoolmistresses, and nine girls recorded as schoolgirls. Although male overseers dominated the department, women began to take on more formal roles. In 1840, Charlotte Pratt was the first woman officially listed as an overseer. By 1843, seven women were recorded as temporary overseers and, by 1857, that number increased to thirty-two, holding either temporary or permanent positions.[59] Overseers were responsible for managing groups of twenty-five 'Liberated Africans' at the Queen's Yard, with duties ranging from conflict mediation to assisting with vocational training and guiding individuals to their sleeping quarters. Female overseers had additional responsibilities, from accompanying women to bathe and teaching children to read, spell, and sew. While overseers were typically drawn from among the settled 'Liberated

54 Ryan, 'A "Very Extensive System"'.
55 Macdonald to Grey, 18 August 1851, SLPA, Governor's Despatches 1851, fol. 64.
56 Census, TNA CO 267/111, fol. 282.
57 Registration No. 33, SLPA, RBF (1857–1860).
58 Fyfe, *A History*, p. 188; For more on Savage, see Cole, 'Liberated Slaves', pp. 383–403.
59 Blue Books of Sierra Leone, 1840, BOA, fol. 60; Blue Books of Sierra Leone, 1831–1862, BOA.

Africans', many, as Maeve Ryan notes, were illiterate, making their instructional duties somewhat 'wishful thinking'.[60] Overall, most female employment remained confined to domestic roles, such as church cleaning, or serving as matrons or schoolmistresses. Women held only 392 (4 per cent) of the 10,951 occupations listed in the Blue Books.

Informal and unrecorded labour, especially that carried out by women, was largely absent from official sources such as the census and government statistics. This included socially condemned activities such as prostitution, the practioners of which were prosecuted for offending the Christian moral order imposed by colonial authorities. On 21 October 1839, William Scott was charged with 'lending his wife for the purpose of prostitution'.[61] The court record does not provide further details, and the name of his wife is not given. However, the 1831 census lists a William Scott, recorded without an occupation, living at 15 Portuguese Town 2 with his wife Betsy Scott, a 'Liberated African' woman, also without an occupational title, and Thomas Morrison, a 'Liberated African' carpenter.[62] It is possible the couple supported themselves through Betsy's sex work, highlighting how some households relied on informal and illicit income sources to survive.

As Adam Jones notes, in some African contexts, prostitution was tied to beer brewing, which enabled women to improve their economic standing. Vanessa Oliveira points out that, in Luanda, taverns where men gathered to drink, gamble, and purchase sex were common.[63] In the 1831 census, only one brewer is listed, Grace Grafton, who lived with Hannah James, a sausage maker. Their cohabitation suggests they may have operated a tavern and perhaps participated in or profited from prostitution activities. Reports from the time also indicate that prostitution involved a range of women. In 1827, Governor Neil Campbell noted that some apprenticed girls lived as prostitutes with soldiers, and others were forced into prostitution by their mistresses. In 1829, a Maroon man was said to have sold his daughter to an officer for this purpose.[64] Prostitution

60 Ryan, 'A "Very Extensive System"'.

61 William Scott, 21 October 1839, SLPA, Police Magistrate Record (27 February 1839 – 10 January 1840), fol. 369.

62 Census, 1831, TNA, CO 267/111, fol. 374.

63 Adam Jones, 'Prostitution, Polyandry or Rape? On the Ambiguity of European Sources for the West African Coast, 1660–1860', in Mariana P. Candido and Adam Jones (eds), *African Women in the Atlantic World: Property, Vulnerability & Mobility 1660–1880* (Woodbridge, 2019), pp. 89–108, at p. 104; Vanessa S. Oliveira, 'Baskets, Stalls, and Shops: Experiences and Strategies of Women in Retail Sales in Nineteenth Century Luanda', *Canadian Journal of African Studies / Revue canadienne des études africaines*, 54:3 (2020), 419–36, at p. 428.

64 Ryan, '"A Moral Millstone"?' 413; *Report*, HC 1842, no. 551, p. 417; Maeve Ryan, *Humanitarian Governance and the British Antislavery World System* (New Haven, 2022), p. 185; *The Barbadian* (20 January 1829), Barbados Archives.

functioned as a significant, though hidden, source of income for some women and households, especially those excluded from formal employment.

While largely absent from demographic records, sex work appears in court documents and police reports, revealing its role in the informal economy. Known to authorities as a prostitute, Betsy Bragger appeared frequently in court for public disturbances linked to her work. She was repeatedly arrested for being drunk on Water and Westmoreland Streets, areas associated with sex work, and was involved in several altercations with individuals she lived with, or was accused of assault. These encounters suggest that Bragger's livelihood was tied to street-based prostitution, and that her visibility in public spaces made her a target of surveillance and regulation.[65]

While society was marked by inequality, certain factors enabled social mobility for some. Education and family background were important in defining access to elite status. Early settler groups, especially the Nova Scotian and Maroon communities, formed the colony's original elite. As Hannah Kilham observed in 1828, Freetown's schools offered 'superior advantages' compared to village schools, largely because most students were children of settlers who already spoke English.[66] This educational advantage enabled them to secure higher-status colonial occupations, which were largely reserved for this group.[67] Charles Shaw, a Maroon, served as a gaoler until his death in 1831 and was succeeded by John Gray, a Nova Scotian settler.[68] The Spilsbury family, of Maroon descent, also illustrates this pattern, with multiple family members holding clerical and merchant roles across decades.[69] Children of Europeans occupied prominent posts, such as John Meheux, the son of a French trader, who became Queen's Advocate and later sheriff, and William Smith Jr., registrar

65 James Villiams v. Betsy Bragger, 10 February 1851, SLPA, Police Court Record (1851–1852); Regina v. James Williams and Betsy Bragger, 16 September 1854, Regina v. Betsy Bragger, 19 October 1854, SLPA, Police Magistrate Record (1 June 1854 – 21 October 1854); Queen v. Betsy Bragger, 23 September 1862, SLPA, Assistant Police Magistrate Record (8 August 1862 – 12 November 1862), fol. 217.

66 Hannah Kilham, *Report on a Recent Visit to the Colony of Sierra Leone* (London, 1828), p. 7.

67 Walker, *The Black Loyalists*, pp. 200–3, 374.

68 Blue Books of Sierra Leone, 1831, BOA, fol. 53.

69 In 1831, Joseph Green Spilsbury worked as a clerk. His son Thomas became second clerk in Customs by 1857. Joseph's cousin, John Sweeney, was a writer in 1860, and his godson Joseph Spilsbury Carew died as a clerk in 1862. Henry Fowler Spilsbury, likely related, was listed as a merchant in 1860 and 1862. See: Census, 1831, TNA, CO 267/111, fol. 322; Registration No. 35, 104, SLPA, RBF (1860–1861); Will of Joseph Green Spilsbury, Merchant of Freetown, Sierra Leone (22 August 1856), TNA, PROB 11/2238/111; Blue Books of Sierra Leone, 1859, BOA, p. 104; Registration No. 271, SLPA, RBF (1861–1862); Registration No. 445, SLPA, Register of Deaths, Freetown district (1861–1862).

at the Mixed Court Commission, who followed his father's footsteps.[70] The connection between education, family lineage, and elite occupation was not unique to the colony of Sierra Leone; comparable patterns existed elsewhere in West Africa, where Western education signified wealth and social standing.[71]

Time spent in the colony gave 'Liberated African' children and children of 'Liberated Africans' better chances at higher-status occupations. From 1824, the Church Missionary Society (C.M.S.) focused on educating colony-born children, founding schools that excluded 'Liberated Africans', and in the hope of turning these children into schoolteachers.[72] Scholars note that colony-born Africans came to dominate teaching professions across West Africa. In Freetown and other cities such as Lagos and Saint Louis, Western education opened opportunities in civil service and Christian missions, typically as lower-level clerks.[73] The 1831 census recorded eight schoolteachers, mostly colonial residents, with only two 'Liberated Africans'. Education and time spent in Freetown also offered greater opportunities for 'Liberated Africans' who arrived as children. George Metzger, taken in as a servant by missionary William Young, lived in Grassfield in 1831 with other servants and pupils. Between 1857 and 1862, two men named George Metzger appear in birth registers, one a clerk and the other a schoolmaster. It is probable the Metzger who lived with Young became the schoolmaster.[74] A well-known example is Samuel Crowther, who disembarked from a slave ship in 1822, became a schoolteacher by 1830, and was appointed the first African Anglican Bishop in 1864.[75]

Education was not the only path to social mobility; knowledge of other languages was another important factor. Thomas George Lawson, son of the

70 Christopher Fyfe, 'The Administration in 1885', *Sierra Leone Studies*, 1 (1955), 226–8, at p. 227; Census, 1831, TNA, CO 267/111, fol. 294; Blue Books of Sierra Leone, 1845, BOA, fol. 94; Blue Books of Sierra Leone, 1853, BOA, fol. 83; Registration No. 252 SLPA, RBF (1857–1860).

71 Pernille Ipsen, *Daughters of the Trade: Atlantic Slavers and Interracial Marriage on the Gold Coast* (Philadelphia, 2015), p. 163.

72 Benjamin N. Lawrance, Emily Lynn Osborn, and Richard L. Roberts, 'Introduction: African Intermediaries and the "Bargain" of Collaboration', in Benjamin N. Lawrance, Emily Lynn Osborn, and Richard L. Roberts (eds), *Intermediaries, Interpreters, and Clerks* (Madison, 2006), pp. 3–36, at p. 5.

73 Hilary Jones, *The Métis of Senegal: Urban Life and Politics in French West Africa* (Bloomington, 2013), p. 98; Mann, *Slavery*, p. 92.

74 Census, 1831, TNA, CO 267/111, fol. 259; Blue Books of Sierra Leone, 1862, BOA, p. 100; Registration No. 472, SLPA, RBF (1857–1860); Registration No. 49, SLPA, RBF (1860–1861).

75 Philip D. Curtin, *Africa Remembered; Narratives by West Africans from the Era of the Slave Trade* (Madison, 1967), pp. 289–90; Jesse Page, *The Black Bishop Samuel Adjai Crowther* (New York, 1909), p. 17.

chief of Little Popo (Aneho, Togo), settled in Freetown in 1825. Though listed as a servant in 1831, by 1846 he became Governor Macdonald's emissary and, in 1852, a government messenger and interpreter, roles that were key to the colonial administration.[76] Similarly, Joseph DeGraft, an educated African immigrant from the Gold Coast, worked as a writer collecting census data in 1831. His familiarity with African societies gave him an advantage over British officials such as Norman Macdonald. Clerks such as Lawson and DeGraft were valued as 'cross-cultural brokers' who bridged colonial and African societies.[77]

Forming strong social and professional connections with more highly placed individuals sometimes enabled people to advance their status. When European Walter William Lewis died on 23 July 1844, he bequeathed £25 to his servant James Lewis.[78] African Barbadian Thomas Carew left a plot of country land near Freetown to Mary Carew, described in his will as 'his domestic shop woman', meaning his 'Liberated African' apprentice, making her a landowner upon his death.[79] Connections could also open broader economic and political opportunities. John Ezzidio benefited from his relationship with Reverend Thomas Dove, General Superintendent of the Wesleyan Mission, who took him to England in 1842. There, he formed partnerships with businessmen from London and Manchester, enabling him to import goods worth £3,000–£4,000.[80]

The socio-economic landscape of Freetown is further revealed through an analysis of residential patterns among different occupational groups. By combining social and occupational descriptions from the census with the inhabitants' addresses, it is possible to trace economic, social, and spatial

76 Kenneth C. Wylie, *The Political Kingdoms of the Temne: Temne Government in Sierra Leone, 1825–1910* (New York, 1977), p. 110; David E. Skinner, *Thomas George Lawson: African Historian and Administrator in Sierra Leone* (Stanford, 1980), pp. 32, 45; David E. Skinner, 'Lawson, Thomas George (1814–1891), Colonial Official and Baptist Leader', *Oxford Dictionary of National Biography* (Oxford, 2008), <www.oxforddnb.com/view/10.1093/ref:odnb/9780198614128.001.0001/odnb-9780198614128-e-53504> [accessed 3 July 2019]; Blue Books of Sierra Leone, 1858 BOA, p. 124; Trina Leah Hogg, *The Paradox of Protection: The Making of Indirect Rule in Southern Sierra Leone, 1850–1915* (East Lansing, 2026), p. 52.

77 Census, 1831, TNA, CO 267/111, fol. 327; Allen M. Howard, 'New Insights', pp. 107, 124; Lawrance, Osborn, and Roberts, 'Introduction', p. 23.

78 Will of Walter William Lewis of Freetown, Sierra Leone (23 July 1844), TNA, PROB 11/2002/103.

79 Will of Thomas Carew, Merchant of Freetown, Sierra Leone (13 October 1848), TNA, PROB 11/2081/362.

80 Fyfe, *A History*, pp. 217, 231; Fyfe, 'The Life', pp. 213–23; Peterson, *Province of Freedom*, p. 294; Everill, *Abolition and Empire*, p. 161; Deveneaux, 'Public Opinion', p. 48; Census, 1831, TNA, CO 267/111, fol. 310; Registration No. 48, SLPA, Register of Deaths, Freetown district (1872–1873).

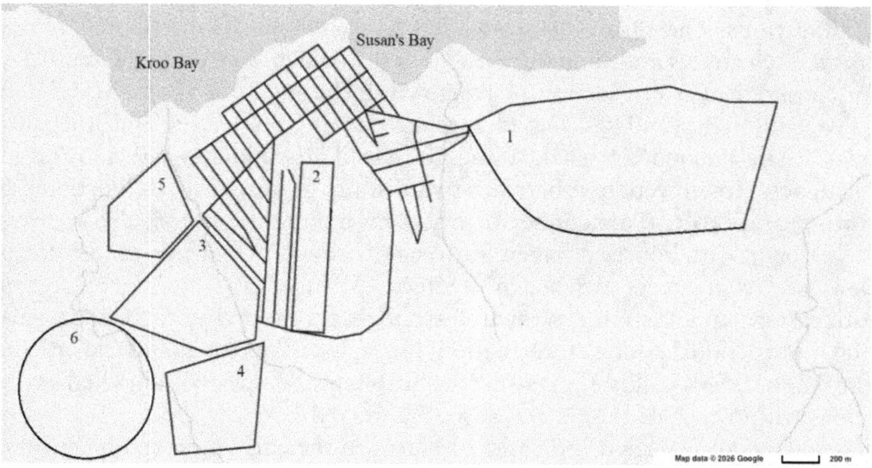

Figure 3.2 Streets and neighbourhoods of Freetown listed in the 1831 census.
1. Grassfield 1; 2. Soldier Town; 3. Grassfield 2; 4. Portuguese Town; 5. Krutown; 6. Grassfield 3.

Source: Map data ©2026 Google; Census of Population and liberated Africans, 1831, TNA, CO 267/111.

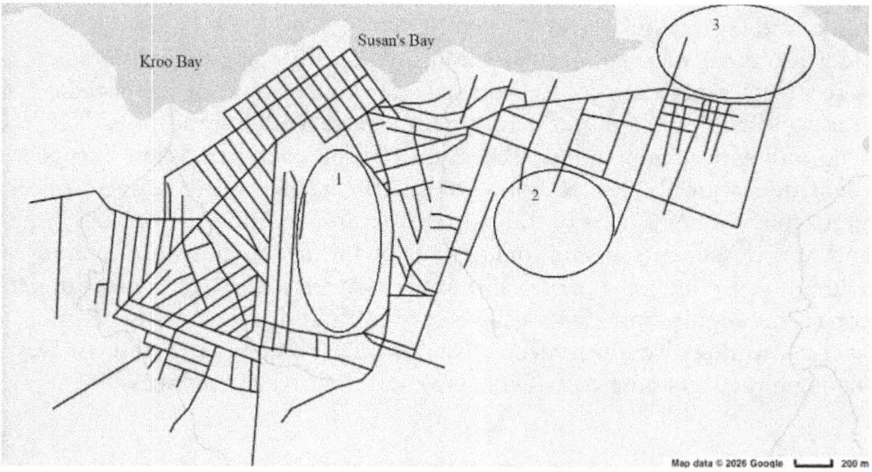

Figure 3.3 Streets of Freetown listed in the birth registers (1857–1862).
1. Government Hill; 2. Fula Town, 3. Cline Town.

Source: Map data ©2026 Google; SLPA, RBF (1857–1860); SLPA, RBF (1860–1861); SLPA, RBF (1861–1862); SLPA, RBF (1862–1863).

stratifications. The 1831 census recorded 8,505 individuals distributed across thirty-seven streets and six main areas, three of which were named Grassfield. For clarity, the eastern section of Freetown, including Fula Town, Mandingo Town, Fourah Bay, and Kissy Road, is referred to as Grassfield 1. The other two areas are designated Grassfield 2 and Grassfield 3 (see Figure 3.2). Houses in Portuguese Town were numbered in two distinct groups: 1 to 38 (Portuguese Town 1) and 1 to 31 (Portuguese Town 2). This numbering system also appears in Krutown, with houses numbered 1 to 99 (Krutown 1) and 1 to 12 (Krutown 2), as well as in streets such as Cross Street, Circular Road, and Fort Street in both eastern and western Freetown. Birth registers from 1857 to 1862 provide even more detailed address information, listing locations for all but five fathers across 180 streets. Unlike the census, the birth registers specify individual street names within each of the six areas (see Figure 3.3).

Residence was a clear indicator of status in the early nineteenth century. Settlers and Europeans lived on parallel streets in Settler Town.[81] By 1831, 63 of the 85 (74 per cent) Europeans listed in the census still lived in this area alongside many settler families (see Appendix F). Maroon William Brown lived on 17 Walpole Street, Nova Scotian John Ellis on 11 Charlotte Street, and Maroon William Libert at 70 Bathurst Street.[82] Settler Town remained the neighbourhood of both the social and economic elite, serving as the epicentre for members of the civil and judicial establishments. Of the 100 inhabitants with administrative occupations, 74 lived in Settler Town (see Appendix G). Several clerks of the Courts of Mixed Commission, along with other clerks, were concentrated on Rawdon Street, Howe Street, Charlotte Street, and Gloucester Street.[83]

Settler Town was the most populous area, with 1,964 inhabitants across its 19 streets, representing nearly one quarter (23 per cent) of the population. Households varied in size and were socially diverse, with Europeans and settlers living with African immigrants, 'Liberated Africans', and Kru. While Europeans and settlers typically headed households, Africans generally occupied subordinate roles. Among the 539 'Liberated Africans' residing there, 394 (73 per cent) were classified as servants or apprentices. Of the 671 individuals employed in domestic service, 339 (51 per cent) lived on streets located in the area underscoring the area's status as a centre of wealth and influence. In 1831, 381 domestic workers were recorded in Freetown East and 290 in Freetown West. The birth registers note 10 fathers employed in domestic service, all residing

81 There were nineteen streets in Settler Town in the census: Charlotte Street, Cross Street 1 to 3 (east), Cross Street 1 to 3 (west), East Street, George Street, Gloucester Street, Howe Street, Little East Street, Percival Street, Pultney Street, Rawdon Street, Trelawney Street, Walpole Street, Water Street (east), and Wilberforce Street.

82 Census, 1831, TNA, CO 267/111, fol. 298, 307, 322.

83 Walker, *The Black Loyalists*, p. 336; Census, 1831, TNA, CO 267/111, fol. 297, 301.

in Freetown East, further indicating the concentration of domestic workers in that area. These inhabitants typically did not own property and lived under the authority of European or settler masters and mistresses.

Occupation determined an individual's place of residence. Wealthier residents were more likely to live near the commercial and administrative centre of Freetown. Within Settler Town, distinct social clusters emerged: for example, 149 (18 per cent) of the African immigrants ('Native Strangers') lived on its streets in large households. Thirteen of them lived at 1 Rawdon Street, ten of whom were gold traders, while three had no recorded occupation.[84] Seventeen African immigrants lived at 24 Pultney Street, eight of them traders. Other examples of Africans who lived in, or close to, Settler Town and not as servants included Joseph DeGraft who lived in a large household on 59 Wellington Street with two writers from the Liberated African Department. Tatlata, a country doctor, possibly a traditional healer, resided in his own house at 16 Charlotte Street.[85] Both men's ability to live in this area reflected the status and income their occupations afforded them.

By 1862, Settler Town remained closely associated with high-status occupations. In 1859, Edward Jones, an African American clergyman of the C.M.S. from South Carolina, resided on Oxford Street (formerly Cross Street). By 1862, William Smith Jr lived with his wife Anne Spilsbury near Settler Town, on Wellington Street.[86] Among the twenty-two clerks recorded in the birth registers, nine lived in Settler Town, with an additional five residing on adjacent streets such as Andrew Street, Liverpool Street, Upper Brook Street, and Wellington Street. This means that around 63 per cent of clerks listed in the registers lived in or near Settler Town. Likewise, of the 22 merchants listed in the birth registers, 15 (68 per cent) lived in Settler Town.

Fyfe noted that the streets in this area were 'guarded jealously' to prevent the settlement of 'Liberated Africans', a control maintained through the passing down of property within families.[87] British merchant Dominic Garel, who died in 1819, divided his estate equally among his children John Balthazer, Maria Antoinetta, and Jane Garel. In 1831, John Balthazer and Maria Antoinetta lived together on 30 Trelawney Street.[88] Herbert Williams, son of Nova Scotian Herbert Williams, lived with his father at 7 George Street, where he was still

84 Census, 1831, TNA, CO 267/111, fol. 293.

85 Census, 1831, TNA, CO 267/111, fol. 298; Roquinaldo Ferreira, *Worlds of Unfreedom: West Central Africa in the Era of Global Abolition* (Princeton, 2025), p. 70.

86 Nemata A. Blyden, *West Indians in West Africa, 1808–1880: The African Diaspora in Reverse* (Rochester, 2000), p. 134; Registration No. 266, SLPA, RBF (1857–1860); Registration No. 474, SLPA, RBF (1861–1862).

87 Fyfe, *A History*, p. 190.

88 Will of Dominic Garel, Merchant of Free Town, Sierra Leone (31 March 1819), TNA, PROB 11/1614/482; Census, 1831, TNA, CO 267/111, fol. 306.

recorded in 1859.[89] Governor Kenneth Macaulay (d. 1831), Maroon Stephen Gabbidon (d. 1839), and African Barbadian Thomas Carew (d. 1848) all bequeathed properties in Settler Town to their children.[90] In 1858 and 1860, John Meheux lived on Kissy Street, the same street where his father lived in 1831. By the time of his death in 1886, John Meheux sold some of his properties but retained land near Kissy Street.[91]

Although Settler Town was primarily an elite area, by the mid-nineteenth century a small number of successful African immigrants, 'Liberated Africans', and their descendants were able to acquire property there. John Ezzidio purchased a house from a Maroon family on George Street in 1841. William Henry Pratt, an Igbo 'Liberated African' who landed in Freetown in 1822, bought properties on Cross Street and was appointed marshal of the Vice-Admiralty Court on 20 November 1859. In 1858, Thomas George Lawson lived on Charlotte Street.[92] Joseph DeGraft's daughter, Anne, who resided with him on Wellington Street in 1831, later moved to Settler Town, living on Wilberforce Street by 1862.[93]

In contrast, the Grassfields and the streets in the south-west of Freetown were considered lower-status areas. These areas had a high concentration of newly arrived 'Liberated Africans' and people who moved from the colony villages, which is reflected in the relatively low number of children recorded as living there.[94] 'Liberated Africans' made up more than half of the population in Grassfield 2 and 3, Portuguese Town, Upper Brook Street, Pademba Road, Soldier Street, Fort Street, and Circular Road in the western part. These areas were among the most densely populated, with Grassfield 2 and 3 accounting for 7 per cent of Freetown's population (617 inhabitants), and the western areas around Pademba Road, Soldier Street, Fort Street, and Henry Street comprising 12 per cent (1,013 inhabitants). Of the 1,630 individuals residing in these areas, 423 (26 per cent) were colonial residents. There were only two Europeans: Wesleyan missionaries J. Keightley and

89 Census, 1831, TNA, CO 267/111, fol. 304; Registration No. 183, SLPA, RBF (1857–1860).

90 Will of Stephen Gabbidon of Sierra Leone, West Africa (17 December 1839), TNA, PROB 11/1920/64; Census, 1831, TNA, CO 267/111, fol. 305, 322, 339; TNA, PROB 11/2081/362; Will of Kenneth Macaulay of Freetown, Sierra Leone (3 January 1831), TNA, PROB 11/1780/280.

91 Registration No. 66, SLPA, RBF (1860–1861); Registration No. 28, SLPA, RBF (1857–1860); Census, 1831, TNA, CO 267/111, fol. 269, Fyfe, *A History*, pp. 279, 471.

92 Fyfe, *A History*, pp. 231–2; Howard, 'New Insights', p. 121; Census, 1831, TNA, CO 267/111, fol. 296; Registration No. 15, SLPA, RBF (1857–1860).

93 Registration No. 104, SLPA, RBF (1862–1863).

94 Howard, 'New Insights', p. 117.

W. Ritchie, both at 119 Pademba Road, serving the 'Liberated African' community at the Wesleyan chapel in Portuguese Town.[95]

Grassfield 1 was the most diverse of the lower-status areas. Its population comprised 164 colonial residents (26 per cent), 244 'Liberated Africans' (38 per cent) and 216 'Native Strangers' (34 per cent). Of the 522 inhabitants listed with an occupation, 290 (56 per cent) were involved in trade as market people, traders, merchants, or milk women. Grassfield 1 encompassed both Fula Town and Fourah Bay, centres of the Muslim community.[96] Fula Town was initially settled by Fula traders engaged in commerce with Fuuta Jalon in cattle, ivory, and gold. Fourah Bay derives its name from 'Foro' or 'Fora Bay' and became home to Muslim Aku in 1833. They settled there after receiving land from William Henry Savage, who acted as their attorney following the Colobo War.[97] Of the thirty-two Muslim fathers identified in the birth registers, fifteen resided in Grassfield 1, while fourteen others lived to the west, on streets such as Goderich Street, Magazine, and Mountain Cut.

The elite were originally concentrated in Settler Town, but by the 1830s the city had begun to expand eastward. While this eastward movement was still limited in scale during the 1830s, it laid the foundation for more pronounced development by the 1850s. In 1831, missionary William Young lived in the developing eastern area with thirteen pupils and three servants. The Church Missionary Society established a church on Kissy Road in 1830.[98] Eight Europeans and three African Europeans were recorded in this area, while none were listed in the other Grassfields. The area also housed colonial officials and professionals, including Robert Dougan, King's Prosecutor; Thomas Pinches, a

95 Census, 1831, TNA, CO 267/111, fol. 349, Blue Books of Sierra Leone, 1831, BOA, fol. 60.

96 Harrell-Bond, Howard, Skinner, *Community Leadership*, pp. 45, 107; Fyfe, *A History*, p. 94; Anderson, *Abolition*, p. 248; Cole, *The Krio of West Africa*, p. 129.

97 In November 1832, a group of Aku 'Liberated Africans', who had settled in Colobo, attempted to attack the villages of Hastings, Waterloo, and Wellington. In response, colonial troops were deployed, resulting in the deaths of fifty Aku, either in combat or by drowning. Four men were charged with high treason and defended by Savage, who argued that the British held no legal jurisdiction in Colobo. He later provided land on his estate at Fourah Bay for the displaced Aku settlers; Cole, *The Krio of West Africa*, p. 144; Anderson, *Abolition*, pp. 227–59.

98 Fyfe, *A History*, 213; Blue Books of Sierra Leone, 1840, BOA, fol. 71; Ademide Adelusi-Adelluyi, *Imagine Lagos: Mapping History, Place, and Politics in a Nineteenth-Century African City* (Athens, 2024), p. 118; Sierra Leone, Plan of Freetown, town plan showing streets (named), principal buildings, named districts ('New Town East', 'New Town West', 'Soldiers Town', 'Kroo Town'), cemeteries; boundary of Ordnance land, encroachments by soldiers; old and new privies, drain; work undertaken by Lieutenant-Governor Campbell. Scale: 7.25 inches to 2,000 feet. Signed by J W Lawson, Assistant Surveyor (1836), TNA, MPH 1/881/11.

Custom House clerk; and Abraham Hazeley, the government printer.[99] By the late 1850s, Fourah Bay had become home to Chief Justice John Carr, as well as merchant Allan Cummings Walker and his wife, Frances Walker.[100] Over time, the area grew increasingly socio-economically diverse. In 1831, the only person listed in agriculture or fishing was a cow-keeper named Damba. However, birth registers later recorded twenty-four farmers and fishermen living on streets in Grassfield 1, including six in Fourah Bay, indicating the growing occupational variety in the eastern part of the city.[101]

Grassfield 3 in western Freetown, Portuguese Town, and Krutown recorded the highest number of individuals without an occupation, with 340 inhabitants in Grassfield 3, 269 in Portuguese Town and 351 in Krutown. These figures represented 61 per cent, 62 per cent, and 95 per cent of their respective populations, suggesting a significant underreporting of occupations. Of the 501 Kru recorded, only 91 had an occupational title, though, given that many Kru came to Freetown seeking work, it is unlikely that more than 80 per cent were unemployed. Writing in 1847 about the C.M.S.'s work, Reverend Samuel Abraham Walker described Kru as the 'boatmen, labourers, out-of-door servants, and cooks of the Colony'.[102]

The scarcity of occupational data in these lower-status western areas stemmed from communication barriers between inhabitants and Norman McDonald, the census enumerator. Many residents may have struggled to convey their occupations, or may have refused to speak English as a way of limiting colonial influence.[103] Occupations recorded in these areas indicate lower social status. In 1831, 73 of the 135 fishermen lived in Portuguese Town and Grassfield 3, on Pademba and Circular Roads. These last two roads also housed a cluster of farmers, with 42 out of 124 (34 per cent) residing there. The birth registers from the late 1850s and early 1860s offer less clarity on these patterns, listing only 99 farmers, with two each on Pademba and Circular Roads. In 1831, 19 farmers were recorded in Grassfield 3, located near the outskirts of the city. Other farmers living further from the city centre were not included in the census.

99 Census, 1831, TNA, CO 267/111, fol. 262.

100 Registrations No. 12, 249, SLPA, RBF (1857–1860).

101 Registration No. 35, 329, 420 SLPA, RBF (1857–1860); Registration No. 20, 22, 156, 182, 191, 236, 322, 422, 493, SLPA, RBF (1860–1861); Registration No. 166, 211, 73, 79, 80, 127, 133, 375, 413, 479, SLPA, RBF (1861–1862); Registration No. 11, SLPA, RBF (1862–1863).

102 Samuel Abraham Walker, *The Church of England Mission in Sierra Leone* (London, 1847), p. xxxv.

103 Jeffrey Gunn, 'Homeland, Diasporas and Labour Networks: The Case of Kru Workers, 1792–1900' (Unpublished PhD dissertation, York University, 2019), pp. 62–3, 109.

Socio-economic clusters of low-income occupations can be identified for those linked to noxious character. In 1831, ten lime burners were recorded to the west of Settler Town on Liverpool Street, Wellington Street, West Brook Street, and Upper Brook Street. Of these, nine were 'Liberated Africans', indicating the lower status associated with the occupation. In the birth registers, two men were recorded as lime burners and lived on Krutown Road and on Edward Street, not far from West Brook Street.[104] A similar trend is seen with tanners. In 1831, three were listed in Soldier Town, Soldier Street, and Mountain Road, and between 1857 and 1862, another three were recorded on Mountain Cut, Sackville Street, and Goderich Street.[105]

As some occupations grew, they stimulated greater spatial mobility. For practical needs, boat builders were initially concentrated in Settler Town, close to the harbour, but as the industry expanded, they spread throughout the city. In 1831, ten of the thirteen ship carpenters recorded in the census lived in Settler Town, as did two of the three sail makers and all nine rope makers. The only two boat builders listed in the census were found together on Circular Road. In the birth registers, of the ten fathers recorded as ship carpenters, only Thomas Frazer lived in Settler Town, and of nine shipwrights, only two resided there. All the eleven tailors in 1831 were located in the eastern part of the city, but by 1857–62, sixteen out of the twenty-six tailors lived in the western part. In 1831, three coopers lived in the western part of the city. By the late 1850s and early 1860s, coopers were more dispersed; of the ten coopers listed in the birth registers, two lived in Freetown East and eight in Freetown West, with no clear clustering by function.[106] This pattern suggests that these occupations became both more numerous and more widely spread. Larger occupations, e.g. trade, were even more dispersed across Freetown. In 1831, traders were recorded on every street except Short Street, Little East Street, and Krutown 1. Between 1857 and 1862, 263 fathers in trade were almost equally distributed, with 138 recorded on streets in eastern Freetown and 125 in the west. Likewise, those in manufacturing were spread throughout the city, with a majority in the western part: in 1831, 127 living in the east and 204 in the west; by 1857–1862, 53 were in the east and 64 in the west.

Wealth disparities did heavily influence the landscape of Freetown, with the appearance of houses serving as clear evidence of unequal living conditions.

104 Census, 1831, fol. TNA, CO 267/111 313–314, 325–326, 333, 336–338; Registration No. 36, 84, SLPA, RBF (1860–1861).

105 Census, 1831, TNA, CO 267/111, fol. 268, 286, 351; Registration No. 182 SLPA, RBF (1857–1860); Registration No. 183, 219, SLPA, RBF (1861–1862).

106 Census, 1831, fol. 297, 308, 342, TNA, CO 267/111; Registration No. 70–71, 88, 291, 362, SLPA, RBF (1857–1860); Registration No. 206, 233, SLPA, RBF (1861–1862); Registration No. 204, SLPA, RBF (1861–1862); SLPA, RBF (1862–1863), Registration No. 40, 45, 95, 120.

According to a report drafted in 1827, 'Liberated Africans', discharged soldiers, and African immigrants lived in houses made from wattle and moistened clay or houses improved with clapboards. In contrast, Nova Scotian and Maroon settlers resided in frame houses, while Europeans and the wealthiest Africans lived in stone houses.[107] These were scarce, with only about 80 in 1827, compared to a total of 2,313 houses (both occupied and unoccupied) listed in the census. During the dry season, fires frequently destroyed houses with grass roofs, prompting the government to pass a law banning grass roofs in 1846, which led to an increase in the number of stone and frame houses. By 1850, Freetown had 350 stone houses, 2,184 frame houses, and 1,873 wattle houses.[108] Designed for formerly enslaved Africans, the colony evolved into a society where successful 'Liberated Africans' were a minority. Living conditions among them diverged significantly from those of the elite. However, some successful 'Liberated Africans' were able to build or move into stone houses by the time they retired, though these cases were exceptional.[109]

Wealth distinctions were further exerted on land and property ownership. With a few exceptions, most 'Liberated Africans' were confined to lower-status areas, where properties were more affordable, further entrenching social and economic divisions. In the late 1830s and 1840s, houses in Settler Town ranged in price from £100 to £505. In 1839, Joseph Green Spilsbury purchased a house at the corner of Rawdon and Kissy Streets for £505, while William Henry Pratt bought a property between George and Trelawney Streets for £300. In the 1840s, Ezzidio acquired a more affordable house on George Street for £100.[110] In 1842, Godfrey Wilhelm, a 'Liberated African', bought property on Percival Street for £180. In contrast, in 1846, Emmanuel Cline, also a 'Liberated African', purchased eleven acres in Fourah Bay for just £55.[111] While the price of land is not comparable to that of property, there is a stark difference between £55 and £505. Many 'Liberated Africans' bought land and built their own houses due to their limited income.[112]

Ownership of land and property participated in the accumulation and transmission of wealth as the most common asset bequeathed by wealthy men. Prominent figures such as Kenneth Macaulay (acting Governor in 1826),

107 *Coms. of Inquiry*, HC 1827, no. 312, p. 7.

108 Macdonald to Grey, 18 August 1851, SLPA, Governor's Despatches 1851, fol. 88–9; Robert B. Clarke, 'Sketches of the Colony of Sierra Leone and its Inhabitants', *Transactions of the Ethnological Society of London*, 2 (1863), 320–63, at p. 323.

109 *Report*, HC 1842, no. 551, p. 253.

110 Fyfe, *A History*, pp. 211, 231; Fyfe, 'The Life', p. 215; Christopher Fyfe, 'View of the New Burial Ground', *Sierra Leone Studies*, 2 (1954), 85–90, at p. 89.

111 Fyfe, 'Four Sierra Leone Recaptives', p. 81; Christopher Fyfe, *Africanus Horton, 1835–1883: West African Scientist and Patriot* (Oxford, 1972), p. 49.

112 Ryan, '"A moral millstone"?' pp. 410–11.

Stephen Gabbidon, Thomas Carew, James Hook (Commissioner in the Courts of Commission), Joseph Green Spilsbury, and John Ezzidio left behind multiple houses, landholdings, or town lots. Their estates were substantial as Gabbidon owned six properties, Macaulay ten, and Spilsbury seven, demonstrating how freehold ownership underpinned elite status.[113] By the 1860s, the significance of property expanded beyond inheritance to include its use as a financial instrument. In Lagos, the practice of mortgaging property to secure commercial credit had become widespread. As Antony Hopkins notes, 'private ownership of landed property was the basis of success in commerce'.[114]

Wives were beneficiaries of their husbands' property until their death or so long as they remained widows. Spilsbury allowed his wife to remain on his property only as long as she did not remarry, reflecting a broader pattern in Maroon communities in Jamaica, where widows were expected to relinquish property to the head of the family.[115] Ezzidio left his properties on George Street and Trelawney Street to his wife, Sarah Ezzidio, but only for the period of her widowhood or natural life. She could not dispose of them, as the properties were to pass to Ezizdio's executors upon her remarriage or death. In the same vein, James Hook bequeathed his freehold estate on Gloucester Street to his wife, Eliza Francis, 'during the time of her natural life'.[116]

Some women benefited from property ownership in ways that enabled economic opportunity and financial independence. Access to land or houses provided them with sources of income and a degree of security uncommon for many women at the time. Daughters sometimes enjoyed greater inheritance rights than their mothers and male relatives. Anne Spilsbury inherited more than her brothers, receiving town lots on Gloucester Street and £1,000, while her brothers, Henry and Thomas, received £200 and some town lots to share. This was not unique to Freetown; in the Portuguese Empire, women had inheritance rights dating back to the late sixteenth century, and daughters were entitled to an equal share of their parents' property.[117] Women also maintained

113 Will of Logan Hook, Collector of Her Majesty's Customs at Sierra Leone of Islington (7 January 1850), TNA, PROB 11/2106/253; Will of James Hook, Her Britannic Majesty's Commissioner in the Courts of Commission established in Sierra Leone and a Member of the legislative Council of this Colony (1 April 1851), TNA, PROB 11/2130/327.

114 Kristin Mann, 'Women, Landed Property, and the Accumulation of Wealth in Early Colonial Lagos', *Signs: Journal of Women in Culture and Society*, 16:4 (1991), 682–706, at p. 689; Hopkins, 'Property Rights', p. 797.

115 Ipsen, *Daughters of the Trade*, p. 141.

116 The Will of John Ezzidio, 18 December 1872, Principal Registry of Her Majesty's Court of Probate; Will of James Hook, Her Britannic Majesty's Commissioner in the Courts of Commission established in Sierra Leone and a Member of the legislative Council of this Colony (1 April 1851), TNA, PROB 11/2130/327.

117 Mariana Candido and Eugénia Rodrigues, 'African Women's Access and Rights to Property in the Portuguese Empire', *African Economic History*, 43 (2015), 1–18, at p. 4.

control of property after marriage in some cases. From 1838 to around 1846, Ann Saunders collected rent from her property in Freetown, and, after her marriage to Daniel Taylor, in around 1846, rent continued to be paid directly to her rather than to her husband, demonstrating that her marital status did not affect her income.[118]

Beyond land and property, household possessions also reflected the wealth and lifestyle of their owners. Items were passed down along gendered lines. Walter William Lewis left books to his sons Walter, Thomas, and Samuel Lewis, while John Ezzidio donated his books to the Wesleyan Missionary Society. Wives typically inherited linen cloth and furniture. Thomas Carew gave his wife Rosetta Carew a silver plate and household linens; James Hook left furniture and linen to his wife Eliza Francis; Joseph Green Spilsbury gave household furniture to his wife Hannah; and Walter William Lewis bequeathed plate furniture to his son and the son's mother.

Furniture itself had become a luxury good in eighteenth-century Britain, replaced every five to six years.[119] In 1842, successful 'Liberated Africans' owned houses with English furniture, a trend mirrored in other European West African settlements where African European women possessed European furniture, silverware, and linens.[120] Wealthier 'Liberated Africans' increasingly adopted European lifestyles and material symbols of success. In 1846, Elizabeth Helen Melville observed that wealthy 'Liberated Africans' had 'good, substantial … and well-furnished houses'.[121] At his death in 1872, John Ezzidio left his wife an extensive collection of household furnishings, including bedroom furniture, linens, chairs, tables, glassware, and kitchen utensils.

Clothing served as another powerful indicator of status, communicating social position, success, and identity. During a visit to the colony in the early 1830s, Mary Church observed that 'liberated African men have completely borrowed their dress from the English, but very few think it necessary to have a full suit; shoes and stockings are only worn by those who consider themselves rich'.[122] Among the Nova Scotian settlers, European-style dress was a visible marker of status and identity. Francis B. Spilsbury compared the clothing of Nova Scotian women to that of Welsh girls.[123] In 1849, Elizabeth

118 Schwarz, 'Adaptation', pp. 23, 26; William Rainy, *The Censor Censured: or, the Calumnies of Captain Burton (Late Her Majesty's Consul at Fernando Po) on the Africans of Sierra Leone* (London, 1865), pp. 48–57.

119 Maxine Berg, *Luxury and Pleasure in Eighteenth-Century Britain* (Oxford, 2005), p. 37.

120 421 *Report*, HC 1842, no. 551, p. 387; Ipsen, *Daughters of the Trade*, p. 10.

121 Norton (ed.), *A Residence*, p. 264.

122 Mary Church, *Sierra Leone, or, The Liberated Africans: in a series of letters from a young lady to her sister in 1833 & 34* (London, 1835), p. 9.

123 Benjamin, *The Texture of Change*, p. 160.

Helen Melville noted that wealthier people wore 'jackets, waistcoats, and trowsers [*sic*] of cloth', while domestic servants typically dressed in 'a white jacket, check shirt, and duck trowsers [*sic*]'.[124] European dress was similarly prized in other West African colonies, such as Senegal and Benguela, where it signified success and prestige.[125]

As a sign of higher status, clothing was frequently included in the wills of influential men. Stephen Gabbidon bequeathed half of his wearing apparel to his son William Gabbidon, with the remainder divided between his cousins Robertson Bonard and Samuel Senior. Kenneth Macaulay bequeathed his wearing apparel to his brother John Macaulay. Jewellery was likewise another symbol of wealth and status. James Hook gave his gold watch to his son James Clarke, and a gold ring to his brother Logan Hook. Kenneth Macaulay gave his watch to his cousin Thomas Babington Macaulay and rings to other cousins. Maxine Berg argues that in eighteenth-century England a watch signified manhood, which may explain Macaulay's choices, since he died when his children were still young.[126]

The value and desirability of clothing made it a common target for theft, from shirts, waistcoats, cotton frocks, and trousers to cloth jackets and flannel trousers. Out of 100 cases of thefts recorded in the police court record between 7 February 1851 and 1 January 1852, 40 were of stolen cloth, cotton, or linen.[127] Some other examples include the case of Mamadoo, who on 8 February 1847, was charged with stealing one stocking, four shirts, one waistcoat, and a pair of drawers from Nova Scotian settler James Wise. On 12 March 1851, Allee Bundo was charged with stealing five basins, three cotton frocks, and three bed sheets from Elizabeth Thompson of Maroon Town.[128] The value of clothing varied considerably with cloth trousers worth 6 pence, shirts £1, cotton frocks £5, and cotton trousers £6, which were prices beyond the reach of many inhabitants, since, as an example, the annual income of laundresses in 1850 was only around £6.[129]

While European styles of dress and material culture were widely adopted as symbols of success, they were not the only markers of wealth and status. African inhabitants also expressed identity and prestige through local and

124 Norton (ed.), *A Residence*, pp. 21–2.

125 Sarah Fee, '"Cloths with Names": Luxury Textile Imports in Eastern Africa, c. 1800–1885', *Textile History*, 48:1 (2017), 49–84, at p. 52; Jones, *The Métis of Senegal*, p. 91; Candido, *An African Slaving Port*, p. 81; Ipsen, *Daughters of the Trade*, p. 164.

126 Berg, *Luxury and Pleasure*, p. 200.

127 SLPA, Police Court Record (1851–1852).

128 Mamadoo, 8 February 1847, SLPA, Police Magistrate Record (31 December 1846 – 18 September 1847); Regina v. Allee Bundo, 12 March 1851, SLPA, Police Court Record (1851–1852).

129 Blue Books of Sierra Leone, 1850, BOA, p. 88.

non-European forms of adornment and dress. Silver jewellery was commonly worn by African inhabitants.[130] Clothing was similarly diverse. Among Muslim communities, both imported and locally woven cloth carried deep symbolic meaning, particularly during religious occasions such as Ramadan. Garments were not only decorative but also conveyed social status, piety, and community belonging.[131]

Conclusion

When established by abolitionists in the late eighteenth century, Freetown and the colony of Sierra Leone were envisioned for formerly enslaved populations, basing the economy on agriculture and commerce. By the third decade of the nineteenth century, Freetown largely developed into an urban trading centre, revolving around commerce and the manufacture of small crafts. Socio-economic divides emerged as individuals worked in similar sectors, but at different levels, thus creating varying degrees of wealth. Europeans and settlers retained the most influential positions, but a small number of 'Liberated Africans' were able to improve their status and become members of the Legislative Council or marshals of the Vice-Admiralty Court. Although successful examples of social mobility, they were exceptions and not typical of the wider experience of 'Liberated Africans'. The experience of women followed a similar pattern with the first female overseer in 1840. Although more occupations were opened to women, they were still excluded from the most influential positions. The socio-economic divides created by differences in social status had consequences on the landscape of Freetown. Settler Town was the wealthiest area, and the Grassfield areas were occupied by residents of lower status. This echoes what Odile Goerg observed of the British Empire in the late nineteenth century where masters 'imposed a more strictly divided vision of urban space, best symbolized by separate residential areas'.[132] In Freetown, this was both deliberately planned and developed organically. The earlier arrival and status achieved by settlers contributed to their residence in wealthy areas. Colonial policies considering 'Liberated Africans' as apprentices or manual workers (farmers or public works) contributed to their residence in distinct areas. These areas became micro-societies with their own clusters according to status and occupations that contributed to, and reinforced, social divisions.

130 Norton (ed.), *A Residence*, p. 21.

131 Benjamin, *The Texture of Change*, p. 151.

132 Odile Goerg, 'From Hill Station (Freetown) to Downtown Conakry (First Ward): Comparing French and British Approaches to Segregation in Colonial Cities at the Beginning of the Twentieth Century', *Canadian Journal of African Studies / Revue canadienne des études africaines*, 32:1 (1998), 1–31, at p. 2.

4

Kinship in the Aftermath of Displacement

By the mid-nineteenth century, most of Freetown's population consisted of 'Liberated Africans' who had been separated from their family members and displaced from their home communities. Upon arrival in the colony of Sierra Leone, they were compelled to form new kinship and family relations with other inhabitants. These bonds were often imposed by the colonial authorities as 'Liberated Africans' were placed in various households according to 'disposal' policies, which included women forcibly married and allocation to households as apprentices. The household emerged as a place where relationships were formed and redefined. This chapter examines the structure of Freetown society at the micro level of the household to offer insights into the process of family formation. Through this lens, it becomes clear that, despite the promotion of British systems and ideologies by colonial authorities, household customs and traditions from the inhabitants' homeland survived. A comparative approach is also adopted to examine similarities and differences with other societies in Africa and with other colonies of the British Empire. The analysis of household organisation reveals not only the cultural complexity of the society but also the nature of daily social interactions among its diverse population.

The chapter begins with an analysis of the importance of marriage and the societal practices associated with it, before moving on to examine the composition and organisation of households in Freetown. The discussion considers how marriage influenced household arrangements and daily life. Next, it discusses the roles individuals held within households based on status and gender. The chapter concludes by linking these insights to pre-enslavement family connections and whether and how such ties were preserved over time.

Marriage operated both as a social institution, and as a colonial economic tool. This becomes evident in the statistical alignment between large numbers of disembarkations of 'Liberated Africans' and the rapid increase in marriages that followed. Graph 4.1 shows that following the arrival of 7,073 'Liberated Africans' in 1836, there were a record 827 marriages in 1837 in the colony, with 202 in Freetown. A similar pattern occurred in 1847–48, with 4,434 arrivals and 255 marriages registered the following year in Freetown and 604 in the colony. Among 'Liberated Africans', colonial authorities actively promoted marriage as a cost-saving measure. Upon arrival, women received a government allowance for three months, after which it ceased, hoping to transfer the financial

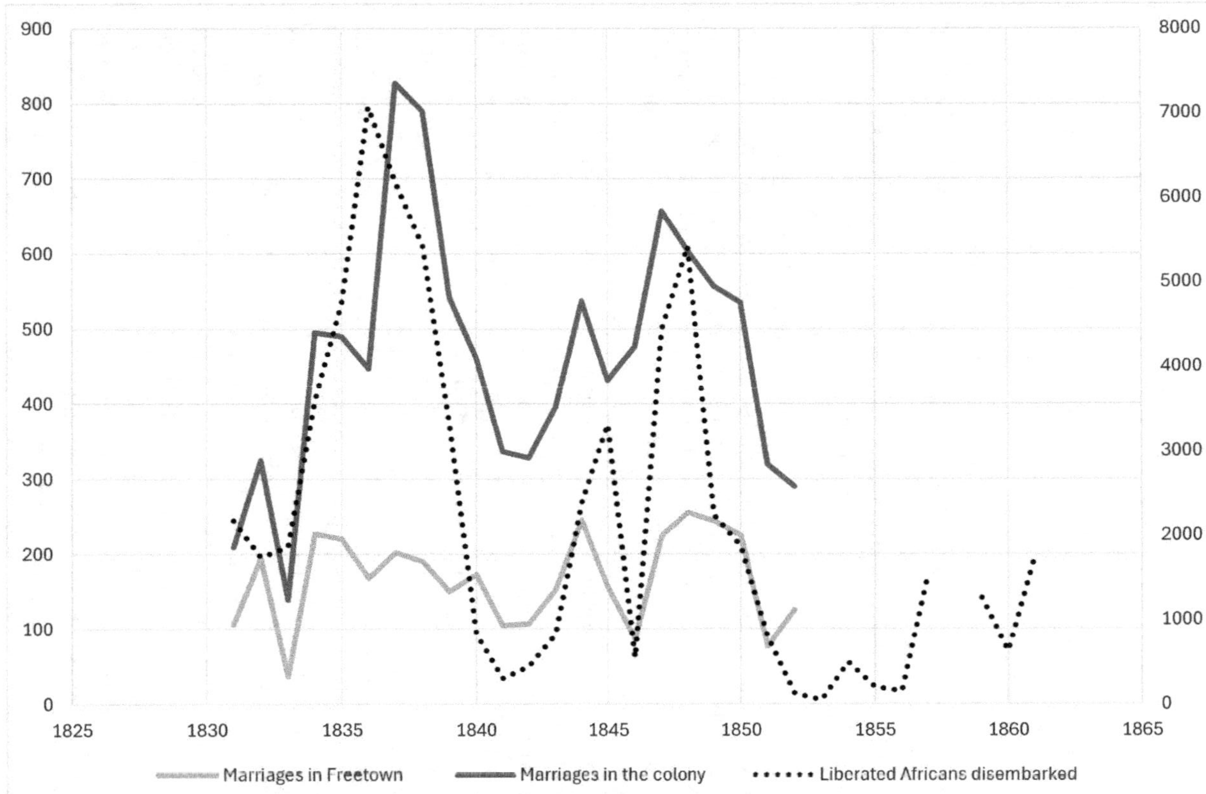

Graph 4.1 'Liberated Africans' disembarked at Freetown and marriages recorded, 1831–1862.

Source: Liberated Africans database <https://liberatedafricans.org/databases/cases.php> [accessed 25 February 2026]; BOA, Blue Books of Sierra Leone, 1831–1862.

responsibility of supporting women from the state to individual men.[1] This was made more feasible by the gender imbalance at the time, women comprising only 46 per cent of the population in 1831 with 3,909 females to 4,584 males. By 1860, women slightly outnumbered men, with 9,080 women and 8,955 men.[2]

In fact, many of these marriages were organised immediately upon disembarkation through the structured system of the Yard, where 'Liberated African' women were sent and quickly paired with men who had applied to take a wife. Men already resident in the colony were brought into the Yard to 'make friends' with the women before selecting a partner.[3] Marriage upon disembarkation served additional colonial objectives since it promoted social stability and furthered the Christianisation and assimilation of 'Liberated Africans'. Framed as a moral and civilising institution, Christian marriage was presented as a step toward adulthood and social respectability, mirroring broader patterns across the Atlantic world.[4] For example, in 1827, Argossee and Ekohmah disembarked from the *NS da Conceição de Maria* and the *Silveirinha*. The clerk of the Liberated African Department recorded their 'disposal' as married to 'Liberated African' men Thomas French and John Craig. By the time of the 1831 census, Thomas French was living with Mary French and John Craig was living with Sarah Craig, the Christian names given to Argossee and Ekohmah upon marriage.[5] Both had taken their husbands' surnames, suggesting the formalisation of these unions within the colony's Christian and administrative order.

1 Daniel Augustine Vonque Stephen, 'A History of the Settlement of Liberated Africans in the Colony of Sierra Leone during the First Half of the 19th Century' (Unpublished PhD dissertation, Durham University, 1963), p. 81; Christopher Fyfe, *A History of Sierra Leone* (Oxford, 1962), p. 230.

2 Census of Population and liberated Africans, 1831, TNA, CO 267/111; *Reports to Secretary of State on Past and Present State of H.M. Colonial Possessions, 1860*, HC 1862, nos 2955–1, p. 24.

3 *Report from the Select Committee on the West Coast of Africa; together with the minutes of evidence, appendix, and index. Part I – Report and evidence*, HC 1842, no. 551, p. 261.

4 Randy M. Browne, *Surviving Slavery in the British Caribbean* (Philadelphia, 2017), pp. 103, 105; Sharla M. Fett, *Recaptured Africans: Surviving Slave Ships, Detention, and Dislocation in the Final Years of the Slave Trade* (Chapel Hill, 2017), p. 180; Lorelle D. Semley, *Mother is Gold, Father is Glass: Gender and Colonialism in a Yoruba Town* (Bloomington, 2011); Manolo Garcia Florentino and José Roberto Góes, 'Slavery, Marriage and Kinship in Rural Rio de Janeiro, 1790–1830', in Paul Lovejoy (ed.), *Identity in the Shadow of Slavery*, 2nd edn (London, 2009), pp. 137–62, at p. 151.

5 'Silveirinha', Liberated Africans database, <https://liberatedafricans.org/databases/event_details.php?EventID=3378> [accessed 26 September 2025]; 'Nossa Senhora da Conceição de Maria', Liberated Africans database, <https://liberatedafricans.org/databases/event_details.php?EventID=3375> [accessed 26 September 2025]; Registration No. 25,444; 25,942, SLPA, RLA 25465–30708 (1827–1829); Census, 1831, TNA, CO 267/111, fol. 321, 349.

Yet the durability of these marriages is far from certain. Although marriage was promoted by colonial authorities as a tool for integration and control, it was not universally embraced by the 'Liberated African' population, and the issue of women's consent further complicates its acceptance. Maeve Ryan notes that many newly arrived women did not speak English, and the speed and structure of the marriage process raised serious doubts about whether these unions were truly voluntary. In 1842, former naval officer William Hamilton testified that he had received complaints from individuals who wished to change partners after being matched in the Yard.[6] In addition, formal Christian marriage ceremonies were relatively uncommon. Europeans such as Harrison Rankin and Robert B. Clarke noted that weddings were uncommon. In 1834, Rankin wrote that many couples chose informal country marriages to avoid paying registration fees, and in 1863, Clarke observed that marriage was not highly valued, writing that it was 'held in but little esteem'.[7] Economic obstacles, such as the inability to afford dowries or licence fees, also discouraged formal unions, resulting in many couples living together outside the bounds of official marriage.

Because many of these unions were arranged quickly and under coercive conditions, both colonial officials and 'Liberated Africans' sought strategies to make the pairings more sustainable. In 1845, eleven women who had been embarked on the slave ship the *Uncas* in Cabinda were married to men from Congo Town, a settlement formed by 'Liberated Africans' from the *Amelia*, which had also departed from Cabinda.[8] As did many formerly enslaved people across the Atlantic world, 'Liberated Africans', sought partners who shared their cultural, ethnic, or religious backgrounds, reinforcing communal ties despite pressures to marry quickly upon disembarkation.[9] This was especially evident among the Yoruba, who formed the largest ethnolinguistic group among the 'Liberated African' population. John Taylor, who disembarked before 1839 and was of Egba origin (a subgroup of Yoruba), married

6 Maeve Ryan, '"It Was Necessary to do Something with Those Women': Colonial Governance and the "Disposal" of Women and Girls in Early Nineteenth-Century Sierra Leone', *Gender & History*, 35 (2021), 491–510, at p. 496.

7 Rankin, F. Harrison, *The White Man's Grave: A Visit to Sierra Leone, in 1834*, vol. 1 (London, 1836), p. 224; Robert B. Clarke, 'Sketches of the Colony of Sierra Leone and its Inhabitants', *Transactions of the Ethnological Society of London*, 2 (1863), 320–63, at p. 332.

8 '*Uncas*', Liberated Africans dabatase <https://liberatedafricans.org/databases/event_details.php?EventID=3525> [accessed 10 October 2025]; Richard Anderson, *Abolition in Sierra Leone: Re-Building Lives and Identities in Nineteenth-Century West Africa* (Cambridge, 2020), pp. 93–4.

9 James H. Sweet, 'Defying Social Death: The Multiple Configurations of African Slave Family in the Atlantic World', *The William and Mary Quarterly*, 70:2 (2013), 251–72, at p. 259.

Sally Taylor, a Yoruba woman also 'liberated' from slavery.[10] Samuel Ladipo Osanyintade Williams, another Egba man, married Ajayi (Lucy), a Yoruba 'Liberated African'.[11]

Family formation among 'Liberated Africans' sometimes emerged from shared experiences of displacement, particularly through bonds formed aboard slave ships. Scholars have documented how enslaved Africans, communicating through a common language, created social relationships during the Middle Passage. Walter Hawthorne argues that slave ships were 'places where individuals died but communities were born', as those on board came to consider one another as kin.[12] In Liberia, Fett found examples of marriages between 'Liberated Africans' who had arrived on the same ship; and in the Rio de la Plata region, Borucki identified grooms and their witnesses from the same slave ship.[13] Although direct evidence of family formation through shipboard bonding in Freetown's archives remains elusive, some family ties may have originated from such shared experiences. Anderson's study of abolition in the colony of Sierra Leone records instances of friendships and bonds among shipmates developing within colony villages.[14]

Stefania Galli's analysis of the 1831 census makes clear that marriage in Freetown was overwhelmingly endogamous, with more than 70 per cent of unions occurring within the same descriptive category, whether among discharged soldiers, colonial residents, 'Native Strangers', or 'Liberated Africans'.[15] As seen above, several factors contributed to this pattern. At the same time, marriages between African women and European men were rare and socially discouraged. The few exceptions involved elite women rather than

10 Memorial to John Taylor, Circular Road Cemetery, Freetown, Sierra Leone, 2 October 1876, University of Hull, Remember Me project; Memorial to Sally Taylor, Circular Road Cemetery, Freetown Sierra Leone, 24 May 1885, University of Hull, Remember Me project; Anderson, *Abolition*, pp. 20, 57, 195–7; Earl Phillips, 'The Egba at Abeokuta: Acculturation and Political Change, 1830–1870', *Journal of African History*, 10:1 (1969), 117–31, at p. 117.

11 Antony Hopkins, *Capitalism in the Colonies: African Merchants in Lagos, 1851–1931* (New Haven, 2024), p. 206.

12 Paul E. Lovejoy, 'Identifying Enslaved Africans in the African Diaspora', in Paul Lovejoy (ed.) *Identity in the Shadow of Slavery* (London, 2000), pp. 1–29, at p. 9; Walter Hawthorne, '"Being Now, As it Were, One Family": Shipmate Bonding on the Slave Vessel Emilia, in Rio de Janeiro and throughout the Atlantic World', *Luso-Brazilian Review*, 45:1 (2008), 53–77, at p. 54; Marcus Rediker, *The Slave Ship* (London, 2007), pp. 305–6; Sidney Wilfred Mintz and Richard Price, *The Birth of African-American Culture: An Anthropological Perspective*, Vol. 2 (Boston, 1992), pp. 43–4.

13 Fett, *Recaptured Africans*, p. 156; Alex Borucki, *From Shipmates to Soldiers: Emerging Black Identities in the Río de la Plata* (Albuquerque, 2015), pp. 74–7.

14 Anderson, *Abolition*, pp. 88–94.

15 Stefania Galli, 'Marriage Patterns in a Black Utopia: Evidence from Early Nineteenth-Century Colonial Sierra Leone', *The History of the Family*, 24:4 (2019), pp. 744–68, at p. 755.

'Liberated Africans'. German missionary Gustavus Reinhold Nyländer married a Nova Scotian settler, and merchant Theodore Amandus Rosenbush married a woman of mixed African–European heritage.[16] These examples are rare, which parallels social norms in Caribbean colonies such as Jamaica, where interracial marriage was frowned upon, but it stood in contrast to other European colonies in Africa, such as Senegal, the Gold Coast, and Angola, where marriages with European men could sometimes offer African women pathways to financial or social mobility.[17]

Children of 'Liberated Africans' who attained elite status used marriage as a means of consolidating wealth and reinforcing social standing across generations.[18] Hannah Carew, the daughter of wealthy 'Liberated Africans' Thomas and Betsy Carew, married Joseph Green Spilsbury, the son of a Maroon woman. As a wedding gift, Thomas and Betsy presented the couple with a home on Rawdon Street valued at £300.[19] This pattern continued with Hannah and Joseph's daughter, Anne Spilsbury, who married William Smith Jr., son of a white English commissioner, in 1858. Similarly, 'Liberated African' William Henry Pratt married Fanny Potts, daughter of a sergeant in the 4th W.I.R. By the time Pratt was serving as Marshal of the Vice Admiral's Court of Sierra Leone, their eldest daughter, Fannie Marietta, consolidated the family's elite status through her marriage in 1862 to James Africanus Beale Horton, M.D. (Edinburgh), the Staff Assistant Surgeon on the Gold Coast and himself the son of 'Liberated Africans'.[20]

Despite the strong endogamous patterns that characterised most marriages in Freetown, there were also households that crossed the descriptive categories imposed by the colonial state. James Lemon, a 'Native Stranger' who had

16 James W. St. G. Walker, *The Black Loyalists: The Search for a Promised Land in Nova Scotia and Sierra Leone, 1783–1870* (London, 1976), pp. 273–4; Fyfe, *A History*, pp. 103, 293, 339, 211; Census, 1831, TNA, CO 267/111, fol. 318; Registration No. 425, 12, 57, 484, SLPA, RBF (1857–1860); 'Ralph Walker', Legacies of British Slave-ownership database <www.ucl.ac.uk/lbs/person/view/2146641913> [accessed 22 June 2020].

17 Daniel Livesay, *Children of Uncertain Fortune: Mixed-Race Jamaicans in Britain and the Atlantic Family, 1733–1833* (Chapel Hill, 2018), p. 385; Hilary Jones, *The Métis of Senegal: Urban Life and Politics in French West Africa* (Bloomington, 2013), p. 74; Suzanne Schwarz, 'Adaptation in the Aftermath of Slavery: Women, Trade and Property in Sierra Leone, c.1790–1812', in Mariana P. Candido and Adam Jones (eds), *African Women in the Atlantic World: Property, Vulnerability & Mobility 1660–1880* (Woodbridge, 2019), pp. 19–37, at p. 33.

18 Mariana Candido, 'African Women in Ecclesiastical Documents, Benguela, 1760–1860', *Social Sciences and Missions*, 28:3/4 (2015), 235–260, at p. 251; Jones, *The Métis*, p. 7.

19 Adelaide M. Cromwell, *An African Victorian Feminist: The Life and Times of Adelaide Smith Casely Hayford 1868–1960* (London, 1986), p. 31.

20 Registration No. 252, SLPA, RBF (1857–1860); Census, 1831, TNA, CO 267/111, fol. 339; *Clonmel Chronicle* (16 July 1862), British Newspaper Archives.

migrated freely, lived in 1831 with his wife Sarah, a 'Liberated African', and their two children.[21] 'Liberated African' James Newman lived with Jane, listed as a 'Native Stranger', and their children, forming a household that crossed categories shaped by different migration experiences.[22] These mixed-background families were not uncommon, and similar patterns appeared among Kru migrants as well. In Portuguese Town, some Kru men lived with women identified as 'Liberated Africans' – a Kru man named Tom lived with Betsy Tom, a woman identified as a 'Liberated African'.[23]

To understand family formation beyond the bounds of endogamous marriage, this chapter draws on Barry W. Higman's 1973 study of household structures on Jamaican plantations. Higman classified households on three estates into thirteen common types, eight of which are applicable to Freetown.[24] The relevance of this comparison lies in the shared experience of forced displacement: just as enslaved Africans in Jamaica were uprooted and reshaped into new social units, so too were 'Liberated Africans' in the colony of Sierra Leone. David Northrup argues that both groups disembarked in a comparable state of physical and psychological dislocation and faced similar challenges in forming new lives. In 1856, the colonial surgeon described the faces of newly arrived 'Liberated Africans' as exhibiting 'suffering, moral and physical, of the most profound agonising nature'. Maeve Ryan describes the redistribution of 'Liberated Africans' as another iteration of the Middle Passage.[25] However, Freetown's case differs from that of the British Caribbean in one critical way, the colonial authorities actively managed the distribution of apprentices and shaped household formation, interfering more directly in the social lives of the freed population.

Household units are not necessarily synonymous with biological families. Armstrong and Higgs describe them as 'co-residing groups' and 'administrative

21 Census, 1831, TNA, CO 267/111, fol. 338.

22 Ibid., fol. 348.

23 Ibid., fol. 374, 375.

24 B. W. Higman, 'Household Structure and Fertility on Jamaican Slave Plantations: A Nineteenth-Century Example', *Population Studies*, 27:3 (1973), pp. 527–50; Michael Craton, 'Changing Patterns of Slave Families in the British West Indies', *The Journal of Interdisciplinary History*, 10:1 (1979), pp. 1–35, p. 2.

25 David Northrup, 'Becoming African: Identity Formation among Liberated Slaves in Nineteenth-Century Sierra Leone', *Slavery and Abolition*, 27:1 (2006), 1–21, at pp. 4–5; Robert Clarke, 'Short Notes of the Prevailing Diseases in the Colony of Sierra Leone, with a Return of the Sick Africans Sent to Hospital in Eleven Years, and Classified Medical Returns for the Years 1853–4. Also Tables Showing the Number of Lunatics Admitted to Hospital in a Period of Thirteen Years, and the Number Treated from 1st April, 1842, to 31st March, 1853', *Journal of the Statistical Society of London*, 19:1 (1856), 60–81, at p. 65; Maeve Ryan, *Humanitarian Governance and the British Antislavery World System* (New Haven, 2022), p. 24.

artefacts', emphasising their structural dimensions. Jane I. Guyer further argues that households are 'constituted by a series of implicit or explicit contracts', rather than by a unified solidarity in which internal relationships are fixed or assumed.[26] Of the 2,049 households recorded in the census, only 921 were headed by 'Liberated Africans'. To provide a broader understanding of household composition in Freetown, this study examines households in three contrasting areas: Settler Town, Grassfield 1 (in the western part of the city), and West Brook Street. These areas differ economically but share a similar number of households led by 'Liberated Africans'. In Settler Town, just 38 of the 363 households were headed by 'Liberated Africans'. In contrast, all 37 households in Grassfield 1 were led by 'Liberated Africans'. On West Brook Street, 31 out of 47 households had 'Liberated African' heads.

In Grassfield 1, Settler Town, and West Brook Street, the two most common household structures among 'Liberated Africans' were a couple without children and a couple with their children. In both Grassfield 1 and Settler Town, no households composed of a couple and their children included apprentices. In contrast, on West Brook Street, five such families did include apprentices (see Table 4.1). There is a significant presence of two-parent households since both parents were identified for 46 of the 72 'infants' listed in the census (64 per cent). Among the 528 clearly identified households consisting of a couple and their children, most had only one or two children: 248 had one child, and 149 had two. The household model of a couple and their children was also typical of formerly enslaved African families in other British colonies. In Cape Town during the 1830s, this structure was actively promoted by the British as a foundational unit of a free society. However, in practice, most families of formerly enslaved Africans there consisted of single parents.[27]

26 W. A. Armstrong, 'The Census Enumerators' Books: A Commentary', in Richard Lawton (ed.), *The Census and Social Structure: An Interpretative Guide to Nineteenth Century Censuses for England and Wales* (London, 1978), pp. 28–81, at p. 52; Edward Higgs, *A Clearer Sense of the Census: Victorian Censuses and Historical Research* (London, 1996), pp. 63, 75; Jane I. Guyer, 'Household and Community in African Studies', *African Studies Review*, 24:2 (1981), 87–137, p. 99; Sarah Delius, 'The Same in All but Name? The Intersections of Marriage and Slavery in Sierra Leone, 1890–1930', *Slavery & Abolition*, 43:2 (2022), 320–45, at p. 328.

27 B. W. Higman, 'The Slave Family and Household in the British West Indies, 1800–1834', *The Journal of Interdisciplinary History*, 6:2 (1975), 261–87, at p. 283; Vertrees C. Malherbe, 'Illegitimacy and Family Formation in Colonial Cape Town, to c. 1850', *Journal of Social History*, 39:4 (2006), 1153–76, at p. 1165.

Table 4.1 Household structure with 'Liberated Africans' as head of households in Grassfield 1, Settler Town, and West Brook Street.

Household structure	Grassfield 1 West	Settler Town	West Brook Street
Couple without children	9	5	3
Couple without children plus one or more adults	4	4	2
Couple and their children	4	5	8
Couple and their children plus apprentices	0	0	5
Couple and their children plus one or more adults	2	4	1
Woman and her children	1	0	1
Woman and her children plus apprentices	0	3	0
Men and children	1	0	0
Single man	7	3	3
Single woman	2	0	0
Males	3	8	3
Females	0	1	0
Males and females	4	5	4
One adult and two apprentices	0	0	1
Total number of households	**37**	**38**	**31**

Source: Census of Population and liberated Africans, 1831, TNA, CO 267/111.

In addition to households formed around couples and their children, more mixed and extended household structures were common. John and Betsy Mellish, living at 9 West Brook Street, shared their home not only with their four children but also with Robert, an apprentice, Cabbarcee, a farmer, and a child named Nancy.[28] Cabbarcee's occupational title suggests he was a more permanent resident, possibly a seasonal labourer or boarder contributing to the household economy. Such households sometimes functioned as informal boarding houses, providing accommodation for seasonal workers or lodgers, typically adult men, who moved in and out according to economic opportunity.[29]

28 Census, 1831, TNA, CO 267/111, fol. 331

29 Laura Channing and Bronwen Everill, 'On the Freetown Waterfront: Household Income and Informal Wage Labour in a Nineteenth Century Port City', *African Economic*

These extended arrangements were not unique to 'Liberated Africans'. At 5 Water Street, Nova Scotian settler Mingo Jordan lived with two adult women, Mrs Jordan and Nancy Jordan, as well as Moses Murray, a fisherman, and Rosannah, a freeborn child. Such household diversity reflects broader patterns in communities shaped by slavery and emancipation. In Nova Scotia, Lieutenant John Clarkson observed that the idea of family extended beyond the British model to include godchildren or other members of the wider community.[30] In other contexts, such as in Cape Town, formerly enslaved households frequently included co-residing families, single parents, boarders, children, elderly people, and short-term visitors.[31]

Adults in households who appeared unrelated might reveal polygynous family structures, especially where several adult males and females lived together. Polygyny was still prevalent among the older Maroons who rejected Christianity and monogamy.[32] Some 'Liberated Africans' also practised it in their homeland. Among 56 'Liberated Africans' married in their home communities and interviewed by Koelle between 1849 and 1850, ten were in polygynous relationships, 'four with two wives, two with three, one each with four, five, seven – and one man, a Mahi/EWE, who "married two wives and on his father's death, inherited, according to the custom of the country, twenty-two more who had been his father's"'.[33] Galli notes that some women recorded as single in the census might have been in polygamous relationships where their husbands lived with other wives.[34] Higman's research on Jamaican slave plantations similarly highlights how polygynist men housed their partners and children in adjacent dwellings, allowing proximity without co-residence.[35]

In the four volumes of birth registers available between 1857 and 1862, fourteen fathers were listed at the same street address with different partners. The name of the street was recorded without a number, which suggests that either a man's wives lived in adjacent houses or in the same one. Out of the fourteen fathers, eight were in clear polygynous relationships. The birth date of the children shows that the women who had children with the same man gave birth in the same house or street. An explicit case is that of Charles Bucknor Bucknor, who fathered children with multiple women living on

History Working, 58 (2020), 1–36, at p. 17; Michael Anderson, 'What Can the Mid-Victorian Censuses Tell Us about Variations in Married Women's Employment?' *Local Population Studies*, 62 (1999), 9–30, at p. 21.

30 Walker, *The Black Loyalists*, p. 85.

31 Malherbe, 'Illegitimacy', pp. 1165, 1167.

32 Fyfe, *A History*, p. 88.

33 P. E. H. Hair, 'The Enslavement of Koelle's Informants', *Journal of African History*, 6:2 (1965), 193–203, at p. 194.

34 Galli, 'Marriage Patterns', p. 17.

35 Higman, 'Household Structure', p. 539.

Westmoreland Street over a span of four years. On 14 January 1859, Diana Cline gave birth to his child, followed just over a month later by Harriet Andy who gave birth to another of his children on 18 February 1859. Harriet had another child by him in December 1859, and Diana again in September 1860. Harriet gave birth a third time in January 1861, followed by Mary Ann Cuthbert in October 1862.[36]

Polygyny was widely practised among Muslim communities and persisted despite colonial efforts to impose Christian, monogamous marriage. Out of the fourteen fathers listed in the birth registers with multiple partners, six were explicitly identified as Muslims ('Mahomedans' in the source) – Aruna, Buboo Coonatch, Lamina Fooray, Momodoo, Momadoo Garankay, and Yellie Binch.[37] According to Islamic law, men are permitted to marry up to four wives, and this principle was upheld by many Muslims in Freetown. Polygyny had long been an accepted part of Islamic family structure in West Africa, especially among communities such as the Mandinka and Yoruba.[38] The persistence of polygynous marriage underscored both the continuity of Islamic cultural and religious practices and the challenges they posed to the Christian marital norms promoted by colonial authorities, particularly among the 'Liberated African' population, who were expected to adopt monogamy as part of their integration into colonial society. The case of Momodoo is especially illustrative. He had a child with Jenny Savage, who, although not explicitly identified in the records as a 'Liberated African', belonged to that group. Her surname, commonly adopted by Muslims in the colony as a tribute to the attorney William Henry Savage, along with her relationship with Momodoo, suggests she was also Muslim. Of the eight men recorded in the registers with the surname Savage, four were explicitly identified as Muslims.

While polygyny was a prominent and culturally recognised marital practice among Muslim communities, other family arrangements indicate informal relationships, particularly involving African women and European men.

36 Registration No. 169, 193, 409, SLPA, Register of Births, Freetown district [hereafter RBF] (1857–1860); Registration No. 133, 245, SLPA, RBF (1860–1861); Registration No. 55, SLPA, RBF (1862–1863).

37 Registration No. 44, 45, 48, 50, 54, 55, 58, 59, 68, 72, 74, 75, 93, SLPA, RBF (1860–1861).

38 Fyfe, *A History*, p. 270; Kristin Mann, 'Marriage Choices among the Educated African Elite in Lagos Colony, 1880–1915', *The International Journal of African Historical Studies*, 14:2 (1981), 201–28, at pp. 208–9; Barbara E. Harrell-Bond, Allen M. Howard, and David E. Skinner, *Community Leadership and the Transformation of Freetown (1801–1976)* (The Hague, 1978), p. 9; Assan Sarr, 'Women, Land & Power in the Lower Gambia River Region', in Mariana P. Candido and Adam Jones (eds), *African Women in the Atlantic World: Property, Vulnerability & Mobility 1660–1880* (Woodbridge, 2019), pp. 38–54, at p. 41; Kristin Mann, *Marrying Well: Marriage, Status and Social Change among the Educated Elite in Colonial Lagos* (Cambridge, 1985), pp. 40, 59; Akinwumi Ogundiran, *The Yoruba: A New History* (Bloomington, 2020), p. 325.

Kenneth Macaulay, a Scottish merchant and acting governor in 1826, acknowledged nine children in the colony of Sierra Leone in his 1831 will. He had three children, John, Margaret, and Charles, with Abisha (also listed as Abba Shaw), a 'Liberated African' woman. In 1831, Margaret and Charles lived on 23 Pultney Street with their mother in a household of seven. Macaulay also had a daughter, Elizabeth (Betsy), with Nelly Reid, who lived at 35 Percival Street with four others, including Betsy. Another daughter, Charlotte, born to Mary Harding, appeared in the census as living at 56 Liverpool Street with colonial resident Sarah Jarrett and two apprentices.[39] European men formed sexual relationships with African women without marrying them, though they frequently acknowledged paternity by giving their children their surnames. British law defined illegitimate children as those born out of wedlock or from common-law unions. However, in Freetown, these children were not labelled as illegitimate because the term imposes a moral and legal framework that fails to account for the population's cultural, religious, and social diversity, where many unions were locally recognised but not formalised under British law.[40] As early as 1863, Robert B. Clarke observed that many couples had children before formalising their unions through legal marriage.[41]

Diverse kinship arrangements included households with children from different partners as well as children placed with godparents or foster families. Across West African societies, as Esther Goody explains, parenthood is understood as a shared, communal responsibility. Practices such as baptism, wardship, and fostering played an important role in child-rearing, involving multiple adults in a child's upbringing. Children were frequently placed with others to gain access to education, to help families manage periods of crisis, or to encourage discipline and good behaviour.[42] These arrangements were typically long-term, with children remaining with foster families from around age five until marriageable age. During this time, foster parents were involved in arranging the child's marriage, usually with the consent of the biological parents, marking an important phase in socialisation into adulthood.[43]

In Freetown, these patterns were evident in both households listed in the 1831 census. For instance, discharged soldier George Mall and his wife

39 Will of Kenneth Macaulay of Freetown, Sierra Leone (3 January 1831), TNA, PROB 11/1780/280; Census, 1831, fol. 310, 312, 317, TNA, CO 267/111.

40 Lisa Forman Cody, 'The Politics of Illegitimacy in An Age of Reform: Women, Reproduction, and Political Economy in England's New Poor Law of 1834', *Journal of Women's History*, 11:4 (2000), 131–57, at p. 136.

41 Clarke, 'Sketches', p. 333.

42 Esther N. Goody, *Parenthood and Social Reproduction: Fostering and Occupational Roles in West Africa* (Cambridge, 1982), pp. 7–8; Jessica Catherine Reuther, *The Bonds of Kinship in Dahomey: Portraits of West African Girlhood, 1720–1940* (Bloomington, 2025), p. 8.

43 Goody, *Parenthood*, pp. 61, 99, 135, 172; Reuther, *The Bonds*, p. 28.

Hannah lived with their daughter Nancy and a 'Liberated African' boy apprentice, Davies Mall. They also cared for another freeborn child, Isabella Eagle. The family lived at 80 Soldier Street. Not far away, at 73 Soldier Street, the household of Mary Eagle, a 'Liberated African' woman, also included colonial residents such as Betsy Eagle (an adult) and several children, Thomas, Fatima, and Jennabou Eagle, along with their servant, Soree. [44] The presence of Isabella in a different household suggests placement through baptism, fostering, or other forms of fictive kinship. Comparable practices existed across the Atlantic and in other African coastal settlements. In the free African communities of Saint Louis and Gorée, baptisms created fictive kin bonds between godparents and godchildren, strengthening social ties beyond blood relations. In Portuguese Angola, particularly in Benguela and Luanda, baptism was used to forge protective relationships through kinship. Elsewhere, in places like Danish Fort Christianborg on the Gold Coast and Portuguese settlements in Guinea-Bissau, christening symbolised children's integration into colonial society while also expanding their social networks through baptismal kinship. African communities adapted and reinterpreted both indigenous and Christian institutions to reinforce extended kinship systems in the colonial context.[45]

Baptism was not simply a spiritual rite but also a means of social mobility that came with financial obligations. In 1835, Nova Scotians Sarah and Isaac Solomon placed their child under the care of Mrs Turner, the godmother, who lived in Settler Town with her husband Aberdeen Turner, the head constable, and son of a prominent Nova Scotian. Although all were part of the Nova Scotian community, the Turners occupied a higher social and occupational status. The Solomons, a workwoman and a fisherman, were of more modest means, and the arrangement suggests an attempt to connect their child to a more influential household. As part of this agreement, the Solomons agreed to pay the Turners for the child's maintenance and education, with Mrs Turner taking responsibility for the child's upbringing in exchange for payment. However, the relationship became contentious when, in 1838, Aberdeen Turner took

44 Census, 1831, TNA, CO 267/111, fol. 353.

45 Jessica Marie Johnson, *Wicked Flesh: Black Women, Intimacy, and Freedom in the Atlantic World* (Philadelphia, 2020), p. 58; Candido, 'African Women in Ecclesiastical Documents', p. 247; Mariana P. Candido and Vanessa S. Oliveira, 'The Status of Enslaved Women in West Central Africa, 1800–1830', *African Economic History*, 49:1 (2021), 127–53, at p. 137; Pernille Ipsen, *Daughters of the Trade: Atlantic Slavers and Interracial Marriage on the Gold Coast* (Philadelphia, 2015), p. 146; Philip J. Havik, *Silences and Soundbites: The Gendered Dynamics of Trade and Brokerage in the Pre-Colonial Guinea Bissau Region* (Münster, 2004), pp. 65, 137–8; Bernard Moitt, *Child Slavery and Guardianship in Colonial Senegal* (Cambridge, 2024), pp. 77–8.

Isaac Solomon to court over an unpaid £10. Their dispute continued for years, leading to a police report in 1843 after Solomon threatened to assault Turner.[46]

The relationship between godparents and godchildren was hierarchical, shaped by clear expectations and responsibilities, including legally recognised obedience. On 3 October 1839, John Kendall brought his godson, John Wise, to the Police Office for refusing to follow his orders; Wise was sentenced to three weeks in the House of Correction.[47] While such relationships could be disciplinary, baptisms were generally beneficial for all parties involved. Godchildren contributed labour to their godparents' households, and their placements offered opportunities for social mobility by enhancing family status and expanding kinship networks. Though there are additional cases of children being placed with Nova Scotian and Maroon settlers, the precise nature of these relationships is not always documented.

Households headed by single mothers represented another different type of family structure, shaped by widowhood, informal partnerships, and child-rearing without co-resident spouses. The 1831 census recorded 104 women with children but no spouse. Some may have been widows left to care for their children after their husband's death. Between 1857 and 1862, the proportion of single mothers can be estimated by examining birth registers, focusing on children whose fathers were not listed. Out of 1,620 births registered during this period, 503 (31 per cent) did not record a father's name. The reasons for this omission are not always clear. Reasons for such concealment could include the nature of the relationship, such as adultery or sexual assault, the father's own desire to remain anonymous, or disapproval of the relationship. Laura Adderley notes that in Tortola, when Sarah, a 'Liberated African' woman, had a child, her mistress requested that the father's identity be concealed.[48] Of the 503 births without a father listed, 49 were reported by the single mothers themselves, 5 by someone present at the birth, 2 had no informant recorded, and 13 were reported by the grandfather. The majority, 434 births, were registered by an 'occupier', a person living in the same household as tenant or owner.[49] The exact relationship between the mother and occupier is unknown; they could have been relatives, lodgers, or otherwise co-resident individuals.

46 Isaac Solomon, 27 July 1843, SLPA, Police Magistrate Record (1 July 1843 – 27 June 1844); Census, 1831, TNA, CO 267/111, fol. 286, 292; Aberdeen Turner v. Isaac Solomon, 8 December 1838, SLPA, Court of Commission for the Recovery of Small Debts (15 September 1838 – 18 January 1840).

47 John Kendall v. John Wise, 3 October 1839, SLPA, Police Magistrate Record (27 February 1839 – 10 January 1840), fol. 344.

48 Laura Rosanne Adderley, 'Household Labor and Sexual Coercion Reconstructing Women's Experience of African Recaptive Settlement', in Richard Anderson and Henry B. Lovejoy (eds), *Liberated Africans and the Abolition of the Slave Trade: Digital Histories of Enslavement and Freedom* (Rochester, 2020), pp. 174–97, at pp. 185–6.

49 'occupier, n.' *OED Online* (Oxford, 2020) <www.oed.com/view/Entry/130187> [accessed 4 January 2021].

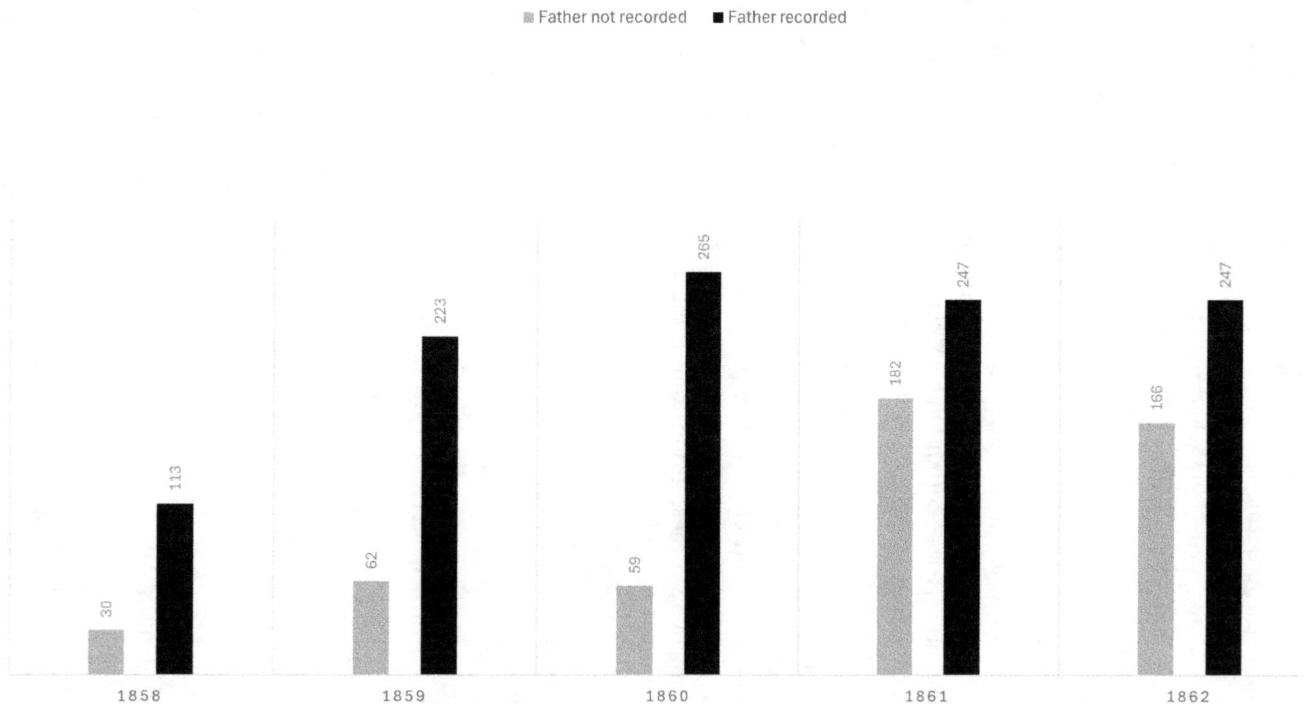

Graph 4.2 Births registered with and without a father in Freetown, 1858–1862.
Sources: SLPA, RBF (1857–1860); SLPA, RBF (1860–1861); SLPA, RBF (1861–1862); SLPA, RBF (1862–1863).

Single mothers tended to live with their parents, forming multigenerational households. Stephen Gabbidon and Nelly Libert had two sons, Samuel and James. While Gabbidon lived on 6 George Street, James and Samuel resided with their mother on 70 Bathurst Street with ten other people, including their grandfather.[50] Court records show that parental separation also contributed to such arrangements, especially when women sought support with family members. On 3 June 1847, William Doherty, a 'Liberated African' man of Egba origin, testified that his wife had left him and gone to live with her sister, Mary Hall. Likewise, on 2 July 1847, Sarah Williams reported that she left her husband and moved in with her mother.[51]

Other multigenerational households emerged when a parent had left or was deceased. John Ellis, who was 91 years old in 1831, lived at 11 Charlotte Street with his wife Susannah, and Jenny Ellis, a freeborn child who might have been their granddaughter. Nova Scotian Diana Weeks lived on 22 Charlotte Street with her grandchildren Sally, George, and Isaac Weeks. As Higman notes, in families of enslaved Africans, grandmothers typically lived with the mother and children unless the mother had died.[52] This would suggest that the parents of Jenny Ellis and of Sally, George, and Isaac Weeks were likely deceased, resulting in extended family households headed by grandparents.

Multigenerational households were particularly common among settler communities, as Nova Scotian settlers arrived in 1792 and Maroon migrants in 1800, meaning by 1831 these groups simply included more generations living together than those who had arrived more recently. These extended households combined elders, adults, and children under one roof in which family responsibilities were shared. Census records show that most older individuals did not live alone. Of the twenty-nine inhabitants described as 'old man/woman', 'very old man/woman', 'blind old woman', or 'helpless old woman', only nine lived independently, while twenty resided with adults, children, or child servants. This pattern was evident among colonial residents such as Nova Scotian settlers Aberdeen Turner and Phillis Colville, and African American immigrant Alexander Harlston.

Having examined the structure and composition of households, it is important to consider the roles played by different members within these units. Upon disembarkation, 'Liberated Africans' individuals were distributed across the colony as apprentices, playing a central role in the formation of what can be described as 'artificial' families.[53] These households were primarily

50 Census, 1831, TNA, CO 267/111, fol. 303, 322.

51 William Doherty v. Mary Hall, 3 June 1847, Sarah Williams v. Thomas Williams, 2 July 1847, SLPA, Police Magistrate Record (31 December 1846 – 18 September 1847).

52 Higman, 'Household Structure', p. 540.

53 Érika Melek Delgado, 'Children, Childhood and Slavery in Sierra Leone: The Experiences of Liberated African Children c. 1808–1834' (Unpublished PhD dissertation, University of Worcester, 2017), p. 182.

economic units, organised around resources, labour, and a central locus rather than genuine kinship ties.[54] In areas such as Grassfield 1 West, Settler Town, and West Brook Street, apprentices were most commonly found in households headed by 'Liberated Africans' and consisting of couples and their children or single women with children. These family structures depended heavily on the labour of 'Liberated Africans' for their economic survival.

Children made up a significant portion of the 'Liberated African' population within these households as apprentices and servants. The 1831 census recorded 1,007 'Liberated African' children, of whom 919 (91 per cent) were servants or apprentices. These children were officially classified as orphans by the Liberated African Department, with their masters and mistresses acting as guardians. Their lack of family ties made them easier to control and more loyal.[55] This cheap, dependent child labour was a cornerstone of the nineteenth-century Freetown economy, as illustrated by the fact that all 'Liberated African' children in discharged soldiers' households in Soldier Town were servants in 1831.[56]

From the late 1840s, there is evidence to suggest that wards, referred to as 'alien' children, began to replace 'Liberated Africans' as a source of domestic labour. These children were sent to the colony ostensibly to 'learn the white man fashion' but in practice, this meant working as unpaid servants in exchange for food, shelter, and informal instruction.[57] Between 26 April and 22 September 1859, 112 children were recorded as arriving in Freetown. Of these, fourteen had parents already residing in the city. Twenty-seven were employed explicitly as domestic servants, and eight were required to learn household tasks such as washing and sewing, together accounting for 31 per cent of all the children who arrived during that time. It is probable that thirty-six children (32 per cent) listed as coming into Freetown for education were employed in domestic service in their respective households. Beyond the colony, the institution of wardship involved children being fed and housed, in exchange for labour in the households in which they were placed.[58] In colonial Senegal, children under

54 Guyer, 'Household and Community', pp. 89, 98.

55 Melek Delgado, 'Children, Childhood', p. 187; Maeve Ryan, '"A Moral Millstone"? British Humanitarian Governance and the Policy of Liberated African Apprenticeship, 1808–1848', *Slavery & Abolition*, 37:2 (2016), 399–422, at pp. 404, 412; Paul E. Lovejoy, *Transformations in Slavery: A History of Slavery in Africa* (Cambridge, 2012), p. 3.

56 Melek Delgado, 'Children, Childhood', pp. 22. 78; Allen M. Howard, 'New Insights on Liberated Africans: The 1831 Freetown Census', in Richard Anderson and Henry B. Lovejoy (eds), *Liberated Africans and the Abolition of the Slave Trade: Digital Histories of Enslavement and Freedom* (Rochester, 2020), pp. 101–26, at p. 117.

57 Christine Whyte, '"Freedom but Nothing Else": The Legacies of Slavery and Abolition in Post-Slavery Sierra Leone, 1928–1956', *The International Journal of African Historical Studies*, 48:2 (2015), 231–50, at p. 233; Fyfe, *A History*, p. 270.

58 Allen M. Howard, 'Pawning in Coastal Northwest Sierra Leone, 1870–1910', in Toyin Falola and Paul E. Lovejoy (eds), *Pawnship in Africa: Debt Bondage in Historical Perspective* (Boulder, 1994), p. 271.

tutelle (freed children arriving in the French colony) became wards of the state and were placed in urban households that required domestic labour.[59]

Although the institution of wardship subjected children to exploitative labour conditions, some attempts were made to regulate their treatment, particularly regarding education. From 1855, regulations mandated that 'alien' children attend school for at least four hours daily, and guardians who failed to ensure this faced prosecution.[60] Evidence of this is found in court records where between November and December 1860, Richard Cathcart was repeatedly warned by the police to send his ward, Mary, to school. Despite these warnings, Cathcart did not comply and was eventually convicted seven months later for failing to do so. At court, he explained that Mary had been staying with his sister due to illness.[61]

Despite regulations aimed at ensuring access to education, hard conditions led several children to leave their assigned household, cases which are recorded in the Register of Alien Children. Four children were recorded as having 'run away' between 1859 and 1870.[62] Alfred Cole, a Sherbro boy, fled after less than a month. The proximity of Sherbro to the colony, combined with the fact that his mother was still alive, might have made return to family both possible and appealing. The other children ran away after two, three, and eleven years respectively. Mary was placed with William Chapman at the age of six and remained there until she was seventeen years old. By then, she was no longer legally considered a child, which might have emboldened her to leave. Her case also suggests that 'alien' children, unlike 'Liberated African' apprentices, were not subject to fixed terms of service, which could result in prolonged and undefined periods of dependency.[63] The long durations before escape reflect both the severity of their circumstances and the risks involved in leaving. Similar patterns were seen elsewhere. In Saint Louis, children under *tutelle* frequently

59 Moitt, *Child Slavery*, p. 73; Cheikh Sène, 'Le décret de l'émancipation des esclaves de 1848 : une application difficile au Sénégal (1848–1905)', *Esclavages & Post-esclavages*, 10 (2024) <https://doi.org/10.4000/12sh5> [accessed 2 December 2024]; Ibrahima Thioub, 'L'abolition de l'esclavage en Afrique française : le principe du sol libérateur à l'épreuve du terrain', in Annie Fitte-Duval (ed.), *Droit et esclavages : Théorie et pratiques en Afrique et dans les Amériques (XVe-XIXe siècles)* (Paris, 2022), pp. 215–40, at p. 220.

60 Philip Misevich, 'Freetown and "Freedom?" Colonialism and Slavery in Sierra Leone, 1790s to 1861', in Paul E. Lovejoy and Suzanne Schwarz (eds), *Slavery, Abolition and the Transition to Colonialism in Sierra Leone* (Trenton, 2015), pp. 189–216, at p. 203.

61 Registration No. 148, SLPA, Register of Alien Children (1859); Queen v. Richard Cathcart, 1 July 1861, SLPA, Police Court Record (1 July 1861 – 31 November 1861), fol. 1–2.

62 Registration No. 77, 13, 37, 97, SLPA, Register of Alien Children (1859).

63 *An Act for the Abolition of the Slave Trade* (1807), 47° GEORGII III, Session 1, Cap. XXXVI.

fled, regardless of age or kinship ties, underscoring the emotional and physical toll of their conditions.[64]

As did the 'alien' children, 'Liberated African' apprentices also resisted mistreatment by running away. Though their legal circumstances differed, their acts of escape similarly reveal the oppressive conditions they endured and their refusal to accept them passively. Authorities firmly recognised their legal ties to masters and attempts to flee were treated as punishable offences. In a sample of seven police court and police office volumes examined, twelve apprentices were brought before the authorities for absconding. On 22 February 1847, for example, Charles Murray was sentenced to two weeks in the House of Correction for leaving the service of Henry Richards. Months later, on 28 June, Peter Renner appeared before the Police Magistrate for running away and refusing to follow his mistress's orders. He was cautioned and sent back.[65]

The legal bond between apprentices and their masters was strongly upheld by the authorities, particularly in cases where pregnancy disrupted an apprentice's ability to work. When an apprentice became pregnant, masters or mistresses were entitled to compensation for the loss of their labour and could seek financial redress from men who denied responsibility for the pregnancy. In 1846, John Yackey took Thomas Richard Joseph to court on this basis. Elizabeth Langley, the apprentice in question, testified that Joseph, a butcher, had promised to take responsibility if she became pregnant. Joseph denied any involvement, claiming he had nothing to do with her. Despite his denial, the court ruled that he must pay a monthly sum to compensate Yackey for the loss of Elizabeth's labour during her pregnancy.[66]

In addition to social status, hierarchies within households were also shaped by gender roles, which were influenced by broader social, economic, and political forces.[67] Catherine Koonar notes that, in the mid-nineteenth-century Gold Coast colony, for example, children were trained in occupations aligned with Christian missionary goals, reinforcing European gender norms. Boys were prepared for trades such as carpentry, weaving, and farming, while girls were taught domestic skills, e.g. sewing, crocheting, and cooking.[68] This gendered division of labour extended into the school system, where boys were

64 Moitt, *Child Slavery*, p. 178.

65 Charles Murray, 22 February 1847, SLPA, Police Magistrate Record (31 December 1846 – 18 September 1847), Peter Renner, 28 June 1847, SLPA, Police Magistrate Record (31 December 1846 – 18 September 1847).

66 John Yackey v. Thomas Richard Joseph, 6 July 1847, SLPA, Police Magistrate Record (31 December 1846 – 18 September 1847).

67 Emily Lynn Osborn, *Our New Husbands are Here: Households, Gender, and Politics in a West African State from the Slave Trade to Colonial Rule* (Athens, 2011), pp. 4–5.

68 Catherine Koonar, '"Christianity, Commerce and Civilization": Child Labor and the Basel Mission in Colonial Ghana, 1855–1914', *International Labor and Working-Class History*, 86 (2014), 72–88, p. 73.

educated as future labourers and girls as home carers. The colonial government actively sought to enforce these ideals by encouraging women to organise and manage the household, at the expense of their education. 'Liberated African' girls sent to missionary schools in Freetown were commonly withdrawn after marriage. Samuel Walker observed that school attendance dropped not only due to apprenticeship demands and illnesses such as smallpox, but also due to early marriages.[69] All this is reflected in the occupational imbalance of the 1831 census, where 925 adult women were listed without an occupational title, compared to 650 adult men.

European ideals of domesticity shaped colonial expectations, but practices sometimes intersected with indigenous norms regarding gender roles and family responsibilities. In both Igbo and Yoruba communities, women were expected to perform domestic labour for their husbands. Gendered expectations also shaped the timing of marriage, with young Yoruba women encouraged to marry early, while men were discouraged from marrying before their twenties.[70] Initiation societies such as Poro and Bundu (also known as Sande) also shaped and reinforced gender roles. These societies guided young people through important rites of passage, instilling moral values and social expectations tied closely to their roles in society. While not solely focused on domestic life, they helped organise household structures by providing vocational training and instruction until marriage. For women, initiation into the Bundu society was particularly significant, as it prepared them for their reproductive and domestic responsibilities. During this initiation, girls learned essential skills related to childcare and motherhood.[71]

Gendered expectations positioned women as the primary caregivers within households, a role that was reinforced through both custom and coercion. These expectations were evident in the way 'alien' children were passed between households, particularly when illness required additional care. In these cases, caregiving responsibilities shifted to women's households,

69 Melek Delgado, 'Children, Childhood', pp. 201–204; Samuel Abraham Walker, *The Church of England Mission in Sierra Leone* (London, 1847), p. 222.

70 Marc Matera, Misty L. Bastian, and Susan Kingsley Kent, *The Women's War of 1929: Gender and Violence in Colonial Nigeria* (London, 2011), p. 18; Mann, 'Marriage Choices', p. 209; Gibril R. Cole, *The Krio of West Africa: Islam, Culture, Creolization, and Colonialism in the Nineteenth Century* (Athens, 2013), p. 135.

71 Katrina Keefer, 'Poro, Witchcraft and Red Water in Early Colonial Sierra Leone: G. R. Nylander's *Ethnography and Systems of Authority on the Bullom Shore*', *Canadian Journal of African Studies / Revue canadienne des études africaines*, 55:1 (2021), 39–55; K. L. Little, 'The Role of the Secret Society in Cultural Specialization', *American Anthropologist*, 51:2 (1949), 199–212; Christine Whyte, 'Mothering Solidarity: Infant-Feeding, Vulnerability and Poverty in West Africa since the Seventeenth Century', *Past & Present*, 246:15 (2020), 54–92, at pp. 61–4; Lynda Rose Day, *Gender and Power in Sierra Leone: Women Chiefs of the Last Two Centuries* (New York, 2012), 16–17.

highlighting the central role women played in nurturing and tending to children's well-being. Richard Cathcart placed his ward Mary with his sister while she was ill, a practice that was not uncommon and is documented in other court records from the period.[72] Evidence from court records, though anecdotal, further reveals clear expectations about gendered behaviour within the household. As an example, on 28 February 1851, Thomas Dublin went to the house of his mother, Sarah, to take her remaining food supplies. She complained to him that it was the only food she had left, and due to her old age and illness, he needed to work to purchase his own. In response, he violently threw her on the sofa.[73]

Cases such as that of Thomas Dublin show that mothers were vulnerable to violence within the household, but court evidence also makes clear that wives faced similar dangers and received little protection from the colonial state. In a sample of fifty-five recorded cases of domestic abuse, forty-two (76 per cent) involved violence between romantic partners, yet in seventeen of these cases husbands were only reprimanded and told to 'keep the peace', a warning that carried no immediate consequence for them but could carry serious consequences that could be life-threatening for the women. In the case of William Taylor, heard in August 1857, police constable Thomas Taylor testified that he heard 'cries of murder' and found Ellen Taylor lying in the gutter after being repeatedly kicked by her husband.[74] Violent assault was a harsh reality for some women, causing some to fear for their lives, even though direct evidence of femicide is absent in the cases analysed. In addition, death records for Freetown between 1860 and 1875 show only two cases of manslaughter, both involving male victims.[75] Women listed in the records died from diseases or complications related to childbirth, with no recorded causes directly linked to femicide. The absence of such records, however, does not mean femicide did not occur.

Regarding children, the law typically upheld fathers as their primary legal guardians, particularly in matters of inheritance, guardianship, and education. Even when mothers remained involved in their children's lives, they were formally excluded from guardianship rights, particularly if they were not married to the father. When Stephen Gabbidon, the father of Nelly Libert's sons, died in 1839, she continued to live with her sons, yet guardianship was granted to the children's older brother, William Gabbidon, and to their father's

72 Registration No. 148, SLPA, Register of Alien Children (1859).

73 Mary Dublin v. Thomas Dublin, 3 March 1851, SLPA, Police Court Record (1851–1852).

74 Regina v. William Taylor, 29 August 1857, SLPA, Police Court Record (1857).

75 SLPA, Registers of deaths, Freetown District (1861–1890); SLPA, Registers of deaths, Freetown District (1870–1871); SLPA, Registers of deaths, Freetown District (1872–1873); SLPA, Registers of deaths, Freetown District (1873–1874); SLPA, Registers of deaths, Freetown District (1874–1875).

cousin, James Robertson Bonard.[76] Following the death of Kenneth Macaulay, guardianship of his sons was assigned to European Jane Nicol and African Barbadian Thomas Carew, rather than to the children's mothers, Abisha, Nelly Reid, and Mary Harding. In another case, Joseph Green Spilsbury made no mention of guardianship in his will but left £500 to John Meheux and William Hirst Wise for the education of his daughter.[77]

However, during the early years of a child's life, women's responsibilities and rights were more clearly acknowledged, especially in matters of care and custody. In 1847, Hannah Crew approached the Police Office seeking the return of her child and charged Thomas Coker, the child's father, with detaining the child. Hannah explained that she had previously lived with Coker and had a child with him, but after their separation, he kept the child and refused to return the infant to her care. By the time of her complaint, Hannah was legally married to another man, while Coker was cohabiting with a different woman. The Police Magistrate ruled in her favour and ordered the child to be returned to her, upholding her maternal rights.[78]

This chapter has explored marriage, household structure, and the roles individuals held within these new family units. However, not all familial connections were newly formed in Freetown, some ties from before enslavement persisted or were actively restored. Despite the trauma and displacement caused by slavery, 'Liberated Africans' sometimes managed to reunite with relatives, demonstrating the resilience of family bonds across time and distance.[79] Upon disembarkation, 'Liberated Africans' could be claimed by relatives as colonial officials believed they were to fare better under familial care than under that of the Department.[80] Such examples can be traced in the Registers of Liberated Africans, although such documented reunions became increasingly rare after 1831. On 15 April 1827, Billegoh was disembarked from the Portuguese vessel *NS da Conceição de Maria*. She was placed with her sister, Mary Barber. By 1831, both women were living at 44 Circular Road 1 in western Freetown, along with Mary's husband and their children.[81] On 17 November 1836, Lackendah

76 Will of Stephen Gabbidon of Sierra Leone, West Africa (17 December 1839), TNA, PROB 11/1920/64.

77 Will of Kenneth Macaulay of Freetown, Sierra Leone (3 January 1831), TNA, PROB 11/1780/280; Will of Joseph Green Spilsbury, Merchant of Freetown, Sierra Leone (22 August 1856), TNA, PROB 11/2238/111.

78 Hannah Crew v. Thomas Coker, 24 August 1848, SLPA, Police Magistrate Record (31 December 1846 – 18 September 1847).

79 Melek Delgado, 'Children, Childhood', p. 208.

80 William Hamilton, 'Sierra Leone and the Liberated Africans', *The Colonial Magazine and Commercial-Maritime Journal*, 6 (1841), 327–34, at p. 330; John Peterson, *Province of Freedom: A History of Sierra Leone, 1787–1870* (Evanston, 1969), p. 194.

81 'Nossa Senhora da Conceição de Maria', Liberated Africans database, <https://liberatedafricans.org/databases/event_details.php?EventID=3375> [accessed 26 September 2025];

disembarked from the Portuguese ship *Quatro de Abril* and within weeks, was placed with her sister.[82] Additional examples of family reunions include the story of Dorokoo. She also disembarked from the *NS da Conceição de Maria* and was placed with William Adams, a soldier who claimed she was his wife in his native country.[83] Family units were further preserved when relatives, such as couples or siblings, were identified together aboard the same ship and subsequently placed in the same household upon arrival.[84]

Geographical proximity to the homeland made it possible for some formerly enslaved individuals to recover links disrupted, but not entirely severed, by enslavement. As Kristin Mann notes, mobility renewed 'family ties that had been interrupted, but clearly not broken, by slaving and the slave trade'.[85] An example is Samba, who was relocated to Freetown in 1813, and later told Koelle that he was 'often visited by relatives and other people from Salum', in present-day Senegal.[86] Another case is Samuel Crowther, who disembarked from a slave ship in 1822. After receiving Christian instruction in Freetown and England, he joined the British Niger Expedition and, in 1843, took part in a mission to Abeokuta, where he was reunited with his mother and sisters, who had been redeemed from slavery by one of his brothers.[87] In a journal entry from 1841, Crowther also recounted how 'Liberated Africans' travelled to trade in Badagry

Registration No. 25,428, SLPA, RLA 25465–30708 (1827–1829); Census, 1831, TNA, CO 267/111, fol. 360.

82 Registration No. 55,668, SLPA, RLA, 54157–57571 (1837); 'Quatro de Abril', Liberated Africans database, <https://liberatedafricans.org/databases/event_details.php?EventID=3356> [accessed 26 September 2025].

83 Registration No. 25,431, SLPA, RLA 25465–30708 (1827–1829).

84 Melek Delgado, 'Children, Childhood', p. 206; Érika Melek Delgado, 'Freedom Narratives: The West African Person as the Central Focus for a Digital Humanities Database', *History in Africa* (2021), 35–59, at p. 39; Registration No. 38,018; 38,058, SLPA, RLA 37430–43537 (1829–1832); 'Nueva Isabelita', Liberated Africans database, <https://liberatedafricans.org/databases/event_details.php?EventID=3197> [accessed 26 September 2025].

85 Kristin Mann, 'Gendered Authority, Gendered Violence: Family, Household & Identity in the Life & Death of a Brazilian Freed Woman in Lagos', in Mariana P. Candido and Adam Jones (eds), *African Women in the Atlantic World: Property, Vulnerability & Mobility 1660–1880* (Woodbridge, 2019), pp. 148–70, at pp. 153–4.

86 Sigismund Wilhelm Koelle, *Polyglotta Africana; or A Comparative Vocabulary of Nearly Three Hundred Words and Phrases in more than One Hundred Distinct African Languages* (London, 1854), p. 17.

87 Jesse Page, *The Black Bishop Samuel Adjai Crowther* (New York, 1909), pp. 95–7; John Flint, 'Crowther, Samuel Ajayi (c. 1807–1891), Bishop of Western Africa and Linguistic Scholar', *Oxford Dictionary of National Biography* (Oxford, 2015), <www.oxforddnb.com/view/10.1093/ref:odnb/9780198614128.001.0001/odnb-9780198614128-e-6836> [accessed 16 June 2020]; Jennifer Lofkrantz, *Ransoming Prisoners in Precolonial Muslim West Africa* (Rochester, 2023).

and Lagos, where they encountered lost family members. They 'found their children, others their brothers and sisters'. While some relatives returned with them to the colony, others sent messages back to their 'parents and relations whom the traders met at Badagry'.[88] Another similar example is found in John Duncan's *Travels in Western Africa in 1845 & 1846*, which recounts the story of a 'Liberated African' man who reunited with his mother in Abomey.[89]

Other histories of family reunions include those of the Saros, a group of Yoruba people who, upon gaining freedom, sought to return to their natal communities. Most Saros who returned to Benin and Nigeria were from Brazil, relatively few came from the Sierra Leone colony. In Benin, many settled along the coast rather than in their original communities due to restrictions imposed by Dahomeyan authorities, who would re-enslave those caught attempting to leave.[90] On 1 April 1839, three 'Liberated' Yoruba from the colony of Sierra Leone sailed on the *Queen Victoria* to Badagry with sixty-seven passengers. They initially settled there before moving inland.[91]

Beyond 'Liberated Africans', some settlers were able to maintain family connections despite the distance, sustaining bonds across the Atlantic Ocean. Thomas Carew, who died in 1848, bequeathed his Freetown properties to two cousins, Mary Hall and Elizabeth Richards, described in his will as 'of the Island of Barbados'. Upon his death in 1856, Joseph Green Spilsbury, of Maroon descent, left £50 to his uncle in Jamaica.[92] While such cases suggest that some settlers preserved transatlantic ties, their wealth indicates that this opportunity was limited to the more affluent. Transatlantic ties to the homeland are also evident in free migration movements back to the Caribbean. In 1841,

88 J. F. Ade Ajayi, *Christian Missions in Nigeria 1841–1891: The Making of a New Élite* (Evanston, 1965), p. 27.

89 'A Sierra Leone Incident', *Douglas Jerrold's Weekly Newspaper*, 66 (1847), p. 1301; John Duncan, *Travels in Western Africa in 1845 & 1846, Comprising a Journey from Whydah, Through the Kingdom of Dahomey, to Adofoodia, in the Interior*, vol. 1, 2nd edn (London, 1847), pp. 264–8.

90 Robin Law, 'Yoruba Liberated Slaves Who Returned to West Africa', in Toyin Falola and Matt D. Childs (eds), *The Yoruba Diaspora in the Atlantic World* (Bloomington, 2005), pp. 349–65, at pp. 349–50, 355; Frederick E. Forbes, *Dahomey and the Dahomans: Being the Journals of Two Missions to the King of Dahomey, and Residence at His Capital, in the Years 1849 and 1850*, vol. II (London, 1851), p. 72.

91 Fyfe, *A History*, p. 212; Kristin Mann, *Slavery and the Birth of an African City: Lagos, 1760–1900* (Bloomington, 2007), p. 92; Bronwen Everill, 'Bridgeheads of Empire? Liberated African Missionaries in West Africa', *The Journal of Imperial and Commonwealth History*, 40:5 (2012), 789–805, at p. 793.

92 Will of Thomas Carew, Merchant of Freetown, Sierra Leone (13 October 1848), TNA, PROB 11/2081/362; Will of Joseph Green Spilsbury, Merchant of Freetown, Sierra Leone (22 August 1856), TNA, PROB 11/2238/111.

591 Maroons returned to Jamaica.[93] The older settlers among them had been absent for nearly forty years, while the majority, the second generation, had never lived there. That same year, the Secretary of State for the Colonies approved the return of African Barbadians exiled in 1819 for their participation in Bussa's Rebellion. However, as Hilary Beckles points out, research has found no evidence that they were ever able to return to their island.[94]

Conclusion

Archival documents provide a rich amount of evidence on the experiences of women in Freetown but also on how family relations were both maintained despite displacement and created in a foreign environment. Marriages and kinship ties were at the basis of the expansion of the port-city in the nineteenth century. British colonial administration interfered and shaped these relations, but the inhabitants found ways to overcome some of these challenges.[95] They tended to marry individuals of their social and cultural group, retained strong connections to their homeland, and sometimes attempted to go back there. These are elements that contributed to the development of Freetown's social and cultural diversity. Within households, gender roles were defined both by the authorities and traditions from home communities. Women fulfilled multiple roles but, as with African women in West and West Central Africa, they were able to overcome socially constructed gender roles.[96] Testimonies traced in the police office and police court records offer insights into family relationships beyond the enumeration of data in the census, birth registers, and various other sources.

93 Jeffrey A. Fortin, '"An Act of Deportation": The Jamaican Maroons' Journey from Freedom to Slavery and Back Again, 1796–1836', in Ana Lucia Araujo (ed.), *Paths of the Atlantic Slave Trade* (Amherst, 2011), p. 94; Jeffrey A. Fortin, '"Blackened Beyond Our Native Hue": Removal, Identity and the Trelawney Maroons on the Margins of the Atlantic World, 1796–1800', *Citizenship Studies*, 10:1 (2006), 5–34, at p. 23.

94 Hilary Beckles, *Great House Rules: Landless Emancipation and Workers' Protest in Barbados* (Kingston, 2004), pp. 91–5.

95 Ryan, '"It Was Necessary"', p. 506.

96 Mariana P. Candido and Adam Jones, 'Introduction', in Mariana P. Candido and Adam Jones (eds), *African Women in the Atlantic World: Property, Vulnerability & Mobility 1660–1880* (Woodbridge, 2019), pp. 1–18, at p. 2.

5

Trade, Kinship and the Afterlives of Slavery

The port and market functions of Freetown encouraged the development of commercial networks both within and beyond the city and across the broader region surrounding the colony. These networks were closely tied to the advancement of abolition and the rise of legitimate trade, even as the area remained entangled with slave trading activities. Scholars such as Walter Rodney and Bruce Mouser have highlighted the role of river systems and waterways in facilitating commerce along the upper Guinea coast, particularly the Northern Rivers, and extending southward to Sherbro and Cape Mount.[1] As a British Atlantic port, Freetown also maintained trading connections with other parts of West Africa, including Calabar and Lagos, as well as with Britain, other European nations, the Caribbean, the United States of America, and Brazil. By the mid-nineteenth century, the city exhibited complex business networks and partnerships, rooted in familial ties or religious affiliations. These relationships provided access to labour, expanded employment opportunities, and helped ensure the reliability of financial transactions.

This chapter examines trading networks in Freetown within the context of abolition. It begins by evaluating business partnerships within the city, focusing on geographic clusters, family ties, and cross-ethnic interactions. It then explores Freetown's role as the colony's commercial centre, linking it to surrounding villages. The next section traces connections to interior trade routes, such as the Northern Rivers, Sherbro, Timbo, and Kangaba. Finally, the chapter turns to Freetown's Atlantic ties, including Lagos, Calabar, and European ports, also highlighting the role of merchants in British diplomacy and abolitionist efforts.

Freetown was a regional and transatlantic centre for trade, yet internal dynamics were shaped by the everyday practices of its inhabitants. In particular, occupational clustering structured both the social fabric and spatial layout of the urban environment. Individuals engaged in the same trade lived on the same street, in the same area, or even within the same household, which facilitated the

1 Walter Rodney, *A History of the Upper Guinea Coast 1545–1800* (New York, 1980); Bruce L. Mouser, 'Continuing British Interest in Coastal Guinea-Conakry and Fuuta Jaloo Highlands (1750 to 1850)', *Cahiers d'études africaines*, 43:172 (2003), 761–90.

exchange of knowledge and skills. Bronwen Everill highlights such examples through ship repair partnerships, noting instances where sailors, carpenters, and boatmen were recorded at the same address. John McCarthy and a man named Charles, the only two boatbuilders listed in the 1831 census, lived together at 12 Circular Road.[2] Everill attributes the growth of the ship repair sector in part to the apprenticeship system, which enabled 'Liberated Africans' to become productive contributors since many of them had prior experience in boatbuilding, a widespread skill in West Africa.[3] Similar occupational patterns emerged among other trades. Coopers, who crafted barrels essential for storing and transporting goods, lived in proximity, allowing them to share tools, techniques, and labour. Fence makers, responsible for constructing enclosures and boundaries in a rapidly expanding urban landscape, also clustered together.[4]

Within households, women maintained important occupational networks as domestic workspaces functioned as informal training grounds and support systems. It was common to find groups of women working together as seamstresses under one roof. Of the sixty-seven seamstresses recorded in the census, fourteen lived with another seamstress.[5] In three cases, mothers shared their trade with daughters, as seen with Anne Fraser and her daughter Maria. The remaining eight shared no apparent familial ties beyond their shared profession. The remaining eight shared no apparent familial ties beyond their shared profession, indicating that skill-sharing and collaboration extended beyond kinship.

Beyond women's collaborative labour, children also sustained household economies and advanced family businesses. Their contributions, ranging from manual labour to clerical support, were instrumental in maintaining commercial operations and forging transatlantic partnerships. The analysis of records from the police court made it possible to uncover detailed histories of such collaborations. One police court case from 1862 comprises fifty-seven pages related to the Lumpkin family shop on Oxford Street.[6] On 12 July 1862, Henry Lumpkin Senior, a Yoruba 'Liberated African' who was initially settled in Aberdeen as a fisherman before becoming a merchant, brought a forgery

2 Bronwen Everill, '"For the Services of Shipwrights, Coopers, and Grumettas": Freetown's Ship Repair Cluster in Nineteenth-Century Sierra Leone', *History of Science* (2020), 1–17, at p. 10; Census of Population and liberated Africans, 1831, TNA, CO 267/111, fol. 272.

3 Everill, '"For the Services"', 6–9.

4 Census, 1831, TNA, CO 267/111, fol. 260, 308.

5 Census, 1831, TNA, CO 267/111, fol. 274, 276, 297, 298, 302, 303, 304, 305, 308, 310, 311, 312, 313, 314, 316, 317, 318, 319, 320, 322, 323, 326, 328, 330, 334, 339, 341, 342, 345, 349, 352, 353, 354, 355, 357, 358, 359, 362, 364, 367, 368, 373, 380. 383.

6 The Queen v. Isaac Nathaniel Williams, 22 September 1862, SLPA, Police Court Record (11 December 1862 – 12 October 1863), fol. 9–66.

case against Isaac Nathaniel Williams.[7] Over the course of ten hearings between July and December, Magistrate John McCormack heard testimony from Lumpkin himself, Williams, and eight witnesses. At the first hearing, Lumpkin explained that he received a half-yearly account from two London merchant firms and discovered unauthorised orders issued to Owen Parsons and Williams. The court proceedings revealed that the shop was a family-run operation. Lumpkin's eldest son, Henry Junior, had previously worked as a clerk before marrying and establishing his own trade, in keeping with Yoruba customs. By 1862, the second son, Moses Maximus Lumpkin, had assumed the clerk role, assisting his father who could barely write his own name. The sons' education in Freetown schools enabled the family to maintain business partnerships with firms in Britain. This model of intergenerational collaboration was not unique since another witness, Lewis Nicol Junior, testified that he too worked alongside his father at their shop on East Street.

Shared geographic background and ethnic communities likewise fostered business partnership and facilitated trade. By the early 1840s, Johann Daniel Eppfenhausen and Johann Gottfried Nagel, two traders from Hamburg, established a partnership in Freetown. A decade later, African Caribbean builders Charles Hazelborg and Charles Clinton were occasionally working together.[8] In May 1843, the theft of an ivory wrist ring from Prince Will's house revealed a chain of transactions rooted in Kru community ties. After spotting Jack Widdow wearing the stolen ring, Prince Will confronted him and learned it had been purchased from a man named Bottled Beer, who had acquired it from a Kru man known as Pea Soup.[9] On 8 June 1843, Pea Soup was brought before Police Magistrate Thomas McFoy on charges of theft. While the records explicitly identify Pea Soup as Kru, the name Bottled Beer reflects a naming convention among Kru seamen, who adopted names derived from alcoholic beverages.[10] Census data from 1831 lists six individuals named Prince Will, all categorised as Kru, suggesting that three of the four men involved in this case were members of the same ethnic group.[11]

Ethnic networks formed business partnerships and sustained credit systems that underpinned the growth of trade. In the absence of formal banking institutions across West Africa, commerce relied heavily on credit arrangements and bills of exchange. Among Yoruba inhabitants, a traditional financial system

7 Christopher Fyfe, 'A Royal Visit in 1860', *Sierra Leone Studies*, 2 (1959), 260–72, at p. 265.

8 Christopher Fyfe, *A History of Sierra Leone* (Oxford, 1962), pp. 250, 302.

9 Prince Will v. Pea Soup, 8 June 1843, SLPA, Police Magistrate Record (1 June 1843 – 27 June 1844).

10 Jeffrey Gunn, *Outsourcing African Labor: Kru Migratory Workers in Global Ports, Estates and Battlefields until the End of the 19th Century* (Berlin, 2021), p. 84.

11 Census, 1831, TNA, CO 267/111, fol. 334, 377, 386, 388.

known as 'Esusu' was adapted to support traders. This system was built on trust among members, typically friends, relatives, or co-workers, who met monthly and contributed varying amounts. Once a year, the pooled contributions were redistributed, with each participant receiving their original deposit multiplied by the number of members. Esusu was transplanted to the colony of Sierra Leone, where it enabled residents to raise capital and navigate the challenges of an unfamiliar economic landscape.[12]

Not all business partnerships, however, were rooted in ethnic or familial connections. In a few instances, professional collaboration emerged across lines of social status and background. Records from the Court Commission for the Recovery of Small Debts reveal such occupational ties with individuals in informal partnerships prior to their legal disputes. In 1831, Thomas Chambers, a 'Liberated African', and Thomas Hunter, a colonial resident, were both masons residing at 106 Pademba Road and 9 James Street, respectively. In 1838, they completed two masonry jobs for a client named Mr Brown, who paid Hunter £5, a sum he failed to share with Chambers. Chambers subsequently brought the matter before the Court, claiming £7. 10s. 0d. as his share of the work performed in partnership. Hunter admitted to withholding the payment, and the Court ruled that he owed Chambers £4.[13] A similar case involved James Solomon and William Senegal, both children in 1831, living at 12 Percival Street and 37 Waterloo Street. Solomon, a servant to seamstress Creshie Ellis and registered as a 'Native Stranger', and Senegal, the son of a discharged soldier, were involved in a dispute over masonry work done for Mr Lewis. In February 1839, Senegal took Solomon to Court, but the case was dismissed after records showed Solomon had been overpaid.[14] Due to the lack of first names and the commonality of surnames, it is impossible to definitively identify Mr Brown and Mr Lewis.

Networks shaped the urban-rural economic life by helping individuals from colony villages secure employment in Freetown. On 22 July 1846, a man named King William brought before the Police Magistrate a labourer named Jim Wilson, who lived in Wilberforce, and accused him of breaching

12 C. Magbaily Fyle, 'The Yoruba Diaspora in Sierra Leone's Krio Society', in Toyin Falola and Matt D. Childs (eds), *Yoruba Diaspora in the Atlantic World* (Bloomington, 2005), pp. 366–82, at p. 379; William R. Bascom, 'The Esusu: A Credit Institution of the Yoruba', *Journal of the Royal Anthropological Institute of Great Britain and Ireland*, 82:1 (1952), 63–9; Richard Anderson, *Abolition in Sierra Leone: Re-Building Lives and Identities in Nineteenth-Century West Africa* (Cambridge, 2020), pp. 170–1; Akinwumi Ogundiran, *The Yoruba: A New History* (Bloomington, 2020), p. 389.

13 Thomas Chambers v. Thomas Hunter, 15 September 1838, SLPA, Court of Commission for the Recovery of Small Debts (15 September 1838 – 18 January 1840).

14 William Senegal v. James Solomon, 9 February 1839, SLPA, Court of Commission for the Recovery of Small Debts (15 September 1838 – 18 January 1840); Census, 1831, TNA, CO 267/111, fol. 275, 311, 329, 348.

his work agreement.[15] Wilson had been hired for three months and received an advancement payment of one dollar and a piece of blue baft, yet he only worked for two days. King William, a Kru man living in Krutown in 1831, was not listed with an occupation in the census. He might have served as a headman, possibly overseeing the recruitment of labourers in Freetown. Labourers like Wilson carried out a number of tasks ranging from work as porters, boat-pullers, lightermen, longshoremen, stevedores, woodcutters, and timber transporters.[16]

Beyond contracted labour, many people from the villages travelled to Freetown to sell goods in the city's markets and streets. Women from nearby villages such as Leicester, Bathurst, and other Mountain communities had the advantage of proximity, allowing them to bring their produce to market daily. They cultivated vegetables, which they carried along steep and uneven terrain. The journey itself was physically taxing; Bathurst, for instance, lies about twelve miles from Freetown. Once there, the work remained demanding, as the city itself is far from flat and women had to navigate hilly streets while carrying their goods to markets and selling points. Women from coastal villages such as Tombo and York also participated in this trade, selling fish both locally and in Freetown. York lacked a substantial market of its own, so women walked to Waterloo to sell their goods or took boats to reach Freetown.[17]

People regularly migrated from rural settlements into the urban centre, relying on networks of trust, shared identity, and mutual support to access housing, employment, and community. In a letter dated 5 April 1841, Elizabeth Helen Melville recounted how she asked her laundress, Dinah, who lived in Regent, to find another servant. Dinah sought candidates from nearby villages and first introduced Eliza, a girl from the Mountain District who had prior experience working for Europeans. However, just three days later, Eliza's mother requested that she return home, needing her daughter's help. After Eliza's departure, Dinah informed Melville of another young girl from the Mountain District who was eager to work for a European household.[18] With both girls, word of mouth and personal connections enabled people from rural areas to access employment opportunities in Freetown. It is possible that Dinah was acquainted with Eliza or her family or had previously worked alongside them in another household.

15 King William v. James Wilson, 22 July 1846, SLPA, Mountain District Magistrate Court Record (5 November 1844 – 26 September 1846).

16 Gunn, *Outsourcing African Labor*, pp. 11–12.

17 E. Frances White, 'Creole Women Traders in the Nineteenth Century', *The International Journal of African Historical Studies*, 14:4 (1981), 626–42, at pp. 627, 629.

18 Caroline Sheridan Norton (ed.), *A Residence at Sierra Leone. Described from a Journal Kept on the Spot, and from Letters Written to Friends at Home* (London, 1849), pp. 33–4.

Within those village ties, religious affiliation served as an additional layer of connection, offering migrants both spiritual community and practical support as they transitioned into life in Freetown. Court records offer valuable insight into how these connections operated. Jabardee, a 'Liberated African' living in Charlotte Town with his wife and children, relocated to Freetown in September 1839, bringing his children while leaving his wife behind. Shortly after, his wife brought a complaint to the court accusing him of desertion. In fact, Jabardee moved to Freetown as he was trying to seek work as a sawyer.[19] There, as a member of the Muslim community, Jabardee settled among Yoruba Muslims. Through this community, Jabardee found housing, social support, and introductions to potential employers or collaborators.

Inhabitants of both Freetown and the surrounding colony villages employed a range of strategies beyond personal networks to secure work and financial support. One of them was the use of written letters delivered door-to-door, in which individuals offered their services or requested employment. These letters were especially common for individuals seeking employment at the service of Europeans. During her stay in Freetown in 1841, Melville recorded six such notes in her journal. One was written by Daniel Davis, who asked to be employed as a messenger. He may have been the same Daniel Davies listed in the 1831 census as the son of 'Liberated Africans' William Davies and Judith White. Melville observed that some colony-born children of 'Liberated Africans' were literate, which supports the possibility that Davies authored the note himself. For those who could not write, scribes were available to compose such letters on their behalf.[20] The letters reveal a variety of employment aspirations. J. S. D. Davies requested access to a farm to hunt birds for personal consumption. John Coffee sought permission to cultivate two or three acres of land, while Moses Johnson applied for work as a horseman. William Kinness, though trained as a cook, expressed willingness to take on any type of employment. Another letter, unsigned, came from a man hoping to be hired as a schoolmaster in one of the colony villages.[21] These written appeals illustrate how individuals actively pursued opportunities not only in Freetown but also across the colony. While none of these examples were authored by women, similar letters were likely written by or on behalf of women, particularly those seeking employment in domestic service or housekeeping roles. Melville herself recalled an instance when a girl came to her home to ask for needlework, offering a glimpse into the informal ways women also sought employment.

19 Jenny Taylor v. Jabardee, 19 September 1839, SLPA, Police Magistrate Record (27 February 1839 – 10 January 1840), fol. 317.

20 Norton (ed.), *A Residence*, pp. 255, 335.

21 Ibid., pp. 333–4; Registration No. 256, SLPA, RBF (1860–1861); Census, 1831, TNA, CO 267/111, fol. 385.

While these individual efforts to secure employment reflect the everyday strategies of urban and rural residents, broader commercial networks were also taking shape, rooted in long-standing social and religious ties. By the 1860s, Freetown was an important centre in what Allen Howard termed the Sierra Leone–Guinea system, a regional trade corridor that exported kola and palm oil. The north-west coastal plain, particularly between the Rokel and Scarcies rivers, served as a major supply zone for kola, a crop deeply associated with Muslim religious rites, initiation ceremonies, and property rights.[22] Sierra Leone lay on the periphery of a trade route stretching from the upper valley of the St Paul River through Kankan and Kissidougou, linking interior markets to coastal export hubs.[23] Trade in Freetown was thus closely intertwined with Muslim identity and community formation, as Islam provided a shared cultural framework that bonded traders across linguistic and ethnic divides.[24]

Muslim traders had long sustained commercial ties between interior markets and the colony, and their presence in Freetown was reinforced by networks of ethnic and religious affiliation. These traders, among which were Fula and Mandinka, arrived from the Northern Rivers, Melakori, Pongo, Nunez, or Scarcies, and landed at Susan's Bay, one of the city's coastal entry points. Colonial authorities recognised and documented the fluid boundaries between permanent settlement and commercial mobility. In 1846, the significance of these traders was indicated by distinguishing between different categories of residents in statistical data. Approximately 1,000 individuals were listed as 'aliens and transient strangers', separate from 1,074 Mandinka, Susu, and Fula, and 1,530 Sherbro and others considered more settled. By 1851, 1,766 'Native Strangers' were accounted for in the race section of the census, and 594 transient traders recorded under trades and occupations.[25]

To navigate the city and conduct business, these transient traders relied on a well-established system of local hosts known as landlords, a role embedded in West African long-distance trade traditions, particularly among Muslim communities engaged in the exchange of livestock, kola, and other commodities. The landlord system, however, was socially diverse and not confined to any single ethnic or religious group. While Fula and Mandinka individuals

22 Rodney, *A History*, p. 206; Paul E. Lovejoy, *Caravans of Kola: The Hausa Kola Trade 1700–1900* (Zaria, 1980), p. 2.

23 Rodney, *A History*, p. 206; Allen M. Howard, 'Mande Kola Traders of Northwestern Sierra Leone, Late 1700s to 1930', *Mande Studies*, 9 (2007), 83–102, at p. 85.

24 Allen M. Howard, 'Trade and Islam in Sierra Leone, 18th–20th Centuries', in Alusine Jalloh and David E. Skinner (eds), *Islam and Trade in Sierra Leone* (Trenton, NJ, 1997), pp. 21–63, at p. 23; Howard, 'Mande Kola', p. 84.

25 *Reports to Secretary of State on Past and Present State of H.M. Colonial Possessions, 1851*, HC 1852, no. 1539, pp. 181–2; *Reports to Secretary of State on Past and Present State of H.M. Colonial Possessions and of the United States of The Ionian Islands, 1847*, HC 1848, no. 1005, p. 198.

frequently acted as trade mediators, Temne, Loko, Limba, and Mende landlords also facilitated regional commerce.[26] Landlords provided a wide array of services, including accommodations, food, livestock care, market intelligence, warehouse space, translation, and short-term credit. In return, they received commissions on their traders' sales.[27]

This landlord-trader relationship was governed not only by proximity but also by linguistic and social familiarity. Dorjahn and Fyfe noted that in the 1840s, when traders arrived in Freetown by canoe, locals would gather around them, and the first person to touch the canoe became the trader's landlord.[28] However, this ignores the importance of shared language and trust. In 1863, Robert Clarke observed that African merchants from surrounding regions held palavers with Freetown merchants and visited their stores before selecting trading partners. Once a relationship was established, landlords were expected to house and feed the traders employing various strategies to prolong their stay.[29] Of the sixty-five inhabitants registered as Fula in the 1831 census, some might have acted as landlords since fifty-six of them were listed as merchants or traders, living with their families. These landlords frequently served as interpreters and facilitators for visiting traders and typically resided in Grassfield 1, near the estuary where canoes arrived. Muslim merchants from Fula Town, Fourah Bay, and surrounding villages established stalls along Kissy Road, close to the harbour.[30]

Landlords' familiarity with Freetown's administrative systems and ability to navigate its social landscape made them indispensable to trade. Mamadoo Yellie, a Mandinka cleric born in Wolof country, arrived in Freetown in 1843 and became a landlord. By the late 1850s, he was employed as a policeman,

26 Howard, 'Trade and Islam', pp. 27–8, 37; David E. Skinner, 'The Influence of Islam in Sierra Leone History: Institutions, Practices, and Leadership', *Journal of West African History*, 2:1 (2016), 27–71, at p. 31; Christopher Fyfe, *A Short History of Sierra Leone* (London, 1979), p. 44.

27 Polly Hill, 'Landlords and Brokers: A West African Trading System (With a Note on Kumasi Butchers)', *Cahiers d'études africaines*, 6: 23 (1966), 349–66, at pp. 350–1; P. Lovejoy, *Caravans*, p. 31; Paul Lovejoy, *Salt of the Desert Sun: A History of Salt Production and Trade in the Central Sudan* (Cambridge, 1986), p. 201; Paul Lovejoy, *Jihād in West Africa during the Age of Revolution* (Athens, 2016), pp. 57–8; V. R. Dorjahn and Christopher Fyfe, 'Landlord and Stranger: Change in Tenancy Relations in Sierra Leone' *Journal of African History*, 3:3 (1962), 391–7, at p. 394; Fyfe, *A Short History*, p. 18.

28 Dorjahn and Fyfe, 'Landlord and Stranger', p. 396.

29 Robert B. Clarke, 'Sketches of the Colony of Sierra Leone and its Inhabitants', *Transactions of the Ethnological Society of London*, 2 (1863), 320–63, p. 328.

30 Gibril Cole, *The Krio of West Africa: Islam, Culture, Creolization, and Colonialism in the Nineteenth Century* (Athens, 2013), p. 99; Barbara E. Harrell-Bond, Allen M. Howard, and David E. Skinner, *Community Leadership and the Transformation of Freetown (1801–1976)* (The Hague, 1978), p. 51.

serving both the colonial administration and the traders he hosted.[31] His dual role illustrates how integration into official structures could enhance a landlord's capacity to support commerce and mediate relationships. Language was central to this function. Koelle, who interviewed two men acknowledging that they acted as landlords, noted that both spoke English fluently, a skill that clearly facilitated trade and strengthened their roles as hosts and intermediaries.

Similar dynamics shaped the labour networks of the Kru, whose migration to Freetown was facilitated by individuals maintaining active ties with their homelands. Kru workers typically operated in organised groups of twenty-five to a hundred men, overseen by a headman responsible for recruitment and discipline along the coast. Young Kru, around thirteen or fourteen years old, were guided by older Kru already working in the colony, especially those who spoke English.[32] As Thomas Coke observed in 1811, English fluency was essential for business, and anyone who could not speak the language was not considered fit to be a chief.[33]

Trading connections in Freetown extended beyond the immediate surroundings, reaching into the interior and linking with the places of origin of 'Liberated Africans'. These individuals maintained strong ties to their homelands and, as some of them became landlords, their networks helped broaden the colony's commercial reach. During interviews for *Polyglotta Africana*, Koelle spoke with 'Liberated Africans' and African immigrants who received visits from relatives and maintained active trade connections. Mohammadu, born in Timbo, the capital of Fuuta Jalon, acted as a trading agent for his countrymen in Freetown. Mahammadu, born in Kaba (Kangaba), south-west of Bamako, traded goods sent by his relatives and served as a broker for fellow Mande traders. Kangaba sat on a major route linking Siguiri and Segou and connected to the Muslim commercial interior via Dinguiraye and Kankan.[34] Other traders, such as Bubu Masare from Masamana in Torong

31 Harrell-Bond, Howard, Skinner, *Community Leadership*, p. 51; Fyfe, *A History*, p. 270; Registration No. 31–2, SLPA, RBF (1857–1860); Registration No. 446, SLPA, RBF (1860–1861).

32 Gunn, *Outsourcing African Labor*, pp. 91–2, 97–9.

33 Thomas Coke, *An Interesting Narrative of a Mission, Sent to Sierra Leone, in Africa, By Methodists, in 1811; To Which is Prefixed, An Account of the Rise, Progress, Disasters, and Present State of that Colony. The Whole Interspersed with a Variety of Remarkable Particulars* (London, 1812), p. 46.

34 Kathryn L. Green, '"Mande Kaba," the Capital of Mali: A Recent Invention?' *History in Africa*, 18 (1991), 127–35; Jan Jansen, 'Habitation and Warfare Strategies in 19th Century Mande – A View from the Kafu', in Allen M. Howard and Richard M. Shain (eds), *The Spatial Factor in African History: The Relationship of the Social, Material, and Perceptual* (Leiden, 2005), pp. 260–89, at pp. 263, 271; Richard L. Roberts, *Warriors, Merchants, and Slaves: The State and the Economy in the Middle Niger Valley, 1700–1914* (Stanford, 1987), p. 62; Howard, 'Mande Kola', p. 90.

country, and John Grey (Fana), who travelled frequently to Vai country, lived in Freetown intermittently while conducting business.[35] These individuals forged links with regions both near, e.g. Timbo, 139 km (86 miles) away, and far, such as Kangaba, 925 km (574 miles) distant.

People in Freetown expanded their trading networks through various channels, some through their roles as landlords, others through leadership positions within migrant labour groups. Muslim communities, in particular, extended their influence by cultivating ties through marriage and religious affiliations with residents of towns along the rivers.[36] In the coastal plains of Sierra Leone and Guinea, trade connections were reinforced not only by religious bonds but also through kinship ties, trade alliances, secret societies, age-grade systems, and other social structures.[37] Marriage served as a strategic tool for economic expansion, as shown in a court case from 1847. A trader from the Scarcies explained that he had married his sister to a long-term resident of Freetown so that his new brother-in-law could trade on his behalf in the colony. He was later able to expand his reach by sending another relative to Freetown to sell wood.[38]

Another kinship-based mechanism that sustained and expanded trade was the institution of wardship, in which children were placed in the care of relatives or trusted associates to strengthen social and commercial ties. Traders frequently hosted wards from their regions of origin, reinforcing connections to home communities while cultivating future intermediaries and traders. Among Muslim families, it was common for boys to be educated by their uncles, a tradition that spanned generations.[39] Comparable arrangements occurred in Freetown, even outside Muslim communities, where family members took responsibility for training and placing children. Lucy Caulker, who lived along the Bompey River, sent her son Thomas Caulker to Freetown, where he was registered on 7 June 1859 to live with Maria Caulker on Horton Street.[40] Thomas was listed as a domestic servant, suggesting that his placement may have been intended to provide access to urban opportunities and future advancement.

35 Sigismund Wilhelm Koelle, *Polyglotta Africana; or A Comparative Vocabulary of Nearly Three Hundred Words and Phrases in more than One Hundred Distinct African Languages* (London, 1854), pp. 2, 3, 17, 18; Lester P. Monts, 'Islam in Liberia', in Ruth M. Stone (ed.), *The Garland Handbook of African Music*, 2nd edn (New York, 2008), pp. 63–87, at p. 63.

36 Howard, 'Trade and Islam', p. 48.

37 Allen Howard, 'The Relevance of Spatial Analysis for African Economic History: The Sierra Leone-Guinea System', *Journal of African History*, 17:3 (1976), 365–88, at p. 374.

38 Karimo, 8 June 1847, SLPA, Police Magistrate Record (1846–1847).

39 Yacine Daddi Addoun and Paul Lovejoy, 'Muhammad Kaba Saghanughu and the Muslim Community of Jamaica', in Paul E. Lovejoy (ed.), *Slavery on the Frontiers of Islam* (Princeton, 2004), p. 201; P. Lovejoy, *Jihād*, pp. 47, 112.

40 Registration No. 92, SLPA, Register of Alien Children (1859).

Although the exact relationship between Lucy and Maria is unclear, Maria may have been Lucy's sister or possibly an older daughter, the arrangement reflects the broader familial logic behind many ward placements.

Education and training from foster parents served clear commercial purposes. As in other European settlements, fostering children created tangible links between coastal merchants and inland communities. Syptine Valentine, a ship carpenter, hosted two boys, William and Buboo, who were sent from their hometown of Port Loko.[41] Valentine relied on their labour to support his trade, thereby strengthening his ties with populations near the forests along the Port Loko Creek and Rokel River. These forests supplied valuable raw materials, especially timber, essential for shipbuilding and repair.[42] Other merchants, such as German trader Theodore Rosenbush and French merchant Charles Brémond, also registered wards in their households. Of 100 children whose places of origin can be traced, 86 came from towns located on rivers, which are key sites for trade and transport. In the 1860s, Rosenbush and fellow merchant Charles Heddle competed for influence along the Melakori and nearby rivers.[43] Five additional children came from Sherbro, a region that connected the Atlantic coast to central forests via river routes. These forests were rich in camwood, a major export commodity for Freetown merchants.[44]

The movement of traders, wards, and labourers, generated increased traffic along the region's rivers. The rivers and tributaries of the upper Guinea coast formed important waterways for local, regional, and long-distance commerce.[45] They supported a dynamic transport system, enabling individuals to travel independently if they owned a canoe or to rent one when needed. Records from the Court Commission for the Recovery of Small Debts (1838–1840) reveal the professional infrastructure surrounding river-based trade with fourteen cases involving canoe rentals, and four concerned lost or damaged canoes. They highlight the informal and sometimes precarious nature of equipment sharing, as well as the embedded social and economic relationships that sustained river transport. They also offer insight into the

41 Philip J. Havik, *Silences and Soundbites: The Gendered Dynamics of Trade and Brokerage in the Pre-Colonial Guinea Bissau Region* (Münster, 2004), p. 139; Registration No. 418, SLPA, RBF (1857–1860); Registration No. 399, SLPA, RBF (1860–1861); Registration No. 47–8, SLPA, Register of Alien Children (1859).

42 Colleen E. Kriger, *Making Money: Life, Death, and Early Modern Trade on Africa's Guinea Coast* (Athens, 2017), p. 182; Everill, '"For the Services"', p. 7; Rodney, *A History*, p. 159.

43 Fyfe, *A History*, p. 339.

44 Rodney, *A History*, p. 158.

45 Gibril R. Cole, 'The History of Sierra Leone', *Oxford Research Encyclopedia of African History* (Oxford, 2021), <https://oxfordre.com/africanhistory/display/10.1093/acrefore/9780190277734.001.0001/acrefore-9780190277734-e-625?rskey=YRgxwo&result=2> [accessed 1 July 2021].

logistics and informal lending practices that underpinned mobility. Ben Coffee rented a canoe from John Wilson for thirty days, suggesting extended use for commercial travel. In another case, Tom Reed lent a canoe that did not belong to him: he had passed on William Weston's canoe to Alexander Grant, who subsequently broke it.[46]

Another option for travel and transport was to hire 'grumettas', maritime labourers who worked along the waterways. In 1851, people identified as 'grumetta' were listed with house servants and predial labourers, who cultivated the land (predial refers to farms and lands).[47] They accounted for 4,121 inhabitants out of a total population of 16,679.[48] Their presence in legal records further illustrates their role in the colonial economy. In the Court Commission for the Recovery of Small Debts, four men claimed wages for working as grumettas, over three-month periods. In separate cases, Jackson Howard, Thomas Davis, and Samuel Wilson each hired Adams J. Burrows as a grumetta to take them to the Nunez River. All three later filed complaints, stating that Burrows failed to return them to Freetown despite having paid for the journey back.[49] Grumettas were not only essential to the movement of goods and people but also embedded in the legal and labour systems of the colony. Their services were widely used, including by villagers who sold produce in town markets. Women from the village of York who cultivated and prepared food reached Freetown by boat. The work of grumettas thus helped sustain a dynamic network of trade and mobility that linked rural production with urban consumption.[50]

Grumettas also transported goods from anchored ships to the shore by canoe. In February 1842, Joseph Reffell, a 'Liberated African' identified as Aku, was brought before the Police Magistrate in Freetown and later tried for placing slave irons aboard the *Ermelinda*, a Brazilian barque, allegedly to secure its conviction. Reffell worked as a canoe man, ferrying goods from

46 John Wilson v. Ben Coffee, 13 October 1838, SLPA, Court of Commission for the Recovery of Small Debts (15 September 1838 – 18 January 1840); Tom Reed v. Alexander Grant, 9 February 1839, SLPA, Court of Commission for the Recovery of Small Debts (15 September 1838 – 18 January 1840).

47 'predial, adj. and n.' *OED Online* (Oxford, 2021), <www.oed.com/view/Entry/149836> [accessed 19 April 2021].

48 Governor Norman William Macdonald to Secretary of State for War and the Colonies, Henry Grey, 3rd Earl Grey, 18 August 1851, SLPA, Governor's Despatches to the Secretary of State (13 July 1851 – 26 December 1851), fol. 64.

49 Jackson Howard v. Adam Burrows, 15 September 1838, SLPA, Court of Commission for the Recovery of Small Debts (15 September 1838 – 18 January 1840); Thomas Davis v. Adam Burrows, 15 September 1838, SLPA, Court of Commission for the Recovery of Small Debts (15 September 1838 – 18 January 1840); Samuel Wilson v. Adam Burrows, 15 September 1838, SLPA, Court of Commission for the Recovery of Small Debts (15 September 1838 – 18 January 1840).

50 E. F. White, 'Creole Women Traders', p. 629.

ships anchored between 100 and 500 yards offshore. Two witnesses called to testify, Thomas Bucknor and Abraham Cole, had been hired by Reffell as grumettas. Bucknor stated that he was hired because he owned a canoe, while Cole explained that his task was to land goods from the *Ermelinda* to the shore using Reffell's canoe.[51]

It is important to recognise that the work and status of grumettas were specific to their local context. Across West Africa, the term referred to individuals of varying social and legal statuses, but within the colony of Sierra Leone, it denoted paid workers associated with trade and maritime labour. The term itself derives from the Portuguese *grumete*, originally a seaman. These individuals could be either free or enslaved. In Lower Senegal, grumettas were African maritime labourers, while in 1792, Royal Navy lieutenant Philip Beaver described them as 'natives who Trade for Europeans in canoes; but is generally applicable to all those who labour, for others, for wages'.[52] In 1793, slave traders H. Jackson and Richard Horrock of the Îles de Los considered grumettas as property.[53] Robert Thorpe wrote in 1815 that, in Sierra Leone, grumettas were 'liberated from slavery as "indented servants"'.[54] In 1848, geographer James Macqueen testified before the Select Committee on the Slave Trade that a grumetta was a domestic slave who could not be sold.[55] Walter Rodney argued that on the upper Guinea coast, a *grumete* was enslaved to a sailor but functioned more as a wage-earner than as chattel.[56]

The term grumetta reflected a distinct labour category tied to trade and maritime activity, which was especially important in Freetown as its economy matured, and its commercial reach extended well beyond the borders of the colony. Grumettas helped facilitate the movement of goods and people, connecting local actors to global trade networks. This interconnectedness is

51 *Report from the Select Committee on the West Coast of Africa; together with the minutes of evidence, appendix, and index. Part I – Report and evidence*, HC 1842, no. 551, pp. 322, 401–10.

52 Kriger, *Making Money*, p. 118; James F. Searing, *West African Slavery and Atlantic Commerce: The Senegal River Valley, 1700–1860* (Cambridge, 1993), p. 95; Walter Rodney, 'African Slavery and Other Forms of Social Oppression on the Upper Guinea Coast in the Context of the Atlantic Slave-Trade', *Journal of African History*, 7:3 (1966), pp. 431–43; Tim Soriano, '"What Rascals!" Perceptions of Free Labor in the Bulama Settlement, 1792–1793', *African Economic History*, 49:1 (2021), 173–91, at pp. 174, 179, 188.

53 Bruce Mouser, 'Shifting the Littoral Frontiers of EurAfrican and African Trade in the Northern Rivers of Sierra Leone, 1794: Opportunities and Challenges from Changing Conditions' (paper presented at Sierra Leone Studies and Liberian Studies Associations Joint Meeting Charleston, South Carolina April 1994), p. 12.

54 Gunn, *Outsourcing African Labor*, p. 60.

55 *Third Report from the Select Committee on the Slave Trade; together with the minutes of evidence, and appendix*, HC 1848, no. 536, p. 190.

56 Rodney, 'African Slavery', p. 438.

evident in the case of Joseph Reffell, noted above, who was accused of placing slave irons aboard a vessel to secure its condemnation, a tactic that enabled ships to be auctioned and repurposed for trade. These condemned ships became valuable assets in the colony's commercial expansion.

More affluent inhabitants, especially European and African European merchants, capitalised on this system. One of the main avenues for building capital were to auction condemned ships at the Courts of Mixed Commission. In the 1820s, merchants such as William Henry Savage and Stephen Gabbidon acquired several of these ships, forging relationships with foreign traders who were barred from bidding directly.[57] On 4 July 1828, Savage purchased the schooner *Esperanza* for £710 on behalf of a Brazilian merchant. William Cole, who served as Commissioner of Appraisal and Sale to the Mixed Commission Court from October 1824 to July 1825, noted that the transaction was conducted in Brazilian dollars and that the ship's papers were issued in the name of a foreigner. This pattern of transnational exchange continued. In 1829, Commodore Collier bought the *Hope*, renamed it *Dallas*, and sold it to Saul Solomons, an Anglo-Jewish merchant based in St Helena. Solomons was part of a broader network of Anglo-Jewish traders with ties to the colony and was one of the largest employers on St Helena, where his shipping and import-export business is still active today.[58]

As Freetown's merchants gained access to maritime assets, they expanded their commercial reach through partnerships with British firms and trade with other European nations. Early on, Macaulay & Babington was the only company with financial capital in London connected to the colony, but by 1838, other firms entered the scene. Scottish merchant Alexander Rae owed his Freetown estate to the London firm Forster and Smith. Matthew Forster, a merchant from the City Chambers, was named executor in Rae's will and tasked with selling the estate to settle outstanding debts.[59] A small number of 'Liberated African' merchants also managed to establish business relationships with British companies.[60] Henry Lumpkin Senior maintained trading agents

57 Padraic X. Scanlan, *Freedom's Debtors: British Antislavery in Sierra Leone in the Age of Revolution* (New Haven, 2017), p. 105; Fyfe, *A History*, p. 196; Leslie Bethell, 'The Mixed Commissions for the Suppression of the Transatlantic Slave Trade in the Nineteenth Century', *Journal of African History*, 7:1 (1966), 79–93, at p. 88.

58 *Charge delivered by Mr. Justice Jeffcott to Grand Jury of Sierra Leone and Correspondence on Slave Trade*, HC 1832, no. 364, pp. 17, 20; Aryo Makko, *European Small States and the Role of Consuls in the Age of Empire* (Leiden, 2019), p. 137; Nigel Browne-Davies, 'Jewry in West Africa', *Transactions of the Historical Society of Ghana*, 19 (2019–2020), 1–60, at p. 15.

59 Will of Alexander Rae, Merchant of Freetown Sierra Leone, West Africa (14 November 1838), TNA, PROB 11/1903/141.

60 Christopher Fyfe, 'Peter Nicholls – Old Calabar and Freetown', *Journal of the Historical Society of Nigeria*, 2:1 (1960), 105–14, at p. 111.

with two London firms and corresponded with them through steam mail.[61] European trade extended beyond Britain: on 29 January 1859, John Mason advertised in *The New Era* for a vessel to transport 240 tons of palm nuts to Marseille, France, a centre of the French soapmaking industry. Rising olive oil prices had increased demand for alternatives such as groundnut and palm oils, driving up the price of groundnuts.[62] Between 1840 and 1850, 16 per cent of the colony's exports went to foreign nations outside Britain, its colonies, or the United States, with France as a leading destination.[63]

The expansion of steamship services opened new commercial routes along the West African coast, allowing merchants to reach distant port cities with greater ease. After British forces bombarded Lagos in 1851, it emerged as a magnet for merchants from the colony of Sierra Leone seeking new opportunities in trade and settlement. Many of these immigrants came from modest backgrounds, yet some had prior ties to British trading firms.[64] Among the most prominent African merchants in Lagos were 'Liberated Africans' and their descendants, such as James Pinson Labulo Davies, whose success was attributed to his personal and professional connections. Born in 1828 in the village of Bathurst to Yoruba parents who had been resettled as 'Liberated Africans', he received training in navigation, took part in the 1851 bombardment under Royal Navy forces, and proceeded to become an influential merchant in Lagos.[65]

Davies's second marriage to Sarah Forbes Bonetta further reflected these elite connections. Born Àìná, she was a Yoruba girl who had been enslaved and 'gifted' to Captain Frederick Forbes by King Ghezo of Dahomey and later raised under the patronage of Queen Victoria. Her story and their wedding in 1862, officiated by the honorary secretary of the C.M.S. in London and attended

61 The African Steamship Company, founded by Scottish shipbuilder Macgregor Laird in 1852, sent regular mail steamers to West Africa with low fares to encourage Africans to do business with Britain. The Company operated seven steamships and carried mail, cargo, and passengers from Liverpool to ports between Freetown and Fernando Po. In 1856, it extended its traffic to London. See: John Flint, 'Laird, Macgregor (1808–1861), Shipbuilder and Explorer', *Oxford Dictionary of National Biography* (Oxford, 2004), <www.oxforddnb.com/view/10.1093/ref:odnb/9780198614128.001.0001/odnb-9780198614128-e-15895> [accessed 2 December 2020].

62 Adam Rovner, *The Jew Who Would Be King: A True Story of Shipwreck, Survival, and Scandal in Victorian Africa* (Oakland, 2025), p. 193.

63 *Reports to Secretary of State on Past and Present State of H.M. Colonial Possessions, 1850*, HC 1851, no. 1421 (London, 1851), pp. 168, 172.

64 Fyfe, 'Peter Nicholls', 105–14; Kristin Mann, *Slavery and the Birth of an African City: Lagos, 1760–1900* (Bloomington, 2007), p. 124.

65 Antony Hopkins, *Capitalism in the Colonies: African Merchants in Lagos, 1851–1931* (New Haven, 2024), pp. 135–46; Henry B. Lovejoy, *Becoming Sarah Forbes Bonetta: A Yorùbá Woman in Queen Victoria's Court* (Toronto, 2026).

Figure 5.1 Portrait of James Pinson Labulo Davies and Sarah Forbes Bonetta. Source: Camille Silvy, James Pinson Labulo Davies; Sarah Forbes Bonetta (Sarah Davies), albumen print, 15 September 1862, NPG Ax61382, © National Portrait Gallery, London.

by Samuel Ajayi Crowther, drew considerable attention in the British press.[66] The portrait of the couple by Camille Silvy, commissioned by Queen Victoria, underscores both their elevated social standing and the visibility of African elites within Victorian society. Silvy further attests to their elevated status and the visibility of African elites in Victorian circles (Figure 5.1). While their story highlights the remarkable reach of merchants, it is highly unrepresentative of the broader population.

J. P. L. Davies was part of a larger group of Saro migrants discussed in Chapter 4, who rose to prominence as the commercial elite of Lagos in the mid-nineteenth century. As some sailed back to their home communities around Badagry, they petitioned the colonial government to establish a settlement that would support their trading ambitions. Others moved to Egba land, where the rise of Abeokuta and Christian missions opened new avenues for economic and social integration.[67] In Lagos, their cultural familiarity, combined with fluency in English, Christian affiliations, and extensive social networks, gave them a distinct edge over other traders. These attributes also granted them privileged access to colonial institutions. Many applied for crown grants, official documents signed by the Governor that validated land claims. J. P. L. Davies secured such grants in the early 1860s, enabling him to obtain credit and expand his trading operations.[68] Two other prominent examples of this Saro merchant class are the George and Doherty families. James George (also known as Osoba), son of Thomas (Masinka), an Egba 'Liberated African', relocated to

66 Mann, *Slavery*, p. 125; Joan Anim-Addo, 'Bonetta [married name Davies] (Ina) Sarah Forbes [Sally] (c. 1843–1880), Queen Victoria's ward', *Oxford Dictionary of National Biography* (Oxford, 2015) <www.oxforddnb.com/view/10.1093/ref:odnb/9780198614128.001.0001/odnb-9780198614128-e-75453> [accessed 2 December 2020]; Henry Lovejoy 'Queen Victoria's "Liberated African": Sarah "Sally" Forbes Bonetta and Her Extraordinary Apprenticeship by the British Royal Family, 1850–1862', *Slavery & Abolition* (2024), 911–34; Hopkins, *Capitalism*, p. 136; Lovejoy, *Becoming Sarah*.

67 Olatunji Ojo, 'Amazing Struggle: Dasalu, Global Yoruba Networks, and the Fight against Slavery, 1851–1856', *Atlantic Studies*, 12:1 (2015), 5–25, at p. 7; Bronwen Everill, 'Bridgeheads of Empire? Liberated African Missionaries in West Africa', *The Journal of Imperial and Commonwealth History*, 40:5 (2012), 789–805; Fyfe, *A History*, p. 212.

68 Antony Hopkins, 'Property Rights and Empire Building: Britain's Annexation of Lagos, 1861', *The Journal of Economic History*, 40:4 (1980), 777–98, at pp. 785, 792; Kristin Mann, *Marrying Well: Marriage, Status and Social Change among the Educated Elite in Colonial Lagos* (Cambridge, 1985), p. 19; Mann, *Slavery*, p. 252; David Lishilinimle Imbua, 'From Captives to Heroes: Liberated Africans in Calabar, 1850–1920', in Vanicléia Silva Santos (ed.) *General History of Africa*, vol. X, *Africa and its Diasporas* (Paris, 2023), p. 989; Ndubueze L. Mbah, 'The Black Englishmen of Old Calabar: Freedom and Mobility in the Age of Abolition in West Africa', *Radical History Review* 144 (2022), 45–75; Hopkins, *Capitalism*, p. 22; Kristin Mann, 'Marriage Choices among the Educated African Elite in Lagos Colony, 1880–1915', *The International Journal of African Historical Studies*, 14:2 (1981), 201–28.

the colony village of Hastings and was educated in Freetown. By the mid-1850s, he had become the Lagos agent for merchant William Lewis and established a substantial business, including operating ships between Freetown and Lagos.[69] William Doherty, from Ilaro, was relocated to Freetown by the Royal Navy in 1826. By 1855, he had moved to Lagos with his family. Already married and with a son born in Freetown, Doherty became a C.M.S. agent at Isaga, further embedding himself, and later his descendants, into the region's intertwined religious and commercial networks. These families, and the broader Saro elite, are explored in detail in A. G. Hopkins's *Capitalism in the Colony*.[70]

'Liberated Africans' sometimes achieved commercial success through the support of missionary networks, English literacy, and strategic relocations across West Africa. These efforts also aligned with British missionary goals. Peter Nicholls, a 'Liberated African' from Old Calabar, benefited from such support in developing his palm oil trade. In 1853, Reverend Edward Jones of the C.M.S. requested permission from local leaders in Old Calabar for Kalabari 'Liberated Africans' to resettle in the region. After approval was granted, the first group arrived in October 1854, with Nicholls following soon after to establish his commercial presence.[71]

For missionaries, facilitating these returns served both religious and economic aims since it reinforced Christian influence while enabling trusted intermediaries to anchor trade in familiar territories. In places like Calabar, local leaders such as Eyo Honesty II welcomed 'Liberated Africans', viewing their British colonial background as an asset to business. They were perceived as intermediaries between African and European spheres, and sometimes even as white or European themselves. However, not all regions responded positively. Resettlement proposals met resistance in Igboland and Bonny, where 'Liberated Africans' were seen more as outsiders than contributors to local trade.[72]

Because of their commercial importance and wide-reaching networks, European and 'Liberated African' merchants in Freetown were not only central to the economy but also increasingly influential in shaping colonial policy. Seeking to represent their interests, they founded the Mercantile Association in 1851, a body first proposed by Savage and Gabbidon in 1827. The Association became a platform for lobbying colonial authorities, with members regularly submitting petitions to the government. In the mid-1850s, when the Liberian government laid claim to the Gallinas and the territory north of it, the Association protested the recognition of this claim, aiming to

69 Hopkins, *Capitalism*, p. 93.

70 Ibid, p. 363.

71 Fyfe, 'Peter Nicholls', pp. 109–10.

72 Mbah, 'The Black Englishmen', p. 51; Imbua, 'From Captives to Heroes', p. 989; Hopkins, *Capitalism*, pp. 21–2.

preserve the area for British trade.[73] Other petitions focused on trade regulations, such as on bonds of imports. On 6 July 1851, Governor Macdonald forwarded a memorandum from the mercantile community to Henry Grey, Secretary of State, advocating for the removal of bonds on goods intended for local consumption, a change Macdonald himself supported.[74] Beyond trade, the Mercantile Association also sought political reform. In 1858, fifty-seven members, all men, petitioned the government for a new constitution that would establish an elected House of Assembly.[75] By demanding greater representation, they challenged the limitations of Freetown's status as a Crown colony, contrasting it with the autonomy enjoyed by self-governing colonies.[76]

While merchants in Freetown were advocating for greater political representation, they were also actively involved in diplomatic negotiations beyond the colony. In 1852, Governor Macdonald appointed Dillet (from the Secretary's office), Denniss (an assistant staff surgeon), and Isaacs (a merchant) to conclude treaties with leaders in the Small and Great Scarcies, north of present-day Sierra Leone.[77] The kola trade in this region opened new commercial links between Freetown and the upper Niger, as juula traders from Segou, Sikasso, and Dinguiraye brought cattle to Freetown and exchanged goods for kola in the Scarcies. Juula were long-distance traders, typically Mande-speaking Muslims, but the term also refers to diverse groups of small- and medium-scale traders

73 Fyfe, *A History*, pp. 259, 307–8.

74 Governor Norman William Macdonald to Secretary of State for War and the Colonies, Henry Grey, 3rd Earl Grey, 6 July 1851, SLPA, Governor's despatches to the Secretary of State (22 April 1851 – 17 July 1851), fol. 91–2.

75 Fyfe, 'Peter Nicholls', p. 112; Governor Hill, Nos 1 to 118, Enclosure in despatch No. 29, Governor Stephen Hill to Secretary of State for War and the Colonies, Henry Labouchere, 17 February 1858, TNA, CO 267/260, 1858, Sierra Leone, vol. 1, January to June.

76 Despite its commercial influence, the Mercantile Association was not a cohesive body and was formally dissolved in December 1863. Its membership was predominantly European but included several prominent 'Liberated Africans', such as Peter Nicholls, John Ezzidio, William Henry Pratt, Isaac Benjamin Pratt, and Henry Lumpkin Senior. By the time of its dissolution, the Association counted 39 members: 14 Europeans, 24 Africans (either immigrants or 'Liberated'), and one African Caribbean man, Charles Hazelborg. Some members did not reside in the colony, including James Burnet, who had left Freetown by 1852, and D. H. Davison, who was based in the Melakori River, both of whom signed the 1858 petition advocating for a House of Assembly. See: Fyfe, *A History*, pp. 269, 319; Fyfe, 'Peter Nicholls', pp. 111–12.

77 Executive no. 137, Governor Norman William Macdonald to Secretary of State for War and the Colonies, Henry Grey, 3rd Earl Grey, 7 August 1851, SLPA, Governor's despatches to the Secretary of States (13 July 1851 – 26 December 1851), fol. 2–7.

who operated within the Sierra Leone–Guinea plain, trading kola, cattle, cloth, and other commodities.[78]

John McCormack, who had traded along the coast since 1808 and settled in Sierra Leone in 1816, was also sent to negotiate with rulers such as Sorin Caesey at the Rokel River.[79] In 1857, Governor Stephen Hill invited McCormack and Charles Heddle, one of Freetown's wealthiest merchants and the son of a Scottish man and an African woman from Gorée, to hold palavers with Temne leaders in Port Loko and Magbeli.[80] By the mid-1850s, Magbeli was emerging as a major commercial centre, eventually surpassing Port Loko in importance by the 1860s.[81] These four-day negotiations had multiple aims, from recognising the authority of the new Alikali of Port Loko, to securing customs for the timber trade, demanding the surrender of criminals from the colony of Sierra Leone, exempting duties, and ending human sacrifice in Temne country.[82] McCormack and Heddle were accompanied by a formal deputation, including lieutenants from the W.I.R., commissariat staff, a military guard, and a militia band.

Merchants' commercial experience and regional knowledge also made them valuable for gathering intelligence. During the Kossoh War (1838–41) – which erupted between Mohammadu Bundu's district in Koya Temne and En Kerry, leader of the Kpa Mende – merchant John McCormack was despatched by John Carr, the Queen's Advocate, to report on the conflict. En Kerry had recruited Mende 'Liberated Africans' living in Koya to fight against the Temne, and by the war's end, those 'Liberated Africans' were expelled from the region. When some returned to retrieve cassava from their farms, they were attacked, and

78 Rodney, *A History*, p. 206; Howard, 'Mande Kola', p. 90; Allen M. Howard, Cross-Boundary Traders in the Era of High Imperialism: Changing Structures and Strategies in the Sierra Leone-Guinea Region', *Journal of Urban Research*, 10 (2014) <https://journals.openedition.org/articulo/2535> [accessed 25 April 2026].

79 Fyfe, *A History*, pp. 125–6, 286.

80 Maeve Ryan, 'A "Very Extensive System of Peculation and Jobbing": The Liberated African Department of Sierra Leone, Humanitarian Governance and the Fraud Inquiry of 1848', *Journal of Colonialism & Colonial History*, 17:3 (2016), <https://doi.org/10.1353/cch.2016.0041> [accessed 25 April 2026]; George E. Brooks, 'Peanuts and Colonialism: Consequences of the Commercialization of Peanuts in West Africa 1830–1870', *Journal of African History*, 16:1 (1975), 29–54, at p. 48; Fyfe, *A Short History*, p. 56; Christopher Fyfe, *Sierra Leone Inheritance* (London, 1964), p. 183; Governor Stephen Hill to Secretary of State for War and the Colonies, Henry Labouchere, 12 March 1857, SLPA, Governor's despatches to the Secretary of States (7 February 1857 – 30 June 1857), fol. 13–16.

81 E. Ade Ijagbemi, 'A History of the Temne in the Nineteenth Century' (Unpublished PhD dissertation, University of Edinburgh, 1968), pp. 78, 104, 159.

82 Hill to Labouchere, 12 March 1857, SLPA, Governor's despatches to the Secretary of State (7 February 1857 – 30 June 1857), fol. 13–16; 'Laws and Treaties', Liberated Africans database, <https://liberatedafricans.org/databases/source_details_AL.php?ObjectID=337> [accessed 4 September 2023].

Figure 5.2 Map of Sierra Leone and its surrounding areas.
Source: Courtesy of Henry B. Lovejoy, African Diaspora Maps Ltd., <www.hlovejoy.wordpress.com/maps-2/> [accessed 26 January 2021], (open access).

six were captured by Temne warriors. McCormack, whose familiarity with the region stemmed from years of trading voyages, was later joined by G. W. Nicol, manager at Waterloo, to conduct a full investigation.[83]

Yet merchants were not always neutral actors. In some cases, they contributed to local tensions. A paper included in the 1842 report of the Select Committee on the West Coast of Africa, written by Sir John Jeremie, described

83 Adeleye Ijagbemi, 'The Kossoh War 1838–41: A Study in Temne/Colony Relations in the Nineteenth Century', *Journal of the Historical Society of Nigeria*, 5:4 (1971), 549–64, at pp. 557–8.

a conflict between two men from the colony (Atkins, a former storekeeper, and Marquis Granby, a retired soldier), who were trading timber near the Rio Pongo. Though details were limited, both men reportedly mobilised armed supporters. Atkins was backed by a local chief, while Granby recruited men from his own social circle. The dispute escalated until Bey Fokey, the ruler in the area, intervened to resolve it.[84]

Beyond formal diplomacy, merchants also played an important part in shaping British abolitionist efforts. Their commercial activities supported the transition from slave-based economies to agricultural exports, and colonial governors relied on their regional connections to negotiate treaties and expand legitimate trade.[85] In 1847, Governor Macdonald consulted with influential merchants before endorsing trade initiatives with Cape Mount.[86] By 1851, he praised the groundnut trade between colony merchants and neighbouring territories as a means of 'extinguishing the slave trade' by providing steady employment to local populations.[87] These developments mirror broader trends in the nineteenth century, as British officials intensified abolitionist efforts and negotiated treaties with African leaders. Rulers from Muslim states sent official trading delegations to British colonial authorities as Freetown was the centre of Britain's negotiations for its abolitionist campaign.[88] Local leaders agreed to end the slave trade, keep paths and waterways open for commerce, and avoid warfare.[89] As Trina Hogg argues, treaties offered protection amid ongoing regional conflicts over land and labour. Because commercial interests were shaped by these conflicts, alliances with Britain emerged as a strategic means of securing military protection.[90] Many of these treaties are now accessible through Henry Lovejoy's Anti-Slavery Legislation digital archive.[91]

84 *Report*, HC 1842, no. 551, p. 288.

85 Suzanne Schwarz, '"A Just and Honourable Commerce": Abolitionist Experimentation in Sierra Leone in the Late Eighteenth and Early Nineteenth Century', *African Economic History*, 45:1 (2017), 1–45, at pp. 1–4.

86 Governor Norman William Macdonald to Secretary of State for War and the Colonies, Henry Grey, 3rd Earl Grey, Registration No. 59, 8 May 1847, SLPA, Governor's despatches to the Secretary of State (2 October 1846 – 12 September 1847).

87 Governor Norman William Macdonald to Secretary of State for War and the Colonies, Henry Grey, 3rd Earl Grey, 18 August 1851, SLPA, Governor's Despatches to the Secretary of State (13 July 1851 – 26 December 1851), fol. 21.

88 Howard, 'Trade and Islam', p. 24.

89 J. J. Crooks, *A History of the Colony of Sierra Leone, West Africa* (London and Dublin, 1903), p. 182.

90 Trina Leah Hogg, *The Paradox of Protection: The Making of Indirect Rule in Southern Sierra Leone, 1850–1915* (East Lansing, 2026).

91 Henry Lovejoy, Liberated Africans database, <https://liberatedafricans.org/databases/laws-and-treaties.php> [accessed 18 September 2023].

Despite Freetown's role as a centre of British abolitionist policy, slave trafficking persisted through local and regional networks that shaped both the colony's social landscape and its legal system. A parliamentary inquiry in 1853 revealed that 117 individuals were enslaved in the colony, and court records show that trafficking was actively prosecuted.[92] Formerly enslaved individuals and witnesses appeared before the police magistrate to accuse residents of participating in the illegal trade, exposing the continuity of these networks. Dorah, Bocaree, Harry Doctor, Jack Davis, Tom, and William Davis testified about their experiences. All of them, except Jack Davis, were sent to locations north of the colony, with Dorah sent to Melakori, Harry Doctor to Rio Pongo, Tom to Candia near Forekaria, and William Davis to Forekaria. Jack Davis was sent to the Shebar Straits and later to the Gallinas. Other inhabitants were kidnapped from the Northern Rivers, such as Nunez and Small Scarcies, or from Koya country, including Magbeli and Robureh. Some testimonies did not specify the place of capture but confirmed that victims were trafficked to the Small Scarcies, Rio Pongo, and Port Loko. As Fyfe noted, slave traders had long been established in the Melakori and Bereira Rivers, the Pongo and Nunez Rivers, and in Sherbro and Gallinas, and regularly came to Freetown to trade.[93] By the 1850s, slave trade linking Sierra Leone to groundnut plantations along the upper Guinea coast peaked. Merchants, especially Muslims, transported enslaved Africans from southern Sierra Leone to plantations near the Northern Rivers.[94]

The persistence of slave trafficking in Freetown was further complicated by the expansion of Portuguese trade along the West African coast. Harry Doctor, Alee Barga, and Bocarry were taken to Rio Pongo, a major slaving port from where twenty-six slave ships departed between 1830s and 1860s.[95] On 23 August 1847, Harry Doctor testified that he had lived at Rio Pongo

92 Sean Kelley, 'Enslavement in Upper Guinea during the Era of the Transatlantic Slave Trade: Biographical Perspectives', *African Economic History*, 48:1 (2020), 46–73; Governor Kennedy No 1 to 60, Despatch no. 49, Arthur E. Kennedy to The Duke of Newcastle, 14 March 1853, TNA, CO 267/231, Sierra Leone 1853, vol. 1, Jan. to March; William Davis, 7 December 1839, SLPA, Police Magistrate Record (27 February 1839 – 10 January 1840); Tom, 7 December 1839, SLPA, Police Magistrate Record (27 February 1839 – 10 January 1840); Jack Davis, 9 April 1839, SLPA, Police Magistrate Record (27 February 1839 – 10 January 1840); Bocaree and Dorah v. Karimo, 8 June 1847, SLPA, Police Magistrate Record (31 December 1846 – 18 September 1847); Harry Doctor, 23 August 1847, SLPA, Police Magistrate Record (31 December 1846 – 18 September 1847).

93 Christopher Fyfe, 'European and Creole Influences in the Interior of Sierra Leone before 1896', *Sierra Leone Studies*, 6 (1956), 113–23, at pp. 114–16.

94 Philip Misevich, *Abolition and the Transformation of Atlantic Commerce in Southern Sierra Leone, 1790s to 1860s* (Trenton, 2019), pp. 157–9, 169–75.

95 Slave Voyages database <www.slavevoyages.org/voyages/MIpzh3TV> [accessed 27 April 2021].

for five months before being placed aboard the Portuguese brigantine *Lebro*, which was captured by the British sloop *Sealark* on 7 August and condemned on 30 August. Doctor was later registered as number 79,897 in the Registers of Liberated Africans.[96] William Reffell, another formerly enslaved individual, was trafficked from further afield. He left Freetown in April 1844 to seek education for his child in Badagry, accompanied by Thomas Parker, a Yoruba acquaintance from the colony of Sierra Leone. In a town near Lagos ruled by a man named Alotto, Parker sold Reffell to Alotto, who then took him to a coastal site called 'Meddoo, where Portuguese people put slave on board ship'. Reffell boarded the Portuguese schooner *Emprendedora* in July 1847, which was intercepted by the British sloop *Grappler* in the Bight of Benin and condemned on 21 August.[97]

Slave trafficking in the colony of Sierra Leone was sustained through personal and familial networks. A series of cases compiled in 1853 and forwarded to the Secretary of State in London reveal how relatives collaborated in the capture, sale, and exchange of enslaved individuals. In March 1852, Moosah Yarankee of Bambara Town agreed to lend Saranako $25 only in exchange for an enslaved girl. Three months later, it was Saranako's brother, Boccari, who brought two enslaved girls from Port Loko to Freetown. Around the same time, Maligeah Seelah of Gibraltar Town purchased a girl named Buoye, and his brother, Sanasee Seelah, proposed to exchange Buoye for Yeara, an enslaved boy he owned.[98] The case of Bocaree, recorded in the police magistrate's records, further illustrates the role of family connections in slave trafficking networks. Bocaree was sold by his brother-in-law, Karimo, and later testified that Sadoo, one of the men aboard the canoe that transported him to Leopard Island, was Karimo's brother.[99]

Conclusion

Family, religion, and ethnic affiliations shaped trade and business networks within and beyond Freetown. These social structures helped residents navigate an unfamiliar environment structured around forced relocation, colonial

96 Harry Doctor, 23 August 1847, SLPA, Police Magistrate Record (31 December 1846 – 18 September 1847); Liberated Africans database, <https://liberatedafricans.org/databases/event_details.php?EventID=3542> [accessed 11 February 2026].

97 William Reffell, 23 August 1847, SLPA, Police Magistrate Record (31 December 1846 – 18 September 1847); Liberated Africans database, <https://liberatedafricans.org/databases/event_details.php?EventID=3538> [accessed 11 February 2026].

98 Governor Kennedy No 1 to 60, Despatch no. 49, Arthur E. Kennedy to The Duke of Newcastle, 14 March 1853, TNA, CO 267/231, Sierra Leone 1853, vol. 1, Jan. to March.

99 Karimo, 8 June 1847, SLPA, Police Magistrate Record (31 December 1846 – 18 September 1847).

oversight, as well as around abolitionist and capitalist ideals. All members of society contributed to economic life: for instance, children supported family enterprises within Freetown and, through wardship arrangements, helped forge connections with distant regions. Some traders extended their networks by travelling to reconnect with home communities and establish new commercial ties, while others remained in Freetown and acted as landlords, hosting and supporting newcomers from across West Africa. Freetown's commercial landscape was influenced by early British involvement on the upper Guinea coast, with Royal Navy patrols and the resettlement of thousands of 'Liberated Africans'. Yet the colony did not exist in isolation. Slave trafficking persisted in hidden forms, sustained by kinship networks and informal exchanges that operated beyond the reach of official scrutiny. Some 'Liberated Africans' endured multiple episodes of enslavement, revealing the fragile boundaries between freedom and captivity. These experiences point to an entangled web of commerce, kinship, and migration, connecting Freetown not only to its immediate hinterland but also to interior villages, coastal trading centres, and transatlantic networks. Trade was never confined to official channels since it was embedded in everyday relationships, shaped by personal histories, and sustained through both visible and underground routes.

6

The Public Sphere and Cultural Expression

Freetown was a multicultural society, home to people from across the Atlantic world, including West Africa, West Central Africa, North America, the Caribbean, and Europe. Communities there formed around shared social, cultural, religious, and ethnic identities, preserving customs from their places of origin. As individuals continued to practise customs from their homeland, British administrators tried to impose their own institutions and Victorian values of religion and morality. This chapter evaluates the cultural diversity of Freetown by scrutinising aspects of public and community life. It examines the extent to which Christianity and British Victorian values, Islam, and the cultural traditions of the Akan, Kru, Temne, Yoruba, and others influenced public identity and shaped social interactions beyond the boundaries of home and work. While previous chapters examined family structures and professional life, this chapter builds on that foundation by turning to the shared public spaces where diverse communities engage with one another. It begins by highlighting the roles of language and names in public life, before looking at Christianity and Islam, to underscore the role of religion in public expression. These two monotheistic traditions were not the only sources of identity, so other practices are evaluated, such as local initiation societies. Yoruba traditions expressed in the public sphere are analysed given the significant number of Yoruba among 'Liberated Africans' and their descendants. Finally, court records provide insight into public spaces and social practices, including night-time dancing, gambling, and other forms of recreation.

Language was one of the first factors that contributed to shaping communities in Freetown – a society where, according to Koelle, more than one hundred languages were spoken.[1] People arrived speaking their native tongues, or languages they had been exposed to earlier and shared, for example Arabic among members of the Muslim community. Language influenced broad social relations in public spaces. David Northrup notes, however, that a common language only produced meaningful communities when there were large

1 Sigismund Wilhelm Koelle, *Polyglotta Africana; or A Comparative Vocabulary of Nearly Three Hundred Words and Phrases in more than One Hundred Distinct African Languages* (London, 1854).

numbers of speakers.[2] This shaped the strength of social bonds in public life, and had consequences on the feeling of alienation, as explained in Chapter 2. Evidence of this is shown in Koelle's interviews for *Polyglotta Africana*. He interviewed eighty-six inhabitants asking whether any other inhabitant spoke the same language. Of these, fifty reported knowing at least one other person who shared their language. Forty-two respondents gave figures ranging from two to one hundred. Among them, twenty-four individuals had fewer than ten countrymen or countrywomen in the colony, seventeen had between ten and fifty, and three had over a hundred. Eight others replied with vague terms such as 'a few', 'many', or 'a great many'.[3]

Just as language provided a framework for community formation, naming practices offered a marker of identity in public life. In the 1831 census, of the 3,381 individuals listed as 'Liberated Africans', 2,618 bore Christian names, most commonly John (397), William (209), Mary (211), Nancy (146), and Hannah (124). These five names alone accounted for 32 per cent of the population and were typically assigned by missionaries rather than chosen by the individuals themselves. In contrast, children born in Freetown were typically named by their parents, and the majority still received Christian names. Of the 614 children born between 1857 and 1862 whose parents were both listed, 530 had Christian names. While familiar names such as John, William, and Mary remained popular, more distinctive biblical names such as Obadiah, Micah, and Zephaniah also appeared.

The presence of a Christian name did not necessarily indicate adherence to Christian beliefs or practices. Christian names were sometimes the result of namesaking, a tradition found in both European and African cultures. Among Maroon and Nova Scotian settlers, 'Liberated Africans', African immigrants, and discharged soldiers, it was common to name children after relatives, particularly fathers. Maroon Herbert William and Nova Scotian Abraham Hazeley were named after their fathers, and 'Liberated African' Samuel Gote gave his own name to his son. African immigrant Quick Wilson and discharged soldier John Moore also named their sons after themselves.[4] Among the Temne, it was customary to name the firstborn child after the father or a paternal relative, and the second after the mother or a maternal relative.[5]

African traditions are also traced in other naming practices. Some Akan people named children according to the day of the week on which they were

2 David Northrup, 'Becoming African: Identity Formation among Liberated Slaves in Nineteenth-Century Sierra Leone', *Slavery and Abolition*, 27:1 (2006), 1–21, at p. 9.

3 Ibid., p. 19; Koelle, *Polyglotta Africana*.

4 Census of Population and liberated Africans, 1831, TNA, CO 267/111, fol. 262, 304, 350, 359, 368.

5 Jerome S. Handler and JoAnn Jacoby, 'Slave Names and Naming in Barbados, 1650–1830', *The William and Mary Quarterly*, 53:4 (1996), 685–728, at p. 711.

born. In the 1831 census, seven male residents were named Quashie, a name given to boys born on a Sunday. Quashie also appeared as a surname for five individuals in the census and one father in the birth registers. The name Phibah, meaning someone born on a Friday in Akan, illustrates how African naming traditions could be obscured or altered in colonial contexts. In some instances, a name that appears Christian might not reflect Christian affiliation at all. Phoebe is commonly associated with Christian naming, but it can originate from the Akan name Phibah. In colonial Barbados, clerks misunderstood or resisted recording African names, substituting them with familiar Christian ones. Phibah was frequently recorded as Phoebe in official documents, though this substitution was not always consistent.[6] Cheryll Ann Cody notes that on the Ball plantations in South Carolina during the eighteenth and nineteenth centuries, Phoebe was used for several children, yet none were born on a Friday. In Freetown, the connection to Akan naming traditions may have persisted. Of the four children named Phoebe in the birth registers, two were born on Fridays, 18 May 1860 and 16 May 1862, indicating that these names could have been derived from Phibah rather than chosen for their Christian connotation.[7]

Names served as visible indicators of religious affiliation, and Muslim names were a clear expression of Islamic identity in the public sphere. Between 1857 and 1862, the births of forty-four children born to Muslim fathers were registered in Freetown. Of these, only four had European names, while the remaining forty bore Muslim names such as Fatmata, Foday, Mamadoo, and Muhamadu. These names signalled not only religious belonging but also cultural continuity, distinguishing Muslim families within a diverse and multi-faith society. The case of Thomas Ansummana, born in 1859 to William and Harriet Coker, underscores this layered nature of identity.[8] His name combined Thomas, a Christian name, with Ansummana, a name of Mandinka and Muslim origin.

This duality reveals how individuals navigated multiple cultural worlds, adopting names that aligned with colonial expectations while preserving African and religious heritage.[9] Inhabitants reclaimed their identities by

6 Ibid., pp. 697, 712.

7 Ibid., p. 700; Cheryll Ann Cody, 'There Was No "Absalom" on the Ball Plantations: Slave-Naming Practices in the South Carolina Low Country, 1720–1865', *American Historical Review*, 92:3 (1987), 563–96, p. 583; Registration No. 27, SLPA, RBF (1860–1861); Registration No. 353, SLPA, RBF (1861–1862).

8 Registration No. 95, SLPA, RBF (1861–1862).

9 Richard Anderson, Alex Borucki, Daniel Domingues da Silva, David Eltis, Paul Lachance, Philip Misevich, and Olatunji Ojo, 'Using African Names to Identify the Origins of Captives in the Transatlantic Slave Trade: Crowd-Sourcing and the Registers of Liberated Africans, 1808–1862', *History in Africa*, 40:1 (2013), 165–91, at p. 185.

giving their children a Christian first name and an African 'house name' as a second name. These house names were rooted in ethnic traditions, Akan, Ibo, Hausa, Yoruba, and others, and served as markers of cultural continuity within families.[10] Such naming practices were part of a broader pattern in which individuals maintained both public and private identities. Oftentimes, Christian names were used in official contexts but abandoned in private life. Women who married upon disembarkation were given Christian names, yet many ceased using them once settled.[11] Of the eighty-six individuals interviewed by Sigismund Koelle, seventy-four provided both their European and African names. As examples, African immigrant John W. Manuel was also known as Bentu and 'Liberated African' George Bailey was called Bira.[12] A similar dynamic was noted by Gwendolyn Midlo Hall in French Louisiana, where enslaved Africans used both their European and African names.[13]

In the public sphere, religious identity was communicated through visible and material expressions of faith. For Christians, memorialisation practices served as prominent public declarations of religious identity. Graveyards and church interiors featured inscriptions that not only honoured the deceased but also reinforced communal aspirations of salvation.[14] These inscriptions emphasised religious devotion and church membership, highlighting the central role of Christianity in public and civic life. The memorial of Henry Lumpkin Senior at Circular Road Cemetery records that he was 'for over 30 years a faithful member in connection with Samaria Chapel U.M.F.C.' (the United Methodist Free Church). The chapel itself was founded in 1844 by Anthony O'Connor, a 'Liberated African' from Dahomey.[15] Likewise, John Ezzidio, a prominent 'Liberated African' figure, requested in his 1868 will that a marble tablet be erected at Wesley Chapel listing his civic roles, thereby linking his public service to his religious identity.[16] Other memorials, such as

10 C. Magbaily Fyle, 'The Yoruba Diaspora in Sierra Leone's Krio Society', in Toyin Falola and Matt D. Childs (eds), *Yoruba Diaspora in the Atlantic World* (Bloomington, 2005), pp. 366–82, at pp. 378–9.

11 Maeve Ryan, '"It Was Necessary to do Something with Those Women": Colonial Governance and the "Disposal" of Women and Girls in Early Nineteenth-Century Sierra Leone', *Gender & History*, 35 (2021), 491–510, at p. 498.

12 Koelle, *Polyglotta Africana*, pp. 1, 19.

13 Gwendolyn Midlo Hall, *Africans in Colonial Louisiana: The Development of Afro-Creole Culture in the Eighteenth Century* (Baton Rouge, 1992), p. 166.

14 Sarah Tarlow, *Bereavement and Commemoration: An Archaeology of Mortality* (Oxford, 1999), p. 138.

15 Memorial to Henry Lumpkin, Circular Road Cemetery, Freetown, Sierra Leone, 25 April 1877. University of Hull, Remember Me project; Christopher Fyfe, *A History of Sierra Leone* (Oxford, 1962), p. 233.

16 The Will of John Ezzidio, 18 December 1872, Principal Registry of Her Majesty's Court of Probate, *Find A Will* <www.probatesearch.service.gov.uk/Calendar?surname=Ezzidio&yearOfDeath=1872&page=3#calendar> [accessed 23 April 2021].

those of John Taylor, Isaac Benjamin Pratt, and William Henry Pratt, included Bible verses, while Henry Benjamin Cummings, Nancy Bishop, and Sally Taylor were commemorated as devoted members of specific congregations.[17] Christopher Fyfe observed that 'Liberated Africans' were particularly receptive to missionary teachings, interpreting their emancipation as a form of divine salvation.[18] Christianity offered a new source of solace and a framework through which to navigate and survive within an unfamiliar society. Samuel Ajayi Crowther's writing published in the *Church Missionary Record* in October 1837, described the day of his own captivity as a 'blessed' one, since it ultimately led him to the service of Christ.[19]

Religion was a guiding authority, framing public identity, social behaviour, and community life. Missionaries emphasised education as a means of strengthening and expanding their communities. Schools were attached to church buildings, serving as classrooms during the week and places of worship on Sundays. At institutions such as the Grammar School and Fourah Bay College, missionaries taught Latin, the Scripture, and Bible history.[20] Through these missionary schools, the colonial government sought to convert and instruct Africans in what were regarded as European values. Christianity was closely bound to colonial authority and the moral vision promoted by British administrators. Missionaries established churches that became central institutions, not only to worship but also to education, moral instruction, and community organisation. Much of daily life revolved around the church, which became a foundation for identity and social cohesion.[21]

Many of the children from outside the colony, referred to as 'alien' children, attended Christian schools such as the Methodist Huntingdonian schools, government schools, and those subsidised by the C.M.S. (Table 6.1). The choice of school depended on households in which the children lived. Those placed with Nova Scotian settlers typically attended Huntingdonian or Baptist

17 Richard Anderson, *Abolition in Sierra Leone: Re-Building Lives and Identities in Nineteenth-Century West Africa* (Cambridge, 2020), pp. 274–5; Suzanne Schwarz, 'African Diaspora, Sierra Leone and Protestant Christianity, circa 1780–1860', in Vanicléia Silva Santos (ed.), in *General History of Africa*, vol. X, *Africa and its Diasporas* (Paris, 2023), pp. 777–88; Memorial to Sally Taylor, Circular Road Cemetery, Freetown, Sierra Leone, 24 May 1885. University of Hull, Remember Me project.

18 Fyfe, *A History*, p. 201.

19 Philip D. Curtin, *Africa Remembered; Narratives by West Africans from the Era of the Slave Trade* (Madison, 1967), pp. 289–316.

20 Robert B. Clarke, *Sierra Leone: A Description of the Manners and Customs of the Liberated Africans* (London, 1843), p. 30; Arthur T. Porter, 'Religious Affiliation in Freetown, Sierra Leone', *Journal of the International African Institute*, 23:1 (1953), p. 6; *Reports to Secretary of State on Past and Present State of H.M. Colonial Possessions, 1850*, HC 1851, no. 1421 (London, 1851), p. 191.

21 Porter, 'Religious Affiliation', 3–14, at p. 7.

schools as these congregations were established with the arrival of Nova Scotian settlers.[22] Lensenee, Laminah, Mormoh, and Jaku lived with Edward Posley Zizer, a man of Nova Scotian descent, and attended a Huntingdonian school. Eliza Morris and Conteh were placed with Henry Elliot Seymour, also of Nova Scotian descent, and both attended the Baptist school. On 23 April 1859, Joe Harris, a six-year-old boy from Wadah in Sherbro, was enrolled in a government school run by Mr Nylander in Grassfield. Two years later, on 5 July 1861, he was transferred to the Wesleyan school on Krutown Road. Joe lived with Jack Ropeyarn, a common Kru name, who was likely a member of the Kru Wesleyan chapel at Warren Memorial.[23]

Just as with Christianity, Muslim communities were also establishing their own centres of learning. By the late 1800s, they had established educational centres in Labe and Timbo, as well as Qur'anic schools in Fourah Bay. Islamic primary schools, known as Karanthe or Ile-Kewu, offered instruction in Arabic, Islamic studies, and surahs from the Qur'an. This religious education was designed to instil moral values and secure adherence to the faith from an early age.[24] Among the eleven 'alien' children who came from regions where Muslim communities were already established, only four were enrolled in Qur'anic schools. Pharah and Merry were placed with Foday Morana, a member of the Muslim community at Gibraltar Wharf. The title Foday denoted a person learned in Arabic letters who devoted himself to teaching Islamic law.[25] Mousu was initially placed with Hannah Morrison on 2 August 1859, but two days

22 Katrina Keefer, 'Mission Education in Sierra Leone, 1793–1820' (Unpublished PhD dissertation, York University Toronto, 2015), pp. 91–2; Will of Gustavus Vassa or Olaudah Equiano, Gentleman of Addle Street Aldermanbury, City of London, 8 April 1797, TNA, PROB 11/1289/78; 'Questioning Equiano: Vassa and Sierra Leone', *Equiano's World: Gustavus Vassa and the Abolition of the British Slave Trade* <www.equianosworld.org> [accessed 14 February 2022]; Fyfe, *A History*, pp. 104, 140, 233; Christopher Fyfe, 'The Countess of Huntingdon's Connexion in 19th century Sierra Leone', *The Sierra Leone Bulletin of Religion*, 4 (1962), 53–61.

23 Registration No. 42, SLPA, Register of Alien Children (1859); Jeffrey Gunn, *Outsourcing African Labor: Kru Migratory Workers in Global Ports, Estates and Battlefields until the End of the 19th Century* (Berlin, 2021), p. 84.

24 Gibril R. Cole, *The Krio of West Africa: Islam, Culture, Creolization, and Colonialism in the Nineteenth Century* (Athens, 2013), p. 104, 158; David Skinner, 'Islam and Education in the Colony and Hinterland of Sierra Leone (1750–1914)', *Canadian Journal of African Studies / Revue canadienne des études africaines*, 10:3 (1976), 499–520, at p. 501, 509; Barbara E. Harrell-Bond, Allen M. Howard, and David E. Skinner, *Community Leadership and the Transformation of Freetown (1801–1976)* (The Hague, 1978), pp. 107–108; David E. Skinner, 'The Influence of Islam in Sierra Leone History: Institutions, Practices, and Leadership', *Journal of West African History*, 2:1 (2016), 27–71, at p. 31; James Steel Thayer, 'Religion and Social Organization among a West African Muslim People: The Susu of Sierra Leone' (Unpublished PhD dissertation, University of Michigan, 1981), p. 222.

25 Thayer, 'Religion', p. 196.

later was transferred to Foday Morana.[26] Mariana, meanwhile, was sent to live with Laminah Furay, a Muslim trader residing on Fisher Street.[27] Although some of these children might have been raised in Muslim households, others were directed toward Christian education. In 1859, Degbar and Bome from Foredugu attended the Huntingdonian school. There were also nine children from Bullom enrolled across five different Christian schools.

Table 6.1 Schools attended by children from outside the colony in 1859.

Schools	Number of children
African Methodist schools	8
Baptist schools	6
C.M.S. schools	11
Government schools	20
Lady Huntingdon schools	21
Qur'anic schools	4
Wesleyan Methodist schools	8
Total	**78**

Source: SLPA, Register of Alien Children (1859).

Religious education related to Islam and Christianity both extended beyond the school system, but Christian moral values were used by the authorities and reinforced through colonial law. As such, many inhabitants were brought before the Police Magistrate for challenging Police and Colonial Acts that regulated social behaviour. Much of social life was restricted to private conviviality, as colonial authorities asserted moral superiority by criminalising behaviours deemed inappropriate in public view.[28] In the sample of cases analysed between the 1820s and 60s, 512 related to public offence and public order, including fighting in the streets, insufficient clothing, and drunkenness.

The 1824 British Vagrancy Act, which convicted 'rogues and vagabonds', and criminalised 'wilfully exposing the person', was applied in Freetown to regulate bodily conduct.[29] Individuals were charged for urinating in public spaces, washing at rivers and bridges, or engaging in sexual intercourse in

26 Registration No. 16, 144, 132, SLPA, Register of Alien Children (1859).

27 Registration No. 166, SLPA, Register of Alien Children (1859); SLPA, RBF (1860–1861), Registration No. 50.

28 Fyfe, *A History*, p. 304.

29 David J. Cox, Kim Stevenson, Candida Harris, and Judith Rowbotham, *Public Indecency in England 1857–1960 'A Serious and Growing Evil'* (London, 2015), p. 23.

public. On 6 July 1854, Betsy Coker and Bocarie were charged with 'committing fornication at the Public Wharf' after being discovered in a long boat by a police constable.[30] Cases of nakedness and insufficient clothing were treated by colonial authorities as signs of indecency.[31] After observing Kru men walking nearly naked, Lieutenant-Governor Henry Dundas Campbell, declared it a public offence to appear unclothed in the streets.[32] On 22 March 1838, eight 'Liberated Africans' were similarly charged with being improperly clothed and sent to the Liberated African Department.[33]

Drunkenness was another recurring offence that the colonial authorities associated with moral degradation, irreligion, crime, and poverty.[34] Alcohol consumption was closely regulated, with sales restricted to licensed grog-shops (public houses), all of which were required to close at 9 p.m. and remain shut on Sundays. Sellers were required to obtain an annual licence issued at the Quarter Sessions, and breaches attracted strict penalties of a £5 fine or four months in prison for a first offence, increasing to £15 or six months for a second. Licensed sellers also had to display a black signboard at the front of their premises showing their name, licence number, and the words 'Licensed to sell spirituous liquors'.[35] A few people continued to sell alcohol in their shops despite their licences having expired, possibly because they lacked the

30 Tom Jumbo, 26 July 1847; James Ledhum, 26 July 1847; Thomas Lloyd, 27 July 1847; Bad Copper, 27 July 1847; No. 42, 3 August 1847; No. 26, 3 August 1847; No. 26, 4 August 1847; Mary, 4 August 1847; Tua, 10 August 1847; William Platt, 21 August 1847; Peter Williams, 23 August 1847; Thomas Pindor, 28 August 1847; Jim John and Naque, 7 September 1847; Maria Bull, 16 September 1847, SLPA, Police Magistrate Record (31 December 1846 – 18 September 1847); Betsy Coker and Bocarie, 6 July 1854. SLPA, Police Magistrate Record (1 June 1854 – 21 October 1854).

31 Clarke, *Sierra Leone*, p. 2; F. Harrison Rankin, *The White Man's Grave: A Visit to Sierra Leone, in 1834*, vol. 1 (London, 1836), pp. 39, 144; T. W. Ramsay, *Costumes on the Western Coast of Africa* (London, 1830); W. L. Neville, *Journal of a Voyage from Plymouth to Sierra Leone* (London, 1858), p. 24; Thomas Coke, *An Interesting Narrative of a Mission, Sent to Sierra Leone, in Africa, By the Methodists, in 1811; to Which is Prefixed, An Account of the Rise, Progress, Disasters, and Present State of that Colony. The Whole Interspersed with a Variety of Remarkable Particulars* (London, 1812), p. 45; Philippa Levine, 'States of Undress: Nakedness and the Colonial Imagination', *Victorian Studies*, 50:2 (2008), 189–219, at p. 192.

32 Fyfe, *A History*, p. 199.

33 William John, Sam Macaulay, John Cole, Thomas William, William Parker, William Young, Capt Cook, Thomas Parker, 22 March 1838, SLPA, Police Court Record (22 August 1837 – 8 May 1838).

34 *Report from the Select Committee Inquiry into Drunkenness with Minutes of Evidence, Appendix*, HC 1834, no. 559, pp. iv, vii.

35 Council, 1827–30: An Act to amend an Act of the Governor and Council of the 6th April 1827, entitled 'An Act for the better regulating and Licensing of Houses for the retailing of Spirituous Liquors', TNA, CO 270/19, fol. 49–53.

financial resources to pay for renewal. In Luanda, African women sold alcohol from their homes for similar reasons.[36] Restrictions on alcohol consumption extended beyond public houses to include appearing drunk in public, which was consistently prosecuted.

By the second half of the nineteenth century, colonial expectations on public behaviour structured elite social life around an imitation of Victorian Britain.[37] Wealthy inhabitants attended government-organised dinners, balls, and parades. In November 1821, Mayor Thomas Carew hosted a festive dinner, reported in the *Royal Gazette*, where a large party enjoyed wine and a 'festive board'. By the 1830s, Mary Church, a European resident of Freetown, recalled the 'dignity balls' attended by wealthy Africans and Europeans.[38] In January 1843, Governor George Macdonald welcomed François d'Orléans, Prince de Joinville, son of the French king, with a dinner during the latter's three-day visit to Freetown.[39] A decade later, in 1855, new Governor Stephen Hill and his wife organised a dress ball to mark his arrival in the colony.[40] Evidence of the continued popularity of such events appears in the 1860s, when ball dresses were advertised for sale in local shops.[41]

The most elaborate occasion came in October 1860, when Prince Alfred, the second son of Queen Victoria, became the first member of the royal family to visit the colony of Sierra Leone. His arrival prompted road repairs, street cleanings, and illuminations of houses and public buildings. The official press reported that schoolchildren dressed in white sang the national anthem, women cheered from public squares, and military parades and regattas were staged in his honour. The visit also became a moment of political representation.[42]

36 Vanessa S. Oliveira, *Slave Trade and Abolition: Gender, Commerce, and Economic Transition in Luanda* (Madison, 2021), p. 44.

37 Leo Spitzer, *The Creoles of Sierra Leone: Responses to Colonialism, 1870–1945* (Madison, 1974), pp. 15–16.

38 Mary Church, *Sierra Leone, or, The Liberated Africans: in a series of letters from a young lady to her sister in 1833 & 34* (London, 1835), p. 14; A. B. C. Sibthorpe, *The History of Sierra Leone*, 1881 (London, 1970), p. 52; Nemata Amelia Blyden, *West Indians in West Africa, 1808–1880: The African Diaspora in Reverse* (Rochester, 2000), p. 91.

39 Sibthorpe, *The History*, p. 61; Caroline Sheridan Norton (ed.), *A Residence at Sierra Leone. Described from a Journal Kept on the Spot, and from Letters Written to Friends at Home* (London, 1849), pp. 136–7; Prince de Joinville, *Vieux Souvenirs, 1818–1848* (Paris, 1894), pp. 278–81.

40 *Royal Gazette and Sierra Leone Advertiser*, 1 December 1821, TNA, CO 271/2, *Royal Gazette and Sierra Leone Advertiser* (1821–1825); Fyfe, *A History*, p. 304.

41 Despatch No. 10590, *The African and Sierra Leone Weekly Advertiser* (19 October 1860), TNA, CO 267/268.

42 Ibid.; Christopher Fyfe, 'A Royal Visit in 1860', *Sierra Leone Studies*, 2 (1959), p. 262; J. J. Crooks, *A History of the Colony of Sierra Leone, West Africa* (London, 1903), p. 203; British Library, *The Illustrated London News* (17 November 1860); Barbados Archives, *The Barbadian* (14 February 1861).

Addresses were presented by the governor's council, a committee of 'Liberated Africans' and their descendants, and a group of African and Muslim rulers. The Liberated African committee, whose address was read by R. V. Joaque, included prominent figures such as John Ezzidio, Henry Lumpkin, and William Henry Pratt, whose memorial at St George's Cathedral commemorates his role as chairman of the reception committee.[43] Another address was presented by twenty-four African and Muslim leaders including Alexander Bai Kanta, King of Koya; Bai Sherbro, King of Kaffu Bullom; and Alimami Fenda Sanessi Modu of Lungi.

The arrivals and departures of governors were staged as public spectacles that further reinforced colonial authority. Such ceremonies of departure and arrival underscored the governor's symbolic role as the colony's representative of imperial power, and the collective gatherings demonstrated how authority was performed in public space. When Governor Arthur E. Kennedy left the colony in October 1854, the *Illustrated London News* published a sketch of his departure on board the steamer *Forerunner*. The image depicted crowds assembled on the public wharf to bid him farewell. Although the accompanying text noted that Kennedy had made some enemies, the crowd was presented as evidence of the respect he commanded within the community.[44]

Many other forms of public events were modelled on cultural practices imported from Britain. Horse racing was organised at the Fourah Bay racecourse, laid out during Governor MacCarthy's time (1814–24), and frequented in the late afternoon by equestrians. By the 1860s, regattas replaced the races, and military sport days were sometimes staged. The Royal Sierra Leone Regatta of October 1860 was held in honour of Prince Alfred's visit.[45] Dramatic societies were founded by Governor Macdonald and by African Caribbean resident William Drape. In 1857, European members of the garrison and their wives staged Shakespeare's *Othello*, although Africans were excluded from the cast.[46]

43 Memorial to William Henry Pratt, St. George Cathedral, Freetown, Sierra Leone, 21 February 1865. University of Hull, Remember Me project.

44 *The Illustrated London News* (23 December 1854), p. 640; M. C. F. Easmon, 'The Departure of Governor Kennedy from Freetown in 1854', *Sierra Leone Studies*, 6 (1956), 110. During his time in the colony Kennedy set up new tariffs, strongly opposed by merchants, on goods circulating in the colony. The Mercantile Association petitioned Parliament against the actions of the Governor. He passed ordinances abolishing Grand Juries and required the registration of alien children, which also led to opposition and petitions from residents. See Fyfe, *A History*, pp. 269–71.

45 Fyfe, *A History*, pp. 294, 380; Christopher Fyfe, *A Short History of Sierra Leone*, 2nd edn (London, 1979), p. 43; *Report from the Select Committee on the West Coast of Africa; together with the minutes of evidence, appendix, and index. Part I – Report and evidence*, HC 1842, no. 551, p. 244; Despatch No. 10590, *The African and Sierra Leone Weekly Advertiser* (19 October 1860) TNA, CO 267/268.

46 Fyfe, *A History*, pp. 304–5.

Missionaries also organised public gatherings and, by the mid-nineteenth century, public lectures. In 1861, Edward H. Beckles, the colonial chaplain, founded the Young Men's Literary Association, while a Literary and Scientific Institution briefly attempted to provide lectures and a library.[47] These entertainments and associations depended on English literacy, which limited participation by newly arrived 'Liberated Africans'. Although elite dinners, balls, and royal visits gave Freetown's public life the appearance of Victorian Britain, this represented only a small portion of everyday experience.

Alongside such displays of British culture, Muslim communities equally asserted their own traditions, identities, and authorities in the colony's shared spaces. Celebrations of Ramadan, Eid al-Fitr, and Eid al-Adha formed central moments of collective life. These festivities were led by almamies, derived from the Arabic *al-Imam*, who were religious leaders whose authority extended well beyond the festival grounds. Almamies provided a parallel structure of authority that regulated daily life independently of colonial oversight.[48] They led prayers, presided over rites of passage, and recited surahs from the Qur'an at naming, house-building, and burial ceremonies. They also visited the sick, comforted mourners, and cared for orphans and the poor, embedding religious leadership into everyday life.[49] In the 1840s, Muslim 'Liberated Africans' marched in the streets of eastern Freetown to celebrate the end of Ramadan, stopping at Government House and presenting gifts at larger residences. By the late nineteenth century, the march had evolved into a lantern parade.[50] In 1858, Almamy Demba, a member of the Modu family in Bullom and headman of the Susu community, led the Ramadan celebrations.[51] Alongside almamies, other Muslim figures such as headmen and Aku Kings offered additional frameworks of leadership. In 1831, Moussa was identified in the census as the 'headman' of Fula Town, a designation used by British authorities but not necessarily adopted by local communities. During the 1840s, Mohamadu Savage served as the Muslim Aku headman of Fourah Bay, indicating the recognition of Islamic power structures by colonial officials.[52]

Beyond ritual authority and community leadership, Muslim identity was also expressed through physical appearance and personal adornment, making religious affiliation visible in everyday life. Members of the Muslim

47 Ibid., p. 253.

48 Cole, *The Krio of West Africa*, pp. 149–50.

49 Thayer, 'Religion', p. 185; A list of almamies from different Muslim communities in Freetown is preserved in Harrell-Bond, Howard, and Skinner, *Community Leadership*, Appendix 1.

50 Fyfe, *A History*, p. 228; Cole, *The Krio of West Africa*, pp. 149–50.

51 *The Illustrated London News* (24 April 1858), pp. 417–18; Harrell-Bond, Howard, and Skinner, *Community Leadership*, p. 53; Fyfe, *A History*, p. 293.

52 Census, 1831, TNA, CO 267/111, fol. 261; Fyfe, *A History*, p. 228.

Figure 6.1 a *&* b T. W. Ramsay's depiction of 'ornaments'.

Source: T. W. Ramsay, Costumes on the western coast of Africa (n. p., 1830). <https://commons.wikimedia.org/wiki/File:(Costumes_on_the_western_coast_of_Africa_(1830)_(14785470793).jpg> [accessed 29 January 2026] (public domain).

communities wore talismans containing Qur'anic verses, which was noted by several Europeans. T. W. Ramsay described 'ornaments seen upon the necks … contain[ing] extracts from the Koran', while Elizabeth Helen Melville wrote that 'men wear, suspended from their neck, an amulet, or, as they call it here, a "gree-gree," usually formed of a scrap from the Koran, hid in a mass of black paste or sewed up in small leather pouches' (Figures 6.1a and 6.1b).[53]

These talismans, known as *ṭilasm*, *tamīna*, *ḥijāb*, or *ḥirz*, were widely traded from the seventeenth century onward.[54] Also referred to as *sebe*, they typically consisted of folded paper inscribed with Qur'anic verses, sewn into leather and worn as necklaces. They were sometimes hung in homes, over doorways or from ceilings, and their inscriptions included prayers, the ninety-nine names

53 Ramsay, *Costumes*, p. 12; Norton (ed.), *A Residence*, p. 21.

54 Matthew Francis Rarey, *Insignificant Things: Amulets and the Art of Survival* (Durham, 2023), pp. 36, 46–7.

of God, names of angels and demons, and references to the Prophet and his companions. Muslims wore them for protection against forces beyond human control – witchcraft, hardship, and danger. Soldiers used them in battle, and women wore them to stabilise pregnancies.[55]

In the context of forced migration across the Black Atlantic, pouch-form amulets, known as *bolsa de mandinga*, were believed to offer protection from violence and even halt the movement of slave ships. Their use expanded alongside the slave trade, becoming symbols of spiritual resilience.[56] One such Islamic talisman is held at the British Museum and was obtained by Thomas Joshua Alldridge, a trader who later joined the colonial administration in the 1870s (Figure 6.2). In 1883, Momodo Wakka, the government Arabic writer, brought talismans to Freetown that had been gifted by Almamy Sattan Lahaie, ruler of Rowula in Upper Scarcies, to Governor Arthur Havelock. One inscription (where 'O' follows the usage conveying appeal, surprise, sorrow) read:

> In the name of the most merciful God I beseech thee O God by your nearest and quickest name; hearer of prayer, open thy blessing and powerful way, and quick answer O, quicker answer to those who may apply to thee, in the right way, O, nearer to those who may ask thee, O, answer to those who call on thee, answer my request quick and carry out my wishes, O, quicker, O, nearer, O, answer, Praise be to God the Lord of all creatures.[57]

The talisman's inscription expresses dependence on God's mercy and responsiveness, asking for help and blessings, while affirming God's greatness. Spirituality could act as evidence of resilience in the face of forced migration, in which faith and material culture intertwined.

Beyond the spiritual authority of Christian missionaries and Muslim almamies, other 'Liberated African' communities organised themselves under secular leaders who embodied ethnic traditions rather than religious ones.

55 Thayer, 'Religion', pp. 205–6; Constant Hamès, 'Problématiques de la magie-sorcellerie en islam et perspectives africaines', *Cahiers d'études africaines* (2008), 81–99, at pp. 93–4; Tewfik Canaan, 'The Decipherment of Arabic Talismans', in Emilie Savage-Smith (ed.), *Magic and Divination in Early Islam*, 2004 (Abingdon, 2017), at pp. 125–78; Alusine Jalloh, 'Muslim Fula Business Elites and Politics in Sierra Leone', *African Economic History*, 35 (2007), 89–132, at p. 55; David Owusu-Ansah, 'Islamic Influence in a Forest Kingdom: The Role of Protective Amulets in Early 19th Century Asante', *Transafrican Journal of History*, 12 (1983), 100–133.

56 Rarey, *Insignificant Things*, pp. 2–6, 16.

57 Translation of written texts placed inside objects, such as a pouch, necklace, or similar – charms brought by Momodo Wakka from Almamy Sattan Lahaie sent to the Governor-in-Chief with a French flag, 15 March 1883, SLPA, Arabic Letter Book (11 March 1883 – 10 December 1885), fol. 6; 'O, Int. & N. (2)'. *OED Online* (Oxford, 2026), <https://doi.org/10.1093/OED/1029282204> [accessed 25 April 2026].

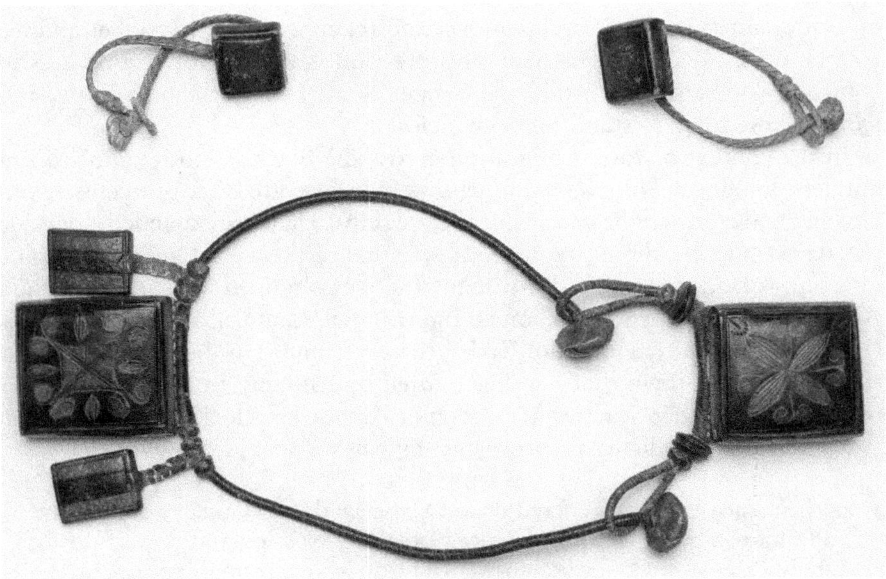

Figure 6.2 Islamic talisman.

Source: Neck ornament, charm; made of leather; leather square decorated with flower design on leather string; two smaller squares hang on braided strip on either side of larger square; knob on each end of string threaded through loops attached to second leather square decorated with flower design. © The Trustees of the British Museum. Shared under a Creative Commons Attribution-NonCommercial-ShareAlike 4.0 International (CC BY-NC-SA 4.0) licence

Among Yoruba groups, this took the form of Aku Kings, whose authority provided a distinctive framework of leadership that mediated between their communities and the colonial state. Recognised figures such as Thomas Will, John Macaulay, and Isaac Benjamin Pratt oversaw networks of headmen who exercised judicial, economic, and political powers, serving as spokespersons for their ethnic communities before colonial officials.[58] Usually, headmen were older residents with long-standing ties to the colony. John Macaulay's headmen included Christopher Taylor and William Lewis, both of Egba origin.[59] By 1850, when he was identified as the headman of the Kongo community during Koelle's interview, Thomas Tob had lived in the colony for forty years.[60]

The Kru community of Krutown was likewise organised under the authority of a headman. A Krutown headman oversaw the administration of the area, received a daily wage of a shilling a day, and was responsible for maintaining

58 Anderson, *Abolition*, pp. 184–7.

59 Fyfe, *A History*, p. 292.

60 Koelle, *Polyglotta Africana*, p. 13.

order within the community and settling disputes. By the 1860s, Kru headmen were responsible for hiring and supplying British captains with ship headmen.[61] Some of their names are documented in the police court records because they identified themselves by the title of headman. On 30 April 1839, Tom Freeman appeared at the police office after a burglary and identified himself as one of Krutown's headmen. On 2 May 1839, Tom Seery was named as a headman in an assault case involving Corporal John Bull of the Royal African Colonial Corps.[62] In hearings from 1854 and 1857, Tom Silly and Black Will aslo identified themselves as head Krumen.[63]

Leadership and community binding was also offered through membership to initiation societies, also known as 'secret societies' since practices remain secret to non-initiates. On the upper Guinea coast, the regional male society, Poro, and its female counterpart, Bundu (also known as Sande), trained youth for adult responsibilities through forest initiations led by masked members, who imparted rituals, symbols, and specialised knowledge.[64] Among the Mende, Humui and Njayei functioned as medicine societies, while the Temne maintained Ragbenle, also known as Maneke, a society closely tied to chiefly authority and central to ceremonies surrounding death, burial, and succession.[65] Evidence of Poro membership appears in the Registers of Liberated Africans, with Katrina Keefer identifying forty-four entries between 1808 and 1821 where Poro was recorded in the description column as 'purrah', suggesting that British clerks recognised its markings.[66] The Bundu society was introduced in Hastings

61 Gunn, *Outsourcing African Labor*, pp. 97–9.

62 Tom Freeman v. John Fisher, 30 April 1839, SLPA, Police Magistrate Record (27 February 1839 – 10 January 1840), fol. 113–14; John Bull v. Tom Seery, Jim, Jim George, 2 May 1839, SLPA, Police Magistrate Record (27 February 1839 – 10 January 1840), fol. 119.

63 Tom Silly v. Thomas Crapin, 20 June 1854, SLPA, Police Magistrate Record (1 June 1854 – 21 October 1854); Regina v. Charles Williams, 13 July 1857, SLPA, Police Court Record (May 1857 – 29 September 1857).

64 Kenneth Little, *The Mende of Sierra Leone: West African People in Transition* (London, 1998), p. 8; Keefer, 'Mission Education', p. 13; Kenneth Little, 'The Political Function of the Poro. Part I', *Africa: Journal of the International African Institute*, 35:4 (1965), 349–65, at p. 249; Christine Whyte, 'Mothering Solidarity: Infant-Feeding, Vulnerability and Poverty in West Africa since the Seventeenth Century', *Past & Present*, 246:15 (2020), 54–92, at p. 62; Katrina Keefer, 'Poro, Witchcraft and Red Water in Early Colonial Sierra Leone: G. R. Nylander's *Ethnography and Systems of Authority on the Bullom Shore*', *Canadian Journal of African Studies / Revue canadienne des études africaines*, 55:1 (2021), 39–55, at pp. 41–3; Trina Leah Hogg, *The Paradox of Protection: The Making of Indirect Rule in Southern Sierra Leone, 1850–1915* (East Lansing, 2026), pp. xxii–xxiii.

65 Fyfe, *A History*, pp. 3, 11; Little, 'The Political Function', p. 249; V. R. Dorjahn, 'The Organization and Functions of the Ragbenle Society of the Temne', *Africa: Journal of the International African Institute*, 29:2 (1959), 156–70.

66 Katrina Keefer, 'Group Identity, Scarification, and Poro among Liberated Africans in Sierra Leone, 1808–1819', *Journal of West African History*, 3:1 (2017), 1–25, at pp. 3, 13, 16.

in 1858 and gained popularity among Muslim women, partly because it offered remedies against smallpox.[67] The Kru community also maintained their own societies, the most documented being the Bo (Boviowah or Gbo), a subgroup of Poro, with rituals carried out in Krutown.[68]

Gibril Cole's study of mid-nineteenth-century Krio society in Sierra Leone reveals that secret societies and cultural institutions were likewise integral to the Yoruba diaspora within the colony.[69] While they were clearly visible by the 1880s in Freetown, they might have emerged in the mid-nineteenth century. Prominent examples included Egúngún (also known as Ojeh), male secret societies, alongside institutions derived from Yoruba divinities (*òrìṣà*), such as Egunuko, Keri-Keri, Gẹlẹdẹ, and Géréfé. Yoruba belief held that Olorun, or Olódùmarè, created the universe and assigned divinities such as Ṣàngó, Ogun, and rṣun to mediate between humans and the divine.[70] Various of the Yoruba-derived institutions also came to be embraced by other groups such as the Temne and Mandinka.[71] Between 1831 and 1871, Ṣàngó, the deity of thunder and lightning, was the most frequently mentioned, in Waterloo, Hastings, Aberdeen, and Freetown, in the C.M.S. archives.[72] Robert B. Clarke observed instances of worship of thunder and lightning by the Aku and noted that worshippers wore black and white bead necklaces.[73]

In public spaces across the colony, the centre of Egúngún activities was Hastings and Waterloo, and in Freetown, it was Fula Town and Fourah Bay, particularly among Muslim Yoruba. The Egúngún masquerade symbolised the return of ancestors through masked figures known as *eku*.[74] These ceremonies were staged during the dry season (roughly November to April), when the absence of heavy rains allowed outdoor gatherings to flourish. They combined prayers with the recitation of names and achievements of the departed, accompanied by drumming and song. A description published in the *Illustrated London News* on 25 October 1856 captured the spectacle, noting the variety of costumes; one sketch depicted a dirty red-hooded cloak adorned with cowrie shells, trousers tucked into old gumboots, and feet bound with dried grass or stockings.[75] Alongside these public performances, families also created

67 Cole, *The Krio of West Africa*, p. 135.
68 Gunn, *Outsourcing African Labor*, pp. 42, 93.
69 Cole, *The Krio of West Africa*, pp. 27–43.
70 Ibid., p. 44, 128; Nemata Amelia Blyden, *African Americans and Africa: A New History* (New Haven, 2019), pp. 45–6.
71 Cole, *The Krio of West Africa*, pp. 39, 42.
72 Ibid., pp. 213–15.
73 Clarke, *Sierra Leone*, p. 150.
74 Cole, *The Krio of West Africa*, pp. 45, 134, 139, 207, 216; Anderson, *Abolition*, p. 221; Akinwumi Ogundiran, *The Yoruba: A New History* (Bloomington, 2020), p. 291.
75 '"Egg-gu-gu" Itinerant Necromancer, and Music', *The Illustrated London News* (25 October 1856), p. 434.

domestic spaces for the Egúngún figure. Rooms within homes were dedicated to hosting the masquerade spirit, where feasts and donations were offered, extending the ritual from the communal square into the private household.[76]

Public ceremonies were marked by their adaptability, shifting to accommodate diverse religious affiliations and social contexts. These practices allowed communities to preserve ancestral traditions while integrating them into Muslim and Christian frameworks. Among the Yoruba, the *àwùjiọ* feast exemplified this flexibility. The ceremony could protect a newborn child, support a marriage, or ease the transition at death, with ritual details adjusted according to faith and personal practice. Sacrifices of chickens, goats, or cows were accompanied by libations, where the oldest woman in the family poured alcohol depending on the habits and beliefs of the person being honoured.[77] Burial rites likewise reflected this adaptability, performed on the third day after death for close relatives, then expanded into larger gatherings on the seventh and fortieth days, culminating in ceremonies that Elizabeth Helen Melville described as filled with crowds, hymns, drumming, and dancing. The first anniversary of death was marked by church services, with mourners dressed in white, showing how ancestral practices could be reframed within Christian liturgy.[78]

Despite this adaptability, not all cultural expressions escaped colonial scrutiny. Night-time drumming and dancing were frequently suppressed and prosecuted, viewed as incompatible with the colonial ideal of Christian tranquillity. Colonial authorities justified these restrictions by claiming they sought to 'improve the morals of the public', a phrase that reveals the colonial mindset on African cultural practices.[79] This language was not neutral but a colonial imposition, used to legitimise prohibitions on drumming at night and to appease Europeans who complained about noise. Across Atlantic colonial settings, drumming and dancing were increasingly regarded as threats to political and moral order, linked to eroticism and disruptive sound.[80] By the nineteenth century, colonial authorities consistently portrayed these performances as improper and unruly, deliberately framing them as the pastime of the lower classes. Spitzer argues that members of the African elite distanced themselves from such practices,

76 *The Illustrated London News* (25 October 1856), p. 436.

77 Spitzer, *The Creoles*, p. 27.

78 Ibid., pp. 34–6, Norton (ed.), *A Residence*, pp. 178–9; Fyfe, *A History*, pp. 139–40; Sibthorpe, *The History*, p. 52; Maeve Ryan, '"A Most Promising Field for Future Usefulness": The Church Missionary Society and the Liberated Africans of Sierra Leone, in W. Mulligan and M. Bric (eds), *A Global History of Anti-Slavery Politics in the Nineteenth Century* (London, 2013), pp. 37–58.

79 J. J. Crooks, *A History of the Colony*, p. 184; Rankin, *The White Man's Grave*, p. 290.

80 Susan A. Reed, 'The Politics and Poetics of Dance', *Annual Review of Anthropology*, 27 (1998), 503–32; Gary A. Donaldson, 'A Window on Slave Culture: Dances at Congo Square in New Orleans, 1800–1862', *The Journal of Negro History*, 69:2 (1984), 63–72.

reinforcing social restrictions to the existing judicial ones.[81] Such judgements were rooted in the colonial mindset that sought to delegitimise African spiritual traditions by casting them as immoral, irrational, and socially disruptive.

Despite colonial efforts to suppress spiritual and cultural traditions, performance remained an important outlet for expression. As official restrictions tightened, inhabitants performed into the night, out of the colonial gaze. When they were noticed, however, performers could find themselves in court. On 31 August 1859, Joseph Atto was brought before the police court for 'beating a Tom Tom at unlawful hour'. He had been drumming at a house on Edward Street while neighbours gathered outside to perform Gumbe dances.[82] Other cases were recorded with less detail, such as that of Betsy Brown, who on 11 November 1839 was charged simply with playing 'goombey' until midnight.[83] Gumbe itself originated in the eighteenth century among Jamaican Maroon communities. In Sierra Leone, it took the form of 'a square frame drum, either of the large bass variety which the player sits upon or as a smaller hand-drum version' and was played by Maroon settlers and 'Liberated Africans' throughout the nineteenth century. As Rachel Jackson notes, the persistence of Gumbe underscores a transatlantic experience that connects colonialism to cultural customs of Africa.[84] Other night songs and dances included one called Koonken or Koonking, introduced by Nova Scotian settlers and Tallala, associated with Maroons. As a man played the drum, refreshments were shared among participants, while women formed a wide circle and danced, turning the night into a space of cultural affirmation and communal joy.[85]

Social spaces were not necessarily grand parties or connected to formal celebrations. These gatherings were sometimes intimate, offering opportunities for everyday sociability rather than spectacle. Court records also show that public houses were important communal spaces where men and women from Freetown and the colony village consumed alcohol and socialised. On Sunday, 4 June 1854, Thomas Williams, a shoemaker from Regent, visited John Thomas's public house ('grog-shop' in the record) in Krutown with his friend James Thompson. The court case is against John Thomas, who was charged with allowing people to remain in his shop after hours. His licence

81 Spitzer, *The Creoles*, pp. 22–3.

82 The Queen v. Joseph Atto, 31 August 1859, SLPA, Police Court Record (13 July 1859 – 14 September 1859), fol. 235–6.

83 Betsy Brown, 11 November 1839, SLPA, Police Magistrate Record (27 February 1839 – 10 January 1840), fol. 393.

84 Rachel Jackson, 'The Trans-Atlantic Journey of Gumbé: Where and Why has it Survived?' *African Music: Journal of the International Library of African Music*, 9:2 (2012), 128–53, at pp. 128, 134–5.

85 Rankin, *The White Man's Grave*, pp. 282–90.

was subsequently forfeited.[86] Taverns were likewise important spaces for the development of social life. Daniel Coker, the son of a pastor from Baltimore, owned one on Charlotte Street.[87] Two taverns had already opened as early as 1795, one operated by Nova Scotian settler Mary Small. Another was established by Richard Blaze on Walpole Street in 1823.[88]

Alongside drinking establishments, various forms of recreation drew communities together, and court records reveal how gambling created additional spaces of sociability. On 21 September 1839, Black Will and Ben Coffee were charged for playing 'jeggy'.[89] Although the record does not describe the game, Thomas Joshua Alldridge later noted that 'jigge' was a gambling game played by the Mende with cowrie shells.

> This is played with four cowrie shells, the convex tops of which have been cut off. One of the players takes the four shells, throws them up with a dexterous twist, clicking his first and second fingers as the shells leave his hands. The shells fall upon the mat which has been spread on the ground; if they fall with two tops or two bottoms up it is a win, all tops or the reverse are also a win, but three tops or the reverse are a lose. Jigge is a terribly gambling game, and half-a-dozen persons or more can play at it, each taking a turn.[90]

Another case heard on 19 August 1859, involved James Ward, James Davis, and Joseph William, who were charged for playing a card game called 'peakup' for half a penny.[91] They explained they had been visiting a sick friend and played the game to pass the time; the court discharged them on account of their young age.[92]

Gambling was not merely recreational but an important social institution within many communities, providing spaces for bonding and competition. On 5 September 1862, Ben Liverpool, a Kru man, was charged with keeping

86 Regina v. John Thomas, 7 June 1854, SLPA, Police Court Record (1 June 1854 – 21 October 1854).
87 Fyfe, *A History*, pp. 132, 257.
88 Vanessa S. Oliveira, 'Baskets, Stalls, and Shops: Experiences and Strategies of Women in Retail Sales in Nineteenth Century Luanda', *Canadian Journal of African Studies / Revue canadienne des études* africaines, 54:3 (2020), 419–36, at p. 428; Fyfe, *A History*, p. 102; BL, BLL01013918484, *The Royal Gazette and Sierra Leone Advertiser*, 29 March 1823, p. 51.
89 Black Will and Ben Coffee, 21 September 1839, SLPA, Police Magistrate Record (27 February 1839 – 10 January 1840), fol. 318.
90 T. J. Alldridge, *A Transformed Colony, Sierra Leone, as it Was, and as it is Its Progress, Peoples, Native Customs and Undeveloped Wealth* (Westport, 1910), p. 229.
91 The Queen v. James Ward, James Davis, and Joseph William, 19 August 1859, SLPA, Police Court Record (13 July 1859 – 14 September 1859), fol. 182–3.
92 Ibid.

a gambling house, as he regularly hosted such parties.[93] Other Kru men were charged for gambling in Krutown. The centrality of gambling to Kru social life is underscored by the fact that disputes over games could escalate into violence; in 1899, a gambling quarrel among Kru men even led to riots.[94] Beyond the Kru community, gambling was also shaped by religious frameworks. Although gambling is forbidden in the Qur'an, it remained widespread in Muslim West Africa. Even in the Sokoto Caliphate, authorities were unable to suppress gambling, where it was described as a 'deeply engrained practice'.[95] Police court testimonies in Freetown, however, do not provide enough detail to determine whether members of the Muslim community were directly involved in gambling. The persistence of gambling despite legal and religious prohibitions highlights its deep cultural roots and the difficulty of eradicating practices that served as important forms of social interaction.

The surviving records from Freetown primarily concern men, underscoring how male sociability was closely tied to gambling. Only men were present at Ben Liverpool's house, and other prosecutions provide further evidence of men gambling. The previously mentioned cases of 'jeggy' and 'peakup' also only involve men. On 7 March 1839, Daniel Preston was charged with gambling with coppers, and on 3 September 1839, William George was charged with gambling money and goods.[96] While many records do not provide details of the games themselves, they nonetheless demonstrate that gambling was a recurring feature of male social life. This does not necessarily mean women were absent from gambling. Instead, it suggests that the evidence is partial. Comparative examples from eighteenth-century Senegambia show that Fula, Mandinka, and

93 Queen v. Ben Liverpool, 5 September 1862, SLPA, Assistant Police Magistrate Record (8 August 1862 – 12 November 1862), fol. 166.

94 Diane Frost, *Work and Community among West African Migrant Workers since the Nineteenth Century* (Liverpool, 1999), p. 127.

95 Per Binde, 'Gambling Across Cultures: Mapping Worldwide Occurrence and Learning from Ethnographic Comparison', *International Gambling Studies*, 5:1 (2005), 1–27, at p. 5; Thomas Q. Reefe, 'The Biggest Game of All: Gambling in Traditional Africa', in William J. Baker and James A. Mangan (eds), *Sport in Africa: Essays in Social History* (New York, 1987), pp. 47–78, at pp. 48, 61.

96 Daniel Preston, 7 March 1839, SLPA, Police Magistrate Record (27 February 1839 – 10 January 1840), fol. 18; Abraham Pratt, William Macaulay, 15 April 1839, SLPA, Police Magistrate Record (27 February 1839 – 10 January 1840), fol. 90; William George, 3 September 1839, SLPA, Police Magistrate Record (27 February 1839 – 10 January 1840), fol. 294; Peter Johnson, Alexander Bucknor, 10 September 1839, SLPA, Police Magistrate Record (27 February 1839 – 10 January 1840), fol. 301; Black Will, Ben Coffee, 21 September 1839, SLPA, Police Magistrate Record (27 February 1839 – 10 January 1840), fol. 318; Queen v. Ben Liverpool, 5 September 1862, SLPA, Assistant Police Magistrate Record (8 August 1862 – 12 November 1862), fol. 166; The Queen v. James Ward, James Davis, and Joseph William, 19 August 1859, SLPA, Police Court Record (13 July 1859 – 14 September 1859), fol. 182–3.

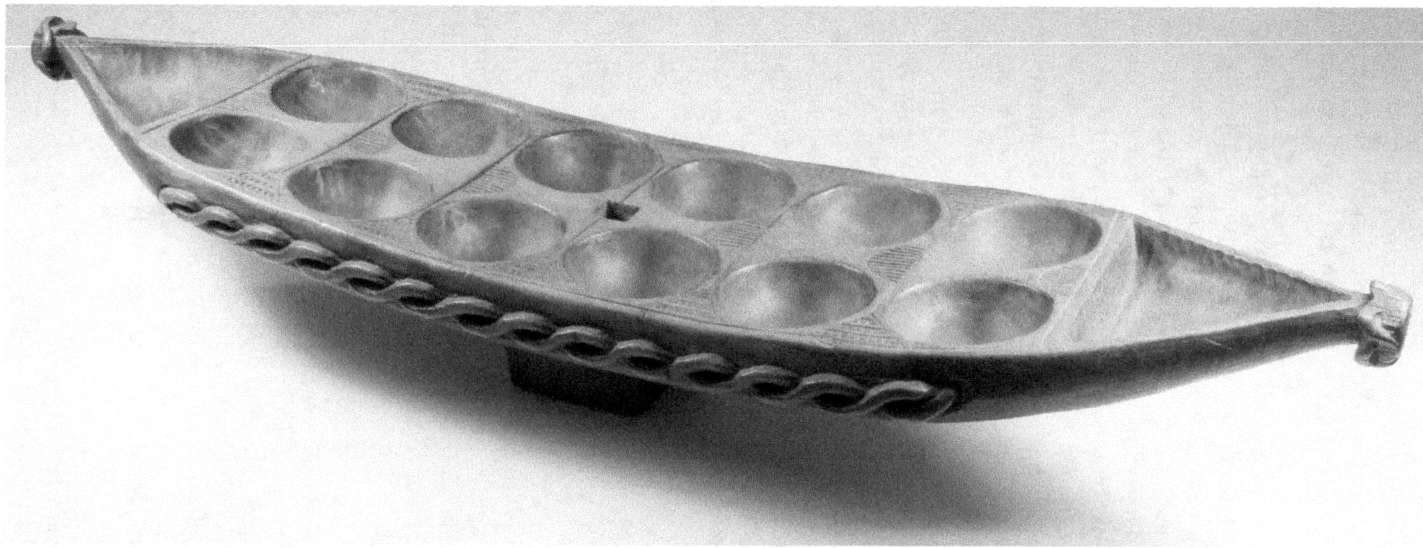

Figure 6.3 Mancala game board from late-nineteenth-century Sierra Leone.

Source: Possibly Bullom. Mancala Game Board, late 19th century. Wood, 25 3/4 x 5 1/2 x 6 ½ in. (65.4 x 14 x 16.5 cm). Brooklyn Museum, Museum Expedition 1922, Robert B. Woodward Memorial Fund, 22.213.

Wolof women were known to gamble separately from men.[97] This does not prove that women in Freetown did the same, but it raises the possibility that gendered divisions in gambling existed, even as they are not directly visible in the court records.

Not all games revolved around gambling. Some games were played purely for entertainment and social bonding. A widespread strategy game among the Yoruba diaspora was *warri* (also known as *ayo*, *oware*, or *okwe*), a two-player *mancala*-style game consisting of a 50-centimetre board with two rows of six cups.[98] In 1841, Rev. Dove, Superintendent of the Wesleyan Mission, observed that non-Christian inhabitants of the colony were playing 'awahrie', and that it was not played for money.[99] *Warri* was widespread across West Africa and had been observed by Europeans as early as 1620 in Gambia by English trader Richard Jobson. It was also played among enslaved African communities in the Caribbean and America. Richard W. Stoffle, Mamadou A. Baro, and Alissandra Cummins note that, in Barbados – although used for recreation – *warri* created a social space important for community bonding.[100] A *mancala* board made in Sierra Leone, possibly by the Bullom in the late nineteenth century, is preserved in the Brooklyn Museum in New York City, clearly indicating its presence near the colony (Figure 6.3). Other games were also observed in Sierra Leone. During his stay in the late eighteenth century, Thomas Winterbottom described several played by the Bullom and Temne, including *k'yungee poo* (the game of bamboos), *k'yungeebel* (the game of palm-nuts), *wur'n keur* (throwing shells), and whipping tops.[101]

Conclusion

Colonial authorities sought to organise many aspects of the inhabitants' lives, yet the public sphere provided space for more organic relationships to develop. Public ceremonies contributed to the growth of an urban popular culture and strengthened community membership. While some individuals

97 Reefe, 'The Biggest Game', p. 66.

98 A. O. Odeleye, *Ayo: A Popular Yoruba Game* (Oxford, 1977), p. viii.

99 *Report*, HC 1842, no. 551, p. 351.

100 Melville J. Herskovits, 'Wari in the New World', *The Journal of the Royal Anthropological Institute of Great Britain and Ireland*, 62 (1932), 23–37, at p. 23; Richard W. Stoffle, Mamadou A. Baro, and Alissandra Cummins, 'Warri's Warriors: From West Africa to Barbados, Men's Social Space from Slavery to Post-Colonial Times', *The Journal of the Barbados Museum & Historical Society*, 65 (2019), 44–68, at pp. 45, 47, 53; Odeleye, *Ayo*, p. viii.

101 Thomas Masterman Winterbottom, *An Account of the Native Africans in the Neighbourhood of Sierra Leone* vol. 1 (London, 1803), pp. 108–23.

observed Christian or Muslim principles, others organised ceremonies rooted in secret societies and maintained connections to their home communities. Public events and gatherings offered opportunities for people of different cultural backgrounds to join in common celebration, though social barriers were rarely erased. Communities continued to gather according to religious beliefs, the languages they spoke, and the cultural heritage of their homelands. The prosecutions of individuals who resisted colonial acts based on Christian moral codes reveal how inhabitants of Freetown did not always conform to imposed behaviours but instead reclaimed their identity. 'Liberated Africans' and other residents of the port-city reconciled their pre-relocation identities with their new status as colonised subjects by sustaining old customs while adopting new cultural elements. In this way, Freetown's public life became a site of negotiation, where colonial authority and African traditions intersected to shape a distinctive urban culture.

Conclusion

The men, women, and children forcibly relocated to the colony of Sierra Leone by the British Royal Navy formed part of the 12.7 million Africans embarked on slave ships between the sixteenth and nineteenth centuries, which is the largest long-distance coerced migration in history.[1] Examining Freetown within this broader history situates its historiography in global patterns of forced migration. Linking these movements to biographical information about individual men and women helps address the scarcity of personal data on people born in Africa during the transatlantic slave trade and fills a gap in the historical record.[2] Colonial records produced in Freetown offer fragmentary evidence that allows for a reconstruction of individual life histories, revealing a wide range of individual experiences that demonstrate that people forcibly transported across the Atlantic cannot be studied as a single, collective demographic.

Biographical information and existing scholarship reveal the adaptability of slavery within an abolitionist framework. Unlike other towns in Africa, such as Lagos, Luanda, or Saint Louis, which remained slave ports into the middle of the nineteenth century, Freetown was an example of an early post-emancipation society that did not rely on enslaved labour. The colony developed as a free-trade centre for kola and palm oil, among other goods, but the experiences of 'Liberated Africans' complicate this picture. Legally freed upon disembarkation, they remained under close surveillance, while British administrators continued to regulate and constrain the course of their lives. After completing apprenticeships, many found low-income occupations and lived in poorer districts such as the Grassfields on the city's outskirts. Enslaved Africans who self-liberated by fleeing to Freetown were likewise confined to the Liberated African Yard, where they became indebted to the imperial system.

1 David Eltis and David Richardson, 'West Africa and the Transatlantic Slave Trade: New Evidence of Long-Run Trends', in David Eltis and David Richardson (eds), *Routes to Slavery: Direction, Ethnicity and Mortality in the Transatlantic Slave Trade* (London, 1997), pp. 16–35.

2 Paul E. Lovejoy, Henry B. Lovejoy, Érika Melek Delgado, and Kartikay Chadha, *Regenerated Identities: Documenting African Lives* (Trenton, 2022), p. 2; Érika Melek Delgado, 'Freedom Narratives: The West African Person as the Central Focus for a Digital Humanities Database', *History in Africa* (2021), 35–59, at pp. 36–7.

The structures imposed by colonial authorities offered few opportunities for social mobility. As Maeve Ryan notes, 'Liberated Africans' were exploited and incorporated into the economy of the empire, demonstrating that legal emancipation did not guarantee economic or social freedom.[3]

This book challenges dominant power paradigms of British colonialism by foregrounding the responses of African people and those of African descent. In Freetown, inhabitants became active in building their lives within the constraints of colonial society, finding ways to assert control and influence through limited means. Navigating life under British control required a strategic understanding of the colonial environment and its institutional frameworks. For adult men, affiliation with Christian institutions sometimes served as a pathway to social mobility. Relationships with missionaries enabled a small number to establish business partnerships in Britain and rise to prominence as merchants. The expansion of Christian missions across West Africa also created opportunities for some 'Liberated Africans' to reconnect with relatives or return to their homelands in places such as Abeokuta, Badagry, and even Bimbia in Cameroon.[4]

Inhabitants drew on trade, language, and legal institutions to navigate the constraints of colonial society. As the largest economic sector, trade placed women at the centre of household economies, whether as single providers or partners in family enterprises. Linguistic skills opened further avenues for professional advancement and geographic mobility, as individuals served as interpreters. Residents also attempted to assert their rights through the British court system in cases involving debt, theft, or domestic abuse, illustrating another way they shaped their lives within a restrictive colonial order.

Amid colonial structures, inhabitants cultivated solidarity through practices such as fictive kinship ties. Through baptism, parents could cultivate influential relationships by selecting prominent individuals as godparents, thereby securing potential avenues of advancement for their children. Family became important in the development of business with children and parents working together and members of the same household having the same occupation. As children acquired English literacy through government or mission schools, they contributed more actively to family enterprises. Court testimonies further reveal the depth of these support networks.

As people built their lives within the community, they still maintained ties to their homelands, expressing these connections in both public and private spheres. Leisure activities, such as traditional games, strengthened social bonds and helped cultural practices from their homelands endure. Public expressions

3 Maeve Ryan, *Humanitarian Governance and the British Antislavery World System* (New Haven, 2022), p. 5.

4 Bronwen Everill, 'Bridgeheads of Empire? Liberated African Missionaries in West Africa', *The Journal of Imperial and Commonwealth History*, 40:5 (2012), 789–805.

of identity were evident in the use of African languages alongside English, as well as in communal observances of Ramadan and festivals. Children born in the colony were given Muslim, Mandinka, or Akan names, while others carried both African and Christian names, moving fluidly across cultural boundaries.

Although this book has focused primarily on the public sphere, the domestic sphere comes into light through the density of the surviving records. The archive does not fall silent here; rather, it offers scattered but revealing traces of household arrangements such as kinship ties or even domestic and professional conflicts. These glimpses are fragmentary, but they are numerous enough to outline the contours of private worlds. Through careful reading of archival sources and scholarship, it becomes possible to see how practices such as polygyny persisted, how rites of passage such as the Yoruba *àwùọ* continued to be observed, and how individuals navigated domestic life within and beyond the structures imposed upon them.

The history of Freetown is as much a story of abolition and colonisation in the Atlantic world as it is of the local actors on the upper Guinea coast. External influences circulated into the colony through interactions with Bullom, Fula, Mandinka, Temne, and other neighbouring communities. Colonial authorities were acutely aware of the prominence of Islam, especially as relations with the interior expanded in the second half of the nineteenth century. The creation of the Aborigine's Branch in 1878, along with Arabic Letter Books (which include both Arabic script and the English translation) documenting official correspondence between the British administration and Muslim leaders, demonstrates the depth of these engagements.[5] Despite this, the archives still exhibit struggles to fully acknowledge and discuss the presence of Muslim communities within Freetown in the mid-nineteenth century. Their visibility in official records remains limited, but scholarship on broader trading networks and community formation in neighbouring regions helps fill these gaps. A similar methodological approach is necessary to recognise the influence of other local actors in shaping identities, particularly for individuals whose lives encompassed diverse experiences before their arrival in Freetown.

The free movement of traders allowed residents to maintain and expand links with communities in the upper Guinea coast and throughout the Sierra Leone–Guinea corridor. Through these connections, members of Freetown's Muslim community and other local actors served as intermediaries, acting as landlords to incoming traders and providing translation services for those who did not speak English. These roles positioned them at the centre of regional

5 Christopher Fyfe, *A History of Sierra Leone* (Oxford, 1962), p. 414; A sample of these documents held at the Sierra Leone Public Archives are available in digitised form through the British Library's Endangered Archives Programme. See EAP project 1366: 'Preserving records of social and political life in nineteenth-century Sierra Leone' <https://eap.bl.uk/project/EAP1366> [accessed 23 December 2025].

commerce and enabled them to benefit from external markers of wealth and authority. At the same time, trade networks allowed people uprooted from their home communities to reconnect with others who shared their cultural or religious heritage.

While these networks enabled Freetown's residents to benefit economically and maintain cultural ties, they also positioned the colony within a wider regional system where slavery, coerced labour, and political influence intersected. In 1843, Britain passed legislation allowing nearby territories to be treated as British possessions without enforcing British law, leaving domestic slavery legal and placing Freetown's inhabitants at risk of kidnapping and enslavement.[6] Slave dealers operated even within the city, sometimes selling children under the guise of education as 'alien' children.[7] Additional limits of the anti-slavery practices of the British Empire relate to exports and businesses that flourished in the mid-nineteenth century. Britain's commitment to international abolition was undermined by the very forms of 'legitimate' trade that depended on slavery and enslaved agricultural labour.[8]

British efforts to curtail the slave trade depended on treaties, commerce, and the involvement of Freetown's influential merchants to extend colonial influence inland. As British authorities sought to persuade African rulers to transition from the slave trade to lawful commerce, they negotiated treaties in Port Loko, Magbeli, Forekaria, and other strategic locations. British engagement with African leaders relied less on military force than on commercial incentives and the growing economic independence of Freetown's inhabitants. Influential members of Freetown, particularly merchants, were involved in these negotiations, conducting business and formalising treaty agreements. Knowledge produced within the colony was crucial for extending British territorial, economic, and material influence. Through these networks, Freetown projected its influence beyond Sierra Leone to the interior, including Kangaba in Mali, as well as to the Gold Coast and Little Popo.

Freetown's rapid demographic growth and diverse population placed it among the main urban centres of West Africa, shaping a social and cultural landscape distinct from other coastal ports. Although quite small by modern

6 John Grace, *Domestic Slavery in West Africa: With Particular Reference to the Sierra Leone Protectorate, 1896–1927* (New York, 1975), p. 27.

7 Sean Kelley, 'Enslavement in Upper Guinea during the Era of the Transatlantic Slave Trade: Biographical Perspectives', *African Economic History*, 48:1 (2020), 46–73; Philip Misevich, 'Freetown and "Freedom?" Colonialism and Slavery in Sierra Leone, 1790s to 1861', in Paul E. Lovejoy and Suzanne Schwarz (eds), *Slavery, Abolition and the Transition to Colonialism in Sierra Leone* (Trenton, 2015), pp. 189–216; Barbara E. Harrell-Bond, Allen M. Howard, and David E. Skinner, *Community Leadership and the Transformation of Freetown (1801–1976)* (The Hague, 1978), pp. 49–50.

8 Philip Misevich, *Abolition and the Transformation of Atlantic Commerce in Southern Sierra Leone, 1790s to 1860s* (Trenton, 2019).

standards, its demographic growth mirrored other major ports. In the 1850s, Saint Louis had about 15,000 inhabitants; Ouidah counted between 18,000 and 20,000; and Lagos had roughly 25,000 residents by 1865.[9] In these West African ports, interactions between European and local populations fostered the emergence of new identities, but Freetown's social and cultural landscape was shaped by the distinctive influence of British suppression policies.[10]

These dynamics of rapid urban and social growth also carried material implications. Freetown's historical sites are directly tied to abolition. Parts of the sites that once housed the Liberated African Yard and the Liberated African Department were repurposed into the Colonial Hospital in 1880, which today remains in use as Connaught Hospital.[11] In contrast, in Lagos, a former slave barracoon was transformed into a public square with breadfruit trees, eventually leading to a street and a church.[12] Freetown's development differed from that of other West African coastal cities, as it did not undergo the transition from the slave trade to legitimate commerce, but its architecture still bears the imprint of its past. These material traces remind us that the city's landscape, similar to its archive, preserves only fragments of the lives that passed through it.

The records that survive were never meant to capture the full experiences of those uprooted, resettled, or born in Freetown, yet their density allows for glimpses of the networks, solidarities, and everyday negotiations that shaped the colony from within. The fragments they contain do not offer complete stories, but they provide enough detail for individuals to emerge, briefly and vividly, from the administrative frameworks that documented them. In closing, Freetown's history reveals not only the limits of the documents that record it, but also the remarkable wealth of material that can be cross-referenced, interpreted, and at times cautiously speculated upon to recover more of the lives that were never fully inscribed in the archive.

9 Robin Law, *Ouidah: The Social History of a West African Slaving 'Port', 1727–1892* (Athens, 2004), p. 73; Catherine Coquery-Vidrovitch, *Histoire des villes d'Afrique noire : Des origines à la colonisation* (Paris, 1993), p. 316; Hilary Jones, 'From Mariage à la Mode to Weddings at Town Hall: Marriage, Colonialism, and Mixed-Race Society in Nineteenth-Century Senegal', *The International Journal of African Historical Studies*, 38:1 (2005), 27–48, at p. 30.

10 Philip D. Curtin and Jan Vansina, 'Sources of the Nineteenth Century Slave Trade', *Journal of African History*, 5:2 (1964), 185–208.

11 'The Gateway to the Old King's Yards', <https://whc.unesco.org/en/tentative-lists/5746/> [accessed 23 May 2025].

12 Ademide Adelusi-Adelluyi, *Imagine Lagos: Mapping History, Place, and Politics in a Nineteenth-Century African City* (Athens, 2024), p. 118.

Appendices

Appendix A: Descriptive Categories in 1831 and Returns of the Population in 1850 and 1860

Table 1 1831.

Categories	Number of inhabitants	Percentage
Europeans	85	1.0%
'Mulattoes'	114	1.3%
Colonial Residents and Freeborn Blacks	3,257	38.3%
Discharged Soldiers and their Families	287	3.4%
Liberated Africans	3,381	39.8%
Krumen	501	5.9%
Native Strangers	826	9.7%
Not Recorded	54	0.6%
Total	8,505	100%

Source: Census of Population and liberated Africans, 1831, TNA, CO 267/111

Table 2 1850.

Categories	Number of inhabitants	Percentage
Europeans	89	0.5%
Maroons	15	0.1%
Nova Scotians	49	0.3%
Liberated Africans	6,898	41.4%

Table 2 continued

Categories		Number of inhabitants	Percentage
Native Creoles		7,565	45.4%
West Indians		90	0.5%
Americans		121	0.7%
Krumen		560	3.4%
Native Strangers		1,292	7.7%
	Total	**16,679**	100%

Source: *Reports to Secretary of State on Past and Present State of H.M. Colonial Possessions, 1850*, HC 1851, no. 1421, p. 184.

Table 3 1860.

Categories		Number of inhabitants	Percentage
Europeans		117	0.7%
Maroons		21	0.1%
Nova Scotians		69	0.4%
Liberated Africans		5,119	29.2%
Colony-born		9,977	56.9%
West Indians		155	0.9%
Americans		50	0.3%
Krumen		338	1.9%
Native Strangers		1,677	9.6%
	Total	17,523	100%

Source: *Reports to Secretary of State on Past and Present State of H.M. Colonial Possessions, 1860*, HC 1862, no. 2955–1, p. 24.

Appendix B: Ethnonyms of 'Alien' Children Registered in 1859

Nations	Register of Alien Children	Percentage	Governor's Despatch	Percentage
Aku	1	0.9%	2	0.6%
American	1	0.9%	1	0.3%
Baggah	2	1.8%	3	0.9%
Bullom	15	13.4%	24	7.3%
Fula/Futa	1	0.9%	2	0.6%
Gallinas	1	0.9%	2	0.6%
Kono			1	0.3%
Koranko			3	0.9%
Kossoh	11	9.8%	23	7.0%
Kru	1	0.9%	1	0.3%
Limba			2	0.6%
Loko	4	3.6%	29	8.9%
Mandinka			3	0.9%
Mende	2	1.8%		
Other			6	1.8%
Popo			1	0.3%
Portuguese	1	0.9%	2	0.6%
Sarakuli	1	0.9%	1	0.3%
Sherbro	19	17.0%	88	26.9%
Susu	14	12.5%	26	8.0%
Temne	38	33.9%	103	31.5%
Wolof			3	0.9%
Unknown			1	0.3%
Total	112	100.0%	327	100.0%

Sources: Despatch No. 1448 (9 February 1859), TNA, CO 267/263; Despatch No. 9141 (1 August 1859), TNA, CO 267/264; Despatch No. 11209 (13 October 1859), TNA, CO 267/264; SLPA, Register of Alien Children (1859).

Appendix C: Occupations in the Birth Registers of Freetown, 1857–1862

Occupations		Number of fathers	Percentage
Administration		85	9.4%
Agriculture and fishing		157	17.3%
Apprentice		0	0.0%
Building		45	5.0%
Domestic Services		27	3.0%
Ecclesiastical		11	1.2%
Education		15	1.7%
Manual labour		94	10.4%
Manufacturing		121	13.4%
Medical		2	0.2%
Military		13	1.4%
Mining		12	1.3%
Not Recorded		15	1.7%
Public Service		0	0.0%
Trade		264	29.1%
Transport		45	5.0%
	Total	906	100%

Sources: SLPA, RBF (1857–1860); SLPA, RBF (1860–1861); SLPA, RBF (1861–1862); SLPA, RBF (1862–1863).

Appendix D: Distribution of Occupations in the 1831 Census

Table 1 Occupations according to the descriptive categories of the census.

Categories of the census	Europeans	'Mulattoes'	Colonial Residents	Discharged Soldiers	Liberated Africans	'Kroomen'	'Native Strangers'	Not recorded	Total
Administration	29	12	41	3	9	2	4	0	100
Agriculture and fishing	0	0	71	21	166	0	6	6	270
Apprentice	0	1	131	10	1,202	1	47	8	1,400
Building	0	3	161	17	182	0	15	4	382
Domestic Services	1	9	433	5	94	62	58	9	617
Ecclesiastical	3	0	3	0	0	0	0	0	6
Education	1	2	35	0	8	0	0	0	46
Manual labour	0	0	109	13	282	21	10	2	437
Manufacturing	0	5	160	12	136	0	21	1	335
Medical	1	0	21	0	1	0	0	0	23
Military	1	0	0	1	1	0	0	0	3
Mining	0	0	13	3	35	0	1	0	52
Not Recorded	10	70	1,833	137	608	410	439	15	3,522
Public Service	1	1	7	5	0	0	0	0	14
Trade	22	10	206	56	598	0	182	7	1,081
Transport	16	1	33	4	59	5	43	2	163
Total	85	114	3,257	287	3,381	501	826	54	8,505

Source: Census of Population and liberated Africans, 1831, TNA, CO 267/111.

Table 2 Occupations according to gender.

Categories of the census	Female	Male	Not Recorded	Total
Administration	0	100	0	100
Agriculture and fishing	0	268	2	270
Apprentice	686	712	2	1,400
Building	0	380	2	382
Domestic Services	473	197	1	671
Ecclesiastical	0	6	0	6
Education	12	34	0	46
Manual labour	59	378	0	437
Manufacturing	74	261	0	335
Medical	20	3	0	23
Military	0	3	0	3
Mining	0	52	0	52
Not Recorded	1,937	1,582	3	3,522
Public Service	0	14	0	14
Trade	648	431	2	1,081
Transport	0	163	0	163
Total	**3,939**	**4,584**	**12**	**8,505**

Source: Census of Population and liberated Africans, 1831, TNA, CO 267/111.

Table 3 Occupations according to age group.

Categories of the census	Adults	Children	Not Recorded	Total
Administration	94	6	0	100
Agriculture and fishing	264	1	5	270
Apprentice	286	1,083	31	1,400
Building	380	1	1	382
Domestic Services	528	135	8	671
Ecclesiastical	6	0	0	6
Education	12	34	0	46
Manual labour	433	3	1	437

Table 3 continued

Categories of the census	Adults	Children	Not Recorded	Total
Manufacturing	333	2	0	335
Medical	22	1	0	23
Military	3	0	0	3
Mining	52	0	0	52
Not Recorded	1,575	1,932	15	3,522
Public Service	14	0	0	14
Trade	1,049	28	4	1,081
Transport	160	1	2	163
Total	5,211	3,227	67	8,505

Source: Census of Population and liberated Africans, 1831, TNA, CO 267/111.

Appendix E: Occupational Breakdown of Freetown Residents, 1851

Occupations	Number of inhabitants
Government officers	31
Merchants and merchant clerks	170
Petty traders, hawkers, pedlars	1,769
Farmers, farm labourers and market people	2,405
Grumettas, predial labourers and house servants	4,121
Fishermen and native seamen	588
Mechanics	721
Miscellaneous, including washerwomen, seamstresses	2,014
Transient traders	923
School children	3,511
Infants	426
Total	**16,679**

Source: Governor Norman William Macdonald to Secretary of State for War and the Colonies, Henry Grey, 3rd Earl Grey, 18 August 1851, SLPA, Governor's Despatches to the Secretary of State (13 July 1851 – 26 December 1851), fol. 64.

Appendix F:
Number of Inhabitants per Street in Freetown, 1831

Street names	Area	Europeans	'Mulattoes'	Colonial Residents	Discharged soldiers	Liberated Africans	'Kroomen'	'Native Strangers'	Not recorded	Total Population
Grass Field 1	FE	5	4	164	0	244	3	216	0	636
Soldier Town	FE	0	0	11	90	16	0	2	0	119
Kissy Road	FE	3	4	86	2	51	0	11	0	157
Circular Road	FE	1	0	109	2	39	0	9	0	160
Sackville Street	FE	0	0	16	0	4	0	6	0	26
Horton Street	FE	0	0	30	0	11	0	0	0	41
James Street	FE	0	0	42	1	15	0	0	0	58
Frederick Street	FE	0	0	35	0	17	0	2	0	54
Henry Street	FE	0	0	31	0	11	0	14	0	56
Regent Street	FE	0	1	55	0	13	0	4	0	73
Lumley Street	FE	0	0	71	0	6	0	3	0	80
Goderich Street	FE	0	0	92	0	29	0	15	0	136
Short Street	FE	0	0	12	0	5	0	0	0	17
Back Street	FE	0	0	12	0	2	0	6	1	21
Mountain Road	FE	0	0	182	0	57	0	17	0	256
Cross Street N1	FE	1	0	57	0	16	3	0	0	77
Cross Street N2	FE	3	2	18	0	17	5	0	0	45
Cross Street N3	FE	0	1	40	0	11	0	0	0	52

Street names	Area	Europeans	'Mulattoes'	Colonial Residents	Discharged soldiers	Liberated Africans	'Kroomen'	'Native Strangers'	Not recorded	Total Population
Little East Street	FE	0	1	60	0	19	1	5	1	87
East Street	FE	3	2	74	0	18	0	8	0	105
Wilberforce Street	FE	2	2	91	0	32	5	0	0	132
Rawdon Street	FE	6	4	97	0	29	3	13	0	152
Howe Street	FE	2	2	77	0	19	8	3	0	111
Charlotte Street	FE	2	4	99	0	24	0	0	0	129
Water Street	FE	10	3	37	0	23	7	0	0	80
Gloucester Street	FW	5	16	62	1	36	12	14	0	146
George Street	FW	3	7	49	0	40	10	10	0	119
Trelawney Street	FW	3	6	19	0	14	3	20	0	65
Walpole Street	FW	11	9	46	0	37	5	10	0	118
Pultney Street	FW	5	9	46	0	48	6	28	0	142
Percival Street	FW	0	13	89	0	50	0	22	0	174
Liverpool Street	FW	0	5	154	2	105	0	28	0	294
Bathurst Street	FW	2	6	145	18	80	5	46	11	313
Wellington Street	FW	4	0	97	20	123	0	54	3	301
Water Street	FW	0	1	50	8	78	0	41	4	182
West Brook Street	FW	0	2	61	14	103	23	9	6	218
Upper Brook Street	FW	0	0	74	0	205	0	7	4	290
Cross Street N1	FW	8	0	4	0	12	12	3	5	44

Street names	Area	Europeans	'Mulattoes'	Colonial Residents	Discharged soldiers	Liberated Africans	'Kroomen'	'Native Strangers'	Not recorded	Total Population
Cross Street N2	FW	4	0	15	0	13	0	7	1	40
Cross Street N3	FW	0	0	36	11	81	7	6	5	146
Pademba Road	FW	2	0	145	27	275	0	13	7	469
Soldier Street	FW	0	3	85	26	182	0	5	3	304
Fort Street	FW	0	0	26	14	64	0	5	1	110
Fort Street 2	FW	0	2	23	9	40	0	0	0	74
Circular Road	FW	0	0	81	22	175	0	4	0	282
Circular Road 2	FW	0	0	24	0	69	0	0	0	93
Circular Road 3	FW	0	0	20	1	63	0	0	1	85
Circular Road 4	FW	0	0	20	0	43	0	0	0	63
Circular Road 5	FW	0	0	26	2	72	0	0	0	100
Circular Road 6	FW	0	0	4	1	21	0	0	0	26
Circular Road 7	FW	0	0	19	4	59	0	1	0	83
Grass Field 1	FW	0	0	13	0	86	0	0	0	99
Grass Field 2	FW	0	0	9	0	33	0	0	0	42
Portuguese Town	FW	0	3	49	8	80	0	1	0	141
Portuguese Town 2	FW	0	2	34	0	47	4	41	0	128
Krutown 1	FW	0	0	18	0	1	300	11	0	330
Krutown 2	FW	0	0	12	0	21	0	16	0	49
Grass Field 3	FW	0	0	104	4	297	79	90	1	575
Total		85	114	3,257	287	3,381	501	826	54	8,505

Source: Census of Population and Liberated Africans, 1831, TNA, CO 267/111.
Key: FE = Freetown East; FW = Freetown West.

Appendix G: Number of Workers on Freetown Streets Listed in the 1831 Census

Categories of the census	Area	Administration	Agriculture and fishing	Apprentice	Building	Domestic Services	Ecclesiastical	Education	Manual labour	Manufacturing	Medical	Military	Mining	Not Recorded	Public Service	Trade	Transport	Total
Grass Field 1	FE	5	1	128	19	3	0	14	25	33	0	1	0	114	1	290	2	**636**
Soldier Town	FE	1	6	23	8	1	0	0	6	7	0	0	0	27	1	38	1	**119**
Kissy Road	FE	0	2	59	6	3	0	0	18	1	0	0	0	41	1	26	0	**157**
Circular Road	FE	1	2	36	16	20	0	0	10	9	0	0	2	41	2	19	2	**160**
Sackville Street	FE	1	1	2	0	1	0	0	6	0	0	0	0	4	0	11	0	**26**
Horton Street	FE	0	0	7	1	4	0	0	4	5	0	0	1	12	0	7	0	**41**
James Street	FE	0	1	16	3	7	0	0	4	1	0	1	2	17	0	5	1	**58**
Frederick Street	FE	4	0	16	2	6	0	0	4	4	0	0	1	10	0	7	0	**54**
Henry Street	FE	0	1	13	3	6	0	0	0	2	0	0	0	23	0	8	0	**56**
Regent Street	FE	2	3	14	4	11	0	0	1	3	0	0	1	25	1	8	0	**73**
Lumley Street	FE	0	2	12	9	16	0	0	6	4	0	0	0	26	1	3	1	**80**
Goderich Street	FE	0	0	40	8	11	0	0	5	11	0	0	2	41	1	14	3	**136**

Short Street	FE	0	0	5	2	4	0	0	0	2	0	0	0	4	0	0	0	**17**
Back Street	FE	0	0	3	2	1	0	0	0	1	0	0	0	13	0	1	0	**21**
Mountain Road	FE	3	4	74	13	38	1	0	6	14	0	0	1	83	0	15	4	**256**
Cross Street N1	FE	1	3	21	0	13	2	1	3	5	1	0	0	26	0	1	0	**77**
Cross Street N2	FE	2	0	20	1	7	0	0	3	0	0	0	0	8	1	3	0	**45**
Cross Street N3	FE	1	0	16	0	4	0	4	4	4	0	0	0	16	0	3	0	**52**
Little East Street	FE	1	1	28	5	17	0	0	2	0	0	0	0	29	0	0	4	**87**
East Street	FE	1	4	28	1	10	0	0	16	5	1	0	0	32	0	4	3	**105**
Wilberforce Street	FE	1	2	39	4	37	0	11	1	3	0	0	0	29	0	3	2	**132**
Rawdon Street	FE	4	0	28	5	48	0	1	2	4	1	0	0	36	0	18	5	**152**
Howe Street	FE	6	0	14	2	46	0	2	1	5	1	0	0	28	0	5	1	**111**
Charlotte Street	FE	4	1	22	6	43	1	8	0	5	6	0	0	26	0	6	1	**129**
Water Street	FE	5	1	16	0	24	0	0	6	2	1	0	0	20	0	4	1	**80**
Gloucester Street	FW	12	2	29	5	17	0	0	2	5	0	1	0	64	0	7	2	**146**
George Street	FW	7	0	37	1	13	0	0	2	3	5	0	0	43	1	4	3	**119**
Trelawney Street	FW	2	0	14	0	5	0	0	0	2	1	0	0	27	0	8	6	**65**
Walpole Street	FW	3	0	25	1	19	0	3	2	4	2	0	0	44	0	7	8	**118**

Categories of the census	Area	Administration	Agriculture and fishing	Apprentice	Building	Domestic Services	Ecclesiastical	Education	Manual labour	Manufacturing	Medical	Military	Mining	Not Recorded	Public Service	Trade	Transport	Total
Pultney Street	FW	3	2	27	4	18	0	0	5	4	1	0	0	56	0	17	5	142
Percival Street	FW	1	3	43	9	12	0	0	0	12	0	0	0	77	0	14	3	174
Liverpool Street	FW	3	8	61	14	28	0	0	3	12	0	0	4	141	0	15	5	294
Bathurst Street	FW	3	9	37	22	36	0	0	7	14	1	0	4	151	0	19	10	313
Wellington Street	FW	5	5	56	23	17	0	0	6	10	0	0	3	144	0	20	12	301
Water Street	FW	1	3	26	12	7	0	0	4	8	0	0	3	96	1	17	4	182
West Brook Street	FW	0	7	26	10	2	0	1	6	5	0	0	8	118	0	32	3	218
Upper Brook Street	FW	0	26	48	16	4	0	0	17	10	0	0	6	113	0	47	3	290
Cross Street N1	FW	5	0	9	0	15	0	0	6	3	1	0	0	0	0	3	2	44
Cross Street N2	FW	1	1	10	1	1	0	0	0	3	1	0	0	15	0	1	6	40
Cross Street N3	FW	2	4	20	9	2	0	0	24	4	0	0	0	54	0	23	4	146
Pademba Road	FW	3	22	95	25	13	2	0	27	18	0	0	2	203	0	51	8	469
Soldier Street	FW	1	13	36	19	17	0	0	17	12	0	0	1	136	0	46	6	304
Fort Street	FW	0	4	15	2	8	0	0	10	5	0	0	1	52	1	11	1	110
Fort Street 2	FW	0	2	5	2	9	0	0	3	1	0	0	0	43	0	7	2	74

Circular Road	FW	2	15	11	19	17	0	0	22	11	0	0	3	118	2	56	6	**282**
Circular Road 2	FW	0	8	4	4	2	0	0	18	5	0	0	0	41	0	10	1	**93**
Circular Road 3	FW	0	6	16	4	2	0	0	9	3	0	0	0	30	0	13	2	**85**
Circular Road 4	FW	0	1	2	3	0	0	0	5	8	0	0	2	29	0	12	1	**63**
Circular Road 5	FW	0	7	4	6	1	0	0	13	7	0	0	1	39	0	22	0	**100**
Circular Road 6	FW	0	2	2	0	0	0	0	4	0	0	0	1	5	0	12	0	**26**
Circular Road 7	FW	2	8	10	4	1	0	0	7	2	0	0	0	34	0	14	1	**83**
Grass Field 1	FW	0	3	1	5	6	0	0	22	2	0	0	2	32	0	18	8	**99**
Grass Field 2	FW	0	0	1	2	0	0	0	1	5	0	0	0	29	0	2	2	**42**
Portuguese Town	FW	0	27	12	4	1	0	1	10	2	0	0	0	74	0	10	0	**141**
Portuguese Town 2	FW	0	3	8	11	3	0	0	2	1	0	0	0	92	0	2	6	**128**
Krutown 1	FW	0	0	0	2	2	0	0	1	3	0	0	0	322	0	0	0	**330**
Krutown 2	FW	0	2	6	5	4	0	0	0	0	0	0	1	29	0	2	0	**49**
Grass Field 3	FW	1	42	24	18	8	0	0	49	21	0	0	0	340	0	60	12	**575**
Total		**100**	**270**	**1,400**	**382**	**671**	**6**	**46**	**437**	**335**	**23**	**3**	**52**	**3,522**	**14**	**1,081**	**163**	**8,505**

Source: Census of Population and liberated Africans, 1831, TNA, CO 267/111.

Key: FE = Freetown East; FW = Freetown West.

Bibliography

Primary Sources

Manuscript and Archival Collections

The British Library, London

BLL01003380621, Ordinances Sierra Leone, 1857, no. 10.

BLL01013918573, *The Royal Gazette and Sierra Leone Advertiser*, Newspapers Nos 1–457 (2 August 1817 – 29 September 1827).

BLL01013918484, *The Royal Gazette and Sierra Leone Advertiser*, Newspapers Nos 135–371 (6 January 1821 – 9 July 1825).

Bibliothèque nationale de France, Paris

Moniteur du Sénégal et Dépendances, 134 (Saint Louis, Sénégal, 19 octobre 1858).

Revue Maritime et Coloniale (Paris, 1862)

Church Missionary Society Archives, Special Collections, Cadbury Research Library, University of Birmingham

Census of Freetown, March 1817.

Sierra Leone Public Archives, Freetown

Arabic Letter Books

Arabic Letter Book (11 March 1883 – 10 December 1885)

Birth Registers

Freetown district (1857–1860)

Freetown district (1860–1861)

Freetown district (1861–1862)
Freetown district (1862–1863)

Death Registers

Freetown district (1861–1862)
Freetown district (1872–1873)

Governors' Despatches to the Secretary of State

(1818 – 1822)
(14 August 1824 – 24 July 1826)
(1 January 1833 – 11 February 1835)
(2 October 1846 – 12 September 1847)
(22 April 1851 – 17 July 1851)
(13 July 1851 – 26 December 1851)
(1 January 1852 – 29 January 1853)
(20 February 1853 – 22 July 1854)

Liberated African Registers

1–3,773 (1808–1812)
3,773–6,274 (1812–1814)
4,684–7,507 (1814–1815)
7,508–9,758 (1815–1816)
8,529–9,758 (1816–1817)
9,759–11,905 (1816–1819)
10,115–15,143 (1816–1822)
11,909 –15,967 (1819–1822)
15,144–19,888 (1822–1825)
19,889–24,205 (1825–1827)
20,514–25,422 (1827)
25,423–30,708 (1827–1829)
30,709–37,429 (1829–1830)
37,430–43,537 (1829–1832)
50,762–54,382 (1835–1836)
54,157–57,571 (1837)
57,572–64,406 (1837–1839)
64,407–67,635 (1839)
75,357–84,420 (1845)

(These records are inconsistent, with many repetitions and overlaps. Several documents are missing and cannot be traced.)[1]

1 See: https://eap.bl.uk/collection/EAP443-1/search?page=11.

Police Court Records
(22 August 1837 – 8 May 1838)
(1851–1852)
(May 1857 – 29 September 1857)
(13 July 1859 – 14 September 1859)
(1 July 1861 – 31 November 1861)

Police Magistrate Records
Assistant Police Magistrate Record (8 August 1862 – 12 November 1862)
Police Magistrate Record (15 February 1839 – 10 January 1840)
Police Magistrate Record (1 June 1843 – 27 June 1844)
Police Magistrate Record (31 December 1846 – 18 September 1847)
Police Magistrate Record (13 November 1849 – 29 May 1850)

Register of Alien Children
(26 February 1859 – 22 September 1859)

The National Archives, Kew, London

CO 267/91, Commissioner's Report, Sierra Leone Commissioners of Enquiry: Appendix A, 1827
CO 267/92, Commissioner's Report, Sierra Leone Commissioners of Enquiry: Appendices B and C, 1827
CO 267/111, Despatches, Census of Population and liberated Africans, 1831
CO 267/231, Despatches, January–March 1853
CO 267/263, Memorial of the Nova Scotians and their descendants, 1859
CO 267/264, Despatches: Sierra Leone, June–December 1859
CO 270/19, Council, 1827–1830
FO 84/1433, Fugitive Slaves Commission: Reception of fugitive slaves on board British ships in foreign territorial waters, 1837–1871
MPH 1/881/11, Sierra Leone, Plan of Freetown, town plan showing streets (named), principal buildings, named districts ('New Town East', 'New Town West', 'Soldiers Town', 'Kroo Town'), cemeteries; boundary of Ordnance land, encroachments by soldiers; old and new privies, drain; work undertaken by Lieutenant-Governor Campbell; Scale: 7.25 inches to 2,000 feet; Signed by J. W. Lawson, Assistant Surveyor, 1836
PROB 11/1289/78, Will of Gustavus Vassa or Olaudah Equiano, Gentleman of Addle Street Aldermanbury, City of London (8 April 1797)
PROB 11/1614/482, Will of Dominic Garel, Merchant of Free Town, Sierra Leone (31 March 1819)
PROB 11/1780/280, Will of Kenneth Macaulay of Freetown, Sierra Leone (3 January 1831)
PROB 11/1903/141, Will of Alexander Rae, Merchant of Freetown Sierra Leone, West Africa (14 November 1838)

PROB 11/1920/64, Will of Stephen Gabbidon of Sierra Leone, West Africa (17 December 1839)
PROB 11/2002/103, Will of Walter William Lewis of Freetown, Sierra Leone (23 July 1844)
PROB 11/2081/362, Will of Thomas Carew, Merchant of Freetown, Sierra Leone (13 October 1848)
PROB 11/2106/253, Will of Logan Hook, Collector of Her Majesty's Customs at Sierra Leone of Islington (7 January 1850)
PROB 11/2130/327, Will of James Hook, Her Britannic Majesty's Commissioner in the Courts of Commission established in Sierra Leone and a Member of the legislative Council of this Colony (1 April 1851)
PROB 11/2238/111, Will of Joseph Green Spilsbury, Merchant of Freetown, Sierra Leone (22 August 1856)

Printed Primary Sources

Contemporary Books and Articles

Alldridge, T. J., *A Transformed Colony, Sierra Leone, as it Was, and as it is Its Progress, Peoples, Native Customs and Undeveloped Wealth* (Westport, 1910).
Booth, Charles, 'Occupations of the People of the United Kingdom, 1801–81', *Journal of the Statistical Society of London*, 49:2 (1886), 314–444.
Bridge, Horatio, *Journal of an African Cruiser* (London, 1848).
Church, Mary, *Sierra Leone, or, The Liberated Africans: in a series of letters from a young lady to her sister in 1833 & 34* (London, 1835).
Clarke, Robert B., 'Short Notes of the Prevailing Diseases in the Colony of Sierra Leone, with a Return of the Sick Africans Sent to Hospital in Eleven Years, and Classified Medical Returns for the Years 1853–4. Also Tables Showing the Number of Lunatics Admitted to Hospital in a Period of Thirteen Years, and the Number Treated from 1st April, 1842, to 31st March, 1853', *Journal of the Statistical Society of London*, 19:1 (1856), 60–81.
——, *Sierra Leone: A Description of the Manners and Customs of the Liberated Africans* (London, 1843).
——, 'Sketches of the Colony of Sierra Leone and its Inhabitants', *Transactions of the Ethnological Society of London*, 2 (1863), 320–63.
Coke, Thomas, *An Interesting Narrative of a Mission, Sent to Sierra Leone, in Africa, By the Methodists, in 1811; To Which is Prefixed, An Account of the Rise, Progress, Disasters, and Present State of that Colony. The Whole Interspersed with a Variety of Remarkable Particulars* (London, 1812).

Duncan, John, *Travels in Western Africa in 1845 & 1846, Comprising a Journey from Whydah, Through the Kingdom of Dahomey, to Adofoodia, in the Interior*, vol. 1, 2nd edn (London, 1847).

Ellis, A. B., *The History of the First West India Regiments* (London, 1885).

Forbes, Frederick E., *Dahomey and the Dahomans: Being the Journals of Two Missions to the King of Dahomey, and Residence at His Capital, in the Years 1849 and 1850*, vol. II (London, 1851).

Hamilton, William, 'Sierra Leone and the Liberated Africans', *The Colonial Magazine and Commercial-Maritime Journal*, 7 (1842), 29–43.

Horton, James Africanus Beale, *West African Countries and Peoples* (London, 1868).

Johnson, Samuel, *The History of the Yorubas*, 1897 (London, 1921).

Kilham, Hannah, *Report on a Recent Visit to the Colony of Sierra Leone* (London, 1828).

Koelle, Sigismund Wilhelm, *Polyglotta Africana; or A Comparative Vocabulary of Nearly Three Hundred Words and Phrases in more than One Hundred Distinct African Languages* (London, 1854).

Neville, W. L., *Journal of a Voyage from Plymouth to Sierra Leone* (London, 1858).

Norton, Caroline Sheridan (ed.), *A Residence at Sierra Leone. Described from a Journal Kept on the Spot, and from Letters Written to Friends at Home* (London, 1849).

Prince de Joinville, *Vieux Souvenirs, 1818–1848* (Paris, 1894).

Rainy, William, *The Censor Censured: or, the Calumnies of Captain Burton (Late Her Majesty's Consul at Fernando Po) on the Africans of Sierra Leone* (London, 1865).

Ramsay, T. W., *Costumes on the Western Coast of Africa* (London, 1830).

Rankin, F. Harrison, *The White Man's Grave: A Visit to Sierra Leone, in 1834* (London, 1836), vols 1 and 2.

Ravenstein, E. G., 'The Laws of Migration', *Journal of the Statistical Society of London*, 48:2 (1885), 167–235.

——, 'The Laws of Migration', *Journal of the Royal Statistical Society*, 52:2 (1889), 241–305.

Sibthorpe, Aaron Belisarius Cosmo, *The History of Sierra Leone*, 1881 (London, 1970).

Walker, Samuel Abraham, *The Church of England Mission in Sierra Leone* (London, 1847).

Winterbottom, Thomas Masterman, *An Account of the Native Africans in the Neighbourhood of Sierra Leone* vol. 1–2 (London, 1803).

Official Documents and Publications

Abstract Statement of Expenditure of Sierra Leone, 1812–28, HC 1830, no. 57.

Charge delivered by Mr. Justice Jeffcott to Grand Jury of Sierra Leone and Correspondence on Slave Trade, HC 1832, no. 364.

Coms. of Inquiry into State of Colony of Sierra Leone, Report (Part I.), HC 1827, no. 312.

Correspondence with British Coms. at Sierra Leone, Havana, Cape of Good Hope, Jamaica, Loanda, and Cape Verd Islands; Reports from British Vice-Admiralty Courts and Naval Officers on Slave Trade: 1845 (Class A), HC 1846, no. 723.

Correspondence with British Coms. at Sierra Leone, Havana, Rio de Janeiro and Surinam, and with Foreign Powers on Slave Trade, 1830 (Class A & B), HC 1831, no. 004.

Extracts from the Report of the Commissioners Appointed for Investigating the State of the Settlements and Governments on the Coast of Africa, HC 1812.

Liberated Africans. Papers relating to liberated Africans located in the colony of Sierra Leone, HC 1826, no. 389.

Report from the Select Committee Inquiry into Drunkenness, with Minutes of Evidence, Appendix, HC 1834, no. 559.

Report from the Select Committee on the Settlements of Sierra Leone and Fernando Po, HC 1830, no. 661.

Report from the Select Committee on the West Coast of Africa; together with the minutes of evidence, appendix, and index. Part I – Report and evidence, HC 1842, no. 551.

Reports to Secretary of State on Past and Present State of H.M. Colonial Possessions, 1848 (Maps and Plans), HC 1849, no. 1126.

Reports to Secretary of State on Past and Present State of H.M. Colonial Possessions, 1850, HC 1851, no. 1421.

Reports to Secretary of State on Past and Present State of H.M. Colonial Possessions, 1851, HC 1852, no. 1539.

Reports to Secretary of State on Past and Present State of H.M. Colonial Possessions, 1854, HC 1856, no. 2050.

Reports to Secretary of State on Past and Present State of H.M. Colonial Possessions, 1860, 1862, no. 2955-1.

Reports to Secretary of State on Past and Present State of H.M. Colonial Possessions and of the United States of The Ionian Islands, 1847, HC 1848, no. 1005.

Sierra Leone. Accounts relating to the duties, exports, imports; population; schools, churches, marriages; &c. of the colony of Sierra Leone, HC 1825, no. 520.

Third Report from the Select Committee on the Slave Trade; together with the minutes of evidence, and appendix, HC 1848, no. 536.

Newspapers and Periodicals

The Illustrated London News (23 December 1854, p. 640)
The Illustrated London News (25 October 1856, pp. 434–6)
The Illustrated London News (24 April 1858, pp. 417–18)
The Illustrated London News (17 November 1860)
The Philanthropist, volume 5, 1815 (New York: Greenwood Reprint Corporation, 1968)

Secondary Sources

Published Sources

Adderley, Laura Rosanne, 'Household Labor and Sexual Coercion Reconstructing Women's Experience of African Recaptive Settlement', in Richard Anderson and Henry B. Lovejoy (eds), *Liberated Africans and the Abolition of the Slave Trade: Digital Histories of Enslavement and Freedom* (Rochester, 2020), pp. 174–97.

——, *'New Negroes from Africa', Slave Trade Abolition and Free African Settlement in the Nineteenth-Century Caribbean* (Bloomington, 2006).

Adelusi-Adelluyi, Ademide, *Imagine Lagos: Mapping History, Place, and Politics in a Nineteenth-Century African City* (Athens, 2024).

Agbelusi, O. O., 'Entangled Landscape: Spatial Discipline and Liminal Freedom in Coastal Sierra Leone', *American Antiquity*, 89:4 (2024), 574–90.

Agiri, B. A., 'When was Ogbomoso Founded? An Analysis of the traditions of origin of an Oyo-Yoruba town with special reference to problems of chronology and feedback', *Transafrican Journal of History*, 5:1 (1976), 32–51.

Ajayi, J. F. Ade, *Christian Missions in Nigeria 1841–1891: The Making of a New Elite* (Evanston, 1969).

Anderson, Michael, 'What Can the Mid-Victorian Censuses Tell Us about Variations in Married Women's Employment?' *Local Population Studies*, 62 (1999), 9–30.

Anderson, Richard, *Abolition in Sierra Leone: Re-Building Lives and Identities in Nineteenth-Century West Africa* (Cambridge, 2020).

——, 'Abolition's Adolescence: Apprenticeship as "Liberation" in Sierra Leone, 1808–1848', *English Historical Review* (2022), 763–93.

——, 'The Diaspora of Sierra Leone's Liberated Africans: Enlistment, Forced Migration, and 'Liberation' at Freetown, 1808–1863', *African Economic History*, 41 (2013), 101–38.

——, 'Uncovering Testimonies of Slavery and the Slave Trade in Missionary Sources: The SHADD Biographies Project and the CMS and MMS Archives for Sierra Leone, Nigeria, and the Gambia', *Slavery and Abolition*, 38:3 (2017), 620–44.

Anderson, Richard and Henry B. Lovejoy (eds), *Liberated Africans and the Abolition of the Slave Trade: Digital Histories of Enslavement and Freedom* (Rochester, 2020).

Anderson, Richard, Alex Borucki, Daniel Domingues da Silva, David Eltis, Paul Lachance, Philip Misevich, and Olatunji Ojo, 'Using African Names to Identify the Origins of Captives in the Transatlantic Slave Trade: Crowd-Sourcing and the Registers of Liberated Africans, 1808–1862', *History in Africa*, 40:1 (2013), 165–91.

Anim-Addo, Joan, 'Bonetta [married name Davies] (Ina) Sarah Forbes [Sally] (c. 1843–1880), Queen Victoria's ward', *Oxford Dictionary of National Biography* (Oxford, 2015), <www.oxforddnb.com/view/10.1093/ref:odnb/9780198614128.001.0001/odnb-9780198614128-e-75453> [accessed 2 December 2020].

Armstrong, W. A., 'The Census Enumerators' Books: A Commentary', in Richard Lawton (ed.), *The Census and Social Structure: An Interpretative Guide to Nineteenth Century Censuses for England and Wales* (London, 1978), pp. 28–81.

Armstrong, W. A., 'The Use of Information about Occupation', in E. A. Wrigley (ed.), *Nineteenth-Century Society: Essays in the Use of Quantitative Methods for the Study of Social Data* (Cambridge, 1972), pp. 191–310.

Ballarin, Marie-Pierre, 'L'esclavage en héritage et l'émergence d'une mobilisation sociopolitique au Kenya', *Politique africaine* 4:140 (2015), 41–59.

Bangura, Joseph, *The Temne of Sierra Leone: African Agency in the Making of a British Colony* (Cambridge, 2017).

Banton, Caree A., *More Auspicious Shores: Barbadian Migration to Liberia, Blackness, and the Making of an African Republic* (Cambridge, 2019).

Banton, Michael, *West African City: A Study of Tribal Life in Freetown* (London, 1957).

Bascom, William R., 'The Esusu: A Credit Institution of the Yoruba', *The Journal of the Royal Anthropological Institute of Great Britain and Ireland*, 82:1 (1952), 63–9.

Bassene, Djiguatte Amédé, 'Continuité de la traite d'êtres humains, de la captivité et de l'asservissement des femmes et des enfants en Sénégambie française du XIXe au début du XXe siècles', in Klara Boyer-Rossol and Marie-Pierre Ballarin (eds), *Les esclavages en Afrique. Passé(s), présent(s) et héritages* (Paris, 2024), pp. 179–94.

Baumeister R. F. and M. R. Leary, 'The Need to Belong: Desire for Interpersonal Attachments as a Fundamental Human Motivation', *Psychological Bulletin*, 117:3 (1995), 497–529.

Beckles, Hilary, *A History of Barbados: From Amerindian Settlement to Caribbean Single Market*, 2nd edn (Cambridge, 2006).

——, *Great House Rules: Landless Emancipation and Workers' Protest in Barbados* (Kingston, 2004).

——, 'Running in Jamaica: A Slavery Ecosystem', *The William and Mary Quarterly*, 76:1 (2019), 9–14.

——, 'The Slave-Drivers' War: Bussa and the 1816 Barbados Slave Rebellion', *Boletín de Estudios Latinoamericanos y del Caribe*, 39 (1985), 85–110.

Bellagamba, Alice, 'Slavery and Emancipation in the Colonial Archives: British Officials, Slave-Owners, and Slaves in the Protectorate of the Gambia (1890–1936)', *Canadian Journal of African Studies / Revue canadienne des études africaines*, 39:1 (2005), 5–41.

Bellagamba, Alice, Sandra E. Greene, and Martin A. Klein (eds), *African Voices on Slavery and the Slave Trade*, vol. 1 (Cambridge, 2013).

Bendt, Veronika, 'Some Aspects of Legal Minority in the Tradition of the Anfoe Ewe, Ghana', *Zeitschrift für Ethnologie*, 104:1 (1979), 155–62.

Benjamin, Jody, *The Texture of Change: Dress, Self-Fashioning, and History in Western Africa, 1700–1850* (Athens, 2024).

Berg, Maxine, 'In Pursuit of Luxury: Global History and British Consumer Goods in Eighteenth Century', *Past & Present*, 182 (2004), 85–142.

——, Maxine, *Luxury and Pleasure in Eighteenth-Century Britain* (Oxford, 2005).

Bethell, Leslie, *The Abolition of the Brazilian Slave Trade: Britain, Brazil and the Slave Trade Question* (Cambridge, 1970).

——, 'The Mixed Commissions for the Suppression of the Transatlantic Slave Trade in the Nineteenth Century', *Journal of African History*, 7:1 (1966), 9–93.

Binde, Per, 'Gambling Across Cultures: Mapping Worldwide Occurrence and Learning from Ethnographic Comparison', *International Gambling Studies*, 5:1 (2005), 1–27.

Blyden, Nemata Amelia, *African Americans and Africa: A New History* (New Haven, 2019).

——, '"Back to Africa": The Migration of New World Blacks to Sierra Leone and Liberia', *OAH Magazine of History* (2004), 23–5.

——, '"We Have the Cause of Africa at Heart": West Indians and African-Americans in 19th Century Freetown', in Mac Dixon-Fyle and Gibril Cole (eds), *New Perspectives on the Sierra Leone Krio* (New York, 2006) pp. 91–105.

——, *West Indians in West Africa, 1808–1880: The African Diaspora in Reverse* (Rochester, 2000).

Borucki, Alex, *From Shipmates to Soldiers: Emerging Black Identities in the Río de la Plata* (Albuquerque, 2015).

——, 'The "African Colonists" of Montevideo: New Light on the Illegal Slave Trade to Rio de Janeiro and the Río de la Plata (1830–42)', *Slavery and Abolition*, 30:3 (2009), 427–44.

Boyer-Rossol, Klara, 'From East Africa to the Mascarenes: The Origins and Life Histories of 140 "Mozambiques" (1810s–1840s)', *Journal of Global Slavery*, 10:2–3 (2025), 223–44.

——, 'Les carnets manuscrits de l'ethnographe Eugène Huet de Froberville (1845–1847) : des noms et des voix de captifs déportés de l'Afrique orientale aux îles Mascareignes', *Esclavages & Post-esclavages*, 9 (2024), <doi.org/10.4000/1109y> [accessed 8 February 2026].

Braidwood, Stephen J., *Black Poor and White Philanthropists: London's Blacks and the Foundation of the Sierra Leone Settlement, 1786–1791* (Liverpool, 1994).

Brignac, Kelly, 'African Indentured Labor in Senegal and Ste. Marie, Madagascar, 1817–1830', *Slavery & Abolition*, 43:4 (2022), 779–97.

——, *Immoral Debt: Abolition, Labor, and the End of Slavery in the French Empire* (Philadelphia, forthcoming).

Brooks, George E., 'Peanuts and Colonialism: Consequences of the Commercialization of Peanuts in West Africa 1830–1870', *Journal of African History*, 16:1 (1975), 29–54.

Browne, Randy M., *Surviving Slavery in the British Caribbean* (Philadelphia, 2017).

Browne-Davies, Nigel, 'Jewry in West Africa', *Transactions of the Historical Society of Ghana*, 19 (2019–2020), 1–60.

Burrill, Emily and Richard Roberts, 'Domestic Violence, Colonial Courts, and the End of Slavery in French Soudan, 1905–12', in Emily S. Burrill, Richard L. Roberts, and Elizabeth Thornberry (eds), *Domestic Violence and the Law in Colonial and Postcolonial Africa* (Athens, 2010), pp. 33–53.

Campbell, Gwyn, Suzanne Miers, and Joseph C. Miller, 'Children in European Systems of Slavery: Introduction', *Slavery and Abolition*, 27:2 (2006), 163–82.

Campbell, Mavis C., *Back to Africa: George Ross & the Maroons – From Nova Scotia to Sierra Leone* (Trenton, 1995).

Canaan, Tewfik, 'The Decipherment of Arabic Talismans', in Emilie Savage-Smith (ed.), *Magic and Divination in Early Islam*, 2004 (Abingdon, 2017), pp. 125–78.

Candido, Mariana P., 'African Freedom Suits and Portuguese Vassal Status: Legal Mechanisms for Fighting Enslavement in Benguela, Angola, 1800–1830', *Slavery & Abolition*, 32:3 (2011), 447–59.

——, 'African Women in Ecclesiastical Documents, Benguela, 1760–1860', *Social Sciences and Missions*, 28 (2015), 235–60.

——, *An African Slaving Port and the Atlantic World: Benguela and its Hinterland* (Cambridge, 2013).

——, 'The Expansion of Slavery in Benguela during the Nineteenth Century', *IRSH*, 65 (2020), 67–92.

——, 'Understanding African Women's Access to Landed Property in Nineteenth-Century Benguela', *Canadian Journal of African Studies / Revue canadienne des études africaines* (2020), 1–23.

——, *Wealth, Land, and Property in Angola: A History of Dispossession, Slavery, and Inequality* (Cambridge, 2022).

——, 'Women, Family, and Landed Property in Nineteenth-Century Benguela', *African Economic History*, 43 (2015), 136–61.

——, 'Women and Slavery in Africa', *Oxford Research Encyclopedia of African History* (Oxford, 2020), <https://oxfordre.com/african-history/display/10.1093/acrefore/9780190277734.001.0001/acrefore-9780190277734-e-466?rskey=E03Wpq&result=1> [accessed 2 July 2021].

Candido, Mariana P. and Adam Jones, 'Introduction', in Mariana P. Candido and Adam Jones (eds), *African Women in the Atlantic World: Property, Vulnerability & Mobility 1660–1880* (Woodbridge, 2019), pp. 1–18.

Candido, Mariana P. and Eugénia Rodrigues, 'African Women's Access and Rights to Property in the Portuguese Empire', *African Economic History*, 43 (2015), 1–18.

Candido, Mariana P. and Vanessa S. Oliveira, 'The Status of Enslaved Women in West Central Africa, 1800–1830', *African Economic History*, 49:1 (2021), 127–53.

Cañizares-Esguerra, Jorge Matt D. Childs, James Sidbury, *The Black Urban Atlantic in the Age of the Slave Trade* (Philadelphia, 2013).

Carter, Marina, Vishwanaden Govinden, and Satyendra Peerthum. *The Last Slaves: Liberated Africans in Nineteenth Century Mauritius* (Port Louis, 2003).

Carvalho Cavalheiro, Daniela, '"I am not a Slave": Liberated Africans and their Usage of the Judicial System in Nineteenth Century Rio de Janeiro', in Vanicléia Silva Santos (ed.), *General History of Africa*, vol. X, *Africa and its Diasporas* (Paris, 2023), pp. 891–900.

Childs, Matt D. and Toyin Falola, 'The Yoruba Diaspora in the Atlantic World: Methodology and Research', in Toyin Falola and Matt D. Childs (eds), *Yoruba Diaspora in the Atlantic World* (Bloomington, 2005), pp. 1–16.

Christopher, A. J., 'The Quest for a Census of the British Empire c.1840–1940', *Journal of Historical Geography*, 34 (2008), 268–85.

Cobley, Alan, 'African Barbadians and Barbadians in Africa', in Kwesi Kwaa Prah (ed.), *Back to Africa*, vol. II, *The Ideology and Practice of the African Returnee Phenomenon from the Caribbean and North-America to Africa* (Cape Town, 2012), pp. 188–206.

Cody, Cheryll Ann, 'There Was No "Absalom" on the Ball Plantations: Slave-Naming Practices in the South Carolina Low Country, 1720–1865', *American Historical Review*, 92:3 (1987), pp. 563–96.

Cole, Gibril R., 'Liberated Slaves and Islam in Nineteenth-Century West Africa', in Toyin Falola and Matt D. Childs (eds), *Yoruba Diaspora in the Atlantic World* (Bloomington, 2005), pp. 383–403.

——, 'Religious Plurality and Economic Sustainability: Muslim Merchants in the Colonial Economy of Nineteenth Century Freetown', *African Economic History*, 36 (2008), pp. 79–93.

——, 'The History of Sierra Leone', *Oxford Research Encyclopedia of African History* (Oxford, 2021), <https://oxfordre.com/african-history/display/10.1093/acrefore/9780190277734.001.0001/acrefore-9780190277734-e-625?rskey=YRgxwo&result=2> [accessed 1 July 2021].

——, *The Krio of West Africa: Islam, Culture, Creolization, and Colonialism in the Nineteenth Century* (Athens, 2013).

Coquery-Vidrovitch, Catherine, *Histoire des villes d'Afrique noire : Des origines à la colonisation* (Paris, 1993).

——, *Les Routes de l'Esclavage : Histoire des Traites Africaines, VI-XX Siècle* (Paris, 2021).

Cox, David J., Kim Stevenson, Candida Harris, and Judith Rowbotham, *Public Indecency in England 1857–1960 'A Serious and Growing Evil'* (London, 2015).

Craton, Michael, 'Changing Patterns of Slave Families in the British West Indies', *The Journal of Interdisciplinary History*, 10:1 (1979), 1–35.

Cromwell, Adelaide M., *An African Victorian Feminist: The Life and Times of Adelaide Smith Casely Hayford 1868–1960* (London, 1986).

Crooks, J. J., *A History of the Colony of Sierra Leone, West Africa* (London and Dublin, 1903).

Cunningham, Andreana, 'Atlantic Crossings: Biosocial Interventions in African Diasporic Bioarchaeological Thought and Practice', *American Journal of Biological Anthropology*, 188:2 (2025), 1–10.

Curtin, Philip D., *Africa Remembered; Narratives by West Africans from the Era of the Slave Trade* (Madison, 1967).

——, 'Epidemiology and the Slave Trade', *Political Science Quarterly*, 83:2 (1968), 190–216.

——, 'The End of the "White Man's Grave"? Nineteenth-Century Mortality in West Africa', *The Journal of Interdisciplinary History*, 21:1 (1990), 63–88.

——, *The Image of Africa: British Ideas and Action, 1780–1850*, vol. 1 (Madison, 1964).

Curtin, Philip D. and Jan Vansina, 'Sources of the Nineteenth Century Slave Trade', *Journal of African History*, 5:2 (1964), 185–208.

Curto, José C., 'Alcohol under the Context of the Atlantic Slave Trade: The Case of Benguela and its Hinterland (Angola)', *Cahiers d'études africaines*, 201 (2011), 51–85.

Daddi Addoun, Yacine, and Paul Lovejoy, 'Muhammad Kaba Saghanughu and the Muslim Community of Jamaica', in Paul E. Lovejoy (ed.), *Slavery on the Frontiers of Islam* (Princeton, 2004), pp. 199–218.

Day, Lynda Rose, *Gender and Power in Sierra Leone: Women Chiefs of the Last Two Centuries* (New York, 2012).

de Haas, Michiel and Ewout Frankema, 'Introduction: The Age of Intra-African Migration – A Synthesis', in Michiel de Haas and Ewout Frankema (eds), *Migration in Africa: Shifting Patterns of Mobility from the 19th to the 21st Century* (London, 2022), pp. 1–34.

de Hart, J., 'Warri', *Sierra Leone Studies* (1918), 35–7.

Delius, Sarah, 'The Same in All but Name? The Intersections of Marriage and Slavery in Sierra Leone, 1890–1930', *Slavery & Abolition* 43:2 (2022), 320–45.

Deveneaux, Gustav Kashop, 'Buxtonianism and Sierra Leone: The 1841 Timbo Expedition', *Journal of African Studies*, 5:1 (1978), 34–54.

——, 'Public Opinion and Colonial Policy in Nineteenth-Century Sierra Leone', *The International Journal of African Historical Studies*, 9:1 (1976), 45–67.

Domingues da Silva, Daniel, David Eltis, Philip Misevich, Olatunji Ojo, 'The Diaspora of Africans Liberated from Slave Ships in the Nineteenth Century', *Journal of African History*, 55:3 (2014), 347–69.

Domínguez, Daylet and Víctor Goldgel Carballo, 'Slavery, Mobility, and Networks in Nineteenth-Century Cuba', *Atlantic Studies*, 18:1 (2021), 1–6.

Donaldson, Gary A., 'A Window on Slave Culture: Dances at Congo Square in New Orleans, 1800–1862', *The Journal of Negro History*, 69:2 (1984), 63–72.

Dorjahn, V. R., 'The Organization and Functions of the Ragbenle Society of the Temne', *Africa: Journal of the International African Institute*, 29:2 (1959), 156–70.

Dorjahn, V. R. and Christopher Fyfe, 'Landlord and Stranger: Change in Tenancy Relations in Sierra Leone', *Journal of African History*, 3:3 (1962), 391–7.

Drury, J., 'The Role of Social Identity Processes in Mass Emergency Behaviour: An Integrative Review', *European Review of Social Psychology*, 29:1 (2018), 38–81.

Easmon, M. C. F., 'The Departure of Governor Kennedy from Freetown in 1854', *Sierra Leone Studies*, 6 (1956), p. 110.

Eltis, David and David Richardson, 'West Africa and the Transatlantic Slave Trade: New Evidence of Long-Run Trends', in David Eltis and David Richardson (eds), *Routes to Slavery: Direction, Ethnicity and Mortality in the Transatlantic Slave Trade* (London, 1997), pp. 16–35.

Everill, Bronwen, *Abolition and Empire in Sierra Leone and Liberia* (Basingstoke, 2013).
——, 'Bridgeheads of Empire? Liberated African Missionaries in West Africa', *The Journal of Imperial and Commonwealth History*, 40:5 (2012), 789–805.
——, '"For the Services of Shipwrights, Coopers, and Grumettas": Freetown's Ship Repair Cluster in Nineteenth-Century Sierra Leone', *History of Science* (2020), 1–17.
Everill, Bronwen and Laura Channing, 'On the Freetown Waterfront: Household Income and Informal Wage Labour in a Nineteenth Century Port City', *African Economic History Working*, 58 (2020), 1–36.
Falola, Toyin and Christian Jennings, *Sources and Methods in African History: Spoken, Written, Unearthed* (Rochester, 2003).
Falola, Toyin and Matt D. Childs, *Yoruba Diaspora in the Atlantic World* (Bloomington, 2005).
Fee, Sarah, '"Cloths with Names": Luxury Textile Imports in Eastern Africa, c. 1800–1885', *Textile History*, 48:1 (2017), 49–84.
Ferreira, Roquinaldo, *Cross-Cultural Exchange in the Atlantic World: Angola and Brazil during the Era of the Slave Trade* (Cambridge, 2012).
——, *Worlds of Unfreedom: West Central Africa in the Era of Global Abolition* (Princeton, 2025).
Fett, Sharla M., *Recaptured Africans: Surviving Slave Ships, Detention, and Dislocation in the Final Years of the Slave Trade* (Chapel Hill, 2017).
Field, Kendra, 'The Violence of Family Formation: Enslaved Families and Reproductive Labor in the Marketplace: Review of *Help Me to Find My People: The African American Search for Family Lost in Slavery* by Heather Andrea Williams: *Slave Breeding: Sex, Violence, and Memory in African American History* by Gregory D. Smithers', *Reviews in American History*, 42:2 (2014), 255–64.
Flint, John, 'Crowther, Samuel Ajayi (c. 1807–1891), Bishop of Western Africa and Linguistic Scholar', *Oxford Dictionary of National Biography* (Oxford, 2015), <www.oxforddnb.com/view/10.1093/ref:odnb/9780198614128.001.0001/odnb-9780198614128-e-6836> [accessed 16 June 2020].
——, 'Laird, Macgregor (1808–1861), Shipbuilder and Explorer', *Oxford Dictionary of National Biography* (Oxford, 2004), <www.oxforddnb.com/view/10.1093/ref:odnb/9780198614128.001.0001/odnb-9780198614128-e-15895> [accessed 2 December 2020].
Flory, Céline, *De l'esclavage à la liberté forcée. Histoire des travailleurs africains engagés dans la Caraïbe française au XIXe siècle* (Paris, 2015).
——, 'L'engagisme africain au prisme du genre en Guyane française après l'abolition de l'esclavage de 1848', *Revue d'histoire du XIXe siècle*, 68 (2024), 107–27.

——, 'Sierra Leone Indentured Workers in Guyana and Martinique in the Nineteenth Century', in Paul Lovejoy and Suzanne Schwarz (eds), *Slavery, Abolition and the Transition to Colonialism in Sierra Leone* (Trenton, 2015), pp. 257–72.

Forman Cody, Lisa, 'The Politics of Illegitimacy in An Age of Reform: Women, Reproduction, and Political Economy in England's New Poor Law of 1834', *Journal of Women's History*, 11:4 (2000), 131–57.

Fortin, Jeffrey A., '"An Act of Deportation": The Jamaican Maroons' Journey from Freedom to Slavery and Back Again, 1796–1836', in Ana Lucia Araujo (ed.), *Paths of the Atlantic Slave Trade* (Amherst, 2011), pp. 71–106.

——, '"Blackened Beyond Our Native Hue": Removal, Identity and the Trelawney Maroons on the Margins of the Atlantic World, 1796–1800', *Citizenship Studies*, 10:1 (2006), 5–34.

Frost, Diane, 'Diasporan West African Communities: The Kru in Freetown & Liverpool', *Review of African Political Economy*, 29:92 (2002), 285–300.

——, *Work and Community among West African Migrant Workers since the Nineteenth Century* (Liverpool, 1999).

Fyfe, Christopher, 'A. B. C. Sibthorpe: A Tribute' *History in Africa*, 19 (1992), 327–52.

——, *Africanus Horton, 1835–1883: West African Scientist and Patriot* (Oxford, 1972).

——, *A History of Sierra Leone* (Oxford, 1962).

—— (ed.), *Anna Maria Falconbridge: Narrative of Two Voyages to the River Sierra Leone during the Years 1791-1792-1793* (Liverpool, 2000 [1794]).

——, 'A Royal Visit in 1860', *Sierra Leone Studies*, 2 (1959), 260–72.

——, *A Short History of Sierra Leone*, 2nd edn (London, 1979).

——, 'European and Creole Influences in the Interior of Sierra Leone before 1896', *Sierra Leone Studies*, 6 (1956), 113–23.

——. 'Four Sierra Leone Recaptives', *Journal of African History*, 11:1 (1961), 77–85.

—— (ed.), *Our Children Free and Happy: Letters from Black Settlers in Africa in the 1790s* (Edinburgh, 1991).

——, 'Peter Nicholls – Old Calabar and Freetown', *Journal of the Historical Society of Nigeria*, 2:1 (1960), 105–14.

——, 'Reflections on a Sierra Leone Bicentenary', *Africa*, 57:4 (1987), 411–21.

——, *Sierra Leone Inheritance* (London, 1964).

——, 'The Administration in 1885', *Sierra Leone Studies*, 1 (1955), 226–8.

——, 'The Countess of Huntingdon's Connexion in 19th century Sierra Leone', *The Sierra Leone Bulletin of Religion*, 4 (1962), 53–61.

——, 'The Foundation of Freetown', in Christopher Fyfe and Eldred Durosimi Jones (eds), *Freetown: A Symposium* (Oxford, 1968), pp. 1–8.

——, 'The Life and Times of John Ezzidio', *Sierra Leone Studies*, 1 (1955), 213–23.

——, 'The Sierra Leone Press in the Nineteenth Century', *Sierra Leone Studies*, 8 (1957), 226–36.

——, 'View of the New Burial Ground', *Sierra Leone Studies*, 2 (1954), 85–90.

Fyfe, Christopher and Eldred Durosimi Jones (eds), *Freetown: A Symposium* (Oxford, 1968).

Fyle, C. Magbaily, 'The Yoruba Diaspora in Sierra Leone's Krio Society', in Toyin Falola and Matt D. Childs (eds), *Yoruba Diaspora in the Atlantic World* (Bloomington, 2005), pp. 366–82.

Galli, Stefania, 'Marriage Patterns in a Black Utopia: Evidence from Early Nineteenth-Century Colonial Sierra Leone', *The History of the Family*, 24:4 (2019), 744–68.

——, 'Socioeconomic Status and Group Belonging: Evidence from Early-Nineteenth-Century Colonial West Africa', *Social Science History* 46:2 (2022), 349–72.

Galli, Stefania and Klas Rönnbäck, 'Colonialism and Rural Inequality in Sierra Leone: An Egalitarian Experiment', *European Review of Economic History*, 24 (2019), 468–501.

——, 'Land Distribution and Inequality in a Black Settler Colony: The Case of Sierra Leone, 1792–1831', *The Economic History Review* (2021), 115–37.

Gantly, Patrick, *Histoire de la Société des missions africaines (SMA) 1856–1907*, tome premier, traduit par Joseph Hardy et Pierre Trichet (Paris, 2009).

Garcia Florentino, Manolo and José Roberto Góes, 'Slavery, Marriage and Kinship in Rural Rio de Janeiro, 1790–1830', in Paul E. Lovejoy (ed.), *Identity in the Shadow of Slavery*, 2nd edn (London, 2009), pp. 137–62.

Garelli, Glenda and Martina Tazzioli, 'Migration and "Pull Factor" Traps', *Migration Studies*, 9:3 (2021), 383–99.

Goerg, Odile, 'From Hill Station (Freetown) to Downtown Conakry (First Ward): Comparing French and British Approaches to Segregation in Colonial Cities at the Beginning of the Twentieth Century', *Canadian Journal of African Studies / Revue canadienne des études africaines*, 32:1 (1998), 1–31.

Goody, Esther N., *Parenthood and Social Reproduction: Fostering and Occupational Roles in West Africa* (Cambridge, 1982).

Grace, John, *Domestic Slavery in West Africa: With Particular Reference to the Sierra Leone Protectorate, 1896–1927* (New York, 1975).

Green, Kathryn L., '"Mande Kaba," the Capital of Mali: A Recent Invention?' *History in Africa*, 18 (1991), 127–35.

Gunn, Jeffrey, *Outsourcing African Labor: Kru Migratory Workers in Global Ports, Estates and Battlefields until the End of the 19th Century* (Berlin, 2021).

Guyer, Jane I., 'Household and Community in African Studies', *African Studies Review*, 24:2 (1981), 87–137.

Hair, P. E. H., 'An Analysis of the Register of Fourah Bay College, 1827–1950', *Sierra Leone Studies*, 7 (1956), 155–60.

——, 'Aspects of the Prehistory of Freetown and Creoledom', *History in Africa*, 25 (1998), 111–18.

——, 'Colonial Freetown and the Study of African Languages', *Africa*, 57:4 (1987), 560–5.

——, 'The Enslavement of Koelle's Informants', *Journal of African History*, 6:2 (1965), 193–203.

——, 'The Spelling and Connotation of the Toponym "Sierra Leone" since 1461', *Sierra Leone Studies* (1966), 43–58.

Hamès, Constant, 'Problématiques de la magie-sorcellerie en islam et perspectives africaines', *Cahiers d'études africaines* (2008), 81–99.

Hamlett, Jane, 'Review of *The Foundations of Female Entrepreneurship: Enterprise, Home and Household in London, c. 1800–1870* by Alison C. Kay', *The Economic History Review*, 64:1 (2011), 310–11.

Handler, Jerome S. and JoAnn Jacoby, 'Slave Names and Naming in Barbados, 1650–1830', *The William and Mary Quarterly*, 53:4 (1996), 685–728.

Hardwick, Julie, Sarah M. S. Pearsall, and Karin Wulf, "Introduction: Centering Families in Atlantic Histories," *The William and Mary Quarterly*, 70:2 (2013), 205–24.

Harms, Robert, 'Sustaining the System: Trading Towns along the Middle Zaire', in Claire C. Robertson and Martin A. Klein (eds), *Women and Slavery in Africa* (London, 1983), pp. 95–110.

Harrell-Bond, Barbara E., Allen M. Howard, and David E. Skinner, *Community Leadership and the Transformation of Freetown (1801–1976)* (The Hague, 1978).

Hartman, Saidiya, 'Venus in Two Acts', *Small Axe*, 26:12/2 (2008), 1–14.

Havick, Philip J., 'Gendering the Black Atlantic: Women's Agency in Coastal Trade Settlements in the Guinea Bissau Region', in Douglas Catterall and Jodi Campbell (eds), *Women in Port: Gendering Communities, Economies, and Social Networks in Atlantic Port Cities, 1500–1800* (Leiden, 2012), pp. 315–56.

Havik, Philip J., *Silences and Soundbites: The Gendered Dynamics of Trade and Brokerage in the Pre-Colonial Guinea Bissau Region* (Münster, 2004).

Hawthorne, Walter, '"Being Now, As it Were, One Family": Shipmate Bonding on the Slave Vessel Emilia, in Rio de Janeiro and throughout the Atlantic World', *Luso-Brazilian Review*, 45:1 (2008), 53–77.

Heap, Simon, '"A Bottle of Gin is Dangled before the Nose of the Natives": The Economic Uses of Imported Liquor in Southern Nigeria, 1860–1920', *African Economic History*, 33 (2005), 69–85.

Herskovits, Melville J., 'Wari in the New World', *The Journal of the Royal Anthropological Institute of Great Britain and Ireland*, 62 (1932), 23–37.

Higgs, Edward, *A Clearer Sense of the Census: Victorian Censuses and Historical Research* (London, 1996).

——, 'Domestic Servants and Households in Victorian England', *Social History*, 8:2 (1983), 201–10.

Higgs, Edward and Amanda Wilkinson, 'Women, Occupations and Work in the Victorian Censuses Revisited', *History Workshop Journal*, 81 (2016), 17–38.

Higman, B. W., 'African and Creole Slave Family Patterns in Trinidad', *Journal of Family History* (1978), 163–78.

——, 'Household Structure and Fertility on Jamaican Slave Plantations: A Nineteenth-Century Example', *Population Studies*, 27:3 (1973), 527–50.

——, 'The Slave Family and Household in the British West Indies, 1800–1834', *The Journal of Interdisciplinary History*, 6:2 (1975), 261–87.

Hill, Polly, 'Landlords and Brokers: A West African Trading System (With a Note on Kumasi Butchers)', *Cahiers d'études africaines*, 6:23 (1966), 349–66.

Hogg, Trina Leah, *The Paradox of Protection: The Making of Indirect Rule in Southern Sierra Leone, 1850–1915* (East Lansing, 2026).

Hopkins, Antony, *Capitalism in the Colonies: African Merchants in Lagos, 1851–1931* (New Haven, 2024).

——, 'Property Rights and Empire Building: Britain's Annexation of Lagos, 1861', *The Journal of Economic History*, 40:4 (1980), 777–98.

Hopper, Matthew S., 'Liberated Africans in the Indian Ocean World', in Richard Anderson and Henry B. Lovejoy (eds), *Liberated Africans and the Abolition of the Slave Trade: Digital Histories of Enslavement and Freedom* (Rochester, 2020), pp. 271–94.

——, *Slaves of One Master: Globalization and Slavery in Arabia in the Age of Empire* (New Haven, 2015).

Howard, Allen M., 'Contesting Commercial Space in Freetown, 1860–1930: Traders, Merchants, and Officials', *Canadian Journal of African Studies / Revue canadienne des études africaines*, 37:2/3 (2003), 236–68.

——, 'Cross-Boundary Traders in the Era of High Imperialism: Changing Structures and Strategies in the Sierra Leone-Guinea Region', *Journal of Urban Research*, 10 (2014) <https://journals.openedition.org/articulo/2535> [accessed 25 April 2026].

——, 'Mande and Fulbe Interaction and Identity in Northwestern Sierra Leone, Late Eighteenth through Early Twentieth Centuries', *Mande Studies*, 1 (1999), 13–39.

——, 'Mande Identity Formation in the Economic and Political Context of North-West Sierra Leone, 1750–1900', *Paideuma*, 46 (2000), 13–35.

——, 'Mande Kola Traders of Northwestern Sierra Leone, Late 1700s to 1930', *Mande Studies*, 9 (2007), 83–102.

——, 'New Insights on Liberated Africans: The 1831 Freetown Census', in Richard Anderson and Henry B. Lovejoy (eds), *Liberated Africans and the Abolition of the Slave Trade: Digital Histories of Enslavement and Freedom* (Rochester, 2020), pp. 101–26.

——, 'Nineteenth-Century Coastal Slave Trading and the British Abolition Campaign in Sierra Leone', *Slavery & Abolition*, 27:1 (2006), 23–49.

——, 'Pawning in Coastal Northwest Sierra Leone, 1870–1910', in Toyin Falola and Paul E. Lovejoy (eds), *Pawnship in Africa: Debt Bondage in Historical Perspective* (Boulder, 1994), pp. 267–84.

——, 'The Relevance of Spatial Analysis for African Economic History: The Sierra Leone-Guinea System', *Journal of African History*, 17:3 (1976), 365–88.

——, 'Trade and Islam in Sierra Leone, 18th–20th Centuries', in Alusine Jalloh and David E. Skinner (eds), *Islam and Trade in Sierra Leone* (Trenton, 1997), pp. 21–63.

Howard, Allen M. and David E. Skinner, 'Network Building and Political Power in Northwestern Sierra Leone, 1800–65', *Africa: Journal of the International African Institute*, 54:2 (1984), 2–28.

Ijagbemi, Adelẹyẹ, 'The Kossoh War 1838–41: A Study in Temne/Colony Relations in the Nineteenth Century', *Journal of the Historical Society of Nigeria*, 5:4 (1971), 549–64.

Imbua, David Lishilinimle, 'From Captives to Heroes: Liberated Africans in Calabar, 1850–1920', in Vanicléia Silva Santos (ed.), *General History of Africa*, vol. X, *Africa and its Diasporas* (Paris, 2023), pp. 987–96.

Ipsen, Pernille, *Daughters of the Trade: Atlantic Slavers and Interracial Marriage on the Gold Coast* (Philadelphia, 2015).

——, 'The Fula and Islamic Education in Freetown, Sierra Leone', *Journal of Islamic Social Sciences*, 14:4 (1997), 51–68.

Jackson, Rachel, 'The Trans-Atlantic Journey of Gumbé: Where and Why has it Survived?' *African Music: Journal of the International Library of African Music*, 9:2 (2012), 128–53.

Jalloh, Alusine, 'Muslim Fula Business Elites and Politics in Sierra Leone', *African Economic History*, 35 (2007), 89–132.

Jansen, Jan 'Habitation and Warfare Strategies in 19th Century Mande – A View from the Kafu', in Allen M. Howard and Richard M. Shain (eds), *The Spatial Factor in African History: The Relationship of the Social, Material, and Perceptual* (Leiden, 2005), 260–89.

Jarrett, H. Reginald, 'Some Aspects of the Urban Geography of Freetown, Sierra Leone', *Geographical Review*, 46:3 (1956), 334–54.

Jean-Baptiste, Rachel, *Conjugal Rights: Marriage, Sexuality, and Urban Life in Colonial Libreville, Gabon* (Athens, 2014).

John, Angela V., *Coalmining Women: Victorian Lives and Campaigns* (Cambridge, 1984).

Johnson, Howard, 'The Liberated Africans in the Bahamas, 1811–60', *Immigrants & Minorities*, 7:1 (1988), 16–40.

Johnson, Jessica Marie, *Wicked Flesh: Black Women, Intimacy, and Freedom in the Atlantic World* (Philadelphia, 2020).

Jones, Adam, 'Prostitution, Polyandry or Rape? On the Ambiguity of European Sources for the West African Coast, 1660–1860', in Mariana P. Candido and Adam Jones (eds), *African Women in the Atlantic World: Property, Vulnerability & Mobility 1660–1880* (Woodbridge, 2019), pp. 89–108.

——, 'Recaptive Nations: Evidence Concerning the Demographic Impact of the Atlantic Slave Trade in the Early Nineteenth Century', *Slavery & Abolition*, 11 (1990), 42–57.

Jones, Hilary, 'Digital History Reviews: Liberated Africans', *Journal of American History*, 105:2 (2018), 473–5.

——, 'From Mariage à la Mode to Weddings at Town Hall: Marriage, Colonialism, and Mixed-Race Society in Nineteenth-Century Senegal', *The International Journal of African Historical Studies*, 38:1 (2005), 27–48.

——, *The Métis of Senegal: Urban Life and Politics in French West Africa* (Bloomington, 2013).

Kandé, Sylvie, *Terres, urbanisme et architecture « créoles » en Sierra Leone, XIIe-XIXe siècles* (Paris, 1998).

Katz, Steven T., *The Holocaust and New World Slavery: A Comparative History*, vols 1 and 2 (Cambridge, 2019).

Keefer, Katrina, *Children, Education and Empire in Early Sierra Leone: Left in Our Hands* (Abingdon, 2018).

——, 'Group Identity, Scarification, and Poro among Liberated Africans in Sierra Leone, 1808–1819', *Journal of West African History*, 3:1 (2017), 1–25.

——, 'Marked by Fire: Brands, Slavery, and Identity', *Slavery & Abolition*, 40:4 (2019), 659–81.

——, 'Poro, Witchcraft and Red Water in Early Colonial Sierra Leone: G. R. Nylander's *Ethnography and Systems of Authority on the Bullom Shore*', *Canadian Journal of African Studies / Revue canadienne des études africaines*, 55:1 (2021), 39–55.

——, 'The First Missionaries of The Church Missionary Society in Sierra Leone, 1804–1816: A Biographical Approach', *History in Africa*, 44 (2017), 199–235.

Kelley, Sean, 'American Rum, African Consumers, and the Transatlantic Slave Trade', *African Economic History*, 46:2 (2018), 1–29.

——, 'Enslavement in Upper Guinea during the Era of the Transatlantic Slave Trade: Biographical Perspectives', *African Economic History*, 48:1 (2020), 46–73.

——, 'Precedents: The "Captured Negroes" of Tortola, 1802–22', in Richard Anderson and Henry B. Lovejoy (eds), *Liberated Africans and the Abolition of the Slave Trade: Digital Histories of Enslavement and Freedom* (Rochester, 2020), 25–44.

Koonar, Catherine, '"Christianity, Commerce and Civilization": Child Labor and the Basel Mission in Colonial Ghana, 1855–1914', *International Labor and Working-Class History*, 86 (2014), 72–88.

Kriger, Colleen E., *Making Money: Life, Death, and Early Modern Trade on Africa's Guinea Coast* (Athens, 2017).

Kuczynski, Robert René, *Demographic Survey of the British Colonial Empire* (London, 1948).

Kup, A. P., 'An Account of the Tribal Distribution of Sierra Leone', *Man* 60 (1960), 116–19.

——, *A History of Sierra Leone 1400–1787* (Cambridge, 1962).

Lambert, David, 'Sierra Leone and Other Sites in the War of Representation over Slavery', *History Workshop Journal*, 64 (2007), 103–32.

Lambert, M. N., T. F. Stillman, J. A. Hicks, S. Kamble, R. F. Baumeister, and F. D. Fincham, 'To Belong is to Matter: Sense of Belonging Enhances Meaning in Life', *Personality and Social Psychology Bulletin*, 39:11 (2013): 1418–27.

Laslett, Peter, *The World We Have Lost* (London, 1968).

Laslett, Peter and R. Wall (eds), *Household and Family in Past Times* (Cambridge, 1972).

Law, Robin, 'Between the Sea and the Lagoons: The Interaction of Maritime and Inland Navigation on the Precolonial Slave Coast (Entre mer et lagune : les interactions de la navigation maritime et continentale sur la Côte des Esclaves avant la colonisation)', *Cahiers d'études africaines*, 29:114 (1989), 209–37.

——, 'Ouidah as a Multiethnic Community', in Jorge Cañizares-Esguerra, Matt D. Childs, and James Sidbury (eds), *The Black Urban Atlantic in the Age of the Slave Trade* (Philadelphia: University of Pennsylvania Press, 2013), pp. 42–62.

——, *Ouidah: The Social History of a West African Slaving 'Port', 1727–1892* (Athens, 2004).

——, 'Trade and Politics Behind the Slave Coast: The Lagoon Traffic and the Rise of Lagos, 1500–1800', *Journal of African History*, 24:3 (1983), 321–48.

——, 'Yoruba Liberated Slaves Who Returned to West Africa', in Toyin Falola and Matt D. Childs (eds), *The Yoruba Diaspora in the Atlantic World* (Bloomington, 2004), pp. 349–65.

Law, Robin and Kristin Mann, 'West Africa in the Atlantic Community: The Case of the Slave Coast', *The William and Mary Quarterly*, 56:2 (1999), 307–34.

Lawrance, Benjamin N., Emily Lynn Osborn, and Richard L. Roberts (eds), *Intermediaries, Interpreters, and Clerks: African Employees in the Making of Colonial Africa* (Madison, 2006).

——, 'Introduction: African Intermediaries and the "Bargain" of Collaboration', in Benjamin N. Lawrance, Emily Lynn Osborn, and Richard L. Roberts (eds), *Intermediaries, Interpreters, and Clerks* (Madison, 2006), pp. 3–36.

Lawton, Richard (ed.), *The Census and Social Structure: An Interpretative Guide to Nineteenth Century Censuses for England and Wales* (London, 1978).

Levine, Philippa, 'States of Undress: Nakedness and the Colonial Imagination', *Victorian Studies*, 50:2 (2008), 189–219.

Levitan, Kathrin, '"Sprung from Ourselves": British Interpretations of Mid-Nineteenth-Century Racial Demographics', in Andrew S. Thompson and Kent Fedorowich (eds), *Empire, Migration and Identity in the British World* (Manchester, 2013), 60–81.

Lindsay, Lisa A., *Atlantic Bonds: A Nineteenth-Century Odyssey from America to Africa* (Chapel Hill, 2019).

Little, Kenneth, *The Mende of Sierra Leone: West African People in Transition* (London, 1998).

——, 'The Political Function of the Poro. Part I', *Africa: Journal of the International African Institute*, 35:4 (1965), 349–65.

Livesay, Daniel, *Children of Uncertain Fortune: Mixed-Race Jamaicans in Britain and the Atlantic Family, 1733–1833* (Chapel Hill, 2018).

Lofkrantz, Jennifer, *Ransoming Prisoners in Precolonial Muslim West Africa* (Rochester, 2023).

Lofkrantz, Jennifer and Olatunji Ojo, 'Slavery, Freedom, and Failed Ransom Negotiations in West Africa, 1730–1900', *Journal of African History*, 53:1 (2012), 25–44.

Lovejoy, Henry B., *Becoming Sarah Forbes Bonetta: A Yorùbá Woman in Queen Victoria's Court* (Toronto, 2026).

——, 'Conceptualizing "Liberated Africans" and Slave Trade Abolition: Government Schemes to Indenture Enslaved People Captured from Slavery, 1800–1920', *Past & Present* (2024), 1–69.

——, 'Condemned for Engaging in the Illicit Traffic: Mapping the Maritime Blockade of the African Slave Trade in Global Perspective, 1800–1902', *International Journal of Maritime History* (forthcoming).

——, 'Queen Victoria's "Liberated African": Sarah "Sally" Forbes Bonetta and Her Extraordinary Apprenticeship by the British Royal Family, 1850–1862', *Slavery & Abolition* (2024), 911–34.

——, 'The Registers of Liberated Africans of the Havana Slave Trade Commission: Implementation and Policy, 1824–1841', *Slavery and Abolition*, 37:1 (2016), 23–44.

Lovejoy, Henry B., Paul Lovejoy, Walter Hawthrone, Edward A. Alpers, Mariana Candido, Matthew S. Hopper, Ghislaine Lydon, Colleen E. Kriger, and John Thornton, 'Defining Regions of Pre-Colonial Africa: A Controlled Vocabulary for Linking Open-Source Data in Digital History Projects', *History in Africa* (2021), 1–26.

Lovejoy, Paul E., 'Ali Eisami's Enslavement in Jihad and Emancipation as a Liberated African', in Richard Anderson and Henry B. Lovejoy (eds), *Liberated Africans and the Abolition of the Slave Trade: Digital Histories of Enslavement and Freedom* (Rochester, 2020), 127–52.

——, *Caravans of Kola: The Hausa Kola Trade 1700–1900* (Zaria, 1980).

——, 'Ethnic Designations of the Slave Trade and the Reconstruction of the History of Transatlantic Slavery', in Paul E. Lovejoy and David V. Trotman (eds), *Trans-Atlantic Dimensions of Ethnicity in the African Diaspora* (London, 2004), pp. 9–42.

——, '"Freedom Narratives" of Transatlantic Slavery', *Slavery & Abolition* 32:1 (2011), 91–107.

——, 'Identifying Enslaved Africans in the African Diaspora', in Paul Lovejoy (ed.) *Identity in the Shadow of Slavery* (London, 2000), pp. 1–29.

——, *Jihād in West Africa during the Age of Revolution* (Athens, 2016).

——, 'Kola in the History of West Africa (La kola dans l'histoire de l'Afrique occidentale)', *Cahiers d'études africaines*, 20:77/78 (1980), 97–134.

——, 'Methodology through the Ethnic Lens: The Study of Atlantic Africa', in Toyin Falola and Christian Jennings (eds), *Sources and Methods in African History: Spoken Written Unearthed* (Rochester, 2003), pp. 105–17.

——, 'Pawnship, Debt, and "Freedom" in Atlantic Africa during the Era of the Slave Trade', *Journal of African History*, 55:1 (2014), 55–78.

——, *Salt of the Desert Sun: A History of Salt Production and Trade in the Central Sudan* (Cambridge, 1986).

——, *Slavery in the Global Diaspora of Africa* (London, 2019).

——, 'The Children of Slavery – The Transatlantic phase', *Slavery and Abolition*, 27:2 (2006), 197–217.

——, 'The Urban Background of Enslaved Muslims in the Americas', *Slavery and Abolition*, 26:3 (2005), 349–76.

——, *Transformations in Slavery: A History of Slavery in Africa* (Cambridge, 2012).

—— (ed.), *Identity in the Shadow of Slavery* (London, 2000).

Lovejoy, Paul E. and Suzanne Schwarz, 'Sierra Leone in the Eighteenth and Nineteenth Centuries', in Paul E. Lovejoy and Suzanne Schwarz (eds), *Slavery, Abolition and the Transition to Colonialism in Sierra Leone* (Trenton, 2015), pp. 1–28.

—— (eds), *Slavery, Abolition and the Transition to Colonialism in Sierra Leone* (Trenton, 2015).

Lovejoy, Paul E., Henry B. Lovejoy, Érika Melek Delgado, and Kartikay Chadha, *Regenerated Identities: Documenting African Lives* (Trenton, 2022).

Lowther, Kevin G. and Joseph Opala, *The African American Odyssey of John Kizell: A South Carolina Slave Returns to Fight the Slave Trade in His African Homeland* (Columbia, 2012).

Lynn, Martin, *Commerce and Economic Change in West Africa* (Cambridge, 1997).

——, 'From Sail to Steam: The Impact of the Steamship Services on the British Palm Oil Trade with West Africa, 1850–1890', *Journal of African History*, 30 (1989), 227–45.

MacCormack, Carol P., 'Wono: Institutionalized Dependency in Sherbro Descent Groups (Sierra Leone)', in Suzanne Miers and Igor Kopytoff (eds), *Slavery in Africa: Historical and Anthropological Perspectives* (Madison, 1977), pp. 181–203.

MacQuarrie, H. and A. Pearson, 'Prize Possessions: Transported Material Culture of the Post-Abolition Enslaved – New Evidence from St Helena', *Slavery & Abolition*, 37:1 (2016): 45–72.

Makko, Aryo, *European Small States and the Role of Consuls in the Age of Empire* (Leiden, 2019).

Malherbe, Vertrees C., 'Illegitimacy and Family Formation in Colonial Cape Town, to c. 1850', *Journal of Social History*, 39:4 (2006), 1153–76.

Mann, Kristin, 'Gendered Authority, Gendered Violence: Family, Household & Identity in the Life & Death of a Brazilian Freed Woman in Lagos', in Mariana P. Candido and Adam Jones (eds), *African Women in the Atlantic World: Property, Vulnerability & Mobility 1660–1880*, eds (Woodbridge, 2019), pp. 148–70.

——, 'Marriage Choices among the Educated African Elite in Lagos Colony, 1880–1915', *The International Journal of African Historical Studies*, 14:2 (1981), 201–28.

——, *Marrying Well: Marriage, Status and Social Change among the Educated Elite in Colonial Lagos* (Cambridge, 1985).

——, 'Shifting Paradigms in the Study of the African Diaspora and of Atlantic History and Culture', *Slavery and Abolition*, 22:1 (2001), 3–21.

——, *Slavery and the Birth of an African City: Lagos, 1760–1900* (Bloomington, 2007).

——, 'Women, Landed Property, and the Accumulation of Wealth in Early Colonial Lagos', *Signs: Journal of Women in Culture and Society*, 16:4 (1991), 682–706.

Marten, James 'Family Relationships', in Colin Heywood (ed.), *A Cultural History of Childhood and Family in the Age of Revolution* (London, 2010), pp. 19–38.

Martí, Yaimara Izaguirre, 'Emancipated Women in Cuba: Strategies of Freedom and Motherhood Inside of the Conflict', *Journal of Science*, 7:1 (2024), 84–93.

——, 'Las estrategias legales de los emancipados en Cuba (1856–1880)', *Oficio. Revista de Historia e Interdisciplina*, 18 (2024), 85–104.

Matera, Marc, Misty L. Bastian, and Susan Kingsley Kent, *The Women's War of 1929: Gender and Violence in Colonial Nigeria* (London, 2011).

Mbah, Ndubueze L., 'The Black Englishmen of Old Calabar: Freedom and Mobility in the Age of Abolition in West Africa', *Radical History Review*, 144 (2022), 45–75.

McGowan, Winston, 'The Establishment of Long-Distance Trade between Sierra Leone and its Hinterland, 1787–1821', *Journal of African History*, 31:1 (1990), 25–41.

Medie, Peace A., 'Women and Violence in Africa', *Oxford Research Encyclopedia of African History* (Oxford, 2019), <https://oxfordre.com/africanhistory/view/10.1093/acrefore/9780190277734.001.0001/acrefore-9780190277734-e-567> [accessed 6 November 2023].

Melek Delgado, Érika, 'Freedom Narratives: The West African Person as the Central Focus for a Digital Humanities Database', *History in Africa*, 48 (2021), 35–59.

——, 'Liberated African "Children" in Sierra Leone: Colonial Classifications of "Child" and "Childhood," 1808–19', in Richard Anderson and Henry B. Lovejoy (eds), *Liberated Africans and the Abolition of the Slave Trade: Digital Histories of Enslavement and Freedom* (Rochester, 2020), pp. 81–100.

Mew, Sophie, 'Trials, Blunders and Profits: The Changing Contexts of Currencies in Sierra Leone', *The Journal of Imperial and Commonwealth History*, 44:2 (2016), 195–213.

Meyer-Heiselberg, R., *Notes from Liberated African Department; Extracts from Sources on the Trans-Atlantic Slave Trade, 1808–1860, from the Archives at Fourah Bay College, the University College of Sierra Leone, Freetown, Sierra Leone* (Uppsala, 1967).

Midlo Hall, Gwendolyn, 'Africa and Africans in the African Diaspora: The Uses of Relational Databases', *The American Historical Review*, 115 (2010), 136–50.

——, *Africans in Colonial Louisiana: The Development of Afro-Creole Culture in the Eighteenth Century* (Baton Rouge, 1992).

——, *Slavery and African Ethnicities in the Americas: Restoring the Links* (Chapel Hill, 2005).

Mintz, Sidney Wilfred and Richard Price, *The Birth of African-American Culture: An Anthropological Perspective*, vol. 2 (Boston, 1992).

Misevich, Philip, *Abolition and the Transformation of Atlantic Commerce in Southern Sierra Leone, 1790s to 1860s* (Trenton, 2019).

——, 'Freetown and "Freedom?" Colonialism and Slavery in Sierra Leone, 1790s to 1861', in Paul E. Lovejoy and Suzanne Schwarz (eds), *Slavery, Abolition and the Transition to Colonialism in Sierra Leone* (Trenton, 2015), pp. 189–216.

——, 'The Mende and Sherbro Diaspora in Nineteenth-Century Southern Sierra Leone', in Philip Misevich and Kristin Mann (eds), *The Rise and Demise of Slavery and the Slave Trade in the Atlantic World* (Rochester, 2016), pp. 247–65.

——, 'The Sierra Leone Hinterland and the Provisioning of Early Freetown, 1792–1803', *Journal of Colonialism & Colonial History*, 9:3 (2008), <https://doi.org/10.1353/cch.0.0032> [accessed 25 April 2026].

Moitt, Bernard, *Child Slavery and Guardianship in Colonial Senegal* (Cambridge, 2024).

Monts, Lester P., 'Islam in Liberia', in Ruth M. Stone (ed.), *The Garland Handbook of African Music*, 2nd edn (New York, 2008), pp. 63–87.

Mota, Thiago H., 'Muslims for and Against Slavery: Debates on the European Abolitionism within the Muslim Elite of Saint-Louis, Senegal (1844)', *Slavery & Abolition*, 46:1 (2025), 230–53.

Mouser, Bruce L., 'Continuing British Interest in Coastal Guinea-Conakry and Fuuta Jaloo Highlands (1750 to 1850)', *Cahiers d'études africaines*, 43:172 (2003), 761–90.

——, 'Landlords-Strangers: A Process of Accommodation and Assimilation', *The International Journal of African Historical Studies*, 8:3 (1975), 425–40.

——, '"Walking Caravans" of Nineteenth Century Fuuta Jaloo, Western Africa', *Mande Studies*, 12 (2010), 19–104.

Nelson, Jennifer, 'Apprentices of Freedom: Atlantic Histories of the *Africanos Livres* in Mid-Nineteenth Century Rio de Janeiro', *Africa in the Atlantic World*, 39:2 (2015), 349–69.

Newbury, C. W., 'Credit in Early Nineteenth Century West African Trade', *Journal of African History*, 13:1 (1972), 81–95.

Newman, Richard S., '"Lucky to be Born in Pennsylvania": Free Soil, Fugitive Slaves and the Making of Pennsylvania's Anti-Slavery Borderland', *Slavery & Abolition*, 32:3 (2011), 413–30.

Nicol, Abioseh, 'West Indians in West Africa', *Sierra Leone Studies*, 13 (1958), 14–23.

Nogueira Da Silva, Cristina and Keila Grinberg, 'Soil Free from Slaves: Slave Law in Late Eighteenth- and Early Nineteenth-Century Portugal', *Slavery & Abolition*, 32:3 (2011), 431–46.

Northrup, David, 'Becoming African: Identity Formation among Liberated Slaves in Nineteenth-Century Sierra Leone', *Slavery and Abolition*, 27:1 (2006), 1–21.

——, 'Identity among Liberated Africans in Sierra Leone', in Jorge Cañizares-Esguerra, Matt D. Childs, and James Sidbury (eds), *The Black Urban Atlantic in the Age of the Slave Trade* (Philadelphia, 2013), pp. 21–41.

——, 'The Growth of Trade among the Igbo before 1800', *Journal of African History*, 13:2 (1972), 217–36.

Nwokeji, G. Ugo, *The Slave Trade and Culture in the Bight of Biafra: An African Society in the Atlantic World* (Cambridge, 2010).

Nwokeji, G., Ugo and David. Eltis, 'The Roots of the African Diaspora: Methodological Considerations in the Analysis of Names in the Liberated African Registers of Sierra Leone and Havana', *History in Africa*, 29 (2002), 365–79.

O'Callaghan, Evelyn, *The Earliest Patriots: Being the True Adventures of Certain Survivors of Bussa's Rebellion (1816 In the Island of Barbados and Abroad)* (London, 1986).

Odeleye, A. O., *Ayo: A Popular Yoruba Game* (Oxford, 1977).

Ogundiran, Akinwumi, *The Yoruba: A New History* (Bloomington, 2020).

Ojo, Olatunji, 'Amazing Struggle: Dasalu, Global Yoruba Networks, and the Fight against Slavery, 1851–1856', *Atlantic Studies*, 12:1 (2015), 5–25.

——, 'Child Slaves in Pre-Colonial Nigeria, c.1725–1860', *Slavery & Abolition*, 33:3 (2012), 417–34.

Oliveira, Vanessa S., 'Baskets, Stalls, and Shops: Experiences and Strategies of Women in Retail Sales in Nineteenth Century Luanda', *Canadian Journal of African Studies / Revue canadienne des études africaines*, 54.3 (2020), pp. 419–36.

——, 'Dona Ana Joaquina Dos Santos Silva: A Woman Merchant of Nineteenth Century Luanda', in Vanicléia Silva Santos (ed.), *General History of Africa*, vol. X, *Africa and its Diasporas* (Paris, 2023), pp. 913–24.

——, 'Gender, Foodstuff Production and Trade in Late-Eighteenth Century Luanda', *African Economic History*, 43 (2015), 57–81.

——, *Slave Trade and Abolition: Gender, Commerce, and Economic Transition in Luanda* (Madison, 2021).

Olu-Wright, J., 'The Physical Growth of Freetown', in Christopher Fyfe and Eldred Durosimi Jones (eds), *Freetown: A Symposium* (Oxford, 1968), pp. 24–37.

Osborn, Emily Lynn, *Our New Husbands are Here: Households, Gender, and Politics in a West African State from the Slave Trade to Colonial Rule* (Athens, 2011).

Owusu-Ansah, David, 'Islamic Influence in a Forest Kingdom: The Role of Protective Amulets in Early 19th Century Asante', *Transafrican Journal of History*, 12 (1983), 100–33.

Page, Jesse, *The Black Bishop Samuel Adjai Crowther* (New York, 1909).

Parkes, J. C. Ernest, *Elementary Handbook of Geography of the Colony of Sierra Leone and its Hinterland* (Freetown, 1894).

Patterson, Orlando, *Slavery and Social Death* (Cambridge, 1982).

Peabody, Sue and Keila Grinberg, 'Free Soil: The Generation and Circulation of an Atlantic Legal Principle', *Slavery & Abolition*, 32:3 (2011), 331–9.

Pearson, Andrew, *Distant Freedom: St. Helena and the Abolition of the Slave Trade, 1840–1872* (Liverpool, 2016).

Peel, J. D. Y., 'Kings, Titles, and Quarters: A Conjectural History of Ilesha I – The Traditions Reviewed', *History in Africa*, 6 (1979), 109–53.

——, Religious Encounter and the Making of the Yoruba (Bloomington, 2003).

Peterson, John, *Province of Freedom: A History of Sierra Leone, 1787–1870* (Evanston, 1969).

Phillips, Earl, 'The Egba at Abeokuta: Acculturation and Political Change, 1830–1870', *Journal of African History*, 10:1 (1969), 117–31.

Porter, Arthur, *Creoledom: A Study of the Development of Freetown Society* (London, 1963).

——, 'Religious Affiliation in Freetown, Sierra Leone', *Journal of the International African Institute*, 23:1 (1953), 3–14.

Price, Richard, 'Maroon Societies in the Americas', *Oxford Research Encyclopedia of African History* (Oxford, 2020) <https://doi.org/10.1093/acrefore/9780190277734.013.935> [accessed 17 April 2026].

Rarey, Matthew Francis, *Insignificant Things: Amulets and the Art of Survival* (Durham, 2023).

Rathbone, Richard, 'Some Thoughts on Resistance to Enslavement in West Africa', in Gad Heuman (ed.), *Out of the House of Bondage: Runaways, Resistance and Marronage in Africa and the New World* (London, 1986), pp. 11–22.

Rediker, Marcus, *The Slave Ship* (London, 2007).

Reed, Susan A., 'The Politics and Poetics of Dance', *Annual Review of Anthropology*, 27 (1998), 503–32.

Reefe, Thomas Q., 'The Biggest Game of All: Gambling in Traditional Africa', in William J. Baker and James A. Mangan (eds), *Sport in Africa: Essays in Social History* (New York, 1987), pp. 47–78.

Reilly, M. C., C. A. Banton, C. Stevens, and C. L. Laurore, 'The Archaeology of Providence Island: Liberian Heritage beyond Settlement', *American Antiquity*, 89:4 (2024), 647–63.

Reuther, Jessica Catherine, *The Bonds of Kinship in Dahomey: Portraits of West African Girlhood, 1720–1940* (Bloomington, 2025).

Ribeiro da Silva, Filipa, *Dutch and Portuguese in Western Africa: Empires, Merchants and the Atlantic System, 1580–1674* (Leiden, 2011).

Richards, Jake Subryan, *The Bonds of Freedom: Liberated Africans and the End of the Slave Trade* (New Haven, 2025).

Roberts, Richard L., *Warriors, Merchants, and Slaves: The State and the Economy in the Middle Niger Valley, 1700–1914* (Stanford, 1987).

Rodet, Marie, 'Continuum of Gendered Violence: The Colonial Invention of Female Desertion as a Customary Criminal Offense, French Soudan, 1900–1949', in Emily S. Burrill, Richard L. Roberts, and Elizabeth Thornberry (eds), *Domestic Violence and the Law in Colonial and Postcolonial Africa* (Athens, 2010), pp. 74–93.

Rodet, Marie, Lotte Pelckmans, Wayne Dooling, and Esteban Salas (eds), *Resistance to Slavery in Africa: Past and Present* (London, 2026).

Rodney, Walter, 'African Slavery and Other Forms of Social Oppression on the Upper Guinea Coast in the Context of the Atlantic Slave-Trade', *Journal of African History*, 7:3 (1966), 431–43.

——, *A History of the Upper Guinea Coast 1545–1800* (New York, 1980).

Roldán de Montaud, Inés, 'The Misfortune of Liberated Africans in Colonial Cuba, 1824–76', in Richard Anderson and Henry B. Lovejoy (eds), *Liberated Africans and the Abolition of the Slave Trade: Digital Histories of Enslavement and Freedom* (Rochester, 2020), pp. 153–73.

Rossi, Benedetta, 'Introduction: African Approaches to the Abolition of Slavery', *Esclavages & Post-esclavages* 10 (2024), <https://doi.org/10.4000/12sh9> [accessed 29 November 2024].

Rovner, Adam, *The Jew Who Would Be King: A True Story of Shipwreck, Survival, and Scandal in Victorian Africa* (Oakland, 2025).

Ryan, Maeve, '"A Moral Millstone"? British Humanitarian Governance and the Policy of Liberated African Apprenticeship, 1808–1848"', *Slavery & Abolition*, 37:2 (2016), 399–422.

——, '"A Most Promising Field for Future Usefulness": The Church Missionary Society and the Liberated Africans of Sierra Leone', in W. Mulligan and M. Bric (eds), *A Global History of Anti-Slavery Politics in the Nineteenth Century* (London, 2013), pp. 37–58.

——, 'A "Very Extensive System of Peculation and Jobbing": The Liberated African Department of Sierra Leone, Humanitarian Governance and the Fraud Inquiry of 1848', *Journal of Colonialism & Colonial History*, 17:3 (2016), <https://doi.org/10.1353/cch.2016.0041> [accessed 25 April 2026].

——, *Humanitarian Governance and the British Antislavery World System* (New Haven, 2022).

——, '"It Was Necessary to do Something with Those Women": Colonial Governance and the "Disposal" of Women and Girls in Early Nineteenth-Century Sierra Leone', *Gender & History* (2021), 491–510.

Salau, Mohammed Bashir, *Plantation Slavery in the Sokoto Caliphate: A Historical and Comparative Study* (Rochester, 2018).

Sandoval-Velasco, Marcela, Anuradha Jagadeesan, Jazmín Ramos-Madrigal, María C. Ávila-Arcos, Cesar A. Fortes-Lima, Judy Watson, Erna Johannesdóttir, Diana I. Cruz-Dávalos, Shyam Gopalakrishnan, J. Víctor Moreno-Mayar, Jonas Niemann, Gabriel Renaud, Katharine A. Robson Brown, Helena Bennett, Andrew Pearson, Agnar Helgason, M. Thomas P. Gilbert, and Hannes Schroeder, 'The Ancestry and Geographical Origins of St Helena's Liberated Africans', *The American Journal of Human Genetics*, 110:9 (2023), 1590–9.

Sarr, Assan, *Islam, Power, and Dependency in the Gambia River Basin: The Politics of Land Control, 1790–1940* (Rochester, 2016).

——, 'Women, Land & Power in the Lower Gambia River Region', in Mariana P. Candido and Adam Jones (eds), *African Women in the Atlantic World: Property, Vulnerability & Mobility 1660–1880* (Woodbridge, 2019), pp. 38–54.

Sauer, R., 'Infanticide and Abortion in Nineteenth-Century Britain', *Population Studies*, 32:1 (1978), 81–93.

Scanlan, Padraic X., *Freedom's Debtors: British Antislavery in Sierra Leone in the Age of Revolution* (New Haven, 2017).

——, 'The Colonial Rebirth of British Anti-Slavery: The Liberated African Villages of Sierra Leone, 1815–1824', *American Historical Review*, 121:4 (2016), 1085–113.

——, 'The Rewards of Their Exertions: Prize Money and British Abolitionism in Sierra Leone, 1808–1823', *Past & Present*, 225 (2014), 113–42.

Schwarz, Suzanne, 'Adaptation in the Aftermath of Slavery: Women, Trade and Property in Sierra Leone, c.1790–1812', in Mariana P. Candido and Adam Jones (eds), *African Women in the Atlantic World: Property, Vulnerability & Mobility 1660–1880* (Woodbridge, 2019), pp. 19–37.

——, 'African Diaspora, Sierra Leone and Protestant Christianity, circa 1780–1860', in Vanicléia Silva Santos (ed.), *General History of Africa*, vol. X, *Africa and its Diasporas* (Paris, 2023), pp. 777–88.

——, '"A Just and Honourable Commerce": Abolitionist Experimentation in Sierra Leone in the Late Eighteenth and Early Nineteenth Century', *African Economic History*, 45:1 (2017), 1–45.

——, 'Fragments of the Life History of Fuseng-Be: A Temne Woman Sold in Freetown, Sierra Leone in the Early Nineteenth Century', in Vanicléia Silva Santos (ed.), *General History of Africa*, vol. X, *Africa and its Diasporas* (Paris, 2023), pp. 977–86.

——, 'Land and Settlement: Temne Responses to British Abolitionist Intervention in Sierra Leone in the Late Eighteenth and Early Nineteenth Centuries', *African Economic History*, 49:1 (2021), 222–48.

——, 'Reconstructing the Life Histories of Liberated Africans: Sierra Leone in the Early Nineteenth Century', *History in Africa*, 39 (2012), 175–207.

——, 'The Impact of Liberated African "Disposal" Polices in Early Nineteenth-Century Sierra Leone', in Richard Anderson and Henry B. Lovejoy (eds), *Liberated Africans and the Abolition of the Slave Trade: Digital Histories of Enslavement and Freedom* (Rochester, 2020), pp. 45–65.

Searing, James F., *West African Slavery and Atlantic Commerce: The Senegal River Valley, 1700–1860* (Cambridge, 1993).

Semley, Lorelle D., *Mother is Gold, Father is Glass: Gender and Colonialism in a Yoruba Town* (Bloomington, 2011).

Sène, Cheikh, 'Le décret de l'émancipation des esclaves de 1848 : une application difficile au Sénégal (1848–1905)', *Esclavages & Post-esclavages* 10 (2024), <https://doi.org/10.4000/12sh5> [accessed 2 December 2024].

Skinner, David E., 'Islam and Education in the Colony and Hinterland of Sierra Leone (1750–1914)', *Canadian Journal of African Studies / Revue canadienne des études africaines*, 10:3 (1976), 499–520.

——, 'Lawson, Thomas George (1814–1891), Colonial Official and Baptist Leader', *Oxford Dictionary of National Biography* (2008), <www.oxforddnb.com/view/10.1093/ref:odnb/9780198614128.001.0001/odnb-9780198614128-e-53504> [accessed 3 July 2019].

——, 'The Incorporation of Muslim Elites into the Colonial Administrative Systems of Sierra Leone, The Gambia and the Gold Coast', *Journal of Muslim Minority Affairs*, 29:1 (2009), 91–108.

——, 'The Influence of Islam in Sierra Leone History: Institutions, Practices, and Leadership', *Journal of West African History*, 2:1 (2016), 27–71.

——, *Thomas George Lawson: African Historian and Administrator in Sierra Leone* (Stanford, 1980).

Sidbury, James, '"African" Settlers in the Founding of Freetown', in Paul E. Lovejoy and Suzanne Schwarz (eds), *Slavery, Abolition and the Transition to Colonialism in Sierra Leone* (Trenton, 2015), pp. 127–42.

Soriano, Tim, '"What Rascals!" Perceptions of Free Labor in the Bulama Settlement, 1792–1793', *African Economic History*, 49:1 (2021), 173–91.

Spitzer, Leo, *The Creoles of Sierra Leone: Responses to Colonialism 1870–1945* (Madison, 1974).

Stinnett, Joseph P., *Out of Virginia: Black Americans' Search for Freedom in Nineteenth-Century Liberia* (Charlottesville, 2026).

Stoffle, Richard W., Mamadou A. Baro, and Alissandra Cummins, 'Warri's Warriors: From West Africa to Barbados, Men's Social Space from Slavery to Post-Colonial Times', *The Journal of the Barbados Museum & Historical Society*, 65 (2019), 44–68.

Strickrodt, Silke, 'African Girls' Samplers from Mission Schools in Sierra Leone (1820s to 1840s)', *History in Africa*, 37 (2010), 189–245.

Sweeney, Shauna J., 'Market Marronage: Fugitive Women and the Internal Marketing System in Jamaica, 1781–1834', *The William and Mary Quarterly*, 76:2 (2019), 197–222.

Sweet, James H., 'Defying Social Death: The Multiple Configurations of African Slave Family in the Atlantic World', *The William and Mary Quarterly*, 70:2 (2013), 251–72.

Tarlow, Sarah, *Bereavement and Commemoration: An Archaeology of Mortality* (Oxford, 1999).

——, 'Introduction: Death and Burial in Post-medieval Europe', in Sarah Tarlow (ed.), *The Archaeology of Death in Post-medieval Europe* (Warsaw, 2015), pp. 1–18.

Thioub, Ibrahima, 'L'abolition de l'esclavage en Afrique française : le principe du sol libérateur à l'épreuve du terrain', in Annie Fitte-Duval (ed.), *Droit et esclavages : Théorie et pratiques en Afrique et dans les Amériques (XVe-XIXe siècles)* (Paris, 2022), pp. 215–40.

Tough, Alistair and Paul Lihoma, 'The Development of Recordkeeping Systems in the British Empire and Commonwealth, 1870s–1960s', *Archives and Manuscripts*, 40:3 (2012), 191–216.

Trimingham, J. Spencer, *Islam in West Africa* (Oxford, 1959).

Trimingham, J. Spencer and Christopher Fyfe, 'The Early Expansion of Islam in Sierra Leone', *The Sierra Leone Bulletin of Religion*, 2:2 (1960), 33–40.

Ukpabi, S. C., 'West Indian Troops and the Defence of British West Africa in the Nineteenth Century', *African Studies Review*, 17:1 (1974), 133–50.

van Leeuwen, Marco H. D., Ineke Maas, and Andrew Miles, 'Creating a Historical International Standard Classification of Occupations an Exercise in Multinational Interdisciplinary Cooperation', *Historical Methods: A Journal of Quantitative and Interdisciplinary History*, 37:4 (2004), 186–97.

Walker, James W. St. G., *The Black Loyalists: The Search for a Promised Land in Nova Scotia and Sierra Leone, 1783–1870* (London, 1976).

White, E. Frances, 'Creole Women Traders in the Nineteenth Century', *The International Journal of African Historical Studies*, 14:4 (1981), 626–42.

——, *Sierra Leone's Settler Women Traders* (Ann Arbor, 1987).

Whyte, Christine, '"Freedom But Nothing Else": The Legacies of Slavery and Abolition in Post-Slavery Sierra Leone, 1928–1956', *The International Journal of African Historical Studies*, 48:2 (2015), 231–50.

——, 'Mothering Solidarity: Infant-Feeding, Vulnerability and Poverty in West Africa since the Seventeenth Century', *Past & Present*, 246:15 (2020), 54–92.

Williams Elliott, Dorice, *The Angel out of the House: Philanthropy and Gender in Nineteenth-Century England* (Charlottesville, 2002).

Williams, Eric, *Capitalism and Slavery* (Chapel Hill, 1944).

Wills, Mary, 'At War with the "Detestable Traffic": The Royal Navy's Anti-Slavery Cause in the Atlantic Ocean', in John McAleer and Christer Petley (eds), *The Royal Navy and the British Atlantic World, c.1750–1820* (London, 2016), pp. 123–46.

——, *Envoys of Abolition: British Naval Officers and the Campaign against the Slave Trade in West Africa* (Liverpool, 2019).

Wolfe, Martin, 'The Concept of Economic Sectors', *The Quarterly Journal of Economics*, 69:3 (1955), 403–20.

Woollard, Matthew, 'The Classification of Occupations in the 1881 Census of England and Wales', *Historical Censuses and Social Surveys Research Group Occasional Paper No. 1* (Essex, 1999), 1–57.

Wrigley, E. A. (ed.), *Nineteenth-Century Society: Essays in the Use of Quantitative Methods for the Study of Social Data* (Cambridge, 1972).

——, 'Urban Growth and Agricultural Change: England and the Continent in the Early Modern Period', *The Journal of Interdisciplinary History*, 15:4 (1985), 683–728.

Wylie, Kenneth C., *The Political Kingdoms of the Temne: Temne Government in Sierra Leone, 1825–1910* (New York, 1977).

——, 'The Slave Trade in Nineteenth Century Temneland and the British Sphere of Influence', *African Studies Review*, 16:2 (1973), 203–17.

Wyse, Akintola J. G., 'On Misunderstandings Arising from the Use of the Term "Creole" in the Literature on Sierra Leone: A Rejoinder', *Africa*, 49:4 (1979), 408–17.

Unpublished Theses

Ali, Myles, '"Here in the Queen's Territory, Every Man and Woman Are Free": Slavery and the Lives of the Enslaved in Late Nineteenth Century Sierra Leone' (Unpublished PhD dissertation, York University, 2020).

Anderson, Richard, 'Recaptives: Community and Identity in Colonial Sierra Leone, 1808–1863' (Unpublished PhD dissertation, Yale University, 2015).

Gunn, Jeffrey, 'Homeland, Diasporas and Labour Networks: The Case of Kru Workers, 1792–1900' (Unpublished PhD dissertation, York University, 2019).

Ijagbemi, E. Ade, 'A History of the Temne in the Nineteenth Century' (Unpublished PhD dissertation, University of Edinburgh, 1968).

Keefer, Katrina, 'Mission Education in Sierra Leone, 1793–1820' (Unpublished PhD dissertation, York University Toronto, 2015).

Melek Delgado, Érika, 'Children, Childhood and Slavery in Sierra Leone: The Experiences of Liberated African Children c. 1808–1834' (Unpublished PhD dissertation, University of Worcester, 2017).

Scanlan, Padraic Xavier, 'Maccarthy's Skull: The Abolition of the Slave Trade in Sierra Leone, 1792–1823' (Unpublished PhD dissertation, Princeton University, 2013).

Shyllon, Leslie Ephraim Telé, 'The Dynamics of Methodism, in Sierra Leone, 1860–1911: Western European Influence and culture in Church Development' (Unpublished PhD dissertation, University of Aberdeen, 1983).

Thayer, James Steel, 'Religion and Social Organization among a West African Muslim People: The Susu of Sierra Leone' (Unpublished PhD dissertation, University of Michigan, 1981).

Vonque Stephen, Daniel Augustine, 'A History of the Settlement of Liberated Africans in the Colony of Sierra Leone during the First Half of the 19th Century' (Unpublished PhD dissertation, Durham University, 1963).

Conference Papers

Mbah, Ndubueze L., 'Abolition Forgery: A History of the Afterlives of Slavery', Radcliffe Fellow's Presentation, Harvard Radcliffe Institute, April 2023 < https://www.radcliffe.harvard.edu/event/2023-ndubueze-l-mbah-fellow-presentation-virtual> [accessed 3 August 2025]

Mouser, Bruce L., 'Shifting the Littoral Frontiers of EurAfrican and African Trade in the Northern Rivers of Sierra Leone, 1794: Opportunities and Challenges from Changing Conditions', Sierra Leone Studies and Liberian Studies Associations Joint Meeting Charleston, South Carolina, April 1994.

Pereira, Clifford, 'Black Liberators: The Role of Africans & Arabs sailors in the Royal Navy within the Indian Ocean 1841–1941', The Slave Route UNESCO Symposium Rabat, 2007.

Schwarz, Suzanne, '"A Just and Honourable Commerce": Abolitionist Experimentation in Sierra Leone in the Late Eighteenth and Early Nineteenth Centuries', The Hakluyt Society Annual Lecture, 2013.

Web-based Sources

The British Library Endangered Archives Programme,

'Archival records from *Nineteenth century documents of the Sierra Leone Public Archives* (EAP443)' <https://eap.bl.uk/project/EAP443/search>

'Preserving nineteenth-century records in the Sierra Leone Public Archives (EAP782)', <https://eap.bl.uk/project/EAP782>

'Preserving records of social and political life in nineteenth-century Sierra Leone (EAP1366)', <https://eap.bl.uk/project/EAP1366>

British Online Archives

Blue Books of Sierra Leone, 1819 to 1862. <https://britishonlinearchives.com/collections/39/volumes/235/sierra-leone-1824–1943>

Find A Will

Principal Registry of Her Majesty's Court of Probate, The Will of John Ezzidio, 18 December 1872, *Find A Will*, <www.probatesearch.service.gov.uk/Calendar?surname=Ezzidio&yearOfDeath=1872&page=3#calendar> [accessed 23 April 2021].

Nineteenth Century Collections Online

'A Sierra Leone Incident', *Douglas Jerrold's Weekly Newspaper* (October 16, 1847), Issue 66, p. 1301.

Other Websites and Databases

Liberated Africans database, <https://liberatedafricans.org>

Oxford English Dictionary, Oxford University Press <www.oed.com>

Slave Voyages database, <https://www.slavevoyages.org>

Index

People, Markets, Goods: Economies and Societies in History

Previously published

1. *Landlords and Tenants in Britain, 1440–1660: Tawney's* Agrarian Problem *Revisited*, edited by Jane Whittle, 2013

2. *Child Workers and Industrial Health in Britain, 1780–1850*, Peter Kirby, 2013

3. *Publishing Business in Eighteenth-Century England*, James Raven, 2014

4. *The First Century of Welfare: Poverty and Poor Relief in Lancashire, 1620–1730*, Jonathan Healey, 2014

5. *Population, Welfare and Economic Change in Britain 1290–1834*, edited by Chris Briggs, P. M. Kitson and S. J. Thompson, 2014

6. *Crises in Economic and Social History: A Comparative Perspective*, edited by A. T. Brown, Andy Burn and Rob Doherty, 2015

7. *Slavery Hinterland: Transatlantic Slavery and Continental Europe, 1680–1850*, edited by Felix Brahm and Eve Rosenhaft, 2016

8. *Almshouses in Early Modern England: Charitable Housing in the Mixed Economy of Welfare, 1550–1725*, Angela Nicholls, 2017

9. *People, Places and Business Cultures: Essays in Honour of Francesca Carnevali*, edited by Paolo Di Martino, Andrew Popp and Peter Scott, 2017

10. *Cameralism in Practice: State Administration and Economy in Early Modern Europe*, edited by Marten Seppel and Keith Tribe, 2017

11. *Servants in Rural Europe, 1400–1900*, edited by Jane Whittle, 2017

12. *The Age of Machinery: Engineering the Industrial Revolution, 1770–1850*, Gillian Cookson, 2018

13. *Shoplifting in Eighteenth-Century England*, Shelley Tickell, 2018

14. *Money and Markets: Essays in Honour of Martin Daunton*, edited by Julian Hoppit, Duncan Needham and Adrian Leonard, 2019

15. *Women and the Land, 1500–1900*, edited by Amanda L. Capern, Briony McDonagh and Jennifer Aston, 2019

16. *Globalized Peripheries: Central Europe and the Atlantic World, 1680–1860*, edited by Jutta Wimmler and Klaus Weber, 2020

17. *Financing Cotton: British Industrial Growth and Decline, 1780–2000*, Steven Toms, 2020

18. *Quakers in the British Atlantic World, c.1660–1800*, Esther Sahle, 2021

19. *The Great Famine in Ireland and Britain's Financial Crisis*, Charles Read, 2022

20. *Family Firms in Postwar Britain and Germany: Competing Approaches to Business*, David Paulson, 2023

21. *Labour Laws in Preindustrial Europe: The Coercion and Regulation of Wage Labour, c.1350–1850*, edited by Jane Whittle and Thijs Lambrecht, 2023

22. *Financial Failure in Early Modern England*, Aidan Collins, 2024

23. *Capitalism: Histories*, edited by Robert G. Ingram and James M. Vaughn, 2025

www.ingramcontent.com/pod-product-compliance
Lightning Source LLC
LaVergne TN
LVHW012335130926
847902LV00028B/403
* 9 7 8 1 8 3 7 6 5 3 0 7 2 *